A Communicative Course in English

BUILDING

ENGLISH

STRUCTURES

Chuck Seibel
Applied English Center
The University of Kansas

Russ Hodge
Zentrales Sprachlabor
Universität Heidelberg

PRENTICE HALL REGENTS
Englewood Cliffs, New Jersey 07632

Library of Congress Cataloging-in-Publication Data

Seibel, Chuck, 1942–
    Building English structures : a communicative course in English /
Chuck Seibel, Russ Hodge.
        p.   cm.
    Includes index.
    ISBN 0-13-085861-7
    1. English language—Textbooks for foreign speakers.   I. Hodge,
Russ, 1961–   .   II. Title.
PE1128.S395   1991
428.2′4—dc20   90-39216
                                                            CIP

Editorial/production supervision and
    interior design: Shari S. Toron
Acquisition editor: Anne Riddick
Manufacturing buyer: Ray Keating, Lori Bulwin
Cover design: Richard Puder Design
Illustrated by: Russ Hodge

©1991 by Prentice-Hall, Inc.
A Division of Simon & Schuster
Englewood Cliffs, New Jersey 07632

Printed in the United States of America
10 9 8 7 6 5 4 3 2 1

0-13-085861-7

Prentice-Hall International (UK) Limited, *London*
Prentice-Hall of Australia Pty. Limited, *Sydney*
Prentice-Hall Canada Inc., *Toronto*
Prentice-Hall Hispanoamericana, S.A., *Mexico*
Prentice-Hall of India Private Limited, *New Delhi*
Prentice-Hall of Japan, Inc., *Tokyo*
Simon & Schuster Asia Pte. Ltd., *Singapore*
Editora Prentice-Hall do Brasil, Ltda., *Rio de Janeiro*

CONTENTS

PREFACE

Building English Structures (BES) is an intermediate/advanced textbook for students of English as a second language. *BES* can be used in a full-year or nine-month course in which students enter at the intermediate level of English proficiency. In a shorter course (for example, 15 weeks), a more advanced group might go through the earlier chapters of the book very quickly—perhaps focusing on oral practices and paragraph writing—in order to have enough time to do a thorough job with the later, more advanced chapters. A less advanced class, on the other hand, might have time to do only selected parts of the later chapters.

The following diagram shows how the chapters are organized.

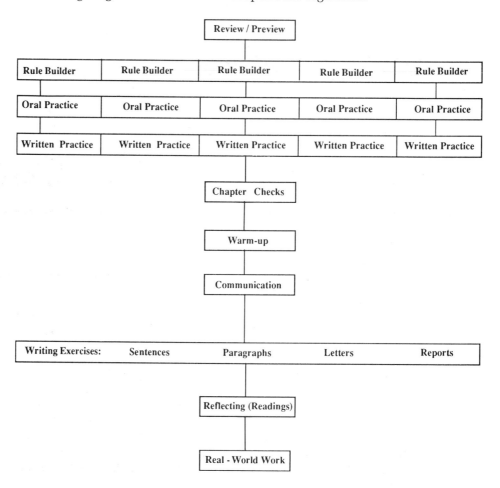

Descriptions of the features illustrated in the diagram can be found in the Teacher's Manual.

We feel that this book is eclectic in the best sense of the word: Aspects of the language are moved in and out of focus for practical, common-sense reasons. This selectivity is reflected in the chapter titles; the focus may be on vocabulary (''Count versus Noncount Nouns''), on inflectional endings (''Agreement''), on syntax (''Objects''), on functions (''Requests, Offers, and Suggestions''), or on notions (''Degree''). We have tried to organize each chapter and the book as a whole so that the course will have a natural flow and a rational progression. At the same time, we have tried to provide a broad assortment of activities which, we hope, will be fun and effective for a wide variety of learners and teachers.

PART ONE: QUESTIONS

1

Tag Questions

PREVIEW

Tags are short yes/no questions that we put at the ends of statements to make **tag questions**. Here are some examples.

> *Americans are individualistic, <u>aren't they</u>?*
> *You live on the second floor of the dorm, <u>don't you</u>?*
> *We don't have a test today, <u>do we</u>?*
> *There won't be a meeting next Friday, <u>will there</u>?*

Tag questions begin with statements, and the speaker expects the listener to agree with the statement. This means saying yes to a positive statement and no to a negative statement.

Of course, the listener does not *have* to agree with the speaker. But if the listener disagrees, he or she usually provides an explanation. For example, if the listener does not agree that Americans are individualistic, the response to tag question 1 could be:

> *No, I don't agree. I think most Americans are conformists.*

Mr. and Mrs. McGill live in an apartment in a large Midwestern city. They are on their first vacation trip in 15 years. Mr. McGill wanted to see the ocean, so he talked Mrs. McGill into going to southern California. Mrs. McGill was not sure that she really wanted to leave their nice apartment and go to California.

Here they are during their first morning on the beach.

1.1 Positive Versus Negative Tag Questions		
Complete these model sentences.	Check.	Complete these rules.
a. Mr. McGill is rather short, _____ **he?** **His wife is quite a bit taller,** _____ **she?**	isn't isn't	A **tag question** is made up of a statement and a tag. When the statement is positive, the tag is _____. When the tag is negative, put the verb and ***not*** together; in other words, make a **contraction.**
b. Mrs. McGill is not having fun, _____ **she?**	 is	When the statement is negative, the tag is _____.
c. Snow is never a problem in southern California, _____ **it?**	 is	***Not*** is the most common negative adverb. Another common negative adverb is _____.

Oral Practice 1:   Using tag questions, find out if you remember your classmates' names correctly. Examples:

Your name is Maria, isn't it?   *You're Reza, aren't you?*

Written Practice 1:   Complete the following tag questions and give the expected answers. The first one has been done for you.

1. Mr. McGill is bald,   _**isn't**_ he?   _**Yes, he is.**_

2. Mrs. McGill isn't very happy, _____ she?   _____

3. He is smoking a cigar, _____ he?   _____

4. She isn't smoking, _____ she?   _____

5. The weather here is unpredictable, _____ it?   _____

6. Newark isn't far from New York, _____ it?   _____

7. The coffee isn't ready yet, _____ it?   _____

8. Riyadh is the capital of Saudi Arabia, _____ it? _____

9. This bus is never on time, _____ it?   _____

10. That bus driver is never pleasant, _____ he?   _____

1.2 Verbs in the Tags		
Complete these model sentences.	Check.	Complete these rules.
a. They are on vacation, _____ **they?**	aren't	The first word in a tag is a **verb.** If the first verb in the **statement** is in the **present tense,** put the **tag verb** in the _____ tense.
b. It wasn't Mrs. McGill's idea, _____ **it?**	was	If the first verb in the statement is in the **past tense,** put the tag verb in the _____ tense.
c. They will be back home soon, _____ **they?** **He hasn't taken many pictures yet,** _____ **he?**	won't has	If the first verb in the statement is • a form of the verb **be** (**am, is, are, was, were)** • a **modal verb** such as _____, • or a form of the **auxiliary verb** *have*, use the same verb in the tag.
d. She seems discouraged, _____ **she?**	doesn't	If the first verb in the statement is not one of the verbs in rule **c**, use the verb *do*. Present and past forms: _____, _____, and _____.
e. She has a frown on her face, _____ **she?**	doesn't	In American English, if *have* is the main verb in a statement, a form of _____ is usually used in the tag. (Some people use *have* in such tags, however.)

NOTE: Look at this sentence:
I'm probably wrong about that, aren't I?
The tags that we put on the end of statements to make questions generally have two words. But there isn't any way to put **am I not** into two words, since we cannot contract **am** and **not**. Therefore, most native speakers of American English use **aren't I** as the tag in this situation. In more formal speech, you might hear **am I not** for the tag.

Oral Practice 2:   You can probably make several good guesses about the daily habits of your classmates, or the way they feel right now. Check your guesses with tag questions. Examples:

You ride the bus to school, don't you?
You feel a little homesick, don't you?

Written Practice 2:   Complete these sentences.

1.   The trip was Mr. McGill's idea, _____ it?

2.   Mrs. McGill won't go next year, _____ she?

3.   The McGills haven't taken a trip for a long time, _____ they?

4.   Mr. McGill has a camera around his neck, _____ he?

5.   Mr. McGill often smokes cigars, _____ he?

6.   Mrs. McGill never smokes cigars, _____ she?

7.   We should work hard this semester, _____ we?

8.   The students introduced themselves yesterday, _____ they?

9.   They haven't really gotten to know each other yet, _____ they?

10.   We have class tomorrow, _____ we?

11.   Teachers almost never forget to give homework, _____ they?

12.   Students usually don't have time to go out during the school week, _____ they?

1.3 Pronouns and *There* in Tags		
Complete these model sentences.	Check.	Complete these rules.
a. Mrs. McGill isn't carrying a camera, is _____? **The McGills are on the beach, aren't _____?**	she they	The **subject** of a tag must be a **personal pronoun**; that is, it must be one of these words: *I, we, you, it, he,* _____, or _____. Make the personal pronoun in the tag agree in person and number with the subject of the statement.

b. That is a heavy bag that Mrs. McGill is carrying, isn't _____? Those are unusual shoes that Mr. McGill has on, aren't _____?	it they	Don't use a **demonstrative pronoun** (*this*, *that*, *these*, and *those*) in a tag. Instead, use _____ (singular) or _____ (plural).
c. There are seashells on the beach, aren't _____?	there	The only word besides the personal pronouns that normally occurs at the end of a tag is _____. Use *there* at the end of the tag when *there* occurs at the beginning of the statement.

Oral Practice 3A: Using tag questions, check on the ownership of things in the classroom. Examples:

> *This is your bag, isn't it?*
> *That bag belongs to you, doesn't it?*

Oral Practice 3B: Think of things that are probably in your teacher's wallet, bag, or brief-case. Then check to see if you have guessed correctly by using tag questions. Examples:

> *There's a picture of your wife in your wallet, isn't there?*
> *There are some books in your briefcase, aren't there?*

Written Practice 3:   Complete these sentences.

1.   The McGills are a rather odd couple, aren't _____?
2.   Mrs. McGill is not enjoying herself, is _____?
3.   That is a pitiful expression on her face, isn't _____?
4.   Those are seashells lying on the sand, aren't _____?
5.   There are no clouds in the sky, are _____?
6.   This is a dangerous but interesting century to live in, isn't _____?
7.   There are students from many nations studying in the U.S., aren't _____?
8.   These students have a variety of reasons for studying abroad, don't _____?

1.4   Making Negative Statements

Of course, to make tag questions when you are expecting no as an answer, you must be able to make *negative statements.*

Complete these model sentences.	Check.	Complete these rules.
a. Mrs. McGill _____ dressed for swimming, is she?	is not/isn't	This is the way to form negative statements: If the first verb is • a form of *be,* • a **modal,** such as _____, • or the auxiliary verb *have,*
She probably _____ go swimming, will she?	will not/ won't	
She _____ started having fun yet, has she?	has not/ hasn't	put _____ immediately after it.
b. She _____ enjoy traveling, does she?	does not/ doesn't	If the first verb is not one of the verbs mentioned in rule **a**, use a form of the verb _____ before *not.* Put the main verb into the **base form**.

Oral Practice 4:   Now make guesses about what is *not* in your teacher's wallet, bag, or case. Examples:

> *You don't have a cup of coffee in there, do you?*
> *There isn't an umbrella in it, is there?*

Written Practice 4:   Look at the tag. Then complete the sentence.

1. The McGills _____ been to the ocean before, have they?
2. Mrs. McGill _____ used to being away from the city, is she?
3. She _____ like to get sand in her shoes, does she?
4. She _____ worry so much, should she?
5. There _____ any English classes on Saturday, are there?
6. We _____ have a test tomorrow, do we?
7. We _____ start chapter 2 tomorrow, will we?
8. The teacher _____ said anything about the final exam yet, has she?

1.5 Chapter Check: Complete these sentences to see how well you have learned this chapter's structures. You should be able to finish the chapter checks without any errors. If you are not sure you have the right answer, or if you just want to check your work, the number of the model sentence and the rule are beside each sentence. Read the model sentence first and then, if necessary, the rule.

1. My friends will be here soon, _____?   [1.1a, 1.2c, 1.3a]

2. These are yours, _____?   [1.1a, 1.2c, 1.3b]

3. That's Tony's backpack, _____?   [1.1a, 1.2c, 1.3b]

4. There's a party at the dorm tonight, _____?   [1.1a, 1.2c, 1.3c]

5. The children couldn't go, _____?   [1.1b, 1.2c, 1.3a]

6. All the guests had a good time, _____?   [1.2d, 1.3a]

7. Americans almost never eat vegetables at breakfast, _____?

   [1.1c, 1.2d, 1.3a]

8. The McGills _____ understand each other very well, do

   they?   [1.4b]

1.6 Chapter Check: Finish sentence B. It should have about the same meaning as sentence A. In this exercise, the A sentences are negative questions. You will learn more about this type of question in the next chapter. They have about the same meaning as tag questions with negative tags. The first one has been done for you.

1. A. Isn't palm oil the principal export of Malaysia today?

    B. Palm oil is   ***the principal export of Malaysia today, isn't it?***

2. A. Isn't oil the principal export of Saudi Arabia?   [1.1a, 1.2c, 1.3a]

    B. Oil is _____

3. A. Don't you think that students worry too much about grades?   [1.1a, 1.2d, 1.3a]

    B. Students worry _____

4. A. Isn't this the first time you've lived away from home?   [1.1a, 1.2c, 1.3b]

    B. This _____

5. A. Aren't there a lot of international students at this university?   [1.1a, 1.2c, 1.3c]

    B. There _____

1.7 Warm-up: Think of things about this class and this semester that you think you know but are not completely sure of. Using tag questions, check this information with your teacher or classmates. Possible topics include: textbooks, days when the class meets and doesn't meet, criteria for grades, tests, holidays, end of the semester, and so on.

1.8 Communication: You and your classmates introduce yourselves to the entire class and tell where you are from, what your native languages are, where you are living now, what your hobbies are, and what you plan to study at this university. Take notes about each student as he or she talks. You can write the information in the spaces on the STUDENT INFORMA-TION SHEET on the following page.

Next, go around the classroom and introduce yourself to each of your classmates individually. Try to learn how to pronounce and spell everyone's name. Using tag questions, check to see if you have correct information about each student.

STUDENT INFORMATION SHEET

Name		
Country		
Language		
Residence		
Hobbies		
Study Plans		
Name		
Country		
Language		
Residence		
Hobbies		
Study Plans		
Name		
Country		
Language		
Residence		
Hobbies		
Study Plans		
Name		
Country		
Language		
Residence		
Hobbies		
Study Plans		
Name		
Country		
Language		
Residence		
Hobbies		
Study Plans		

1.9 Sentence Writing: Think of the tag questions that you would use in the following circumstances. Say each question orally before writing it.

1. You think that a person you see in the dorm is in your calculus class, but you're not positive.
2. You don't think the person you're talking to is taking Chemistry 101, but you're not sure.
3. You think your roommate can drive, but you decide to check with him or her.
4. You don't think you and your roommate will be late to the party, but you're a little worried.
5. You assume that a new friend of yours has seen the *Star Wars* movies, but you want to see if your assumption is correct.
6. You doubt that your roommate has borrowed your pen, but you decide to ask anyway.
7. You're fairly certain that your new friend likes pizza, but you want to make sure before you suggest going to a pizza place.
8. You wonder if your roommate likes to bowl. You doubt it. You expect him or her to say no.
9. You are getting on a bus. You think that it goes to the shopping center, but you check with the driver to make sure.

1.10 Sentence Completion: If you use tag questions and you don't really know if your listener agrees with you, the questions might seem aggressive. Tags are sometimes used in advertising, and sometimes they can make us angry. Complete the tag questions and their short answers in the following cartoon.

1.11 Reflecting: At the end of most chapters in this book, you will find a section called "Reflecting." Each "Reflecting" section is an episode of a story—a mystery about a detective named Stern and a missing person. Each episode contains structures that you have worked on in that chapter. Read the passage. Then reread it, looking at the way the structures have been used. Your teacher may give you special instructions for classroom work or homework.

Read the first episode of the mystery story. Examine the way tag questions are used. Can you find some places where tag questions could have been used but weren't?

> I walked into the elevator just behind a young woman in a business suit. We tried to push the fifth-floor button at the same time. She smiled at me. When we got out we walked to the same office. The door said, "Stern Detective Agency."
>
> "You need a detective, don't you?" I asked her.
>
> "Yes," she said.
>
> I got my keys out of my pocket and unlocked the door. I held it open for her.
>
> "You're Stern, aren't you?" she said.
>
> "That's right. Hey, you could be a detective."
>
> We went inside. I put my coat on the desk and she sat down. "You have already been here today, haven't you?" the woman asked.
>
> "No. I was last here on Friday. Why?"
>
> "Your coffee machine is still on."
>
> I looked at the machine. She was right again. The coffee was very black. "Do you want a job?" I asked.
>
> "No," she laughed.
>
> "Too bad. Do you want a cup of coffee?"
>
> "No!"
>
> I poured a cup for myself and sat down behind the desk. "You must be a client, then," I said.
>
> "My name is Deanne Miller. I want you to find my husband. You can help me, can't you?"
>
> "I'm sure you have already talked to the police."
>
> "Yes," she answered. "They couldn't find him."
>
> "Tell me about it," I said. I found a pencil on the floor.
>
> "That coffee is terribly strong, isn't it?"
>
> "I like my coffee black," I said, and smiled at her.

1.12 Real-World Work

THINK/PRACTICE

Between now and your next class, practice making up tag questions in your mind while you are walking, riding in buses, and so on. Look around you and make up sentences like "That's a beautiful car, isn't it?", "He looks tired, doesn't he?", and "There are a lot of students on campus this morning, aren't there?". If you find that you don't know the correct tag for a particular statement, remember to ask your teacher.

LOOK/LISTEN

If possible, watch an English language TV program this evening—a situation comedy or a drama. Have a pen and a piece of paper ready. Listen for tag questions. Write down the tag questions and the responses you hear. Make a note of the purpose of the tag. Is the person expressing an opinion or checking on a fact? Or maybe the person is just trying to start a conversation or keep a conversation going, or is expressing interest, humor, or surprise.

USE

You are probably often in situations where you are not completely sure that you are doing the right thing. Use tag questions to find out. For example, ''This bus goes to Lester Hall, doesn't it?'', ''This movie is free, isn't it?'', ''There is no pork in this soup, is there?''. Tag questions can be very useful.

2

Yes / No Questions

REVIEW

Imagine that you are trying to find an apartment. You find an ad in the newspaper for an apartment that sounds interesting. You call the number given to get some more information. Fill in the blanks in the conversation.

> I will purchase an '86 or newer motor scooter for $235. 555-7614.

> **ROOMMATE WANTED** for 3 bdrm. house in quiet neighborhood close to campus. Rent is $130/mo. plus shared utilities. Non-smoker grad. student preferred. Call Joe at 555-3084 or 555-8156 anytime.

JOE: Hello.

YOU: Hello. Is this Joe?

JOE: Yes, it is.

YOU: I'm looking for a new place to live. I saw your ad in the paper about the house. Could I ask you a few questions about it?

JOE: Sure.

YOU: Okay. This house has a kitchen,

_____?

JOE: Yes.
YOU: And I could use the kitchen,

_____?

JOE: Sure.

PREVIEW

You used tag questions to ask about the kitchen because you were fairly sure what the answers would be. But now you need to ask some ordinary questions in order to learn:

if the house is close to downtown,

_____***Is the house***_____close to downtown?

whether there is a washing machine in the house,

_____ **a washing machine in the house?**

and if you really have to be a graduate student to live there,

_____ **I really have to be a graduate student to live there?**

The sentences you have just completed are **yes/no questions.**

The man in the picture is named Oscar. His wife died several years ago, and he has lived alone since then. The woman's name is Sadie. She has been alone since her husband's death over 10 years ago. Recently, a mutual friend introduced these two people to each other.

They have just run into each other at the laundromat. Oscar has decided to ask Sadie to go out on a date.

2.1 *Yes/No* Questions With *Be*, Modals, And the Auxiliary *Have*		
Read Sadie's answers. Then complete Oscar's questions.	Check.	Complete these rules.
a. Oscar: _____ _____ **busy tonight?** **Sadie: No, I'm not.** **Oscar:** _____ _____ **like to go to a movie?** **Sadie: Yes, I would. That sounds like fun.** **Oscar:** _____ _____ **seen *King Kong* yet?** **Sadie: No, I haven't. I'd like to see it.**	Are you Would you Have you	This is how to make a **yes/no question** from a statement: If the first verb in the statement is • a form of the verb *be*, • a modal verb, such as _____, • or a form of the auxiliary verb *have*, put the verb _____ the subject. To answer **yes/no** questions, you can use this structure: *Yes or* _____ **+ subject + first verb.**
b. Oscar: _____ **there any other movies in town that you would rather see?** **Sadie: No, no. Let's go to *King Kong*.**	Are	To make a question from a statement beginning with ***there*** and a form of the verb *be*, simply move the form of the verb *be* to the _____ of the sentence.

Oral Practice 1A: Find out whether your classmates can do various things. Example:

Can you swim?

Oral Practice 1B: Ask a question beginning with *Is* or *Are* about a classmate's country or hometown. Example:

Is basketball popular in Indonesia?

Written Practice 1:   Complete these sentences. Read the answer before trying to complete the question.

1. Oscar: _____ we go to the early show or the late show?

   Sadie: We should go to the early show, I think. I usually go to bed early.

2. Sadie: _____ ever been to that theater?

   Oscar: Yes, I have. It's very nice.

3. Sadie: _____ going to pick me up?

   Oscar: Yes, I am. Let's say at 6:30, and then we'll have time to get something to eat.

4. Student: _____ going to be many tests in this course?

   Teacher: There are going to be three major exams.

5. Student: _____ be open-book tests?

   Teacher: No, they won't.

6. Teacher: _____ enough textbooks for this course in the bookstore?

   Student: No, there aren't. They were all gone yesterday.

7. Teacher: _____ bought your book yet?

   Student: No, I haven't. I tried yesterday, but they were all sold out.

2.2 Yes/No Questions With *Do*		
Oscar and Sadie are in Oscar's car on the way to the movie.		
Read Sadie's answers. Then complete these model sentences.	Check.	Complete these rules.
a. Oscar: _____ you go to movies very often? **Sadie: No, I don't, but I usually enjoy them when I do.**	Do	Here are some rules for making a **yes/no question** from a statement. Remember: When the first verb is **be**, the auxiliary **have**, or a modal, put that first verb before the subject in a question. If the verb is something else, put a form of the verb _____ before the subject. (When **do** is used, the main verb is always in the _____ form.)
b. Oscar: _____ _____ _____ any brothers or sisters? **Sadie: I have one sister.**	Do you have	**Have** is not always an auxiliary verb. It is often the **main verb** in the sentence. In American English, when **have** is the main verb, a form of the verb _____ is usually used in questions.
c. Oscar _____ _____ live in this area? **Sadie: No, she doesn't. She lives in Chicago.**	Does she	If the subject is **he, she, it,** or a singular noun, the correct present tense form of **do** is _____.
d. Oscar: _____ _____ ever eaten at Mike's Cafe? **Sadie: Yes, I have eaten there several times. I like it—even though I shouldn't eat greasy food.**	Have you	**REMEMBER:** If **have** is an **auxiliary** verb in the question, don't use **do**. Put the appropriate form of _____ before the subject.

Oral Practice 2A: Ask one of your classmates whether another classmate likes something (food, colors, types of clothing, singers, movie stars, the weather here, and so on.) If the person you ask doesn't know, he or she should ask the other classmate. Example:

Does Marta like spaghetti?
I don't know. I'll ask her.
Marta, do you like spaghetti?

Marta should answer and then ask the next question.

Oral Practice 2B: Find out what your classmates' rooms or apartments have in them. Example:

Does your room have a refrigerator?

Written Practice 2:   Complete these sentences. Read the answer before trying to complete the question.

1. Sadie: _____ here for a long time, Oscar?

    Oscar: Yes, I've lived here since 1946.

2. Sadie: _____ live in an apartment, or _____ have a house?

    Oscar: I have a nice little house that I bought soon after coming here.

3. Sadie: _____ you to live in a house by yourself?

    Oscar: Sometimes it bothers me, but usually I enjoy the peace and quiet.

4. Student: _____ late homework?

    Teacher: Yes, I accept it, but your grade will be lowered if the homework is late.

5. Student: _____ out the lowest test score as some teachers do?

    Teacher: No, I don't throw out any test scores.

6. Student: _____ any prerequisites?

    Teacher: No, this course has no prerequisites.

2.3 Negative *Yes/No* Questions

Now Oscar and Sadie are walking from the theater back to Oscar's car.

Read Sadie's answers. Then complete these model sentences.	Check.	Complete these rules.
a. Oscar: _____ **that a good movie?** **Sadie: Yes, that was a very good movie.**	Wasn't	A **negative yes-no question** is like a regular yes-no question except that it starts with a negative verb. The negative verb is a **contraction.** Sometimes negative questions are used when the speaker has an opinion and wants to find out if the listener _____.
b. Oscar: _____ _____ **afraid?** **Sadie: No! I wasn't afraid at all.**	Weren't you	Sometimes negative questions are used when the speaker is fairly certain about something and wants to find out if he or she is _____. Negative questions that are asked for the two purposes mentioned in rules **a** and **b** could be replaced with tag questions. For example, in model sentence **a**, Oscar could have said: ''That was a great movie, _____ ____?''
c. When they get back to the car, Sadie is surprised to find that Oscar didn't lock it. **Sadie:** _____ _____ _____ **your car?** **Oscar: No, I never do, but I probably should.**	Don't you lock *or* Didn't you lock	Negative questions sometimes show that the speaker is surprised by a situation that is apparently different from what he or she expected.

d. Now refer to model sentences **a**, **b**, and **c**. To answer a negative yes/no question say,
Yes **+ a positive statement**
or
_____ **+ a negative statement.**
In other words, answer negative yes/no questions the same way that you answer positive yes/no questions.

Oral Practice 3:   Check your memory concerning your classmates' names, countries, languages, residences, hobbies, and study plans. Use negative questions. Example:

> *Samir, aren't you from Algeria?*
> *Doesn't Yasuyo study computer science?*

Written Practice 3:   Complete these **negative** questions. Read the answer before trying to complete the question.

1. Sadie: _____ beautiful clothes?

    Oscar: Yes, she had very beautiful clothes.

2. Sadie: _____ enormous?

    Oscar: Yes, he was a big fellow.

3. Sadie: _____ frightened if you saw him?

    Oscar: I would be terrified.

4. Teacher: _____ your homework?

    Student: No, I don't have it today. _____ you say that it was due tomorrow?

5. Teacher: No, I said today. _____ an assignment book to help

    you remember this kind of information?

    Student: No, I don't have one. I guess I should get one.

2.4 Chapter Check: Complete these sentences. *Use at least two negative questions in this exercise. If you are unsure of an answer, check the indicated model sentence and rule.*

1. _____ there an index in this book?

    Yes, _____.   [2.1b]

2. _____ the food that is served in university cafeterias?

    No, I don't like it very much.   [2.2a]

3. _____ remember the first time you went to a movie theater?

    Yes, I can remember it very well.   [2.1a]

4. _____ in Europe?

    No, but I have traveled all over the United States.   [2.1a]

5. _____ an extra pencil that I could borrow?

    Yes, I have several pencils. Take your pick.   [2.2b]

6. _____ Liddy _____ with her parents?

    No, she lives in an apartment.   [2.2a & c]

7. Mary seems to spend a lot of time alone. _____ any friends?

    Yes, she has a lot of friends. She just enjoys being by herself.   [2.3]

8. _____ that an exciting game?

    Yes, I agree. It was a very exciting game.   [2.3]

2.5 Chapter Check: Write sentence B so that it has about the same meaning as sentence A.

1. A. Zebras are in the same family as horses, aren't they?

    B. Aren't _____?   [2.3b]

2. A. English is a Germanic language, isn't it?

    B. _____ a Germanic language?   [2.3b]

3. A. American involvement in Vietnam ended in 1975, didn't it?

    B. Didn't _____?   [2.3b]

4. A. The 1988 Winter Olympics were held in Canada, weren't they?

    B. _____ in Canada?   [2.3b]

5. A. Alexander Graham Bell invented the telephone, didn't he?

    B. _____ Alexander Graham Bell _____?   [2.3b]

6. A. Is Harry a firefighter?

    B. _____ fight fires for a living?   [2.2c]

7. A. Aren't there 26 letters in the English alphabet?

    B. _____ English have _____ in its alphabet?   [2.2b & c, 2.3b]

8. A. Is this the first time you've eaten pizza?

    B. _____ ever eaten pizza before?   [2.2d, 2.3]

9. A. I'm very surprised that you don't know Adrienne.

    B. _____ Adrienne?   [2.3c]

10. A. I had expected Charley to be here by now, but it seems that he isn't.

    B. _____ yet?   [2.3c]

2.6 Warm-up: You want to rent an apartment for next semester. The following checklist shows what you want in the apartment. Pair up with another student. Pretend that this student has an apartment for rent. Ask him or her if the apartment meets your requirements, as follows:

The apartment must be near the university.
The apartment must allow pets and children.
The apartment should have a laundry and swimming pool.
The apartment should have two bedrooms.
The apartment should be near a grocery store or directly on a bus route to downtown.

2.7 Communication: You work for the Office of Student Financial Aid. Your job is to do the preliminary interview of students applying for scholarships. Interview several of your classmates. Using *yes/no* questions, get the information needed to fill out these forms.

SCHOLARSHIP APPLICATION FORM

NAME:_____

    LAST   FIRST   MIDDLE

• MOVED RECENTLY?   __ YES __ NO

• EMPLOYMENT __ WORK __ DON'T WORK

• FULL-TIME STUDENT? __ YES __ NO

• MARITAL STATUS __ MARRIED __ UNMARRIED

• CHILDREN?   __ YES   __ NO

• TUITION __ IN-STATE __ OUT-OF-STATE

• MAJOR DECIDED? __ YES __ NO

• GRADUATE THIS YEAR? __ YES __ NO

NAME:_____

    LAST   FIRST   MIDDLE

• MOVED RECENTLY?   __ YES __ NO

• EMPLOYMENT __ WORK __ DON'T WORK

• FULL-TIME STUDENT? __ YES __ NO

• MARITAL STATUS __ MARRIED __ UNMARRIED

• CHILDREN?   __ YES   __ NO

• TUITION __ IN-STATE __ OUT-OF-STATE

• MAJOR DECIDED? __ YES __ NO

• GRADUATE THIS YEAR? __ YES __ NO

NAME:_____

    LAST   FIRST   MIDDLE

• MOVED RECENTLY?   __ YES __ NO

• EMPLOYMENT __ WORK __ DON'T WORK

• FULL-TIME STUDENT? __ YES __ NO

• MARITAL STATUS __ MARRIED __ UNMARRIED

• CHILDREN?   __ YES   __ NO

• TUITION __ IN-STATE __ OUT-OF-STATE

• MAJOR DECIDED? __ YES __ NO

• GRADUATE THIS YEAR? __ YES __ NO

NAME:_____

    LAST   FIRST   MIDDLE

• MOVED RECENTLY?   __ YES __ NO

• EMPLOYMENT __ WORK __ DON'T WORK

• FULL-TIME STUDENT? __ YES __ NO

• MARITAL STATUS __ MARRIED __ UNMARRIED

• CHILDREN?   __ YES   __ NO

• TUITION __ IN-STATE __ OUT-OF-STATE

• MAJOR DECIDED? __ YES __ NO

• GRADUATE THIS YEAR? __ YES __ NO

NAME:_____

    LAST   FIRST   MIDDLE

• MOVED RECENTLY?   __ YES __ NO

• EMPLOYMENT __ WORK __ DON'T WORK

• FULL-TIME STUDENT? __ YES __ NO

• MARITAL STATUS __ MARRIED __ UNMARRIED

• CHILDREN?   __ YES   __ NO

• TUITION __ IN-STATE __ OUT-OF-STATE

• MAJOR DECIDED? __ YES __ NO

• GRADUATE THIS YEAR? __ YES __ NO

2.8 Sentence Writing: Write the yes/no questions that you might ask in the following situations. Some of the questions should be negative. Example: You want to know if tonight's movie is free, so you call the student union and ask this question:

Is tonight's movie free?

1.   You think Shakespeare was born in the sixteenth century, but you want to make sure, so you ask your teacher.
2.   You want to know if your friend can meet you at the restaurant at 7, so you ask him or her.

3. You think dinosaurs were extinct long before humans appeared on earth, but you decide to check with your roommate.
4. You want to know whether the word *almost* means "nearly" or "mostly," so you ask a native speaker.

2.9 Sentence Writing: Americans routinely ask certain questions of one another when they talk on the telephone. You may have noticed that telephone habits in American English are different from those in your native language. If you have trouble with the following exercise, you might ask an American acquaintance for help. Write questions that would be appropriate in these telephone situations.

1. You are trying to call your friend Mila on the phone. A woman answers. You think that it might be Mila, but you are not sure. Hint: You should not say, "Are you Mila?" in this situation.
2. The woman says that she is not Mila. You want to know if Mila is home.
3. The woman says that she thinks Mila is home. You want to speak to her.
4. The woman tries to find Mila. When she comes back, she says that she is sorry, but Mila is not there. You want the woman to take a message.
5. The woman says she will take a message. You give her the message. You want to make sure that she has written it all down. It would sound impolite to say, "Did you write all that down?" Can you think of a polite way to make sure that she has the important information?

2.10 Sentence Writing: Once in a while, it's effective to begin a paragraph or an essay by asking the reader a yes/no question. This is sometimes a good way to involve your reader in the topic. In this exercise you can practice this kind of introduction.
Example: You are going to explain how to use chopsticks, and you begin by asking if the reader has ever been afraid to try to use them in public.

Have you ever been afraid to use chopsticks in public?

1. You are going to explain how to use chopsticks, and you begin by asking if the reader knows how to use them.
2. You are going to write about a famous person from your native land, and you begin by asking whether the reader has ever heard of that person.
3. You are going to write about abortion, and you begin by asking if abortion can ever be justified on moral grounds.
4. You are going to write about the discovery of America by the Vikings, and you begin by asking if Christopher Columbus really discovered America.

2.11 Letter Writing: You are looking for an apartment. You see this poster in the student union and decide to write for further information. You wonder whether the apartment is furnished and whether it has a kitchen. You hope that the utilities are included in the rent, that you can have a pet, and that the neighborhood is quiet. You want a place that is close to campus and on the bus route. Finally, you want to know whether you have to sign a long-term lease.

Write a letter to the landlord, Jim Daniels. Begin the letter this way:

> Dear Mr. Daniels,
>
> I saw your poster about the apartment and am interested in more information. Could you please answer the following questions for me?

Then write a numbered list of at least eight questions that you would like answers to.

End the letter this way:

> You may write me at the address below. Thank you for your prompt reply.
>
> > Sincerely,
> >
> > (Your Name)
> >
> > (Your Address)

2.12 Reflecting: Read the second episode of the mystery story. Examine the ways yes/no questions are used. Can you find a place where a negative question could have been used but wasn't?

> "My husband has been gone three weeks, Mr. Stern," Deanne Miller told me. "The police couldn't find him. I thought a detective could try. Can you help me?"
>
> "I can try," I said. "First I need some information. Does he have a job?"
>
> "Yes," she said. "He works for an insurance company."
>
> "Does he sell insurance?"
>
> "No. He's a detective, too. He investigates cases against doctors. When a patient says a doctor did something wrong and wants to sue the doctor, my husband finds out if the patient is right. Then the company decides how much money to offer the patient."
>
> "Can you give me the name of the company?"
>
> Mrs. Miller found one of her husband's cards in her purse and gave it to me.
>
> "Did your husband act strangely before he disappeared?"
>
> "No."
>
> "Was he happy with his job?"
>
> "Fairly happy," she said. "Is any job perfect?"
>
> "Only my job," I smiled. "Do you know what he was working on before he disappeared?"
>
> "You'll have to ask the company," she said.
>
> "Did he talk about his work?"
>
> "Not very much."
>
> We talked about her husband for an hour. "I can't promise you anything," I said. "Usually the police can do this kind of work better than I can."
>
> "Please call me when you find something," Deanne Miller said.
>
> "How did you get here?" I asked. "Can I call you a cab?"
>
> "I drove," she answered.
>
> "And you found a parking place? To park in this city, you usually need a shoehorn."

2.13 Real-World Work

THINK/PRACTICE

Between now and your next class, ask yourself a lot of yes/no questions about the people and things you see around you. For example, "Will that guy get to class on time?" "Did I make any mistakes on my homework?" "Has my bus already gone by?" "Isn't it a beautiful day?"

LOOK/LISTEN

Rhetorical questions are not questions in the normal sense. They don't require responses. They are used to make a point. For example, a speaker arguing for higher taxes in a legislative session might say,

Is it wise to allow our nation to go deeper and deeper into debt?

The speaker has used a question form, but it is obvious that he or she is using the question to make the point that it is unwise to allow this to happen.

Try to find an example of a rhetorical question in print. One good place to look is the editorial pages of newspapers and magazines. Bring the example to class and explain why it was used.

USE

1. Try to ask other people questions about things you are curious about. Listen to people talking, and notice their questions. Listen for negative questions especially.

2. Think of some products that you're interested in buying. Call some businesses in town to see if they have these products. (''Do you have . . . ?'' ''Do you know who might have one?'' and so on.)

3. If you don't know what to say in a situation, such as when you are talking on the phone, ask an American friend, ''Should I say . . . ?'' ''Is it all right to say . . . ?''

Information Questions

REVIEW

Oscar is driving Sadie home after *King Kong*. Write the yes/no questions he would ask her in the following situations.

Oscar wants to know if he should turn at the next stoplight:

_____

Oscar thinks that the movie was exciting, and he wants to find out if Sadie agrees, so he says,

_____

Oscar sees an ice cream shop as they ride, and he wants to know if Sadie wants to stop for an ice cream cone, so he asks,

_____

After they have ordered their ice cream, Oscar discovers that he doesn't have any money left, so he asks Sadie,

_____

PREVIEW

After they leave the ice cream store, Oscar drives Sadie the rest of the way home, and they ask each other questions. Complete their questions with one of the suggested answers.

OSCAR: When _____ you again?
         A.   I can see   B.   can I see   C.   can see I

SADIE: Oh, I don't know. What _____ next weekend?
         A.   are you doing   B.   you are doing   C.   you doing

OSCAR: Oh, I don't know. _____ you free on Saturday?
         A.   When do   B.   What time are   C.   What is time

Questions which begin with words such as **when** and **what** are called **information questions.**

Before doing the first rule builder, read the following story.

Stan, an unmarried saxophone player, is talking on the phone with Mr. Grimes, who is the manager of an apartment building. Stan is looking for an apartment.

STAN: When can you show me the apartment?
MR. GRIMES: I can show it to you right away. I'm meeting some other people in the same building in a few minutes. Could you come over now?
STAN: Sure. I'm downtown right now. How far is your building from downtown?
MR. GRIMES: It's just a few blocks.
STAN: How long will it take me to walk there?
MR. GRIMES: It shouldn't take more than 15 minutes.
STAN: How often does a bus go that way?
MR. GRIMES: Once every 45 minutes. You should probably walk.

Mr. and Ms. Jones are going to look at an apartment in the same building. They are getting ready to go.

MS. JONES: When is our appointment with Mr. Grimes?
MR. JONES: At 8:30.
MS. JONES: Why is the appointment so early?
MR. JONES: It was the only time Mr. Grimes could fit us in.
MS. JONES: Where is the apartment located?
MR. JONES: On Elm Street on the block between 4th and 5th. How should we get there?
MS. JONES: Let's walk. It's not far, and it's a nice day.
MR. JONES: How much time do we have to get there?
MS. JONES: We have about 20 minutes. It's just about 10 after.
MR. JONES: How many blocks do we have to walk?
MS. JONES: Only about five. We can make it easily. Come on.

3.1 Common Information Question Structures		
Complete these model sentences.	Check.	Complete these rules.
a. **When _____ _____ show me the apartment?**	can you	The rules for making most **information questions** are just like those for making yes/no questions except that a question word, such as **why, where,** or _____, comes _____ the first verb.
b. **How _____ is your building from downtown?** **How _____ will it take me to walk there?** **How _____ does a bus go that way?**	far long often	Here are some question words for measurements: distance: ***how far*** length of time: _____ _____ frequency: _____ _____
c. **_____ is our appointment with Mr. Grimes?** **_____ is the appointment so early?** **_____ is the apartment located?** **_____ should we get there?**	When Why Where How	Here are some more questions words: time: _____ reason: _____ place: _____ manner: _____
d. **_____ _____ time do we have?** **_____ _____ blocks do we have to walk?**	How much How many	Here are some more question expressions: amount: _____ _____ number: _____ _____

Oral Practice 1A: Pair up with a classmate. Ask each other questions about the following.

- *how long it takes to fly to your classmate's country,*
- *how long he or she has lived here,*
- *what time it is in your classmate's country,*
- *and how often your classmate talks to his or her family.*

Oral Practice 1B: Think about things you have noticed your classmates doing. For example, Sandra always sits in the front row. Or look at the STUDENT INFORMATION SHEET in chapter 1 to remind yourself of things you know about your classmates—for example, Mahmoud lives in a dorm. Ask your classmates why they do these things. Examples:

> *Why do you always sit in the front row?*
> *Why do you live in a dorm?*

Written Practice 1:   Complete these sentences. *Read the answer* before trying to complete the question.

Mr. and Ms. Jones and Stan arrived at the apartment building at about the same time. The manager, Mr. Grimes, has told the Joneses to start looking around and takes Stan upstairs to see an apartment.

1.   Stan: _____ is the lease for?

     Mr. Grimes: It's for 12 months.

2.   Stan: _____ catch a bus for downtown?

     Mr. Grimes: At the corner of 3rd and Elm.

3.   Stan: How _____ is that from here?

     Mr. Grimes: About a block and a half.

4.   Stan: How _____ the garbage picked up?

     Mr. Grimes: It's picked up twice a week.

5.   Stan: _____ the temperature?

     Mr. Grimes: You can control it by adjusting the thermostat in the dining

                  room.

6.   Stan: _____ any restrictions on playing musical in-

                  struments?

     Mr. Grimes: No, there aren't any.

Then Mr. Grimes rushes downstairs to talk to Mr. and Ms. Jones.

Complete the questions they ask.

7.   Mr. Jones: How _____ is the rent?

     Mr. Grimes: It's $350.

8.   Ms. Jones: _____?

     Mr. Grimes: It's due on the first of the month.

9.   Mr. Jones: _____ there no lock on the door?

     Mr. Grimes: Because we always change locks when someone moves out.

10.   Mr. Jones: _____ are there in this building?

     Mr. Grimes: There are 15 other units.

11.   Ms. Jones: _____ loud noise in this building?

     Mr. Grimes: No, we don't allow any loud noise.

3.2 **Questions About Ownership**		
Complete this model sentence.	Check.	Complete this rule.
Teacher: _____ test in this? **Student: That's mine. I'm sorry, I forgot to put my name on it.**	Whose	To find the owner of something, use the question word _____.

Oral Practice 2:   Look around at objects you see in the room. Find out the owners of these objects by asking **whose** questions. Example:

   Whose pack is this?

Written Practice 2A: Complete these sentences. Read the answer before trying to complete the question.

   Now Mr. Grimes has gone back upstairs to see Stan. While they are talking, Mr. Crumm, the assistant manager, rushes in.

1.   Mr. Crumm: _____ red sports car is parked out in front of the building?

      Mr. Grimes: That's *my* car.

2.   Mr. Crumm: And _____ blue station wagon was parked on the other side of the parking lot?

      Stan: That's mine.

      Mr. Crumm: Your station wagon just rolled across the lot and hit Mr. Grimes's car.

3.   Stan: Oh no! _____ the damage?

      Mr. Grimes: *Your* insurance will cover it, or else you'll find another apartment.

Written Practice 2B: Read the answer; then write the appropriate **whose** question.

1.   It's the *landlord's* responsibility to clean up the hallway.
2.   We're going in *Fahad's* car.
3.   I think the professor was referring to *Reynaldo's* paper.

   Before doing Rule Builder 3.3, read some more of the conversation between the Joneses and Mr. Grimes.

Mr. Jones: Who makes the repairs in this building?
Mr. Grimes: A man named Cliff makes all the repairs.
Ms. Jones: *(informal)* Who should we call if we need to have something fixed?
      (more formal) Whom should we call if we need to have something fixed?
Mr. Grimes: You should call me.

Stan has already started practicing on his saxophone.

MR. JONES: What is that awful noise?
MR. GRIMES: I don't know. I'll try to find out.
MR. JONES: What did you say?
MR. GRIMES: (*loudly*) I said I'll try to find out.

3.3 Questions With *Who, Whom,* and *What*		
Complete these model sentences.	Check.	Complete these rules.
a. _____ **makes the repairs in this building?** (*informal*) _____ **should we call if something needs to be fixed?** *or* _____ **should we talk to if something needs to be fixed?**	Who Who Who	***Who*** may be the subject or (in **informal** English) the object of a sentence. ***Who*** does not refer to things; ***who*** refers to _____.
b. (*formal*) _____ **should we call if something needs to be fixed?** *or* _____ _____ **do we talk if something needs to be fixed?**	Whom To whom	In **formal** English, don't use ***who*** as an object; use _____. In formal English, a preposition, such as _____, can come before ***whom*** in a question.
c. _____ **is that awful noise?** _____ **did you say?**	What What	***What*** may be either the subject or an object in a question. ***What*** refers to _____.

Oral Practice 3A: Find out what your classmates did last weekend and who they did these things with (that is, with whom they did these things).

Oral Practice 3B: Find out the names and times of your classmates' favorite television programs. Ask for other information about these programs, too.

Written Practice 3:   Complete these sentences. Read the answer before trying to complete the question.

1.   (*informal*) _____ if I smell something burning?

     You should call the fire department.

2.   _____ the fire department's number?

     It's 911.

3.   _____ come if I call that number?

     A team of firefighters will come.

4.   (*formal*) _____ if I think there was a mistake on my grade?

     You should see someone in the Office of Student Assistance.

5.   _____ responsible for mailing my transcripts to another university?

     The staff of the Office of Admissions and Records is responsible.

6.   _____ about that?

     You should talk to the secretary in the office.

7.   _____ ask me if I want to apply for health insurance?

     They will ask you some general questions about your health history.

3.4 Questions with *Which*, *What*, and *What Kind of* + Noun		
Complete these model sentences.	Check.	Complete these rules.
a. _____ apartment is larger, the one upstairs or the one downstairs?	Which	When you ask someone to identify something, he or she has to pick it out from a small group of things or a large group of things. When the choice is from a small number of known items, use this structure: _____ + **noun**
b. _____ musical instrument does Stan play?	What	When the choice is made from a large group of items, use this structure: _____ + _____

| c. _____ _____ of car does **Mr. Grimes have?**

_____ _____ of *cars* **do you see on the street outside?** | What kind

What kinds | We also ask people to classify things: to identify the group that a thing belongs to. To do this, we can use this structure:

_____ *kind(s)* _____ + **noun**
We can use **which kind of** for a very limited choice:
Which kind of keyboard does your computer have, standard or extended? |

Oral Practice 4A: If it is appropriate in your class, find out which dorms your classmates live in.

Oral Practice 4B: Find out what courses your classmates are taking and which buildings their classes are in.

Oral Practice 4C: Find out which seasons and what kinds of weather your classmates like best.

Written Practice 4:   Complete these sentences.

1. _____ closet does Ms. Jones want for her clothes?

2. _____ of job does Mr. Jones have?

3. _____ floor is Stan's apartment on, the first or second?

4. _____ telephone number do you dial to report a fire?

5. _____ country does your roommate come from?

6. _____ parties do you like?

7. There are three Halloween parties this evening; _____ one do you want to go to?

8. _____ time do the parties begin?

3.5 More *What* Questions		
Complete these model sentences.	Check.	Complete these rules.
a. _____ **does your father do for a living?** **He's a university professor.**	What	The question word ***what*** is used in several expressions. To ask about a person's profession or job, you can say, ***What*** _____ ***he/she*** _____ ***for a living?***
b. _____ **is he like?** **He's somewhat old-fashioned and conservative, but very kind.**	What	To ask about the qualities or character of a person or thing, you can say, ***What*** _____ ***he/she/it*** _____?
c. _____ **does he look like?** **He's tall and slender and has rather long silver hair.**	What	To ask for a physical description of a person or thing you can say, _____ _____ ***he/she/it*** _____ _____?

Oral Practice 5:   Everyone should think about his or her favorite aunt, uncle, or other favorite adult relative. Then ask each other about these people's appearances, qualities, and professions or jobs. Use questions beginning with ***what***.

Written Practice 5A: Complete these sentences. Read the answer before trying to complete the questions.

1. _____ Mr. McGill look like?

   He's bald and rather short.

2. _____ Mrs. McGill _____?

   She's quiet and shy.

3. _____ Mr. McGill _____ for a living?

   I think he's retired.

Written Practice 5B: Complete these sentences.

You are Mrs. Buck, the owner of the building that Mr. Grimes manages. You want to find out if Stan will be a good renter, so you call up one of his references.

1. First, you want to find out what kind of work Stan does. You say,

   _____ living?

2. You want to find out what kind of person Stan is. You say,

   _____ like?

3.   You think that you may have met Stan sometime in the past. To find out, you ask for a

physical description of Stan:

_____?

3.6 Chapter Check: Complete these sentences. Read the answer before trying to complete
the question. If you are unsure of an answer, check the indicated model sentence and rule.

1.   Q: _____ materials were used in the construction of that building?

A: Mostly steel and glass.   [3.4b or c]

2.   Q: _____ designed it?

A: An architect named Peter Gray.   [3.3a]

3.   Q: _____ money did it cost to build it?

A: $100 million.   [3.1d]

4.   Q: _____ did it take to build it?

A: Nearly two years.   [3.1b]

5.   Q: _____ was it finished?

A: In 1989, I believe.   [3.1c]

6.   Q: _____ is it to the restaurant?

A: About five blocks.   [3.1b]

7.   Q: _____ do you think we should get there?

A: Let's drive.   [3.1c]

8.   Q: _____ car should we take?

A: We can take mine.   [3.2]

9.   Q: _____ people does your car hold?

A: Five.   [3.1d]

10. Q: _____ is this restaurant _____?

A: It's very modern, but it has a friendly atmosphere.   [3.5b]

3.7 Chapter Check: Finish sentence B. It should have about the same meaning as
sentence A.

1.   A.   Who is the owner of this electric saw?

B.   _____ is this?   [3.2]

2.   A.   What is Mr. Ferguson's job?

B.   _____ for a living?   [3.5a]

3.   A.   Can you describe Ms. Ferguson for me?

B.   _____ Ms. Ferguson look _____?   [3.5c]

4. A. What is the population of Singapore?

   B. _____ people _____?   [3.1d]

5. A. What is the distance from Chicago to Philadelphia?

   B. _____ is it from Chicago to Philadelphia?   [3.1b]

6. A. Tell the reason why you came to this country to study.

   B. Why _____?   [3.1a]

7. A. What is the price of this blue jacket?

   B. _____ this blue jacket cost?   [3.1d]

3.8 Warm-up: Form small groups. One student looks at the STUDENT INFORMATION SHEET in chapter 1. He or she quizzes the other members of the group about the information. Listen carefully to the information questions, and help out if your classmate has trouble. Examples:

> *What country does Bin come from?*
> *Whose native language is Turkish?*
> *How many students are from Japan?*
> *Where is Freddie living?*

3.9 Communication: Imagine that your job is to call students and get information from them for your school's record-keeping office. Use the following form to interview some classmates. *Be sure to get the correct spelling of names.* Set up a time for the student to come in for an information meeting about his or her major. Try to find a time that is convenient for both you and the student. Imagine that you are speaking over the telephone, so the other student cannot see the form.

NAME	STUDENT NUMBER	AGE	HEIGHT	DATE OF BIRTH	DATE OF U.S. ENTRY	NAME OF A RELATIVE	MAJOR OR CAREER PLANS	APPT. TIME

3.10 Communication: Identify each of the following things. Compare your answers with your classmates' answers. If you think you know the answer but aren't certain, check by using a tag question. If you don't know the answer, ask a normal information question.

1.   The governor of the state you live in: _____

2.   The largest city (*by population*) of this state: _____

3.   The nearest large body of water: _____

4.   The location of the mail box nearest where you are now:

     _____

5.   The price of an airplane ticket to Hawaii: _____

6.   The most expensive restaurant in town: _____

7.   America's three most popular sports: _____

8.   The meaning of ''to catch 40 winks'': _____

3.11 Sentence Writing: Write four information questions about important and well-known facts concerning your native country. (Suggestions—cities (the capital, the largest city, the second largest city); geography (oceans, rivers, neighboring countries); principal exports; population; history; and so on.) You can probably think of many more categories. Try to make the questions challenging but not too difficult. You will quiz your classmates with some of these questions in the next class period. If everyone in the class is from the same country, you can make questions about other countries in the world.

3.12 Letter Writing: You have received a reply from Jim Daniels about the apartment you are interested in. (*See 2.11 Letter Writing.*) In the letter, Jim tells you that the apartment is completely furnished and has a kitchen with all the appliances, including a dishwasher. He says that utilities are not included in the rent and that pets are not allowed, but that the neighborhood is very nice and quiet. He adds that the apartment is only two blocks from campus and that the bus that connects downtown and campus stops right in front of the apartment building.

     Now you are very interested. You didn't really want to have a pet anyway. But you realize that you still have several questions. You don't know how much the initial deposit and the rent are, or what the average monthly cost for utilities is. You don't know the number of bedrooms, the size of the kitchen, how long a lease you must sign, or who you can call in case of problems. You want to know how many single men/women live there. You would like to know when the apartment will be available. You can probably think of a few other things you would like to know about the place.

     Write another letter to Mr. Daniels in which you ask another list of 10 questions.

3.13 Communication: You and your classmates can ask each other some of the questions you prepared for 3.11 Sentence Writing. You could do this as a ''College Bowl'' competition, with two or three teams trying to answer questions that other members of the class ask.

3.14 Reflecting: Read the next episode of the mystery story. Examine the way information questions are used. At the end of the passage, Farmer says, ''I wonder why.'' He could have asked an information question beginning with **why**. What would that question have been?

> After Deanne Miller left, I read my mail and watered my dying plants. The plants were there when I moved into the office, and I'm sure they will be there when I move out.
>
> Then I went to work. I called a friend of mine in the police department. His name was Ted Farmer, and he worked in the missing persons department. We had worked together several times.
>
> ''Hello, Stern,'' he said on the phone. ''What do you want?''
>
> ''I just wanted to say hello.''
>
> ''Hello,'' he said. ''Now what do you really want?''
>
> ''Where is Carl Miller?'' I asked.
>
> ''Oh,'' he said. ''When did Mrs. Miller come to see you?''
>
> ''This morning.''
>
> ''I tried to talk her out of hiring a detective. We couldn't find him.''
>
> ''How long did you look?'' I asked.
>
> ''I had that case for two weeks.''
>
> ''And who is working on it now?''
>
> Farmer sighed. ''Nobody. We're pretty busy.''
>
> ''I understand,'' I said.
>
> ''Wait a second, okay? I'll go find that file.'' Farmer was gone for two minutes. I sang several loud songs into the phone while he was gone. When he came back he said, ''What was that horrible noise?''
>
> ''You're a funny man, Farmer.''
>
> ''It sounded like someone was dying.''
>
> ''You probably found that file quickly,'' I said. ''Then you listened to my whole concert.''
>
> ''People say you're a good detective,'' Farmer said. ''I wonder why.''

3.15 Real-World Work

THINK/PRACTICE

Ask yourself information questions whenever you think about it, and try them out on other people. Don't be afraid to ask when you need something! Asking questions is a great way to learn.

LOOK/LISTEN

Newspapers definitely contain more statements than questions. But there are some features where you can find information questions. Most newspapers have columns in which readers ask experts questions about their social life, finances, or health. Another good place to look for questions is the comic strip page. Find some interesting information questions in a newspaper, cut them out, and bring them to class.

USE

1. In the front of phone books you will often find the numbers to dial when you want information. Your town may have numbers to call to get information about movies, concerts, and so on. If you don't find these numbers in the phone book, ask someone who is more familiar with your town or city. Examples:

   When does the early movie start this evening?
   What time . . . ?
   How long . . . ?

2. If you plan to do any traveling soon, call up a bus or train station, an airline, or a travel agency to find out about times, costs, and so on. Example:

   How much does it cost to fly to . . . ?

3. Make a list of things that you need, or kinds of food that you are used to eating and have not been able to find in a store. Ask a friend where you might find these things.

4

Requests, Offers, and Suggestions

REVIEW

Your roommate, Bill, goes to work early in the morning. He needs the job to pay his way through school. Recently he has been late to work several times. He is late when he doesn't get to bed on time. Bill is going to stay up late tonight because he has to type a paper for class.

After reading the answer, try to complete each question.

YOU: _____ do you have to go to work tomorrow morning?
BILL: Seven.

YOU: _____ aren't you in bed?
BILL: Because I have to type a paper tonight.

YOU: _____ pages long is this paper?
BILL: Ten.

YOU: Maybe you could hand it in late. _____ is your teacher like?
BILL: She hates late papers, if that's what you mean.

PREVIEW

If Bill doesn't get to sleep, he will be late for work. If he's late again, he will be fired. If he's fired, he won't be able to help you pay the rent. Make an offer to type his paper for him.

Can _____?

Bill gladly accepts your offer, but after a few minutes he comes out of his bedroom and says that he is too tense to go to sleep right away. You make a suggestion:

_____ don't you listen to some music?

Bill puts on some music, but he has the stereo turned up so loud that it shakes the house. You make a request.

Could _____?

Questions can be used to obtain new information, as you have seen in previous chapters. They can also be used to make **requests, offers,** and **suggestions,** as in this preview.

Ms. Jones, whose first name is Doris, is Dean of Students at a small college. She is giving some instructions to Sarah, her secretary, while Sarah's co-workers, Cindy and Harold, are busy in the outer office.

4.1 Using Imperatives to Make Requests and Suggestions		
Doris wants Sarah to type a letter to international students about some visitors from abroad who are going to visit the campus soon.		
Complete these model sentences.	Check.	Complete these rules.
a. Sarah, please _____ the letter that I dictated yesterday. We need to get 50 copies of it in the mail by 3:00. **_____ very careful about spelling the visitors' names correctly.**	type Be	To make **requests** (or give **orders**), you can simply use the **base form** of the verb. This verb form is called the **imperative**. To make an imperative sentence more polite, use the word _____. An imperative sentence can also be used to make a **suggestion** or give **advice**. Example: *Take* **good notes in Professor Cox's class.**
b. _____ copy the letter until I've seen it. In fact, let's make that an office rule. *Always* show me a letter after you've typed it. *Never* send out a letter until I've had a chance to read it.	Don't	To make an imperative sentence **negative**, put _____ *not* (contraction: _____) in front of the base form of the verb. The opposite of *always* + the base form of the verb is _____ + the base form.

Oral Practice 1:   Imagine that a new student who has just arrived in this country joins the class. Using imperatives, give this student helpful advice about finding a place to live, getting a roommate, and getting enrolled in classes. Be sure to tell him or her *not* to do certain things.

Written Practice 1:   One of your classmates has just bought a new car, but he/she doesn't know any of the rules for safe driving. Complete these sentences to give your friend safety tips. Use ***always*** and ***never*** where necessary.

1. _____ when you are going to turn.
2. _____ when you come to an intersection.
3. _____ at night.
4. _____ when you are following another car.
5. _____ if you see a drunk driver.
6. _____ when you are driving by a school.
7. _____ when the road is wet or icy.
8. _____ if you are involved in an accident.

4.2   Requesting Permission

Sarah has told Doris that she will make sure that everything gets done. Now she has a request to make. She wants to leave a few minutes early this afternoon so that she can meet a friend at the airport. There are several expressions Sarah could use.

Complete these model sentences.	Check.	Complete these rules.
a. _____ **I leave a few minutes early today?**	May/ Could/ Can	To request **permission,** we use the _____ verbs ***may, could,*** and ***can. May*** and _____ are considered more polite than _____. The verb after a modal verb is always in the _____ form.
b. Do you mind _____ **I leave a few minutes early today?** *or* **Would you mind if I** _____ **a few minues early today?**	if left	Another structure used in requesting permission is: _____ ***you mind if*** + **subject** + **simple present verb** Here is a more polite and formal structure with the same meaning: ***Would you mind if*** + **subject** + **simple PAST verb**

Oral Practice 2:   Ask the teacher for special permission to do something that is not normally allowed in this course. There's a good chance that the answer will be no. Have some fun with this exercise. Example:

I'm getting a little bored. Could I leave a few minutes early today?

Written Practice 2:   Write the questions you would ask in order to get permission to do something in the following situations. Use a variety of expressions.

1. You would like to use your classroom for a short meeting of a student organization at 4:00 P.M. tomorrow. What do you say to your teacher?
2. Your picture has been printed in the campus newspaper, and you would like a copy of the photograph, so you call the office. What do you say?
3. You want to borrow your roommate's bicycle to run some errands. (You often do this, and he always says, ''Sure.'') What do you say to your roommate?
4. You are out of eggs, and you want to bake a cake, so you go to your next-door neighbor's to borrow some. What do you say?
5. You are supposed to give a speech in your English class tomorrow, but you don't think you'll be ready until the next day. What do you say to your teacher?

4.3 Asking Someone to Do Something		
Now Sarah is in the outer office with her co-workers. She has finished typing the letter, and she wants Harold to photocopy it.		
Complete these model sentences.	Check.	Complete these rules.
a. Sarah: _____ you make 50 copies of this, Harold? **Harold: _____.**	Will/Can/ Would/Could Certainly/ Sure/Okay/ Of course/ All right/Yes	To ask someone to do something for you, use the modal **will** or _____, or the past forms of those verbs: _____ and _____. The past forms are considered more polite. Notice that there are several ways to answer a request that all mean ''yes.''
b. Sarah: Would you mind _____ 50 copies of this? **Harold: Not at all.**	making	Another structure used in making requests is: _____ *you* _____ + *ing* form of verb A common answer to such a request is _____ _____ _____.

Oral Practice 3A: Think of a favor you want a friend or an acquaintance to do for you. Tell the class what your relationship with this person is, and then tell what you will say in making this request.

Oral Practice 3B: Ask a classmate to lend you something that you need in class and that you might have left at home.

Written Practice 3:   Write the requests you would make in the following situations.

1. You want your wife or husband to empty the garbage.
2. You would like your teacher to write you a letter of recommendation.
3. You are talking to a friend on the phone, and someone knocks on your door. You want your friend to wait a minute while you answer the door.
4. You would like your teacher to stay a few minutes after class to help you with a home-work assignment.
5. You want your roommate to drop you off at school on his or her way to a party.

4.4   Making Suggestions

Cindy has a suggestion to make. She thinks they should send the letters by campus mail to the teachers and let the teachers give them to the students. They won't have to pay for postage if they do that. Cindy could use several expressions.

Complete these model sentences.	Check.	Complete these rules.
a. I think we _____ send the letters by campus mail.	should	To make a **suggestion**, you can simply make a statement that begins, *I think we/you/she/etc.* _____ . . .
b. _____ we send the letters by campus mail?	Shall/Should/ Could/Can	You can also make a suggestion by asking a question beginning with one of these _____ verbs: *shall, should, could,* and *can*. The most formal is _____ *I/we.*
c. _____ send the letters by campus mail. **Why _____ we send the letters by campus mail?** **Why not _____ the letters by campus mail?** **How about _____ the letters by campus mail?**	Let's don't send sending	Here are some other structures that are used in making suggestions: • *Let's* + the _____ form of the verb • _____ *don't we/you/I* + the _____ form • *Why _____* + the _____ form • *How about/What about* + the _____ form

Oral Practice 4A: Pretend that your class is going to have a party this weekend. Have a class discussion to come up with ideas. Better yet, plan a real party!

Oral Practice 4B: Think of a problem that you are facing. Perhaps your next-door neighbor is too noisy, or lunch is costing you too much money. Tell a classmate about the problem and ask for a suggestion.

Written Practice 4: Write the suggestions you might make in the following situations. *Write two versions of each suggestion, using two different structures from Rule Builder 4.4.*

1. Your roommate, who is bored, is bothering you. You are trying to study for a test.
2. A friend asks you for the best way to study for a structure test.
3. You are going to a 7:30 movie with Oscar and Sadie, and they want to know what time to pick you up. Suggest a time for them to pick you up.
4. There are no groceries in the house, and your roommate wants to know what to do about dinner.

4.5 Making Offers		
In order to know who the students' teachers are, someone must check the students' schedules. Sarah starts to do this, and Harold wants to help. There are several expressions he could use.		
Complete these model sentences.	Check.	Complete these rules.
a. I _____ help you, Sarah.	will/can/ could	The simplest way to make an **offer** is to make a statement beginning with *I will*, _____, or _____.
b. _____ I help you?	May/Can/ Could/Shall	You can also make an offer by asking a question beginning with *May I*, _____ _____, _____ _____, or _____ _____.
c. _____ don't I help you?	Why	Finally, you can make an offer by using the expression: _____ _____ _____.

Oral Practice 5A: Read the following paragraph.

Your roommate or spouse is always very helpful to you, but today she (or he) needs help. She has 25 library books to return, a test to study for, and a paper to write. In addition, one of the tires on her car is flat, there's no food in the kitchen, and this is her night to wash the dishes. Furthermore, she has nothing to wear to class tomorrow because all of her clothes are dirty, and she needs some medicine for a bad cold that she is suffering from. Finally, she needs to wake up early tomorrow morning to study, but her alarm clock is broken.

Now make some offers to your roommate.

Oral Practice 5B: Often the answer to a polite request is an offer.

Could you shut that window?
Sure, I'll do that for you.

An offer can sometimes be followed by a request.

Could I hold the door for you?
Would you mind? I'd appreciate it.

Make an offer or a request to a classmate. He or she should respond politely in one of these ways.

Written Practice 5: Write some offers that you might make in the following situations. Use a variety of expressions.

1. You know your roommate needs a ride to the laundromat.
2. A friend wants to go to the movies, but he's out of money and his bank is closed.
3. The apartment is a mess; your roommate is busy studying for final exams.
4. You don't feel like making dinner, but your spouse or roommate comes home tired and upset after a hard day.

4.6 Chapter Check: Complete these sentences. If you are unsure of an answer, check the indicated model sentence and rule.

1. Would you mind _____ more slowly, please? My English is poor. [4.3b]
2. Shall I _____ the teacher why you are absent? [4.5b]
3. _____ please tell me how to get to the post office? [4.3a]
4. How about _____ to a movie tonight? [4.4c]
5. _____ I hand in my composition tomorrow? [4.2a]

4.7 Chapter Check: Finish sentence B. It should have about the same meaning as sentence A.

1. A. May I look at your dictionary?
   B. _____ if I look at your dictionary? [4.2b]
2. A. Would you please let me use your pencil sharpener?
   B. _____ I _____ your pencil sharpener? [4.2a]
3. A. Could you please not smoke while my mother is here?
   B. Would you mind _____ while my mother is here? [4.3b]
4. A. Shall we dance?
   B. _____ dance. [4.4c]
5. A. Could I help you move that table?
   B. Why _____ move that table? [4.5c]

4.8 Warm-up: Think of five favors that someone could do for you to help you this week. Ask a classmate to do one or two of them. If someone asks you, remember to answer politely.

4.9 Communication: You and your partner are waiting for Mr. Cooper, your teacher, outside his office. He is very late. Following the guide below, develop a dialog. Your teacher may want some of the pairs to present their dialogs to the whole class.

1. Person A suggests leaving.
2. Person B suggests waiting for a few more minutes.
3. Person A agrees and offers either some gum, some candy, or a cigarette to Person B.
4. Person B either refuses or accepts.
5. You wait a little longer.
6. Person A says that he or she has to leave. (He or she explains why.) Person A asks Person B to explain the situation to Mr. Cooper if he comes.
7. Person B agrees to do that and suggests that they meet somewhere this evening to study for tomorrow's test.
8. Person A agrees and suggests a meeting place. Person A leaves.

4.10 Sentence Writing: In the picture above, Mr. Beasely and his son are sitting in the waiting room in a doctor's office. The gentleman who is sitting by the open window has fallen asleep, but Mr. Beasely doesn't know this. It's starting to get windy, and Mr. Beasely would like the man to close the window. At first he makes his request very politely, but he becomes less polite with each request. Write the four requests.

1. Excuse me, sir. _____

_____

2. Sir, _____

_____

3. _____
   _____
   _____

4. _____
   _____

4.11 Sentence Writing: Write an appropriate command, request, offer, or suggestion for the given situation.

1.   You want your roommate to turn his stereo down.
2.   You suggest a class writing topic to your teacher.
3.   You are talking to your best friend; you suggest going bowling this evening.
4.   You have just finished having dinner at the home of your friend's parents. You are talking to your friend's mother. You offer to wash the dishes.

4.12 Note Writing: You are going out of town for a few days. You want your good friend who lives next door to do a few things for you while you are gone: feed your cat every morning and evening, water your plants on Saturday afternoon, and bring in your newspaper and mail every day. Think of other things that might need to be done. Write a note to your friend requesting him or her to do these things for you. Use a variety of request expressions.

4.13 Reflecting: Read the next episode of the mystery story. Look at the way requests, offers, and suggestions are made. What are some other ways each of the offers and suggestions could have been made? At the end of the passage, Stern tells us that he offered to take Farmer out to dinner. What are some of the ways he could have made that offer?

> "Read me your file," I said.
>
> "Ask politely," Farmer said, "and I may."
>
> "Oh, sorry," I said. "Would you please read me your file on Carl Miller, sir?"
>
> "You should take lessons in manners," Lieutenant Farmer told me. I heard him move some papers around.
>
> Farmer told me the police had done their normal routine in looking for my client's husband. "We talked to all of Miller's relatives. We looked through his desk at his office. I talked to his boss about the case Miller was working on. And we looked pretty carefully at Mrs. Miller, too."
>
> "And you didn't find anything?" I asked.
>
> "We don't know where he is. You could check into Mrs. Miller a little more. She may be involved."
>
> "How about checking on girlfriends?" I asked.
>
> "I'm pretty sure he doesn't have any," Farmer told me. "The marriage seemed good. Why don't you talk to his boss again? You might check out the last investigation he was working on more deeply."
>
> I offered to take Farmer out to dinner sometime, and we said good-bye.

4.14 Real-World Work

THINK/PRACTICE

1. While you are walking to class today, think of some things a friend or a teacher could do for you and that you could do for someone. Think of several ways you could make these requests and offers.
2. Think of a situation that could be improved—your living space, perhaps, or a class or a club that you belong to. Think of the suggestions you might make to the other people involved.

LOOK/LISTEN

1. If you are living in the U.S., pay attention to the way people make offers, requests, and suggestions. Pay attention to how people who work in shops, restaurants, and other businesses and offices talk to you. Also, listen to how good friends ask favors and make offers and suggestions. Note the different structures that are used when students talk to teachers. In order to use expressions appropriately, you must develop a feeling for the different levels of formality. For example, if you are having lunch with some classmates, it would sound a little funny to say, ''Would you mind passing me the salt, please?'' On the other hand, it would be inappropriate to ask a professor to repeat something by saying, ''Explain that point again.''
2. There are also many ways to make *impolite* suggestions, especially if someone is bothering you. Some of these are humorous: ''Go jump in a lake,'' or ''Go fly a kite.'' Pay attention to the way native speakers do this, too.

USE

1. Do you have a friend who is having trouble studying? Make some polite suggestions. If you have a chance to do someone a favor, use one of the structures you've learned for making offers. Have you been afraid to ask a teacher to explain something because you weren't sure how to make that request politely? Go ahead and ask; you know several ways to make polite requests now.

2. As you saw in 2.9 Sentence Writing, in chapter 2, there are a lot of times when you need to make requests, offers, or suggestions on the telephone. Some common things you might need to say are the following:

    Could I take a message?
    You could try calling again in an hour.
    Why don't you call back in an hour?
    Would you mind giving me that number?
    Could you wait just a minute?

3. You are probably very good at asking questions in English now. You should use this ability to get information from native speakers about grammar, vocabulary, and appropriateness. Examples:

    Could you tell me the word for . . . ?
    Is it all right to say . . . ?
    What should I say when . . . ?
    Is this sentence grammatical? How should I say that?

5

Question
Review

5.1 Part One Check: Complete these sentences. If you are unsure of an answer, check the indicated model sentence and rule. Some of the questions are followed by answers in parentheses. *If an answer is given, read it before you complete the sentence.*

1. Americans talk a lot about the weather, _____?   [1.2d]

2. Southern Asia has a long rainy season, _____?   [1.2e]

3. There are beautiful Buddhist temples in Thailand, _____?   [1.3c]

4. Americans _____ as much rice as most Asians, do they?   [1.4b]

5. _____ dollar that I could borrow? (No, I'm sorry, I don't.)   [2.2b]

6. _____ will it take to fix my car? (About five hours.)   [3.1b]

7. _____ motorcycle do you have? (A Honda.)   [3.4c]

8. Please _____ call after 11. That's when we usually go to sleep.   [4.1a]

9. _____ time will the movie start?   [3.4b]

10. _____ coat should I wear: the brown one or the blue one?   [3.4a]

5.2 Part One Check: Complete sentence B so that it has about the same meaning as sentence A. If you have trouble, check the indicated model sentence and rule.

1. A. Isn't Seoul the capital of South Korea?

    B. Seoul _____?   [1.1a]

2. A. Aren't those Riad's books?

    B. Those _____?   [1.3b]

3. A. Is he a science teacher?

    B. _____ teach science?   [2.2c]

4. A. Who does this scarf belong to?

    B. _____ is _____?   [3.2]

5. A. The teacher asked for a description of the building.

    B. The teacher said, "_____ look like?"

    [3.5c]

6. A. Could you turn that light off?

    B. Would you mind _____?   [4.3b]

7. A. May I smoke?

    B. _____ if I smoke?   [4.2b]

8. A. Let's go out to eat tonight.

    B. Why _____?   [4.4c]

9. A. Always remember to copy your computer files!

    B. _____ forget to copy your computer files!   [4.1b]

5.3 Sentence Writing: If your friend told you that he or she was going to Europe, you would probably have many questions about the trip. Write five questions you would ask your friend.

5.4 Sentence Writing: Imagine that you are going to have an interview with a person who might be interested in hiring you when you get out of school. It is always a good idea before interviews like this to try to anticipate the questions the person might ask. Make a list of questions your "future employer" will probably ask. He or she will probably want information about your studies and interests, your personal life, and your personality.

5.5 Sentence Writing: Write an appropriate request, offer, or suggestion that you might make in these situations.

1. You want your teacher to stop talking and give you the quiz.
2. You see two people trying to carry an enormous bookcase up the stairs.
3. You think your friend ought to study more.
4. Someone calls and wants to speak to your roommate, who isn't home.
5. The class is planning a party. You ask your teacher for permission to discuss the party during class time.
6. You want Roberto to bring his tape player and some of his tapes to the class party.
7. A friend who is passing through town doesn't have a place to stay.

5.6 Letter Writing: Your university is closing soon for a month-long holiday, and you haven't decided yet how you will spend the time. One of your friends tells you that there is a university in the state of North Carolina which offers a special program in English during this month. Write a letter to the admissions office of this university asking for specific information about its English program. You also want information about tuition, housing, and the climate of the region.

5.7 Letter Writing: You have received this letter from your friend Theresa. Before you could read it, a child used it to draw on. Now you must write back to Theresa, asking her for the missing information.

5.8 Paragraph Writing: Write a set of rules for a common household appliance. Tell the buyer what *not* to do with the appliance. Here is an example of such instructions. Complete this model before writing your own. Use *never* for the most important rules.

Your new microwave oven should give you many years of good service if you follow these safety guidelines. _____ put metal pans or foil wrapping inside the oven. _____ leave foods in the oven after they have finished cooking. _____ forget to clean the inner surfaces after each use. _____ allow the oven to come in contact with water. Most plastic, ceramic, and pottery dishes are microwave-safe, but _____ use a favorite dish unless you are sure it is safe.

Reread the preceding model paragraph, and then write your set of rules for another common appliance.

5.9 Note Writing: In chapter 4 you wrote a note to a friend requesting him or her to do some things around your apartment while you were out of town for a few days. Now your friend has told you that he or she is going to Europe for two weeks. Write another note to your friend, offering to do some helpful things during this two-week period. Use a variety of expressions to make these offers.

6

Agreement

REVIEW

Imagine that you are carrying a large box and you need someone to open a door for you. How will you make this request

if you are talking to your best friend (informal),

_____

if you are talking to an acquaintance (polite),

_____

if you are talking to a stranger who is older than you (very polite)?

_____

PREVIEW

In the preceding sentences, you probably used some of these words: **can**, **could**, **will**, and **would**. These, as you know, are modal verbs. You probably know several other modal verbs, such as **should**, **may**, **might** and so on. These English verbs are special because you don't have to change them if you change the subject of the sentence. We say, "I can," and we also say, "She can." Other English verbs may change if we use them with different subjects. Complete these sentences:

> I get up early, but my wife _____ up late.
> We were late, but he _____ on time.
> We are going to the party, but she _____ not.

We use the terms **agreement** when discussing the relationship between subjects and verbs. Read the following passage, paying attention to the underlined verbs.

Bernard <u>lives</u> on the twenty-second floor of a huge apartment building. Every morning he <u>leaves</u> his apartment, <u>gets</u> into the elevator, <u>travels</u> to the ground floor, and <u>leaves</u> the building. When he <u>comes</u> home, he <u>gets</u> into the elevator on the ground floor, <u>rides</u> up to the fourteenth floor, <u>gets</u> out of the elevator, and <u>walks</u> up the stairs to his apartment on the twenty-second floor. He <u>must</u> always use the elevator and stairs this way. Can you think of an explanation for this?

You and your classmates should try to figure out this riddle.

6.1 Agreement With *Be*: Present and Past; After *There*		
Complete these model sentences.	Check.	Complete these rules.
a. Bernard's apartment building **_____ very tall.**	is	The verb ***be*** has many forms. These are the forms of ***be:*** **Present Tense**　　　　　　　**Past Tense** **I _____ we _____**　　**I ____ we _____** **you _____**　　　　　　　**you _____** **he/she/it _____**　　　　**he/she/it _____** **they _____**　　　　　　　**they _____**
b. There _____ twenty-six floors in the building.	are	***There*** is not a noun or pronoun, so it cannot be the subject of a verb. In sentences beginning with ***there***, make the verb agree with the noun that comes _____ the verb.
c. Last week there _____ a fire on the nineteenth floor. **Within 10 minutes, there _____ 12 fire trucks on the scene.**	was were	The only English verb that has more than one form in the past tense is the verb _____.
d. Luckily, everyone _____ able to get out safely.	was	Most indefinite pronouns, such as _____, are singular. Indefinite pronouns are made by combining ***every***, ***some***, ***any***, or ***no*** with ***one***, ***body***, or ***thing***. Examples: ***somebody***, _____, and _____.

Oral Practice 1A: What are some of the things on your desk at home? (Use ***there***.)

Oral Practice 1B: Using the STUDENT INFORMATION SHEET in chapter 1, make ***there*** sentences about the kinds of people in the class. Example:

> *There is one student from Panama in the class.*
> *There are four Spanish speakers in the class.*

Oral Practice 1C: Describe what you see when you look out a window of a room in the building where you live. Use ***there is*** and ***there are***.

Written Practice 1:   Complete these sentences with a past or present form of the verb ***be***. These sentences make a story. Pay attention to the meaning. *Some of the sentences should be negative.*

1.   Harry _____ a university student who lives in an apartment.

2.   There _____ several movie theaters near his apartment.

3.   Because of that, it _____ unusual for him to go to several movies a week.

4.   There _____ anything else to do last night, so Harry went to a new adventure movie.

5.   There _____ too many people there, so he got a great seat.

6.   Unfortunately, in Harry's opinion, the movie _____ worth seeing.

7.   He thought that the plot _____ unbelievable and the performances _____ poor.

8.   However, everyone else in the audience apparently _____ satisfied.

6.2 Agreement With Other Verbs: *-s, -es, -ies, Does, Goes, Has*		
Complete these model sentences.	Check.	Complete these rules.
a. While Bernard _____ **breakfast, he usually** _____ **TV.** **T.V. cartoons** (*amuse*) _____ **him.**	eats watches amuse	To make most verbs agree with a singular third-person subject, simply add _____. If the verb ends in *s, x, z, sh,* or *ch,* add _____. If the subject is plural, do _____ add *-s.*
b. He always (*try*) _____ **to get to school on time.**	tries	If the verb ends in a consonant plus *y,* change the *y* to _____ and add _____. If you see a vowel plus *y,* as in the word buy, then just add _____.

c. Bernard (*go*) _____ **to one of the best schools in town.**	goes	The third-person singular forms of ***do*** and ***go*** are _____ and _____.
d. Bernard (*have*) _____ **a lot of friends at school.**	has	The third-person singular form of ***have*** is _____.

Oral Practice 2:   What are some of the things that your roommate or spouse does everyday?

Written Practice 2:   Write the correct present-tense form of the verb in each sentence.

Many professional musicians (*suffer*) _____ from stage fright. This nervous condition (*affect*) _____ their ability to perform even easy passages in the music. A good friend of mine (*have*) _____ a routine that he (*go*) _____ through on the day of a concert. During the day he (*relax*) _____ by performing simple physical tasks. For example, sometimes he (*wash*) _____ his car or (*cut*) _____ firewood. Just before the performance he (*breathe*) _____ deeply, (*do*) _____ some exercises, and (*try*) _____ to concentrate only on pleasing the audience. He (*enjoy*) _____ performing in public.

6.3 Agreement With *Every and Each*		
Complete these model sentences with forms of ***have***.	Check.	Complete these rules.
a. Every classroom in Bernard's school _____ **a computer.** **Each classroom in the school** _____ **a computer.**	has has	***Every*** and ***each*** are always singular. A noun that comes immediately after one of these words is always in the _____ form.
b. Each of the classrooms _____ **a computer.** **Every one of the classrooms** _____ **a computer.**	has has	***Each*** or ***every one*** may also be followed by ***of*** + a definite determiner (such as ***the***) and a noun in the _____ form. The verb is still in the _____ form, however.

Oral Practice 3A: Say something that is true of every student in this class.

Oral Practice 3B: Think of some things that each citizen of your country has to do or is supposed to do.

Written Practice 3:   Finish sentence B. It should have about the same meaning as sentence A.

1. A.   All the students in the class are allowed to use the computer every day.

    B.   Every _____ to use the computer every day.

2. A.   All the computers in the school have printers.

    B.   Each of _____ a printer.

3. A.   All the students enjoy working with computers.

    B.   Every one _____ working with computers.

4. A.   All the students are responsible for protecting the computers from damage.

    B.   Each _____ for protecting the computers from damage.

5. A.   All the other schools in the district plan to follow the example of Bernard's school.

    B.   Every _____ to follow the example of Bernard's school.

6.4 Agreement: Negative Sentences and Questions with *Do*		
Complete these model sentences.	Check.	Complete these rules.
a. When Bernard comes home from **school, he _____ not ride up** **to the twenty-second floor.**	does	To make questions and negative sentences in the simple present tense, use the auxiliary verb ***do*** with the main verb. ***Do*** must agree with the subject of the sentence. With third-person subjects (*Mr. Clampett*, *she*, *the car*, and so on) the form of ***do*** is _____.
b. How does he (*go*) _____ **up** **to that floor?**	go	When the auxiliary ***do*** is used, the main verb is in the _____ form.

Oral Practice 4A: A good friend does many things for you. For example, he or she listens to your problems and lets you borrow things. But now let's talk about what a good friend does *not* do. Example:

> *A good friend does not tell your secrets to others.*

Oral Practice 4B: Your teacher will tell you what time he or she does certain things (for example, gets up, eats breakfast, leaves for school, arrives at school). Test your classmates' memories by asking questions about your teacher. Because you are practicing subject-verb agreement, all questions and answers must be complete sentences. Example:

> *What time does Ms. Reynolds go jogging in the park?*
> *She goes jogging at 6:30 in the morning.*

Written Practice 4A: You think that the following statements about the Arabic language are true, but you are not certain. Remember that if you want to check something that you think is true, you can ask a tag question or a negative question. Write the **negative** questions you might ask to check your facts. Example:

> *The Arabic language differs considerably from English.*
> *Doesn't the Arabic language differ considerably from English?*

1. The verb often comes first in written Arabic.
2. Arabic has more consonants than English.
3. Written Arabic runs from right to left.
4. Adjectives follow nouns in Arabic.

Written Practice 4B: Complete these sentences. *To be true, some must be negative.*

1. Bernard (*live*) _____ in a large apartment building.

2. Bernard (*live*) _____ in a one-family house.

3. Bernard (*ride up*) _____ to the twenty-second floor.

4. Bernard (*walk up*) _____ to the twenty-second floor.

5. In the simple present tense, a verb (*must + agree*) _____ with its subject.

6. If the subject is in the third person and singular, a simple present verb (*end*)

   _____ in -s.

7. However, the form of a modal verb (*change*) _____ when the subject is in

   the third person and singular.

6.5 Unchangeable Modal Verbs		
Complete this model sentence.	Check.	Complete these rules.
The boys can almost reach the button for the fifteenth floor.		**Modal verbs,** such as _____, do not have a special third-person-singular form. And the verb after a modal is always in the
The boy _____ almost	can	
_____ the button for the fifteenth floor.	reach	_____ form.

Oral Practice 5:   What are some things that a good teacher **should** or **must** do or **should not** or **must not** do?

Written Practice 5: Complete these sentences. To be true, *some must be negative.*

1. Bernard (*can + reach*) _____ the button for the fourteenth floor, but he _____ the button for the twenty-second.

2. Bernard (*must + get out*) _____ on the fourteenth floor and (*walk*) _____ up the stairs to the twenty-second floor.

3. A careful writer (*should + proofread*) _____ his or her work carefully.

4. The writer (*must + forget*) _____ to check the verb forms.

6.6 Agreement: Collective Nouns		
Complete these model sentences.	Check.	Complete these rules.
a. Bernard's family is not very large; _____ _____ **made up of Bernard, his mother, and his father.**	it is	*Family* is a special kind of noun called a **collective noun**. You can think of a family as one thing (a unit) or as a collection of individuals. In sentence **a**, the noun *family* refers to the family as a _____. Because of that, the pronoun used to take the place of the noun is _____.
b. Bernard's family _____ not like living on the twenty-second floor.	does	In sentence **b**, the noun *family* refers to the individual members. (This is usually the case when we use verbs of emotion, such as *like, want, hope,* and so on.) In American English a verb with a collective noun subject is usually in the _____ form even if the noun refers to individual members.
c. _____ want to move to an apartment on a lower floor if one becomes available.	They	However, a pronoun which takes the place of a collective noun referring to individual members is usually in the _____ form.

Written Practice 6: Complete these sentences with appropriate pronouns and verb forms.

An American softball team (*be*) _____ usually a very strange collection of people. _____ normally (*consist*) _____ of people who are over 30.

_____ (belong) _____ to the team for various reasons: _____

(need) _____ exercise, perhaps, or _____ (appreciate) _____

belonging to a group. A softball team (be) _____ more than an athletic club;

_____ (be) _____ a social organization.

Oral Practice 6:   Using the Written Practice 6 paragraph as a model, work with your classmates on a paragraph about a typical class in this English program. Your teacher can write the
paragraph on the board as you and your classmates decide what it should say.

6.7 Special Agreement Problems		
Complete these model sentences.	Check.	Complete these rules.
a. The police _____ **now certain that all three people** _____ **innocent.**	are are	*The police* and *people* are plural nouns. If one of these nouns is the subject of a sentence, the verb is in the _____ form. The singular form of *people* is **one** _____. The singular form of *the police* is **one** _____.
b. This morning's news _____ **terrible.** **Linguistics** _____ **the study of language.**	was is	There are some nouns in English that end in *s* but are not plural. One example is _____. Many areas of study, such as _____, end in *s*. Can you think of others?
c. A good pair of shoes _____ **essential for a hiking trip. Good shoes** _____ **worth the extra cost.**	is are	Many things come in **pairs**. Some examples are _____, pants (trousers, jeans, shorts), glasses (eyeglasses), and scissors. When we begin the subject with **a pair of**, the verb is in the _____ form. When the noun stands alone, as in *good shoes*, the verb is _____.
d. Five miles _____ **a long way to hike if you are not in good shape.**	is	Expressions of distance, time (*three months*), and money (*five dollars*) are plural in form but they usually take a _____ verb.

Oral Practice 7A: What are some things that people do at weddings in your hometown?

Oral Practice 7B: Think of some areas of study that end in *s* (such as *linguistics*), and define them. Example:

Linguistics is the study of language.

Oral Practice 7C: Write down short answers to the following questions. Then tell your answers to the class in complete sentences. Begin each sentence with the time, distance, or measurement you have written. Example:

Twenty-five dollars is a reasonable price for a pair of pants.

1.   Average height of men in your country: _____

2.   Average height of women in your country: _____

3.   A reasonable price for a pair of pants: _____

4.   A fast time for a race of one mile or 1,500 meters: _____

5.   An amount of weight that is too much for you to lift: _____

6.   The best age to be: _____

7.   An average weekly reading assignment in a history class (number of pages): _____

Written Practice 7:   Complete these sentences.

1.   People who worry all the time _____ usually not as healthy as calm people.

2.   Physics (*scare*) _____ a lot of people, but I find it quite easy.

3.   There _____ a lot of people at the picnic yesterday.

4.   I had hoped to find something happy when I picked up yesterday's paper, but all the news _____ bad.

5.   A good pair of sunglasses _____ essential if you plan to drive across New Mexico.

6.   Glasses _____ necessary if you have bad eyesight and want a driver's license.

7.   If a person is not used to walking, 10 kilometers (*seem*) _____ endless.

8.   Aerobics _____ becoming very popular in many places around the world.

9.   We enjoyed our visit to France, but 21 days _____ enough time to get to know the country.

10.   Ten dollars _____ the usual fine for parking in this lot without a permit; the police _____ very strict about giving tickets in this lot.

6.8 Chapter Check: Complete these sentences. If you are unsure of an answer, check the indicated model sentence and rule.

1. South America _____ the most distinctive bird population in the world. [6.2d]

2. That _____ why people _____ it "the bird continent."   [6.1a,6.7a]

3. More than 1,600 species of birds _____ in Colombia alone.   [6.2a]

4. There _____ 319 species of hummingbirds in the world, and most of them can _____ found only in South America.   [6.1b]   [6.5]

5. A visitor to the South American rain forest usually (*notice + not*) _____ the birds immediately because it is so quiet.   [6.4]

6. The harpy eagle _____ at over 40 miles per hour while chasing monkeys through the trees. It (*catch*) _____ them with its mighty talons.   [6.2a&b]

7. Forty miles per hour _____ an incredible speed for a bird to fly.   [6.7d]

8. In South America, everyone _____ proud of the wonderful variety of birds living there.   [6.1d]

6.9 Chapter Check: Finish sentence B. It should have about the same meaning as sentence A.

1. A.   Nearly everyone thinks of snakes when he or she hears the word *tropics*.

    B.   Most people _____

    _____.   [6.7a]

2. A.   More of these creatures exist in tropical areas than in any other life zone.

    B.   There _____

    _____.   [6.1b]

3. A.   But even professional collectors have trouble finding these snakes.

    B.   But even a professional _____

    _____.   [6.2d]

4. A.   Most people have heard of the anaconda, the largest snake in the world.

    B.   Almost everybody _____,

    the largest snake in the world.   [6.1d,6.2d]

5. A.   A large anaconda is capable of swallowing a small calf.

    B.   A large anaconda can _____.   [6.5]

6. A.   Many people believe that anacondas crush their victims.

    B.   Many people believe that an anaconda _____ its victim.   [6.2a]

7. A. But now it is known that they suffocate their victims or cut off their victims' blood circulation.

    B. But now it is known that it _____ its victim or _____ its victim's blood circulation.   [6.2a]

8. A. It's not unusual for an anaconda to be seven meters long.

    B. Seven meters _____ not an unusual length for an anaconda.   [6.7d]

6.10 Warm-up: Think of somebody who does something that most people don't do, or who doesn't do something that most people do. Your sentence should begin with *most*. Examples:

Most American women wear two earrings, but my roommate wears only one.
Most people I know put ketchup on their French fries, but one friend of mine puts mayonnaise on his.

6.11 Communication: The activity this time is a guess-who game. On a piece of paper, write down the information asked for. Be sure to number your answers. When you have finished, your teacher will pick up the pieces of paper and redistribute them. When the teacher calls on you, look at the piece of paper you were given and give the answers to the first five questions. ("This person likes rice and hates salad. This person plays tennis." and so on.) Then ask one of your classmates to guess who the person is. If the person is wrong, give the answer to number 6 and let someone else try. If necessary, go on to number 7 and number 8. Try to find the champion guesser in your class.

1. Name one kind of food you like.
2. Name one kind of food you hate.
3. What sports do you play?
4. Name one TV program that you enjoy.
5. What do you want to do for a living?
             * * * * * * *
6. Are you male or female?
7. What language do you speak (besides English)?
8. What country are you from?
9. What is your name?

6.12 Paragraph Writing: Ted Pearson is a printer. He prints fine books in a traditional way. A reporter is interviewing him about the process. Read the interview, and then write a paragraph describing what Ted Pearson does.

   Begin like this: *Ted Pearson uses a traditional process to print fine books. First, he has to handset the type . . .*

   "Could you explain the basic process for me?"
   "Yes, certainly. First I have to handset the type, letter by letter, into a form. Of course, I must set it backwards. Then I clamp the lines of type in the form. Next I ink the type with a roller and center the paper on top of the form. I push the form along the track until it's under the platen, which is a flat metal plate. I then pull the lever to lower the platen, which presses the paper against the type at 500 pounds of force per square inch. Finally, I hang the paper on the line to dry, unclamp the form, and sort the letters so that I can do the next page."

6.13 Paragraph Writing: Write a paragraph about someone who has an interesting daily routine, an interesting job, or an interesting hobby. Describe what this person does. Be sure to make your verbs agree with the subjects.

6.14 Reflecting: Read the next episode of the mystery story. Look at subjects and verbs; do they agree with each other? The word **team** is a collective noun. Verbs agree with it as if it were a singular noun, but sometimes a singular pronoun is used to take its place, and sometimes a plural pronoun is used. Find examples of verb and pronoun agreement with **team.**

> Monday night I locked the office and drove out to the sports center. I had a date to see a softball game. I was happy to be able to forget about the Carl Miller case for a few hours. I met my father at the gate, and we went to sit down beside one of his old friends.
>
> One of the teams was the South Bend Golden Age Softball Team. It consists of people like my father and mother who live in the South Bend Retirement Village. To be on the team you have to be at least 55 years old. My father doesn't play because his legs aren't very good. But my mother is a star. She was the pitcher that day.
>
> The other team was from another retirement village a couple of hundred miles away. They had arrived by bus an hour before the game.
>
> "The other team has been warming up, and I've been watching them," said my father's friend. "They have a good pitcher."
>
> "So do we," my father said.
>
> Everyone else at the game was older, except for me and a couple of other children of team members. I think the audience came to the games to shout a lot. At the end I was deaf in one ear because my father spent the whole game cheering and shouting.
>
> My mother's team lost by one run.
>
> I drove my parents home. My mother was angrily silent. As she got out of the car, she said, "That other team didn't play fair. Their pitcher couldn't have been a day older than 50."

6.15 Real-World Work

THINK/PRACTICE

If you leave the *-s* off your verbs and nouns when you write, you probably aren't careful about the final /**s**/ or /**z**/ sounds when you speak. Today, while you are walking or riding along or standing around, make up sentences about what you see, and pronounce those final sounds very carefully: "Those are very tall trees(zzz)." "She speaks(sss) English very well."

LOOK/LISTEN

1. Practice pronouncing the *-s* and *-es* endings by reading some paragraphs from a book, magazine, or newspaper. This may help both your speaking and writing because you will see and pronounce these endings at the same time.

2.   Look in a catalog of the classes at your school or university and find the names of departments. Which ones have *s* at the end and are singular words?

USE

1. Ask a new friend or acquaintance about his or her family. He or she will probably ask you about yours. When talking about your family, be careful to make the verbs agree with the subjects.

2. We often have to describe something to another person who can't see what we're describing. For example, you may need to tell your roommate over the phone where to find your keys in your desk. When giving directions to your apartment, you may have to describe landmarks on the way. You can use **there is** and **there are** in these situations.

3. Ask a native speaker of English if he or she can think of many things that come in pairs. You already found some of these things in Rule Builder 6.7 (a pair of glasses, shoes, and so on), but there are many more.

Dr. Hubbard and his Time Machine.

7

Present Time

REVIEW

You have used verbs to refer to the present time throughout the first chapters on questions and agreement. Let's review some of what you learned. Complete these multiple-choice items.

1. What _____ for a living?

    a. Stan does   c. does Stan do

    b. does Stan   d. do Stan

2. What _____ right now?

    a. Stan is doing   c. is doing Stan

    b. is Stan doing   d. Stan is he doing

3. Stan's family _____ in shame; . . .

    a. lives   c. does live

    b. live   d. do live

4. . . . _____ Stan to go back to school and find a new career.

    a. it wants   c. they wants

    b. it want   d. they want

PREVIEW

In this chapter we will focus on verbs which refer to the present time. You will work with the tense which is often called the "simple present":

Stan _plays_ *the saxophone for a living.*

You will also work with the tense which is often called the "present progressive":

Right now Stan _is practicing_ *in his room.*

For a warm-up, write the correct form of the verb **be** in the blanks.

The Midwest _____ not my favorite place to be at any time of the year. The weather _____ always very unusual. Summer _____ always too hot; spring _____ usually too rainy for my taste; and winter _____ too cold. Right now it _____ snowing, and the roads _____ becoming very slick. The snowplows _____ working overtime to clear them.

In most of the sentences in the preceding passage, the verb **be** is the **main verb**, but in three places it is an **auxiliary verb** for the present progressive tense. Circle the three forms of **be** that are in present progressive structures.

7.1 Action Verbs—Present Progressive		
Look around the room that you are in, or look out a window. Listen. Write down two things that are happening right now.	Check.	Complete these rules.
a. _____ _____ _____ _____	Circle the verbs in your sentences. You should have a form of the verb *be* first and then the -ing form of the main verb; for example, *is walking* or *are writing.*	When an event is in progress at a certain time, use a **progressive** verb tense: a form of the verb **be** (past, present, or future) followed by the _____ form of the main verb. When an event is in progress right now, use the **present progressive**: **present tense of *be* + *-ing* form** Only verbs which describe events or actions (such as _____) can be used in the progressive. We can call these verbs "action verbs."

Give the -ing forms of these verbs.		
b. study _____ **write** _____ **plan** _____ **listen** _____	studying writing planning listening	To make the **-ing** forms of most verbs (including verbs that end in **y**, such as *study*), simply add _____ to the base form. If the base form ends in **e**, drop the _____ and add _____. To make the **-ing** forms of verbs that end in this way: **consonant + vowel + consonant**, double the final consonant and add _____. This rule does **not** apply if a two-syllable verb is stressed on the first syllable, as with *listen*.

Oral Practice 1:   Figure out what time it is in another student's hometown right now. Find out what people there are probably doing at this moment.

Written Practice 1:   Complete these sentences with correct forms of the verbs in parentheses. Imagine that a space shuttle is in space at this moment and the astronauts are working.

Right now the astronauts aboard the space shuttle (*complete*) _____ their second series of experiments. They (*measure*) _____ the amount of solar radiation which (*strike*) _____ a panel of the shuttle at this very moment. NASA scientists (*try*) _____ to determine if the astronauts are adequately protected from the radiation. In another ongoing experiment, Commander Smith (*attempt*) _____ to capture neutrinos—subatomic particles which continually stream out of the sun. These particles (*be*) _____ very hard to observe.

7.2 Stative Versus Action Verbs—Simple Present Versus Present Progressive		
Complete these model sentences.	Check.	Complete these rules.
a. At this moment, the director of the English Center (be) _____ **in the English grammar classroom. She** (see) _____ **several students that she** (know) _____. **When she** (hear) _____ **the students' responses, she** (feel) _____ **certain that most of them will succeed.**	is sees knows hears feels	Some verbs normally don't go into the progressive even when we are talking about the present moment. These verbs cannot refer to an event in progress; they cannot describe "happenings." Let's call these verbs **stative verbs** because they describe states of being, or conditions of a situation, rather than actions. When these verbs are used to refer to present states, they are in the _____ _____ tense. The most common stative verb is _____. Many stative verbs are verbs of perception, both sensory (such as _____ and _____) and mental (such as _____ and _____). Other perception verbs are listed in the following box.

Here are some common verbs of sensory or mental **perception.**

remember	believe	think	like	mind	hear
recall	trust	suppose	dislike	need	see
forget	distrust	agree	love	want	feel
imagine	doubt	disagree	hate	desire	taste
understand	forget	differ	detest	wish	notice
recognize	know	prefer	care		smell
	wonder				

Some of the verbs listed can also refer to sensory or mental actions; that is, they can answer the question, "What is that person doing?" The ones most commonly used with this other meaning are **think** ("use one's mind"), **taste**, and **smell** ("use those senses"). Compare these sentences:

I *think* I will come with you.
Bill *tastes* something strange in his soup.
Bill's soup *tastes* strange.

I *am thinking* about my family.
Now the cook *is tasting* the soup to see what is wrong.

b. Right now the students *(look)* _____ _____ **at** **some model sentences on the board** **and** *(listen)* _____ **to their** **teacher. In a moment, they will be** **using the new structures to communi-** **cate with their classmates.** **The teacher** *(consider)* _____ _____ **whether to play a** **game or have a debate today.**	are looking listening is considering	Many other verbs express sensory and mental actions rather than states. The subject is really *doing* something, not just experiencing something. They can be used to answer the question, ''What is that person doing?'' Some examples are _____ , _____ , and _____ . When these verbs are used to refer to what is going on right now, they are in the _____ _____ tense.

Here are some verbs of sensory or mental **action**. They may be used to indicate an action. They may be used to answer the question, ''What is that person doing?''

look (at)	*consider*	*study*
watch	*think about*	*learn*
listen (to)	*analyze*	*memorize*
examine	*look forward to*	*compare*
observe		*contrast*
inspect		*judge*

Oral Practice 2A: Ask a classmate a question using one of these verbs. Notice that you are asking about **states of being** when you use these verbs—***not*** activities.

want	like	remember	appreciate	believe	see
need	dislike	care	know	think	hear
hope	prefer		understand	agree	

Oral Practice 2B: Ask your classmates some questions about some of their current activities. You may want to use the expression *these days* in your questions. (Here are some verbs you might want to use: *look at, watch, listen to, think about, look forward to, study, learn, memorize.*) Example:

> *Are you watching much TV these days?*
> *What are you studying in your psychology class these days?*

Written Practice 2:   Complete these sentences with the verbs in parentheses.

Many students (*understand + not*) _____ English verb tenses

very well. The students in my class (*make*) _____ some progress,

though, because they (*understand*) _____ that there is a difference

between action verbs and stative verbs. They (*need*) _____ to learn

this distinction because it will help them decide when to use the progressive verb forms.

They (*look*) _____ closely at the problem in class right now. I am

sure that most of them (*see*) _____ the difference now.

NOTE: Look at this sentence:
    My parents *live* in Bogota. (Permanent residence)
    I *am living* in a scholarship hall this semester.
Some verbs can be used as stative or action verbs without much difference in meaning.
Some common examples are *live, hope,* and *plan.* Sometimes we use them in the progressive to show that they are temporary situations. The simple present form shows that the situation has a more permanent feel.

7.3 Stative Verbs of Relationship and Measurement		
Complete these model sentences.	Check.	Complete these rules.
a. Hiroshi's English class (*consist of*) _____ _____ **students from around the** **world. It** (*have*) _____ **students from 10 countries.**	consists of has	Verbs of relationship are usually **stative.** The most common verb in this group is _____. Another is _____ _____.
b. Some of the students in the class are _____ **trouble adjusting to** **the new culture. Others** _____ _____ a **great time.**	having are having	The verb ***have*** is not always stative, however. It is an action verb in many expressions, such as ***have*** _____, _____, ___ _____ _____, ***have difficulty,*** ***have fun, have a party, have dinner, have a nice day,*** and so on.
c. How much (*cost*) _____ **it** _____ **to study abroad?**	does cost	Another small group of statives are verbs of measurement and cost. Examples are ***weigh*** and _____.

Here are some common verbs of relationship and measurement.

have	*consist of*	*lack*	*weigh*
own	*involve*	*need*	*fit*
possess	*include*	*require*	*equal*
contain	*belong to*		*cost*

NOTE: There are a few other stative verbs that don't fit neatly into the categories of perception, relationship, and measurement. Two of these are *deserve* and *matter*.

I think that young thief *deserves* a second chance.

Claire hopes the job will give her good experience; the size of the salary *doesn't matter* to her.

Oral Practice 3A: Tell your classmates some facts about your family. Use *consist of* and *have*.

Oral Practice 3B: Tell about some things you own and love. Then mention some things you lack and want or need. How much do these things cost?

Written Practice 3: Complete these sentences using the correct forms of the verbs in parentheses.

1. This record (*belong to*) _____ me, but that one (*belong to* + *not*)

   _____ me.

2. The pair of shoes I want to buy (*cost*) _____.

3. A _____ team (*consist of*) _____.

4. A liter of water (*weigh*) _____.

5. A student who does his or her best (*deserve*) _____.

6. Studying English (*involve*) _____.

7. This jacket (*fit* + *not*) _____ me very well.

8. This school (*require*) _____ all students to take courses in _____.

   It (*require* + *not*) _____ courses in _____.

7.4   Habitual Actions: Simple Present Versus Present Progressive; Frequency Adverbs; Adverb Clauses: *When* Versus *While*

In the first three rule builders, we were talking about right now. In this rule builder, we are concerned with a typical night in Stan's and Mr. and Ms. Jones's apartments.

Complete these sentences.	Check.	Complete these rules.
a. Every night Stan (*play*) _____ **his saxophone, Mr. Jones** (*watch*) _____ **the news on TV, and Ms. Jones** (*read*) _____ **in bed.**	plays watches reads	When action verbs, such as *play*, *watch*, and _____, describe habitual actions, they are in the _____ _____ tense.
b. Mr. Jones usually (*go*) _____ **to bed at 10:35 every night. Before that, he always** (*close*) _____ **the windows, and** (*lock*) _____ **the door.**	goes closes locks	These words are called **frequency adverbs**: *never*, *rarely*, *seldom*, *hardly ever*, *occasionally*, *often*, _____, and _____. They generally go before a simple present verb.
c. Hobbies, such as reading, watching TV, and making music, (*give*) _____ **people a chance to relax.**	give	General, timeless truths are usually expressed with the _____ _____ tense. (Another example: **People around the world enjoy the sport of soccer.**)

<table>
<tr><td>

d. What is happening at 10:20 every night? Stan (*play + always*)

_____ _____

_____ **the saxophone. Ms.**

Jones (*read + often*) _____

_____ _____ **a mystery novel.**

</td><td>

is always

playing

is

often reading

</td><td>

In these sentences, the action verbs *play* and *read* describe actions which are in progress at a certain time (10:20 every night). Therefore,

they are in the _____ _____ tense. In a progressive construction, frequency adverbs usually go _____ the **main verb.**

</td></tr>
<tr><td>

e. When Mr. Jones (*go*) _____ **to bed, Stan** (*play + still*)

_____ _____

_____ **the saxophone. In other words, Mr. Jones**

_____ **to bed while Stan**

_____ _____

_____ **the saxophone.**

</td><td>

goes

is still

playing

goes

is still

playing

</td><td>

Adverb clauses are subordinate clauses that begin with words such as **because**, **although**, **if**, **when**, or **while**. **When** and **while** both begin adverb clauses of **time**. To refer to a point in time, use a clause beginning with

_____. To refer to a longer period of time, use _____.

</td></tr>
</table>

Oral Practice 4A: Very briefly describe a typical day in the life of your best friend, roommate, brother, or sister. Then tell what that person is usually doing on a typical day at 8:15 A.M., 2:45 P.M., 6:25 P.M., and at midnight.

Oral Practice 4B: Tell the class several things that you rarely (seldom/hardly ever/never) do because of your busy schedule, but which you enjoy very much.

Oral Practice 4C: Think of some general truths and share them with your classmates. Examples:

> *Pears grow on trees.*
> *Water freezes at 0° Celsius.*

Written Practice 4:   Complete these sentences using the correct forms of the verbs in parentheses.

Samuel (*need*) _____ help to get through his day-to-day life. Every morning his wife (*select*) _____ the clothing he will wear that day. When he (*return*) _____ to the bedroom after his morning shower, his clothes (*lie*) _____ on the bed. He (*get*) _____ dressed, (*eat*) _____ breakfast, and then (*drive*) _____ his car to Mr. Able's house. Mr. Able (*wait + always*)

_____ in front of his house at 7:50. When Mr. Able (*come*)

_____ with Samuel, it (*take*) _____ only five minutes to get to the plant

where they (*work*) _____. If Mr. Able cannot come, it (*take*) _____ Sa-

muel half an hour to get to work because he must take a route where there are no stoplights,

only stop signs. Why (*need*) _____ Samuel _____ this help from his wife

and Mr. Able? Can you guess?

7.5 Shortened Clauses After *But* and *And*		
Complete these model sentences.	Check.	Complete these rules.
a. Every night at 11:00 P.M., Mr. and Ms. Jones are trying to sleep, but Stan **_____; he's playing his saxophone.** **Mr. and Ms. Jones normally don't stay up until 2:00 A.M., but Stan** **often _____.**	isn't does	When two clauses are joined with a conjunction such as _____, we usually leave out words in the second clause that would be the same as in the first clause. The shortened clauses in these model sentences consist of a subject and an _____ verb.
b. Mr. Jones goes to bed early, and so **_____ his wife.** **At 11:00 P.M. Mr. Jones is trying to** **sleep, and _____** **_____ his wife.**	 does so is	If you have two **positive** sentences that are the same except for different subjects, you can join them in this way: **Sentence 1, *and* _____ + auxiliary + subject 2**
c. Mr. Jones goes to bed early, and his **wife _____ too.** **At 11:00 P.M., Mr. Jones is trying to** **sleep, and his wife _____** **_____.**	 does is too	Another way to join identical positive sentences with different subjects is to use this structure: **Sentence 1, *and*, + subject + auxiliary +** **_____**
d. Mr. Jones does not stay up late, **and neither _____ his wife.** **At 11:00 P.M. Ms. Jones is not making** **music, and _____ _____** **her husband.**	 does neither is	If two **negative** sentences are identical except for the subject, you can join them in this way: **Sentence 1, *and* _____ + auxiliary + subject 2**

| e. **Mr. Jones does not stay up late, and** **his wife** _____ **either.** **At 11:00** P.M., **Ms. Jones is not making music, and her husband** _____ _____. | **doesn't** **isn't either** | Another way to join the negative sentences is to use this structure: **Sentence 1,** _____ **+ subject 2 +** **auxiliary +** _____ *either* |

Oral Practice 5A: Turn to the STUDENT INFORMATION SHEET in chapter 1. Make sentences about things two of your classmates do or are doing. Use *and* with *so* and *too*. Examples:

> *Rosa speaks Spanish, and so does Laura.*
> *Rika is staying in a dorm, and Mei is too.*

Oral Practice 5B: Make a list of things you don't like or don't do or aren't interested in (for example, kinds of food, kinds of weather, activities). Then get together with two or three classmates, exchange papers, and make sentences comparing your classmates' and your tastes. Examples:

> *Abdul isn't interested in baseball, but I am.*
> *Abdul doesn't drink alcohol, and neither do I.*

Written Practice 5A: Look at the STUDENT INFORMATION SHEET in chapter 1. Using *too*, write two sentences about things that two classmates have in common.

Written Practice 5B: Now rewrite the sentences from 5A, this time using *so*.

Written Practice 5C: Write two sentences about things that two of your classmates don't do or don't like. Use *either*.

Written Practice 5D: Now rewrite the sentences from 5C, this time using *neither*.

7.6 *Whenever, When,* and *If* with the Meaning "Anytime That"; Punctuation in Sentences with Adverb Clauses		
Complete these model sentences.	Check.	Complete these rules.
a. Whenever it _____ rainy, I *(carry)* _____ **an umbrella.**	is carry	*Whenever* means "anytime that." It introduces a situation (for example, "it is rainy") during which something is always true (for example, "I carry an umbrella"). Since the action (carrying an umbrella) is habitual, the verb is in the _____ _____ tense.
b. When it _____ rainy, I _____ **an umbrella.** **If it _____ rainy, I** _____ **an umbrella.**	is carry is carry	*When* and *if* are often used to refer to situations in the future, but they can also be used like *whenever* to mean "anytime that." In that case, the verb in the main clause is usually in the _____ _____ tense.
c. I _____ an umbrella when- **ever it _____ rainy.** *or . . .* **when it _____ rainy.** *or . . .* **if it _____ rainy.**	carry is is is	Clauses that begin with words such as *if,* *when* and _____ are called **adverb** clauses.

d. Now read all the model sentences in this rule builder again, and look at the punctuation to complete this rule:

An adverb clause is separated from the main clause with a comma when the adverb clause comes

_____ _____ _____ _____.

Oral Practice 6:   Think of something that a friend (or a member of your family) does which annoys you. Tell the class how you react whenever this person does this.

Written Practice 6A: Complete these sentences.

1.   Whenever the teacher _____, I _____.

2.   I always _____ when my friend _____.

3.   Whenever the weather is _____, the Williams

_____.

4.   If Laura's son _____, she usually _____.

5.   I _____ whenever the mailman _____.

6.   When I have a test, I _____.

7.   I _____ if I _____ a low grade.

Written Practice 6B: Add commas wherever they are needed.

1. If I get a headache I usually take a couple of aspirins.
2. All of the students get excited whenever the football team has a game.
3. When you don't understand something that the teacher says you should raise your hand and ask questions.
4. I always try to help my friends if they are in trouble.
5. Whenever you learn something new about American culture you should write it in your journal.

7.7 Using Modals to Express Present Possibility, Probability, and Ability		
Complete these model sentences.	Check.	Complete these rules.
a. It is *very likely* that Pablo is ill. = Pablo _____ be ill today. **It is *possible* that Pablo is ill.** = Pablo _____ be ill today. **It is *possible* that Pablo is not ill.** = Pablo _____ _____ **be ill today.** **It is very unlikely that Pablo is ill.** = Pablo _____ be ill today. **It is *impossible* that Pablo is ill.** = Pablo _____ be ill today.	must may/might/ could may not/ might not must not cannot/ could not	**Modal verbs** can be used when you **draw conclusions** from evidence. They indicate that things are probable, possible, or impossible. The following scale shows the range from probability to impossibility. Probably so: **must** Possibly so: _____ or _____ or _____ Possibly not: _____ _____ or _____ _____ Probably not: _____ _____ Impossible: _____ or _____ _____ The verb after a modal is always in the _____ form.
b. Pablo's phone is busy; he might (*talk*) _____ _____ **to his** **doctor.**	be talking	To say that it is likely or possible that something *is happening right now*, use this structure: **modal +** _____ **+ the** _____ **form of the verb**
c. Pablo can _____ **Italian, but** **he** _____ _____ **French.**	speak cannot speak	To indicate a present ability, we use the modal verb _____. We use _____ to indicate a lack of ability.

Oral Practice 7A: Look at an object or some objects that your teacher or classmate allows the students to pass around. Using modal verbs, make guesses and draw conclusions about it. Examples:

It might be made of real gold.
It can't be very old.

Oral Practice 7B: Think of someone you know who lives far away. What time is it there? What may/might/could/must this person be doing at this moment? What can't/couldn't he or she be doing?

Oral Practice 7C: Tell your classmates something you can do and something you can't do.

Written Practice 7:   Complete the following sentences.

1.   Ms. Branson's car is not in her driveway. She must _____ at home.

2.   It's 6:30. We shouldn't call now because the Wongs might be _____ dinner.

3.   Her name is Kyoko. She _____ be from Japan.

4.   Listen to that loud music coming from Ben's room. He _____ really be study-
     ing.

5.   Snow in July? You _____ be serious!

6.   There are several possible explanations for Mick's unfriendly behavior toward Sue. He
     _____ be afraid of her. He _____ be trying to get her attention. Or he
     simply _____ like her.

7.8 Chapter Check: Complete these sentences. *Do not use modal verbs in this exercise. If you need help, check the indicated model sentences and rules.*

1.   In the picture an elderly couple (*walk*) _____
     in a city.   [7.1]

2.   They (*take + often*) _____ walks like this.   [7.4a & b]

3. At this moment both of them (*wear*) _____ hats and

    overcoats and both (*carry*) _____ umbrellas.   [7.1]

4. She (*be + not*) _____ in a hurry and

    _____ he.   [7.5d]

5. They (*look*) _____ into a shop window, and apparently they (*see*)

    _____ something that interests them.   [7.1,7.2a]

6. They (*have*) _____ plenty of money.   [7.2]

7. So _____ they (*notice*) _____ something that they

    (*like*) _____, they (*buy + usually*) _____

    _____ it.   [7.6,7.2a]

7.9 Chapter Check: Finish sentences B and C. They should have about the same meaning
as sentence A.

1. A. Sometimes Mr. Jones falls asleep while his wife is still reading.

    B. Sometimes _____ Mr. Jones falls asleep, his wife is still

        reading.   [7.4e]

    C. Sometimes Ms. Jones is still reading _____

        _____.   [7.4e]

2. A. Now it's 11.00 P.M., and Stan is playing his saxophone, so he is probably enjoying

        himself.

    B. Now its 11.00 P.M., and Stan is playing his saxophone, so he _____

        probably _____ fun.   [7.2b]

    C. Now it's 11:00 P.M., and Stan is playing his saxophone, so he must

        _____ fun.   [7.7b]

3. A. The Joneses worry if their daughter isn't home exactly at 10:25.

    B. Whenever _____

        _____.   [7.6a&d]

    C. _____ when _____

        _____.   [7.6b&d]

4. A. Neither Mr. Jones nor Ms. Jones enjoys Stan's late-night playing.

    B. Mr. Jones _____

        neither _____.   [7.5d]

    C. Mr. Jones _____, and

        Ms. Jones _____.   [7.5e]

5.   A.   Both the man and the woman in the picture are wearing hats.

     B.   The man in the picture _____ a hat, and _____ the

        woman.   [7.5b]

     C.   The man in the picture _____, and the woman

        _____.   [7.5c]

7.10 Warm-up: Study the following library scene and prepare some questions for your classmates about what the people in the picture are doing. Example:

What is the maintenance worker on the ladder doing?

You may want to ask about:

the maintenance worker in the polka-dot shirt
the maintenance worker with glasses
the maintenance worker with a thermos bottle
the maintenance worker wearing a hat
the man with a beard
the woman with glasses
the reference librarian
the female librarian
the student with a French book
the female student with blond hair
the male student sitting in the back
the male student next to the girl with a Walkman®

After you and your classmates have studied the picture carefully and thought of good questions to ask, close your books and test each other's memory.

7.11 Communication: Imagine an activity that someone is doing. Your classmates will try to guess the activity that you are thinking of. Think of some clues (some pieces of information) that you can give your classmates to help them guess what the person is doing. When it is your turn to guess what another student is thinking, use **may/might/could/must** + **be** + **-ing** form. Example:

> *"I'm thinking of a woman who's doing something. She has a pen in her hand."*
> *"She might be writing a composition." "She could be drawing a picture."*
> *"No. Next clue: She's making another person unhappy."*
> *"She might be putting a bad grade on a student's paper."*
> *"Good guess, but that's not right. She's wearing a uniform."*
> *"She might be a policewoman."*
> *"Maybe so. But what is she doing?"*
> *"She must be writing a traffic ticket."*
> *"Right!"*

7.12 Communication: Children in different countries often have different games, habits, and ways of spending time. Interview three classmates to find out *how often* children in their countries participate in the activities listed in the following chart. Add one or two activities that are very common among children in your country. Try to use complete sentences in asking and answering questions. Record the information in the chart.

NAME/COUNTRY	_____	_____	_____
play soccer	_____	_____	_____
study	_____	_____	_____
skip rope	_____	_____	_____
play marbles	_____	_____	_____
play video games	_____	_____	_____
_____	_____	_____	_____
_____	_____	_____	_____

Report briefly to the class on the activities of children in countries other than your own.

7.13 Sentence Writing: What time is it in your native country right now? Write down that time: _____

Write five sentences about what people you know are probably or possibly doing right now in your country. Use **may** and **must** at least once.

7.14 Sentence Writing: Go to a place where you can see several people. Look at them carefully; then write four sentences about some of these people. The first should contain **may**; the second, **must**; the third, **must not**; and the fourth, **cannot**.

7.15 Sentence Writing: Write sentences explaining what the following types of workers do: an orthodontist, a mechanic, a plumber, an astronomer, a composer, an architect, a photographer, a geologist, a detective. Use your dictionary if necessary. Example:

An orthodontist straightens teeth.

7.16 Sentence Writing: Write sentences about six things that both you and someone else (for example, your sister, roommate, friend) know or don't know, understand or don't understand, believe or don't believe, remember or don't remember, need or don't need, own or don't own. Use a different verb in each sentence, and be sure to use the right tense. Use each of these structures at least once: *and neither, and so, and . . . either, and . . . too.* Example:

My roommate doesn't know how to drive, and neither do I.

7.17 Paragraph Writing: Write a paragraph describing the following picture. Be careful with your verbs.

7.18 Report Writing: Write a brief report on what you learned in 7.12 Communication about activities of children in countries other than your own.

7.19 Reflecting: Read the next episode of the mystery story. Examine the use of the present progressive tense with action verbs. The passage also contains several stative verbs. Can you find them? What tense are these verbs in?

> On Tuesday I got up early to start working on the Miller case. I made breakfast and fed my cat. Then I looked up the phone number of the insurance company where Carl Miller had worked before he disappeared. I called them from my house. A young man answered the phone.
>
> "My name is Stern," I said. "I'm working for Deanne Miller, Carl Miller's wife."
>
> "I know Deanne," the young man said.
>
> "You're lucky. I'm looking for her husband."
>
> "I don't know where he is."
>
> Sometimes I want to reach into my phone and slap the person on the other end. "That's fine," I said patiently. "Can I speak to your boss?"
>
> "You need to talk to Mrs. Jackson," he said. "Can you wait just a minute?"
>
> "Don't put me on hold." I said, but it was too late. The telephone entertained me with music. I didn't like the music. Five minutes later he came back.
>
> "I'm sorry," the young man said. "She's talking to a client now."
>
> "I'll call back later," I said.
>
> In the the phone book I found the names of all of the insurance executives in the office. Mrs. Jackson's first name was Andrea. I called the office again and made my voice very deep.
>
> "Hello?" the young man answered the phone.
>
> "How are you?" I said in a very deep voice. "This is Bill Smith. Let me talk to Andrea. And fast, because I'm calling from California."
>
> In a minute I was talking to Mrs. Jackson.
>
> "I thought this was a client from California," she said when I told her my real name.
>
> "I think your secretary got the lines mixed up," I said.

7.20 Real-World Work

THINK/PRACTICE

1. As you walk or ride around, make up sentences about the events and situations that you see. This will help you discover verbs that you don't know in English. Examples:

    That fellow is listening to music on his Walkman®.
    The student in the red jacket seems worried; she must be thinking about final exams.

2. Look around and notice what two things or people have in common. Make up sentences with *too, so, either,* and *neither.* Examples:

    That guy isn't wearing socks, and neither is his friend.
    That blue car has a little rust, and the red one does too.

LOOK/LISTEN

Find the classified pages of today's newspaper. Find an ad that interests you—perhaps under the heading "Computers," "Apartments," "Automobiles," "Motorcycles," or "Personals." When people put ads in the paper, the newspaper charges them for each line of print, so the person who writes the ad makes it as short as possible. Many words are left out. Try to translate these ads into real English sentences. If you don't understand something in an ad, ask a friend for help. Your teacher may ask you to bring an ad to class.

USE

1. Have a conversation about school (in English, of course) with an acquaintance. You can talk about how things **are going** this semester, what courses you **are taking**, what else you **are doing** this semester, and what you **are planning** to do next semester. You will probably also talk about how you **feel** about your classes, whether you **like** or **dislike** your teachers, how well you **understand** your course work, what you **want** or **hope** to do, how much homework your teachers **assign**, how often they **give** tests, how often you **miss** class, and so on.

2. If you keep a journal, write down some notes about how your classes are going so far and how you feel about them.

Dr. Hubbard
in the Past.

8

Past
Time

REVIEW

Write yes/no questions that you would ask in these situations:

1. You want to know if Oscar took Sadie out last night:

    _____

2. You want to know if Mike fired his cook last week:

    _____

3. You want to know if Stan played his saxophone until 3:00 A.M.:

    _____

PREVIEW

In all the questions you have just written, the verb is in the **simple past tense.** In this chapter we will work with that tense and other verb tenses and adverbs that we use to refer to the past. We will make sentences like these:

> *Sadie and Oscar both used to be married, but their spouses passed away years ago.*
> *Last week Sadie and Oscar went to a movie together.*
> *While they were watching the movie, Oscar took Sadie's hand in his.*
> *They have decided to go out again.*

The verb in the last sentence is in the **present perfect tense** (*have* + **past participle**).

Do you know the simple past and past participle forms of the following verbs?

	Past	Past Participle		Past	Past Participle
call	*called*	*called*	shout	_____	_____
say	_____	_____	cry	_____	_____
buy	_____	_____	eat	_____	_____
drink	_____	_____	wear	_____	_____
go	_____	_____	take	_____	_____

Oscar and Sadie are on their second date. They are at Mike's Cafe.

8.1 The Simple Past Tense; Irregular Verbs		
Complete these model sentences.	Check.	Complete these rules.
a. Oscar: What did you do last night, Sadie? **Sadie: Nothing very exciting. I** (*fix*) _____ **dinner around 6. I** **even** (*bake*) _____ **a cake for dessert.**	fixed baked	To tell about things that happened at a certain time in the past, use the **simple past tense**. To make the simple past of most verbs, simply add _____ to the base form. If the base form ends in e, simply add _____.

b. **Then I** (knit) _____ **and** (listen) _____ **to music for a** **while.**	knitted listened	To make the simple past of verbs that end in this way: **consonant + vowel + consonant,** double the final consonant and add _____. For example, the simple past of *stop* is _____. (In model sentence **a** the *x* in *fix* is not doubled because it represents **two consonant sounds**— [k] + [s].) This rule does *not* apply if a two-syllable verb is stressed on the first syllable. An example is _____.
c. **Around 10:30 I** (try) _____ **to read.**	tried	To make the simple past of verbs that end in **consonant + y**, change the **y** to _____ and add _____.
d. **But I** (be) _____ **too tired, so** **I** (go) _____ **to bed.**	was went	Some verbs have irregular simple past forms. Two examples are _____ and _____. See Appendix 1.
e. **I** (wake up + not) _____ _____ _____ _____ **until** **8 this morning.**	did not wake up	In the negative, all verbs except *be* have the same simple past form: _____ + *not* + **the** _____ **form of the verb.**
f. **Oscar: I haven't** (do) _____ **anything very exciting lately either.**	done	The verb form that comes after the auxiliary verb ***have*** is called the **past participle**. The past participles of **regular verbs**, such as *fix*, are the same as the _____ _____ forms. But for **irregular** verbs, such as _____, the past participle may be different. See Appendix 1 for a list of common irregular verbs.

Oral Practice 1:   You and your classmates can quiz each other on irregular simple past and past participle forms. Example:

*What's the past form of **think**?*   It's **thought**.
*What's the past participle of **think**?*   It's the same—**thought**.

Written Practice 1A: In this exercise, you will write the simple past form (which is also the past participle) of each verb listed. Review spelling rules 8.1b and 8.1c. Then try to apply the spelling rules to the other verbs. For some verbs, you need to know which syllable is stressed. If you are not sure, use your dictionary.

1.	receive	_____	2.	snow	_____
3.	beg	_____	4.	trip	_____
5.	permit	_____	6.	taste	_____
7.	offer	_____	8.	hug	_____
9.	wait	_____	10.	argue	_____
11.	help	_____	12.	reply	_____
13.	box	_____	14.	enjoy	_____
15.	study	_____	16.	control	_____
17.	play	_____	18.	fry	_____
19.	open	_____	20.	admit	_____
21.	refer	_____	22.	visit	_____
23.	step	_____	24.	return	_____
25.	listen	_____	26.	need	_____
27.	plan	_____	28.	fan	_____
29.	walk	_____	30.	hope	_____

Written Practice 1B: Look at Appendix 1. Cover the answers in the right hand column, and try to write the simple past and past participle forms of the irregular verbs. Check yourself, and clearly mark the base forms of all the verbs that gave you trouble. The verbs that you have marked are the ones you must work on. As you work on this chapter, quiz yourself every day. Once you have learned all the irregular verbs, it is a good idea to test yourself from time to time.

8.2 Present Perfect Versus Simple Past		
Complete these model sentences.	Check.	Complete these rules.
a. Oscar: *(win)* _____ **you ever** _____ **a prize?**	Have won	When we want to ask if an event has taken place (or a state has existed) *anytime before now*, we usually use the **present perfect tense**: _____ (or **has**) + **the past participle**.

b. Sadie: Yes, I have. When I was a child, I _____ a prize for being the best speller in my school. I **(receive + not) _____ _____** **_____ any money, but I (get)** **_____ a little trophy.**	won did not receive got	To indicate that an event took place (or a situation existed) during a *period of time which ended in the past*, don't use the present perfect. Use the _____ _____ tense. Underline the clause in model sentence **b** that indicates that the event happened in a period that ended in the past.
c. Oscar: Well, I _____ never **_____ a prize. But my name** **(be) _____ _____** **in the paper several times.** **Sadie: Oh, why?**	have won has been	When we say that something has (or has not) happened *anytime before now*, we usually use the _____ _____ tense. In these sentences there may not be any time expression at all.
d. Oscar: Well, for instance, it **_____ in the paper just last** **Friday because I was a volunteer at the benefit fair for underprivileged children.**	was	When we indicate *the specific time* when something happened, we use the _____ _____ tense. Underline the expression in model sentence **d** that indicates the specific time that Oscar's name was in the paper.

Oral Practice 2A: Ask your classmates if they have done certain things. If they have, ask them when they did them and if they enjoyed them.
Example:

*Have you ever seen **Batman**?*	*Yes, I have.*
When did you see it?	*I saw it a couple of years ago.*
Did you enjoy it?	*No, I didn't like it very much.*

Oral Practice 2B: Ask your classmates if they have visited certain well-known places. If the answer is yes, find out when they were there, and what they did there. This would be a good small-group conversation.

Written Practice 2A: Complete these sentences using the correct forms of the verbs in parentheses.

Last Saturday, Oscar (park) _____ his car in front of a gift shop. He (intend)

_____ to run in quickly to buy a small present for Sadie. Unfortunately, there (be)

_____ a fire hydrant right where he left his car. While he (be) _____

in the shop, he (get) _____ distracted by a television set that (be) _____ tuned to a football game. While he was watching the game, the police (*tow*) _____ his car away. When he (*come out*) _____, his car (*be*) _____ gone, of course.

Written Practice 2B: Complete these sentences. Use the **present perfect** whenever possible.

Sadie (*take up*) _____ several new hobbies since her husband (*die*) _____ in 1979. For example, she (*learn*) _____ how to swim. Yesterday she (*spend*) _____ two hours swimming in the indoor pool at the Community Center. Also since her husband's death, she (*buy*) _____ a computer. The first evening that she had it, she (*learn*) _____ enough about it to write a short program. Finally, she (*begin*) _____ taking Spanish lessons. She and her husband (*go*) _____ to Mexico in 1975; she (*be*) _____ sorry then that she (*know + not*) _____ Spanish. She (*learn + already*) _____ to ask simple questions and make simple statements.

8.3 Present Perfect With *Yet, Already,* and *Just*		
Complete these model sentences.	Check.	Complete these rules.
a. Oscar: (*have*) _____ **you** _____ **dinner yet?**	Have had	The **present perfect** is often used to refer to *recently completed* actions. In questions about recently completed actions, the present perfect often occurs with the adverb _____ .
b. Sadie: Yes, I _____ .	have	In short answers to present perfect questions, we use only the auxiliary verb _____ .
c. Oscar: I (*eat*) _____ **already** _____ **, too, but I** (*have + not*) _____ _____ _____ **dessert yet. Let's have some of Mike's famous apple pie.**	have eaten have not had	In positive statements about recently completed actions, the present perfect often occurs with the adverb _____ . When we want to say that an action has not been completed, but we expect it to be completed, we often use the adverb _____ .

d. **Sadie: Good idea. Oscar,** *(read)* _____ **you** _____ **any good books recently?**	have, read	Other adverbs that often occur with the present perfect are **lately** and _____ .
e. **Oscar: Yes, I** *(finish)* _____ **just** _____ **a great book of poetry. I'd like to lend it to you.**	have finished	To emphasize the recentness of an action, we often use the present _____ with the adverb _____ .

Oral Practice 3:   Find someone in the classroom who has not been at this school or in this town very long. Think of things that people like to do here, and find out if the person has done them yet. Example:

> *Have you been to Clinton Lake yet?*

Written Practice 3:   Imagine that you have a classmate who has not been in class for a couple of weeks and really doesn't know what has been going on. The classmate asks you some questions that show how little he or she knows about class activities. You will try to inform the student. Pretend that the following statements are facts:

> *While the student was gone, the class had a test on the present tenses.*
> *While the student was gone, a guest speaker from the History Department came to class.*
> *While the student was gone, the teacher announced the date of the TOEFL test.*
>
> *Later in the semester, the class will have a class picnic.*
> *Later in the semester, the teacher will give you a quiz on irregular verbs.*
> *Later in the semester, the class will start working on future time structures.*

Use **already** and **yet** in your answers. Do *not* tell specific times, such as *last week* or *next week*. Examples:

> *When do we start chapter 6?*
> *We've already finished chapter 6.*
>
> *When did we work on adjective clauses?*
> *We haven't worked on adjective clauses yet.*

1. When do we start chapter 7?
2. When did the teacher explain the conditional structures?
3. When is that speaker from the History Department going to come?
4. Was the class picnic fun?
5. Is the teacher going to announce the TOEFL date soon?
6. How did you do on the irregular verb quiz?
7. Are we going to have a test on the present tenses soon?
8. When did you work on future time structures?

8.4 Past Habits and Situations: *Used To*		
Complete these model sentenes.	Check.	Complete these rules.
a. Sadie: What did you do for a living before you retired, Oscar? **Oscar: I** (*own*) _____ **a flower shop.** *or* **I** _____ **to own a flower shop.**	owned used	The simple past tense is the most common structure for past situations, but another common way to refer to a past situation which has now changed is with this structure: _____ *to* + the _____ **form of the verb.**
b. Sadie: Oh, really? What flower shop _____ **you** _____ _____ **own?** **Oscar: The one on 24th Street. It's called Pete's Flowers now.**	did, use to	Since the verb ***used*** in this expression is in the simple past tense, make questions (and negatives) with the auxiliary verb _____ and change *used* to the _____ form.
c. Sadie: (*sell*) _____ **you** _____ **live plants as well as flowers?** *or* _____ **you** _____ _____ **sell live plants as well as flowers?** **Oscar: Sure. Potted plants were our specialty.**	Did sell Did use to	We can also refer to a past habitual action with the simple _____ tense or with this structure: ***used to*** + the _____ **form of the verb.**

Oral Practice 4:   What are some things that you used to do and do not do anymore?

Written Practice 4:   Complete these sentences with a construction which shows that the activity was habitual or that the situation has now changed.

1.   When Sadie was a girl, her family (*take*) _____ trips to the ocean on weekends.

2.   Her parents (*own*) _____ an enormous house in a small town in Virginia.

3.   She (*see*) _____ her brothers and sisters often. Now she sees them only on holidays.

4. They (*live*) _____ nearby; now they live in distant states.

5. I used _____.

6. When my favorite aunt visited me, she _____

    _____.

8.5 Past Progressive Versus Simple Past; *When* Versus *While*		
Complete these model sentences.	Check.	Complete these rules.
a. Oscar: What _____ you doing in 1939? **Sadie: I _____ teaching school in Chicago. How about you?**	were was	When referring to an event that was in progress at a certain time in the past, we use the **past** _____ **tense**: ***was*** (or ***were***) + **the _____ form**
b. Oscar: I (*work*) _____ _____ **for my father. He** (*own*) _____ **a grocery store over on 32nd street.**	was working owned	Remember that stative verbs are not usually used in the progressive. An example of a stative verb is _____. (See Rule Builders 7.2 and 7.3)
c. I bought the flower shop in 1940 _____ **I was still working for my father.** *or* **I was still working for my father in** **1940 _____ I bought the flower shop.**	 while when	When a time clause refers to a long period of time (for example, the time Oscar was working for his father), it often begins with _____. When a time clause refers to a point in time (for example, when Oscar bought the flower shop), it often begins with _____.

Oral Practice 5A: Ask your classmates what they were doing at specific times in the past (30 minutes ago, at 9:00 last night, last Sunday at 8:00 in the morning, in 1983, and so on).

Oral Practice 5B: Think of something surprising that happened recently. For example, perhaps your parents called you, or the fire alarm in your building went off. Tell your classmates what you were doing when this happened. Use both of these structures:

> *I was washing the dinner dishes last Tuesday when my parents called.*
> *My parents called last Tuesday while I was washing the dinner dishes.*

Written Practice 5:   Complete these sentences using the correct forms of the verbs in parentheses.

In the early 1960s, my Uncle Norris, a journalist, (*go*) _____ to

Egypt. There he (*find*) _____ hundreds of archaeologists, who (*dig*)

_____ day and night. This frantic work (*go on*)

_____ because at the same time thousands of workers (*hurry*)

_____ to complete the Aswan Dam. The archaeologists (*try*)

_____ to save incredible historical treasures. They (*have* + *not*)

_____ much time before the entire region would be flooded.

8.6 Manner Adverbs		
Complete these model sentences.	Check.	Complete these rules.
a. When Oscar and Sadie left Mike's Cafe, it was snowing _____, **so Oscar had to drive his car** **_____.**	hard carefully/ slowly	We can tell how something was done (or is done, has been done, and so on) by using a **manner adverb**. An example is _____. The most common position for a manner adverb is _____ the object or, if there is no object, immediately after the _____ _____.
b. When they reached Sadie's house, Sadie thanked Oscar _____ warmly.	very	To make an adverb stronger, put _____ before it. This word is often called an **intensifier**.
Change the following adjectives to adverbs.		
c. careful _____ **proud** _____	carefully proudly	To make an adverb from most adjectives, add _____ to the adjective.
d. happy _____	happily	If the adjective ends in *y* change the *y*, to _____ and add _____.
e. scientific _____	scientifically	If the adjective ends in *ic*, add _____.

f. public _____	publicly	An exception to the preceding rule is the adverb _____.
g. hard _____ fast _____	hard fast	Two adverbs that do not end in **-ly** are _____ and _____. They have the same form as the adjectives. (The adverb **hardly** has a different meaning. It means "almost not" or "barely.") Compare these sentences: **I was so tired that I could *hardly stay awake.*** **I *hardly know the other people in my building.*** **He works very *hard* in school.**

Oral Practice 6:   Think of something you did earlier today or earlier this week. Tell what you did, how you did it, and when you did it.

> *I studied hard last night.*
> *I played badminton aggressively last Saturday.*

Written Practice 6:   These sentences all contain prepositional phrases which explain how something was done. Circle the adverbial phrase in each sentence. Rewrite the sentence, changing the phrase to a one-word adverb. Example:

> *The disposal team handled the bomb with a great deal of care.*
> *The disposal team handled the bomb very carefully.*

1.   The post office delivered the package with promptness.
2.   The professor explained the grading system with a lot of patience.
3.   The government handled the crisis with a great deal of intelligence.
4.   He outlined his argument with logic.
5.   The director did not discuss the problem in public.

8.7 An Introduction to the Simple Past in the Passive Voice		
Complete these model sentences.	Check.	Complete these rules.
a. People often say that America _____ **discovered by Columbus.**	was	We often put simple past verbs in the **passive voice** when we tell about discoveries, inventions, and works of art and the people who were responsible for them. The structure is as follows:
Movable type _____ **invented by Gutenberg.**	was	
Mona Lisa _____ **painted**	was	_____ **or** *were* + **the** _____ **participle**
_____ **Leonardo da Vinci.**	by	
b. Columbus _____ **sent on his voyage of discovery by the king and queen of Spain.**	was	Of course, the subject of a passive sentence is not always a discovery, an invention, or a work of art. As you see in model sentence **b**, the subject of a passive verb can even be a person. You will work more with the passive in chapter 21.

Oral Practice 7A: Work with your classmates at matching the discoverer or inventor with the discovery or invention in the following box. Use passive sentences to find and agree on the answer. Examples:

Oxygen was discovered by Priestly, wasn't it?
Yes, I think it was.

Was printing for the blind invented by Morse?
No, it was invented by Braille.

The law of falling bodies	Kepler
Radium	Marconi
Vulcanized rubber	Newton
The radio	Galileo
Polio vaccine	Goodyear
Printing for the blind	Priestly
The laws of motion	The Curies
The phonograph	Braille
The telegraph	Edison
Oxygen	Salk
The laws of planetary motion	Morse

Oral Practice 7B: To get practice switching from active to passive voice, you and your classmates can ask each other questions about the discoveries and inventions that must be answered negatively. Example:

> *Was the radio invented by Edison?*
> *No. It was invented by Marconi. Edison invented the phonograph.*

Written Practice 7A: The following sentences are about some famous American artists. Rewrite each of them in the passive voice, making the work of art the topic of the sentence.

1.   Aaron Copland composed *Appalachian Spring*.
2.   Richard Wright wrote *Native Son*.
3.   Frank Lloyd Wright designed the Imperial Hotel in Tokyo.
4.   Jackson Pollack painted *Autumn Rhythm*.
5.   Spike Lee directed *Do the Right Thing*.

Written Practice 7B: Write five passive-voice sentences about the inventions and discoveries discussed in Oral Practices 7A and 7B.

8.8 Chapter Check: Complete these sentences. If you are unsure of an answer, check the indicated model sentence and rule.

1.   The first 13 states of what is now the United States _____ to be British

colonies.   [8.4a]

2.   In 1773, American revolutionaries (*protest*) _____ the British tax on tea by

dumping cargoes of tea overboard in the Boston Tea Party.   [8.2b]

3.   Almost every American schoolchild (*hear*) _____ of the Boston Tea

Party.   [8.2c]

4.   Fighting between revolutionaries and British soldiers (*begin*) _____ in

1775.   [8.2d]

5.   While the Revolutionary War (*go on*) _____, the Declaration of

Independence was written.   [8.5a]

6.   America (*have* + *not*) _____ a constitution during the

Revolution.   [8.2b,8.1e]

7.   Most Americans (*read*) _____ the Declaration of Independence.   [8.2c]

8.   When Sadie was a child, she (*memorize*) _____ the Declaration of Indepen-

dence.   [8.2b]

9.   (*study*) _____ you ever _____ about the American Revolu-

tion?   [8.2a]

8.9 Chapter Check: Finish sentence B. It should have about the same meaning as sentence A.

1. A.   Albert Einstein discovered photons in 1921.

    B.   Photons _____

    _____.   [8.7a]

2. A.   His Special Relativity Theory made him famous.

    B.   He _____ by his Special Relativity Theory.   [8.7b]

3. A.   His life was very simple and modest.

    B.   He lived very _____.   [8.6]

4. A.   He spoke out against war with a great deal of calmness and courage.

    B.   He spoke out against war very _____. [8.6]

8.10 Warm-up: Look at the picture story and try to explain what happened. You may want to give the main character a name. Take some notes. Your teacher may ask you to prepare a written version of this story as part of your homework assignment (8.18 Paragraph Writing).

8.11 Communication: Form groups. Take turns with your classmates asking how many people in the group have been to the places in the chart on the following page. Ask each person who has been to a place **when** and **how long** he or she was there. Example:

> How many of you have been to Paris? (Two people hold up their hands.)
> Anna, when did you go to Paris?
> How much time did you spend there?
> How about you Saleh? When were you in Paris? How long did you stay there?

Write the information in the chart.

Place	Name	Year	Length of Stay
Los Angeles			
Dallas			
Tokyo			
Teheran			
Bogota			
Mexico			
London			
Moscow			

8.12 Communication: Imagine that you are in charge of finding someone to do a certain job. Decide what the job is. It can be anything—auto mechanic, bank teller, waiter, bus driver. Use your imagination. Decide what skills, what kind of education, and what kind of experience a person should have to do this job—make a list. Get together with a partner and do job interviews; take turns being the interviewer and the interviewee. Examples:

Have you finished high school?   *Yes, I have. I graduated . . .*
Have you ever done computer programming?   *No, I haven't, but I have . . .*
Have you ever driven a bus?   *Yes, I have. I used to . . .*

8.13 Sentence Writing: Write whether you have or have never done the following things. If you have done something, indicate how many times (once, twice, many times, and so on) you have done it. Then write another sentence telling about a specific time when you did it.
   Example 1:

climb a mountain
I have never climbed a mountain.

Example 2:

> *go water skiing*
> *I have gone water skiing several times.*
> *Last Sunday I went water skiing at Clinton Lake.*

1. ride a motorcycle
2. eat Chinese food
3. watch the TV show *L.A. Law*
4. fall asleep in class
5. go to Los Angeles

8.14 Sentence Writing: Finish sentence B. It should have about the same meaning as sentence A.

1. A. Mary and I both went to the carnival.

   B. Mary went to the carnival, and so _____.

2. A. Carl and Claire each recently bought a new car.

   B. Carl recently bought a new car, and Claire _____.

3. A. Neither Joan nor I found the answer to the first question.

   B. Joan _____ the answer to the first question, _____

   _____ I.

4. A. Neither my brother nor I have decided on a field of study yet.

   B. My brother _____ on a field of study yet, and

   I _____.

5. A. Both Italian and Spanish descended directly from Latin.

   B. Italian _____, and _____

   _____.

6. A. Spanish and Italian have both borrowed some words from English.

   B. Italian _____,

   and _____.

8.15 Sentence Writing: Write about four things that you used to do but no longer do. Tell why you don't do these things anymore. Example:

> *I used to smoke cigarettes. I don't smoke cigarettes anymore because I started worrying about my health.*

8.16 Paragraph Writing: Write a paragraph about the things you **have learned** about this country, city, or school since you came here.

8.17 Paragraph Writing: Think of an event that had an important effect on your life—for example, meeting someone, reading a book, taking a class. Tell why it was important to you, and how things have been different for you since it happened.

8.18 Paragraph Writing: Write a paragraph about what happened in the picture story from 8.10 Warm-up.

8.19 Paragraph Writing: Write a short report based on the information in the chart for 8.11 Communication. Your report should contain sentences like these:

> *Two of the students in the class have visited Paris. Anna was there for three weeks in 1989, and Saleh spent a month there in 1987.*

8.20 Reflecting: Read the next episode of the mystery story. There are many verbs in the simple past tense. But there are also a few verbs in the present perfect and the past progressive. Do you understand why the author did not use the simple past in those cases?

> After lunch on Tuesday I drove my green Chevrolet to the insurance office where Carl Miller worked. I had an appointment with Andrea Jackson, his boss, at two. When I walked in, a young man was sitting at the reception desk. He made me wait 15 minutes. I read a magazine about life insurance until I got to see Mrs. Jackson.
>
> I sat down in a chair and she smiled at me.
>
> "How can I help you, Mr. Stern?"
>
> "I'm looking for Carl Miller," I said. "The police suggested talking to you. What was Mr. Miller working on when he disappeared?"
>
> "You know that Carl Miller worked on malpractice suits, don't you? There is a doctor in town who has insurance with our company. Recently a man claimed that Doctor Weber—that's his name—made a serious mistake in surgery. As a result, the man's mother died. The man has sued Weber. Carl Miller was checking out the facts of the case. His investigation was supposed to show us what to do about our client. If Weber did something wrong, we would pay the man a settlement. But perhaps there was no mistake. In that case we would not pay, and a court would decide."
>
> "What did Miller find out?" I asked.
>
> "He said that he thought Weber was innocent, but his report wasn't finished." She paused. "Do you think his disappearance is related to the case?"
>
> "I don't know," I said. "But I'll find out. Could I look at your file on the malpractice suit?"
>
> "I have already made you a copy," she said. She gave me the file, and I took it with me.
>
> Outside, her secretary was sleeping on his typewriter. He was wearing a yellow tie. I rolled the end of his tie very quietly into the typewriter and tiptoed out.

8.21 Real-World Work

THINK

As you are walking along today, practice making sentences about the past. Think about things you have done many times, and then make sentences like these:

I have gone bowling many times.
For example, I went bowling with my friend Tim just last week.

You can also make up sentences about things you **used to do** but don't do anymore. Finally, you can tell yourself what you **were doing** at certain times in the past (midnight last night, 3:00 yesterday afternoon, and so on.)

LOOK/LISTEN

Most news stories are about events that occurred in the past, usually the very recent past. Read some articles in today's newspaper, and find verbs in the simple past, past progressive, and present perfect tenses. Ask yourself why particular tenses were used to refer to events or situations.

USE

1. As you look through the newspaper, you will probably find some stories that seem very interesting to you. Interesting news stories provide good material for conversations. Tell a friend (in English, of course) about one of the stories you have read in the paper. Your teacher may want you to make a report on a news story that you have read.

2. The next time you want to take a trip, you might want to get advice before you make your plans. Ask around and find someone who has been to this place already. You might ask,

    Have you ever been to Alaska?

    You could also ask for advice about something else you have never done before. You might ask,

    Have you ever renewed your visa?
    Have you ever made couscous?

    Get the person to tell you what he or she did to make the process easier. You could save yourself a lot of time and trouble.

3. Sometimes you call someone or stop at someone's place and find that the person is not home. When you talk to that person later, you may want to say something like this:

    I tried to call you last night at nine o'clock, but you weren't home. What were you doing then?

9

Dr. Hubbard in the Future.

Future
Time

REVIEW

This paragraph contains a number of errors. Proofread the paragraph and correct any mistakes you find.

At this moment, an author is sit at his desk. He trying to write a great book about the history of the United States. He doesn't knows what to write about because he is having too much information. He hopes he will has an idea soon. In the meantime, he will playing some tennis and trying to forget about his book.

PREVIEW

The first three sentences of the paragraph you have just corrected are about the present time. The last two sentences are not about the present, however; they are about the _____. English does not have a true future tense. Many languages have a special form for each verb to show a future meaning. As we will see in this chapter, English uses a variety of verb constructions in talking and writing about the future. In the preceding paragraph, the writer referred to the future by using the **modal verb** _____. He made some mistakes because he forgot that in English a verb that comes after a modal verb is always in the _____ form.

In this chapter we will be talking and writing about the future and using verb constructions like those underlined in the following sentences.

My friend Rosa <u>is coming back</u> from her trip to California tonight.
Her plane <u>arrives</u> at 9:15. <u>I am going to pick her up</u> at the airport.
The weather <u>should be</u> good; the weatherman says the skies <u>will be</u> clear.

We will also work with adverb clauses that refer to the future. Here are some examples:

<u>If the plane is delayed in California</u>, she is going to call me.
We will come back to the dorm as soon <u>as we leave the airport</u>.

9.1 Plans		
This is not a typical day for Stan. He has a date for this evening with his friend Rhonda. These are their plans.		
Complete this model sentence.	Check.	Complete these rules.
a. **Stan and Rhonda are going to** _____ **dinner at a nice restaurant.**	have	The most common way to talk about plans that have already been made is to use this structure: **be going to** + the _____ **form of the verb.**
b. **After dinner, Stan and Rhonda** _____ **meeting their friends Charley and Bev at a concert in the park.**	are	To tell about a plan in the near future, you can use the present _____ tense instead of **be going to.** There is usually a time adverbial such as *after dinner.*
c. **According to their plan, Stan and Rhonda are** _____ _____ **be by the water fountain at 8:30.**	going to	**REMEMBER:** Stative verbs, such as _____ in this model sentence, do not normally go into the progressive. To tell about plans with stative verbs, use the expression **be** _____ **to.**
d. **The four friends may** _____ **a walk on the beach after the concert.**	take	When plans are not certain, use the modal verb _____ (or **might**) + the _____ form of the verb.

Oral Practice 1:   Find out about your classmates' plans for the future—next weekend, during the next vacation, after graduation, and so on. After you receive an answer, ask a follow-up question to get more information. Examples:

> *What are you going to do on Saturday night, Carlos?*
> *I'm going to go dancing.*
> *Where are you going to go dancing?*
> *I'm not sure. I may go to the new club downtown.*
>
> *What are you going to do during the spring break, Tan-Ming?*
> *I'm going to Dallas, Texas.*
> *How long are you going to stay there?*
> *I'm going to spend six days there.*

Written Practice 1A: Complete these sentences about yourself and your friends. Use *be going to* in each sentence.

1.   After classes today, I _____.

2.   _____ dinner at _____ o'clock.

3.   After dinner, _____ and I _____.

4.   Next weekend, my friend _____ is _____.

5.   During the next vacation, my friends _____ and _____

_____.

Written Practice 1B: Rewrite the sentences from 1A using the present progressive instead of *be going to* wherever possible.

9.2 **Requests and Offers**		
It's about two hours before Stan's and Rhonda's date. Rhonda has just called Stan up. Stan has offered to lend Rhonda a cassette tape that she is interested in, and she wants to remind him to bring it.		
Complete these model sentences.	Check.	Complete these rules.
Rhonda: Stan, will you please bring that tape this evening? **Stan: Sure. And _____ bring along a couple of others that you might like.**	I'll	As you learned in chapter 4 (Rule Builders 4.3 and 4.5), _____ is one of the modals that can be used in making requests and offers. ***Will*** is used when the meaning is "be willing."

Oral Practice 2:   Form a group with some classmates. Imagine that you are going to have a picnic. Use requests and offers to get organized.
Example:

> *Nadir, will you bring a six-pack of soda?*
> *I'll make some cupcakes.*

Written Practice 2: Write a short dialogue between two roommates who have decided to have a party in their room. They must decide who will clean up the room, buy some food and drinks, borrow a tape player and some tapes, and invite their friends.

9.3 Scheduled Events		
Complete these model sentences.	Check.	Complete these rules.
Stan and Rhonda are going to go to a concert. The concert *(start)* _____ **at nine o'clock.** **Classes at Stan's music school** *(begin)* _____ **in September.**	starts begin	We can talk about when future *scheduled* events begin or end by using the _____ _____ tense. There is almost always a time adverbial in these sentences, such as *at nine o'clock* or _____ _____.

Oral Practice 3: Imagine that your school is having a series of special seminars for international students. One seminar ends today, and another begins the day after tomorrow. Tomorrow many students will arrive at and depart from the nearby airport. Using the following schedule, ask a classmate when a certain flight arrives or departs. Examples:

What time does the flight from Atlanta arrive?

Arrivals		Departures	
San Francisco	7:45 A.M.	Kansas City	8:30 A.M.
Los Angeles	9:30 A.M.	Chicago	10:15 A.M.
Atlanta	11:05 A.M.	Philadelphia	11:33 A.M.
Chicago	12:14 P.M.	San Francisco	12:45 P.M.
New York City	2:07 P.M.	Atlanta	1:52 P.M.
Denver	4:10 P.M.	Los Angeles	2:18 P.M.
Kansas City	5:40 P.M.	New York City	3:15 P.M.
Philadelphia	7:05 P.M.	Denver	5:24 P.M.

Written Practice 3: Using the airline schedule for information, complete these sentences.

1. Boon's flight from Atlanta _____.

2. Chin's plane to San Francisco _____.

3. Ahmad's plane from Denver _____.

4. Dan Mei's flight to Philadelphia _____.

5. Patricia's plane to New York City _____.

Look at the cartoon. Then do Rule Builder 9.4.

9.4 Predictions		
Complete these model sentences.	Check.	Complete these rules.
a. The cold front _____ move down from the north tomorrow.	will/ is going to	When you are making predictions and you are rather certain, use the modal _____ or the expression ***be going to***.
b. Suppose that someone asks you, "Will it rain tomorrow?" Since you are not a meteorologist, but you think it is possible that it will rain, your answer would probably be: **It _____ rain tomorrow.**	may/might/ could	When you are not very certain, use the modal _____, _____, or _____.
c. Now suppose that the weatherman is not quite certain enough to say *will*. He knows more than you do, though, so he probably would not say *may*. He would probably say: **The cold front _____ collide with this warm front at about noon tomorrow. So we** **_____ see the first signs of rain at about 12:30. Until then we** **_____ be safe.**	should should should	When you expect something to happen but you are not quite certain, you can use the modal _____.

Oral Practice 4:   Make some predictions and guesses about the near future of some of your classmates. What are you sure of? Use **will**. What do you expect to happen? Use **should**. What do you think is possible? Use **may**, **might**, or **could**.

Written Practice 4:   Complete these sentences.

1. You don't know if there will be a test in your math class next week, but you think it's possible, so you say to your roommate:

    There _____ in math next week.

2. Both you and your classmates have been working hard, so you expect to do well. You say:

    We _____ on the test if there is one.

3. You and your classmate are certain of getting at least a B in the course, so you say:

    We _____ at least a B in the course.

4. You know that a lot of people will come to the basketball game tonight. You say:

    _____ a big crowd at the game tonight.

5. You expect your university's team to win easily tonight. You say:

    Our team _____.

6. You think it's possible for your team to win the league championship this year. You say:

    Our team _____.

7. You expect the team to be at least in the top three. You say:

    Our team _____.

9.5 *If* **Clauses and Time Clauses that Refer to the Future**		
Complete this model sentence.	Check.	Complete these rules.
a. If the cold front from the north (move) _____ **faster than** **expected, it** (start) _____ _____ **raining in the** **morning.**	moves will/may start	Model sentences **a** begins with an *if* **clause** that describes a real possibility in the future. In such a clause use the _____ _____ tense. In the **main clause** use _____ or _____ + the base form.
b. When it (start) _____ **raining, the temperatures** (become) _____ _____ **much** **cooler.**	starts will/may become	Future **time clauses** begin with words such as _____, **before, after,** and **as soon as.** These clauses are similar to *if* clauses. Use the _____ _____ tense.

Oral Practice 5A: Ask another classmate about his or her plans for the rest of the day. When the person mentions an activity, ask what he or she is doing (or is going to do) after that activity (or when he or she finishes that activity). Examples:

> *What are you doing when this class is over?*
> *When this class is over, I'm going to my writing class.*
>
> *What are you going to do after that class ends?*
> *After that class ends, I'm going to have lunch at the union.*
>
> *What are you going to do after you eat?*
> *After I eat, I might go to the library and study.*

NOTE: The **present perfect tense** is often used in time clauses that refer to an action that will be completed. In the second and third examples in Oral Practice 5A the present perfect could be used without changing the meaning:
   After that class *has ended*, I'm going to have lunch. . .
   After I *have eaten*, I might go to the library. . .

Oral Practice 5B: Think of something in the future that you are not sure about. For example, you may have applied for a scholarship, but you don't know whether you will receive it or not. Make an *if* sentence to tell what will occur if this future event happens or doesn't happen.

> *If I get that scholarship, I'm going to quit my part-time job.*
> *If I don't get that scholarship, I'll feel terrible.*

Take notes so that you can do Written Practice 5B.

Written Practice 5A: Complete these sentences.

1. When Stan (*have*) _____ enough money in his savings account, he (*quit*)

    _____ his job and (*go*) _____ to New York to study music.

2. Before you (*take*) _____ the test, you should study.

3. I don't want you to leave before Sam (*arrive*) _____.

4. As soon as class (*be*) _____ over, most of the students (*go*) _____ over

    to the Student Union to watch the big game.

Written Practice 5B: Write six *if* sentences about what your classmates said in Oral Practice 5B.

9.6 Events That Will Be In Progress		
Complete these model sentences.	Check.	Complete these rules.
a. Stan and Rhonda's dinner date is for 6:30 tonight, so we can assume that **at 7:00, they _____** **_____ eating dinner.**	will be	When we indicate that an event will be **in progress** at some future point in time, we use this structure: *will* + *be* + **the _____ form of the verb** We can use *be going to* instead of *will*: **At 7:00, Stan and Rhonda are** *going to be eating* **dinner**.
b. Stan _____ _____ studying music in New York for the next two or three years.	will be	We use the same structure when we tell how long a future action will *be going on*.

Oral Practice 6A: Ask a classmate what he or she will be doing at a certain time.

Oral Practice 6B: Tell the class something that you will or will not be doing for the next few months or years. Example:

> *I will be paying for my new motorbike for the next three years.*
> *I won't be swimming in the ocean for the next few years.*

Written Practice 6:   Tell about some of your plans or make some predictions about your future. Tell about activities that you will be involved in at a particular time or for a certain length of time. Write about things that will be in progress at these times.

1.   Tomorrow at _____, I will be participating in my English class.

2.   Tomorrow night at 8:45, I _____.

3.   At this time next year, _____.

4.   For the next four years, _____.

5.   In 10 years, _____.

6.   In 20 years, _____.

9.7 Chapter Check: Complete these sentences. If you are unsure of an answer, check the indicated model sentence and rule.

1.   From a weather forecast in a newspaper: Today it _____ cloudy with a 40 per-

cent chance of rain.   [9.4a]

2.   "What _____ you _____ do after the movie tonight?"   [9.1a]

or "What _____ doing after the movie tonight?"   [9.1b]

"I don't know. I _____ go home right away and study."   [9.1d]

3. I'm not *absolutely* certain, but I _____ graduate in two years. [9.4c]

4. Harry agreed to meet us here. He said, "I _____ meet you in front of the theater at 7:15." [9.2]

5. _____ you help me move this box? Other possible modals: _____

    _____. [9.2]

6. Stan and Rhonda will _____ a nice time tonight if Stan (*get* + *not*)

    _____ too nervous. [9.5a]

7. In this course, we _____ working on Part Two of the book for at least three

    more days. [9.6b]

9.8 Chapter Check: Finish sentence B. It should have about the same meaning as sentence A.

1. A. Why don't we ask Stan to stop playing?

    B. Shall _____? [4.4b]

2. A. No, I expect that he will stop playing soon.

    B. No, he _____. [9.4c]

3. A. Doris Jones's parents are leaving tomorrow after a five-day visit.

    B. Doris Jones's parents are _____ to leave tomorrow after a five-day

    visit. [9.1a]

4. A. They will visit their other daughter in Houston for a few days. Then they will go

    back to Connecticut.

    B. They will go back to Connecticut after they _____

    in Houston for a few days. [9.5b]

5. A. It is possible that Doris's parents will be home by the first of the month.

    B. Doris's parents _____ by the first of the month. [9.4b]

6. A. What time is their plane scheduled to take off?

    B. What time does _____? [9.3]

7. A. We plan to have a picnic tomorrow. Of course, bad weather will make us change

    our plans.

    B. We'll _____ a picnic tomorrow if the weather _____

    nice. [9.5a]

8. A. Next week at this time, we will be in the middle of the first noun phrase

    chapter.

    B. Next week at this time, we (*work*) _____ on the first

    noun phrase chapter. [9.6a]

9.9 Warm-up: Get together with one or two classmates. Try to get the following information. Begin your questions as indicated.

1. The other students' plans for this evening. "What are you . . . ?"
2. What the other students will be doing at exactly 2:45 tomorrow afternoon. "What do you think you . . . ?"
3. The weather forecast for this weekend. "What's the weather going to be like . . . ?"
4. The winner of the next World Cup championship (or another sports competition that you are interested in). "Who do you think will . . . ?"
5. The date of the beginning of the next semester. "When does . . . ?"
6. The date and time of a good film in the student film series (if there is one) or of a good TV program. "When . . . ?" or "What time . . . ?"

9.10 Communication: Class has just ended, and you and your partner have a conversation. Following the guide below, develop the dialogue. Your teacher may want some of the pairs to present their dialogues to the whole class.

1. Person A finds out the ending time for Person B's last class tomorrow.
2. A asks B about his or her plans after that class.
3. B doesn't have any plans. B asks about A's plans.
4. A has some interesting plans and tells B about them (for example, an evening picnic at the nearby lake or a shopping trip at the mall). A tells B what time this will happen and asks if B would like to do it, too.
5. B agrees to come along and asks A for a ride from his or her apartment or room.
6. After the transportation has been arranged, B asks A about tomorrow's weather.
7. A and B make sure their plans are set and say good-by.

9.11 Sentence Writing: Write 10 true sentences telling what you are doing, are going to do, may do, and so on, at the times given. Use the following expressions in your answers.

1. Right now
2. After that
3. Tomorrow
4. When the semester ends
5. In a few years
6. After I finish my homework
7. Before I go to bed
8. When I have time
9. During the upcoming weekend
10. Before the next century begins

9.12 Sentence Writing: Write four true *if* sentences telling what you will or may do under certain conditions. Remember that adverb clauses (in this case, the *if* clauses) may go before or after the main clauses. Remember the punctuation rules for adverb clauses. Example:

If my grades are not good this semester, I may quit my job.
I may quit my job if my grades are not good this semester.

9.13 Sentence Writing: Think of four temporary activities that you are presently engaged in. Tell how long you will be doing these activities. Example:

I will be studying at this school for three more years.

9.14 Paragraph Writing: Find the weather report in today's newspaper. It will probably consist of only nouns and adjectives rather than complete sentences. Rewrite this forecast in paragraph form. If you cannot find a newspaper weather report, use the following:

Tonight, clear, low 62, east winds 4-8 mph. Saturday, mostly sunny, high 88, southeast winds 6-12 mph. Saturday night, partly cloudy, chance of rain, low 65, southeast winds 5-10 mph.

9.15 Paragraph Writing: You have just bought a telephone answering machine that will take messages from callers when you are not home. Now you have to record a short message that your callers will hear. Write the message that callers will hear when they get your answering machine. All of the members of the class may want to read their messages aloud.

9.16 Paragraph Writing: Imagine that one of your good friends from another town may arrive this weekend for a visit. Tell the things that you will or won't do, or might do, if your friend comes. Describe how your schedule will change if this visitor shows up.

9.17 Paragraph Writing: Write a paragraph about what you think the next century will be like. You can write about the United States, your country or area, another country or area, or the world in general. Limit the paragraph to *one topic*. Suggestions for the topics:

Space exploration   Weather control
Communication   Political changes
Transportation   War
Agriculture   Clothing styles
Food   Computers

You can probably think of other topics. Choose one that interests you, give the paragraph a title (for example, ''Transportation in Iran in the Twenty-first Century''), and write at least 75 words. When you finish, check your verbs carefully.

9.18 Reflecting: Read the next episode of the mystery story. Many of the sentences in the passage refer to the future. Look at the way **be going to**, the **present progressive tense**, and the modals **will, should**, and **may** are used. Can you find the one **if** sentence that refers to the future?

I decided to go back to my office and read the insurance file. On my way downtown I stopped at a phone booth. I found a quarter and called my girlfriend Linda.

"It's me," I said.

"I thought you had forgotten me," Linda said.

"I'll never forget you."

"Hah," she said.

"What are you doing tonight?" I asked.

"I am probably doing something with you."

"I'll take you out to dinner," I told her.

Linda laughed. "That should be interesting. The last time you took me to dinner, you forgot your wallet. I had to pay."

"I'm going to check to make sure I have it this time."

"I hope so," she said. "And the time before that, somebody saw your gun and called the police."

"I won't bring my gun this time," I promised.

"What time are you going to come by?"

"I'm going to do some reading in my office, and then I may go see somebody about my new case. I should get to your place around seven."

"See you then," she said. "Don't forget our date. If you forget, I'll never speak to you again."

"I won't forget," I said.

9.19 Real-World Work

THINK/PRACTICE

1. As you walk around today, make up sentences about the future—your plans for the immediate future (tonight, tomorrow, this weekend), your plans for the more distant future (the next vacation, next year, after you graduate), and predictions about the future—things that will, should, or may happen in your life and in the world.

2. Find a schedule of baseball games, movies, concerts, or television programs in a newspaper. Read the schedule using complete sentences. Examples:

    The Athletics play the Royals tonight at 7:30 in Kansas City.
    Rambo 8 *starts at 8:00.*

Your teacher may want you and your classmates to bring the schedules that you find to class.

LOOK/LISTEN

1. If there is a telephone number that you can call for movie information in English in your town, call it and listen carefully to the way the times of the films are given.

2. Call the weather information number and listen carefully to the way the weather forecast is made. Also, watch the forecast on the TV evening news.

USE

1. It's always interesting and fun to dream about the future with friends and acquaintances. Ask an English-speaking acquaintance about his or her plans for the future. You might end up having a good conversation.

2. Is there a concert, sports event, or film that you are interested in seeing? Call to find out when it starts and when it is over.

10

Verb and Adverb Review I

10.1 Part Two Check: Complete these sentences. If you are unsure of an answer, check the indicated model sentence and rule.

1. There _____ a lot of policemen at yesterday's demonstration. [6.1b]

2. The average American child _____ TV over four hours a day. [6.2a]

3. Shelly doesn't _____ time to go to the movie with us. [6.4b]

4. Shelly usually _____ to movies only on weekends. [6.2c]

5. Everyone _____ on time for yesterday's meeting. [6.1d]

10.2 Part Two Check: Complete this dialogue.

1. Sadie: Do you want some coffee?

   Oscar: No, I _____ any coffee now, thank you. [6.4a]

2. Sadie: You don't drink coffee very often, do you?

   Oscar: No, as a matter of fact, I (*drink* + *never*) _____ it any-

   more. My doctor says that I (*can* + *not* + *drink*) _____

   it. [7.4b, 6.5]

3. Sadie: How about some dessert?

   Oscar: No, thank you. I (*eat + seldom*) _____ dessert. I (*eat*

   + rarely) _____ anything with sugar in it.   [7.4b]

4. Sadie: Shall we take a walk?

   Oscar: That sounds great! I (*take + often*) _____ a walk after

   dinner.   [7.4b]

10.3 Part Two Check: Referring to the cartoons on pages 119–121, complete these senten-ces about ***every evening*** in the apartment building. If you need help, check the indicated rule.

1. Mr. Jones (*watch + always*) _____ the news

   on TV.   [7.4 a&b]

2. At 10:15, when the commercials (*come on*) _____, Mr. Jones (*get up*)

   _____ to feed the cat.   [7.4a]

3. At 10:20 every night, Ms. Jones (*read*) _____ and Mr. Jones (*watch*)

   _____ TV.   [7.4d]

4. At about 10:25 every night, Ms. Jones (*hear*) _____ the door open.   [7.2a]

5. _____ Lisa (*walk in*) _____ at about 10:25 every night, Mr. Jones

   (*greet*) _____ her.   [7.4 e&a]

6. If Lisa (*be + not*) _____ too tired, she (*listen + often*) _____

   _____ to music in her room before she (*go*) _____ to

   sleep.   [7.6b, 7.4a&b, 9.5b]

10.4 Part Two Check: Referring to the cartoon, complete these sentences about **tomorrow evening** in the apartments. If you need help, check the indicated rule.

1. Mr. Jones's favorite TV news program (*start*) _____ at 10:00 P.M.   [9.3]

2. Stan's plans are no different from usual; he (*play*) _____ his saxophone from 10:00 till 12:00.   [9.1a]

3. Occasionally Lisa misses her bus and is late, so we cannot be certain, but she _____ be home at about 10:25 tomorrow night.   [9.4c]

4. When Ms. Jones (*hear*) _____ her daughter come in tomorrow night, she (*lay down*) _____ her book.   [9.5b, 9.4a]

5. Lisa (*listen*) _____ to music for a while before she (*go*) _____ to bed, but she may be too tired.   [9.1d, 9.5b]

10.5 Part Two Check: Referring to the cartoon, complete these sentences about **last night** in Stan's and the Joneses' apartments. If you need help, check the indicated rule.

1. Last night at 10 o'clock, Mr. Jones (*turn on*) _____ the TV.   [8.1a]

2. _____ Mr. Jones watched TV, his wife read a book in bed.   [8.5c]

3. _____ Lisa (*get*) _____ home last night, Stan (*play*) _____ _____ his saxophone.   [8.5c, 8.1b, 8.5a]

4. _____ Lisa (*get*) _____ home last night, her father (*say*) _____ ''Hi'' to her.   [8.5c, 8.1a]

10.6 Part Two Check: Finish sentences B and C. They should have about the same meaning as sentence A. If you need help, check the indicated rule.

Before you start, read the definitions of these terms:

inflection   a change in the form of a word according to grammatical use
tone language   a language in which different tones, or pitches, can change the meaning of a word
inversion   a reversal of the normal order of words

1. A. Neither the Chinese language nor the Vietnamese language has inflections.

    B. Chinese doesn't _____ inflections and _____

        _____ Vietnamese.   [7.5d]

    C. Chinese _____ inflections and Vietnamese

        _____.   [7.5e]

2. A. Both Chinese and Vietnamese are tone languages.

    B. Chinese _____, and _____

        Vietnamese.   [7.5b]

    C. Chinese _____, and Vietnamese

        _____.   [7.5c]

3. A. Neither Chinese nor Vietnamese uses inversion in questions.

    B. Chinese _____ inversion in questions, and neither

        _____.   [7.5d]

    C. Chinese _____,

        and Vietnamese _____.   [7.5e]

10.7 Sentence Writing: Imagine that you hear each of these sentences in a conversation. What question would you ask if you wanted to know how many times the person(s) had done this thing? Example:

I went skiing in the Alps last summer.
How many times <u>have you skied</u> there?

1. She went to New York City last weekend.
2. They ate at that good restaurant on the square.
3. Sheila has changed roommates again this month.
4. He read his favorite book again.

10.8 Sentence Writing: Think of four things that *suddenly* happened to you. Perhaps you hurt yourself, heard some good or bad news, found something that you had lost. Perhaps someone called you on the phone, got angry at you, or gave you something. In your sentence, tell what you **were doing** when this event took place. Write a ***while*** sentence, and then put the same information in a ***when*** sentence. Example:

While I was driving to school yesterday, my car broke down.
I was driving to school yesterday when my car broke down.

10.9 Paragraph Writing: Pretend that you have two roommates; one is easy to live with and one is very difficult. Explain why living with the first is easy while living with the second is difficult by referring to their good and bad habits and the frequency of those habitual actions. Here is an example of the kind of sentences that the paragraph might contain:

Tom almost always leaves his dirty dishes in the sink.

10.10 Paragraph Writing: This is a page from Ms. Jones's appointment book for tomorrow. Write a short paragraph describing her agenda.

AY	FRIDAY	S.
	2 337/29 10 – staff meeting 10³⁰ – Dean's Council 12³⁰ – lunch, Dr. Crowe call Housing Office before 4:00 5³⁰ – pick up Lisa 7³⁰ – reception for honor students	**3** 338/28

10.11 Reflecting: Read the next episode of the mystery story. Examine the way verb tenses are used.

In my office I read Carl Miller's file on his investigation into the malpractice suit. The first page in the file was a note from Miller to his boss.

The note read: "Andrea, I think the company is not going to have to pay. I don't think Dr. Weber made any mistakes when he operated on Daniels's mother."

When I looked through the file, I saw that Troy Daniels was the name of the man who wanted to sue Dr. Weber. I found Daniels's address and copied it onto a piece of paper. Maybe Daniels was involved in the insurance man's disappearance. It was possible that Miller told Daniels the insurance company wasn't going to pay. Maybe Daniels got angry.

I couldn't find Doctor Weber's address in the file, though, so I called Lieutenant Farmer at the police department. He found the address and gave it to me.

"It won't help you, though," Farmer said. "He's gone. He's traveling in Greece."

"That's funny," I said. "Why is he taking a vacation when he has this malpractice trouble?"

I hung up. Maybe Weber wasn't involved. He might not be worried about the case because he might know something about Miller's disappearance.

I decided to visit his house anyway.

11

Count
and Noncount
Nouns

REVIEW

Two friends, Jacob and Jean, have just run into each other in front of the student union. Complete their dialogue.

JACOB: Have you (*see*) _____ Brenda around? I'm (*pick*)

_____ her up here and (*take*) _____ her downtown.

JEAN: Sorry, but I (*think + not*) _____ I know her.

JACOB: Really, I (*be*) _____ sorry I haven't introduced you to her.

JEAN: How long have you (*know*) _____ her?

JACOB: We've known each other since June, when she (*move*) _____ here.

PREVIEW

Choose between the words in parentheses. Cross out the word that is wrong.

JACOB: Brenda doesn't have (*much/many*) friends yet.

JEAN: It's difficult to get adjusted when you don't know (*much/many*) people. And I'll bet she doesn't have (*much/many*) time, either, since she's a student.

JACOB: Actually, she's not taking (*much/many*) classes. But she's very busy; she has to work full-time because she doesn't have very (*much/many*) money.

The words that require *many* are called **count nouns**; the words that require *much* are called **noncount nouns**. You will practice using count and noncount nouns in this chapter.

As you work with count and noncount nouns, you will review irregular noun plurals and the use of *a*, *an* and *some*.

11.1 Tangible Nouns: Count Versus Noncount

Complete these model sentences with the singular or plural forms of these words. Use the words in this order: *sandwich, meat, cheese, bread, hamburger, ketchup, mustard, onion,* and *tomato.*	Check.	Complete these rules.
Mike sells a lot of _____ **at his cafe, so he needs to buy a lot of** _____, _____, **and** _____. **The most popular sandwiches are** _____. **Since customers like to put a variety of things on them, Mike has to buy a lot of** _____, _____, _____, **and** _____.	sandwiches meat, cheese bread hamburgers ketchup mustard onions tomatoes	Tangible nouns refer to things that can be touched. Some of these things can be counted; others cannot. **Nouncount nouns**, such as _____, are normally used only in the singular form. **Count nouns**, such as _____, may be singular or _____. To make most **count nouns** plural, add _____ or ____.

Write each noun from the preceding model sentences in the appropriate list. Then add these nouns to the lists: *apple, sugar, rice, water, chair, coffee, pan, milk, dirt, oil.* Put the count nouns in their plural forms.

COUNT	**NOUNCOUNT**	
sandwiches	*meat*	
_____	_____	_____
_____	_____	_____
_____	_____	_____
_____	_____	_____
_____	_____	_____
_____	_____	_____

Oral Practice 1:   Tell the class what you had for dinner last night.

Written Practice 1:   Underline the *nouns* in the sentences. Then rewrite the sentences, making the nouns plural wherever possible.

1.   A hamburger is not very nutritious.
2.   Milk is essential for a baby.
3.   Always serve wine in a clean glass.
4.   I am surprised that rice is eaten with a fork here.
5.   A machine needs oil.
6.   Sugar is often kept in a special bowl.

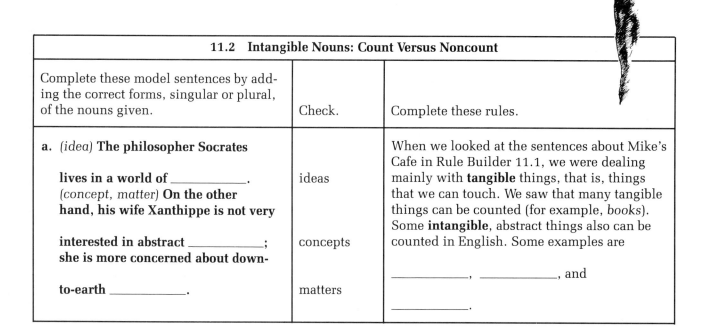

11.2 Intangible Nouns: Count Versus Noncount		
Complete these model sentences by adding the correct forms, singular or plural, of the nouns given.	Check.	Complete these rules.
a. *(idea)* **The philosopher Socrates** **lives in a world of** _____. *(concept, matter)* **On the other hand, his wife Xanthippe is not very** **interested in abstract** _____; **she is more concerned about down-** **to-earth** _____.	ideas concepts matters	When we looked at the sentences about Mike's Cafe in Rule Builder 11.1, we were dealing mainly with **tangible** things, that is, things that we can touch. We saw that many tangible things can be counted (for example, *books*). Some **intangible**, abstract things also can be counted in English. Some examples are _____, _____, and _____.

b. *(love, justice)* **Socrates thinks about** _____ **and** _____.	love, justice	Many intangible nouns refer to abstract things that cannot be counted in English. Two examples are _____ and _____.
c. *(news)* **His wife would rather listen to music and read the** _____.	news	Some noncount nouns end in s, but they are not plural. For example, we must say, ''The news _____ good today.''

Here are some **count** nouns that cause trouble for some students of English.

ideas	*suggestions*	*plans*
concepts	*recommendations*	*decisions*
matters	*proposals*	*choices*
assignments	*remarks*	*mistakes*
problems	*reports*	*prices*
ways	*climates*	*advertisements*

Here are some **noncount** nouns that give some students trouble.

information	*evidence*	*music*
knowledge	*progress*	*fun*
vocabulary	*confusion*	*work*
slang	*trouble*	*weather*
research	*advice*	*scenery*
homework	*permission*	

Here are a few of the **noncount** nouns that end in s that give students trouble.

news	*linguistics*	*mathematics*
	economics	*genetics*

Oral Practice 2A: What are some interesting things to read about? Examples:

Love is interesting to read about.
Scientific experiments are interesting to read about.

Oral Practice 2B: You and your classmates should spend a few minutes talking about your favorite school subjects and your favorite types of entertainment. Remember that some nouns are count and some are noncount. Examples:

Mathematics is my favorite subject.
Movies are my favorite type of entertainment.

Written Practice 2:   Use each term in a sentence that ends with the expression "has/have always interested me." *You will have to make some of the nouns plural.* Example:

philosophical idea
Philosophical ideas have always interested me.

1.   scientific knowledge
2.   classical music
3.   mathematical problems
4.   political news
5.   TV advertisement
6.   nuclear physics

11.3 Plurals with *-es* and *-ies;* Irregular Plurals		
Write the plural of these nouns.	Check.	Complete these rules.
a. onion _____	onions	To form the plural of most nouns, simply add _____ .
b. sandwich _____ **dish** _____ **glass** _____ **tomato** _____ **box** _____ **quiz** _____	sandwiches dishes glasses tomatoes boxes quizzes	Add *-es* if the noun ends in *ch* _____, _____, _____, _____, or _____. There are some exceptions to this rule, such as *stomachs, pianos,* and *radios.* Double the **z** in *quiz* before you add -es.
c. French fry _____ **turkey** _____	French fries turkeys	If the noun ends in **y** preceded by a consonant, change **y** to _____ and add _____. But if the **y** is preceded by a vowel, simply add _____. An example is the word _____ .

d. knife _____ shelf _____ belief _____	knives shelves beliefs	If the noun ends in *f* or *fe*, change the *f* or *fe* to ____ and add _____. There are a few exceptions to this rule, however: *proofs,* *roofs,* and _____.
e. crisis _____	crises	Most nouns ending in **-is** are made plural by changing the -*is* to _____.
f. child _____ woman _____ man _____ foot _____ tooth _____ goose _____ mouse _____	children women men feet teeth geese mice	Some nouns have completely irregular forms. A few examples are the nouns *woman, man,* *foot, tooth, goose, mouse,* and _____. Do you notice anything similar about these plural forms?
g. means _____ sheep _____	means sheep	Some nouns, such as *means* and _____, have the _____ form in the plural as they do in the singular.

Oral Practice 3:   Make a list of nouns that have tricky plurals. Try to think of nouns that are from the categories in Rule Builder 11.3 but are not given in the Rule Builder—for example, *watch* and *spy*. You and your classmates can quiz each other. Your class may want to have a plural noun spelling bee, that is, a contest to see who is the best speller in the class.

Written Practice 3:   Write the plural form for each of the following nouns.

1.	calf	_____	2.	foot	_____
3.	potato	_____	4.	analysis	_____
5.	basis	_____	6.	life	_____
7.	wife	_____	8.	child	_____
9.	embargo	_____	10.	tooth	_____
11.	hero	_____	12.	means	_____
13.	baby	_____	14.	bunch	_____

15.	toy	_____	16.	army	_____
17.	inch	_____	18.	fox	_____
19.	roof	_____	20.	woman	_____
21.	leaf	_____	22.	thesis	_____
23.	echo	_____	24.	self	_____

11.4 *A/An* Versus *Some*		
Complete these model sentences.	Check.	Complete these rules.
a. Two customers are at Mike's Cafe. **Charley: Mike, I'll have _____ American cheese sandwich.** **Jacques: I'd like _____ hamburger.**	an a	As we saw in Rule Builder 11.1, count nouns, such as *sandwich* and *hamburger*, can be singular or _____. And, as we saw, we usually make a count noun plural by adding _____. To make a count noun singular, we put _____ or _____ in front of it. We use **an** when the word after it begins with a _____ sound.
b. Jacques: I'd also like _____ **French fries and _____ milk to drink, please.** **Mike: I'm sorry. We don't have** **_____ milk today. How about** **_____ coffee?**	some some any some	*A* and **an** are used only with singular _____ nouns. Before noncount nouns, such as *milk*, and plural nouns, such as *French fries*, we often use the word _____. Or, after a negative adverb, like *not*, we can use _____.
c. Jacques: Okay, I'll have _____ cup of coffee—and is it possible to **order _____ slice of cheese?**	a a	*Coffee* and *cheese* are _____ nouns. Although nouns like these are not usually counted, they can be divided into units which can be counted. To do this, we can use "container" words, such as *glass*, *can*, or _____, "piece" words, such as *piece* or _____, or "measurement" words, such as *quart*, *pound*, or *liter*.

Oral Practice 4A: Think for a minute about your favorite simple recipe—maybe for something as simple as a sandwich. Explain the recipe to the class. Be sure to tell the quantity of each ingredient that you need.

Oral Practice 4B: Imagine that you're going on a camping trip this weekend. Tell the class what equipment you will take along and what you will not take.

Written Practice 4A: Complete these sentences.

Yesterday I went into _____ store and saw _____ man trying on _____ large hat. For security reasons, this store had a closed-circuit TV system, and the man was looking at _____ image of himself on _____ TV monitor. Later, I saw the same man in _____ restaurant across the street. He asked for _____ piece of pie and _____ of milk. They were out of milk, so the customer ordered _____ of tea instead.

Written Practice 4B: When people make shopping lists, they often do not indicate *how many* or *how much* they want to buy. If I want a pound of hamburger and two quarts of milk, for example, I might just write down *hamburger* and *milk*. Here is a typical U.S. supermarket shopping list. Imagine that it is yours.

```
hamburger      cereal
milk           dog food
sugar          cheese
shampoo        bread
soap           butter
```

Now add the quantities you want to the list. The first two have been done for you.

_____*a pound of*_____	hamburger
_____*two quarts of*_____	milk
_____	sugar
_____	shampoo
_____	soap
_____	cereal
_____	dog food
_____	cheese
_____	bread
_____	butter

11.5 Tangible Nouns that Can Be Both Count and Noncount		
Complete these model sentences by adding the correct form of the noun given.	Check.	Complete these rules.
(hamburger) **Every week Mike must buy nearly 100 pounds of** _____. (hamburger) **Every week Mike sells over 400** _____.	hamburger hamburgers	Many nouns are noncount when they refer to a substance but count when they refer to (1) a serving of a food or drink substance, such as _____, (2) a piece of material, such as *rock*, or (3) a whole from which pieces are cut and eaten—often the name of an animal or vegetable, such as *chicken* and *cabbage*. Some examples of each of the three categories follow.

1. Food/Drink → a Serving
   soda → a soda
   cola, etc. → a cola, etc.
   beer → a beer
   hamburger → a hamburger
   steak → a steak
   aspirin → an aspirin

2. Material → a Piece
   stone → a stone
   rock → a rock
   wire → a wire
   rope → a rope
   cord → a cord
   string → a string
   thread → a thread
   cloth → a cloth

3. Food ← a Whole
   cake ← a cake
   pie ← a pie
   pizza ← a pizza
   chicken ← a chicken
   turkey ← a turkey
   lamb ← a lamb
   salmon ← a salmon
   trout ← a trout
   tuna ← a tuna
     etc.
   coconut ← a coconut
   cucumber ← a cucumber
   melon ← a melon
     etc.

Oral Practice 5A: Choose a noun from the preceding list and make two sentences with it. In the first sentence use it as a noncount noun, and in the second as a count noun. Examples:

Maria's blouse is made of very fine cloth.
After putting wax on your car, wipe it off with a dry cloth.

Oral Practice 5B: With your classmates, try to think of other vegetables and animals that fit into Rule Builder 11.5. Nouns in this category are count nouns when they refer to the whole animal, vegetable, or fruit, but noncount when they refer to the serving of food on our plate. Tell something about the vegetable, fruit, or animal and then something about the food. Example:

> *Sharks have very sharp teeth.*
> *Grilled shark tastes a lot like beef.*

NOTE: Some noncount nouns, especially food and drink words, can be used as count nouns with the meaning ''a kind of X.'' Examples:
   Burgundy is a French **wine.**
   Thyme is a **spice**.

Oral Practice 5C: Refer to the menu on the following page to answer these questions:

1.   How much does a turkey sandwich cost at Mike's?
2.   What can you get for exactly 90 cents?
3.   Is there any mustard on the hamburgers that Mike serves?
4.   How much does Mike charge for beer?

Now you and one or two of your classmates can ask each other similar questions based on the menu.

****MIKE'S CAFE****

the best little sandwich
place in town

SANDWICHES

Hot Roast Beef. 2.35
Turkey 2.35
Ham 2.25
Sloppy Joe 2.10
Hoagie 2.10
Chicken 2.50
Fish 2.65
Cheese (20¢ extra)
    American
    Swiss
    Cheddar
    Longhorn
The turkey and ham come with
lettuce, mayonnaise, pickles,
and tomatoes. If you don't like
these dressings, you can scrape
them off.

Grilled Cheese (1 slice). . . . 1.50
 extra cheese . . . . .20¢ each

SIDE ORDERS

Plate of French Fries. 85
    More than you can eat.
    If it isn't, I'll make you more.
Mashed potatoes 85
    Brown or white gravy
Corn on the cob (summer
only) .75
    Ears as long as your arm
    and as thick as your wrist.

HAMBURGERS

Single Hamburger. 1.45
Single Cheeseburger. 1.70
Double Hamburger 2.50
Double Cheeseburger 2.75

My hamburgers are a quarter
pound of the best beef you can get
around here. If you aren't hungry,
don't order a double. Kids eat
about half of a single. All burgers
come with onions, lettuce, to-
mato, and ketchup. The mustard's
on the table.

HOT DOGS

Standard 1.25
Fat foot-long 1.90
Mike's special 2.75

The special is two dogs wrapped
in a hoagie bun with ketchup,
mustard, and horseradish, etc. All
that is covered with my special
chili recipe. If you order the special, I'll bring a pitcher of water to
the table.

DESSERTS

Pie
    by the slice 90
    whole pies 5.50

We have various kinds. It depends
on what Mabel made today.

DRINKS

I have never sold beer and I never
will, so don't ask for any. If you
wanted beer you should have
gone across the street.
Pop   (glass) 60
       (bottle). 75
Milk .45
Coffee (bottomless cup) 60

Written Practice 5:   Write *a* or *an* in the blanks wherever necessary.

1. I really can't tell the difference between _____ Coke® and _____ Pepsi®, but when I'm in a restaurant, I automatically say, "I'd like _____ Coke, please."

2. This sofa is covered with _____ specially treated cloth. If something is spilled on the sofa, it can be wiped clean with _____ damp cloth.

3. _____ aspirin is probably the most widely prescribed medicine. Thousands of times a day, the world's doctors say, "Take _____ aspirin or two, and go to bed."

4. I have to write _____ paper for my history class, but I don't know what kind of _____ paper I should write it on.

11.6 Intangible Nouns that Can Be Count or Noncount		
Complete these model sentences with ***a*** or ***an*** if an article is needed.	Check.	Complete these rules.
One of the things that distinguish human beings from the other animals is _____ language. **Many people believe that English is _____ very important language to know.**	no article a	Many intangible nouns can be either noncount or count. An example is _____. Do you see a difference in the way this noun is used in the two model sentences? When these nouns are noncount, they have a more abstract meaning. When they are count, they are more concrete. Following is a list of common nouns that are noncount when they have an abstract meaning and count when they have a more concrete meaning.

ability	*imagination*	*reason*
action	*improvement*	*religion*
adventure	*joy*	*responsibility*
agreement	*language*	*rest*
color	*law*	*sacrifice*
compromise	*life*	*skill*
conflict	*marriage*	*society*
crime	*movement*	*space*
custom	*noise*	*speech*
desire	*organization*	*strength*
disease	*pain*	*style*
duty	*personality*	*talent*
exercise	*pleasure*	*thought*
fear	*proof*	*tradition*
friendship	*punishment*	*truth*
habit	*quality*	*weakness*
hope		
illness		

Oral Practice 6:   Look through the preceding list and find a noun whose count and non-count meanings you understand. Demonstrate the abstract and concrete meanings by using the noun in two sentences. Examples:

*The doctor said I needed plenty of **rest**.*
*I had a nice **rest** after lunch.*

Written Practice 6:   Write *a* or *an* in the blanks wherever necessary.

1.   Smallpox is _____ disease that used to kill many children in this country.

2.   _____ disease is a major problem in many parts of the world.

3.   Another of the major problems in the world today is _____ crime.

4.   Just last week _____ serious crime, a robbery, was committed in our neighborhood.

5.   We do many things every day out of _____ habit.

6.   Smoking is _____ very dangerous habit.

7.   It is important to study philosophy, the history of _____ thought.

8.   _____ thought concerning your problem has just occurred to me.

9.   Taking care of children is _____ very serious responsibility.

10.   To be mature, a person must learn to take _____ responsibility.

11.7 **Noncount Category Nouns**		
Complete these model sentences.	Check.	Complete these rules.
a. Chairs, desks, and tables are some **examples of** _____.	furniture	Some **noncount** nouns are names for categories or collections of things that can be counted. An example of this type of noun is _____. (You can refer to machinery and clothing with the plural nouns *machines* and *clothes*. *Machine* is an ordinary count noun; it can be singular or plural. *Clothes* is a rather strange noun; it is used only in the plural form).
Apples, bananas, and pears are **kinds of** _____.	fruit	
Flasks, beakers, and Bunsen burners **are kinds of lab** _____.	equipment	
Engines, pumps, and lathes are **types of** _____.	machinery	
Rings, necklaces, and bracelets are **kinds of** _____.	jewelry	
Shirts, pants, and coats are **examples of** _____.	clothing	

b. **A chair can be called a piece of**		You can refer to individual things in the category without specifying which one by
_____. **You can call an apple and a banana**	furniture	using the expression **a** _____ **of** or
two _____ **of** _____.	pieces, fruit	the plural _____ _____.

Oral Practice 7A: Put the items listed in the correct category. Example:

A blender is a type of (a kind of) kitchen equipment.

coffee table	sweater	brooch (an ornamental pin)
fig	toaster	tennis racket
sofa	pineapple	teeter-totter
plum	blouse	combine

Oral Practice 7B: Point to something in the classroom that belongs to one of these categories: furniture, fruit, equipment, machinery, jewelry, and clothing. Make a sentence using the expression **a piece of.** Example: Holding up an orange, you say,

This is a piece of fruit.

Oral Practice 7C: Now quiz one another. Think of something that falls into one of the categories in Rule Builder 11.7 or point to something and ask a classmate what it is. Example:

What is an earring? or What is this?
It's a kind of jewelry. or It's a piece of jewelry.

Written Practice 7:   Complete these sentences.

1. _____ is a piece of furniture.

2. A typewriter is _____ office equipment.

3. A bulldozer is _____.

4. An earring is _____.

5. _____ of clothing.

6. _____ fruit.

7. In a modern office, a computer is an important _____.

8. A lathe is a _____ that is used to shape wood or metal.

9. A _____ is _____ jewelry that goes around the neck.

10. A pair of pants is _____.

11.8 Chapter Check: Write the correct forms of the nouns in the blanks. Add *a* or *an*, *some*, and *any* wherever necessary. If you are unsure of an answer, check the indicated model sentence and rule.

1. (*robot, factory, plant*) By the end of 1984, there were about 1,300 _____ in

    American _____ and 40,000 in Japanese _____.   [11.1, 11.3c]

2. (*robot, machinery, machine*) Of course, most factories still did not have _____

    in 1984, but more and more companies had started to replace old-fashioned

    _____ with these new ''smart'' _____.   [11.1,11.7a]

3. (*object, brick, egg*) Some robots even have a sense of touch; when they pick up

    _____, they can tell if it's _____ or _____ and apply just

    the right amount of pressure.   [11.4]

4. (*experimental robot, plastic block, toy airplane*) General Electric has

    _____ that talks with the operator. ''What do

    you want?'' the robot asks. ''Three airplanes,'' the operator answers. The robot takes

    _____ and builds three _____.   [11.4a]

11.9 Chapter Check: Complete these sentences with the correct forms, singular or plural, of the nouns given.

1. (*remark*) The speaker made some interesting _____.   [11.2]

2. (*advice, suggestion*) The counselor gave me some valuable _____ and some

    good _____.   [11.2]

3. (*progress, homework*) My teacher said that I am making some _____, but she

    said that I would improve even faster if I did all of my _____.

    [11.2]

4. (*habit*) Fred can be very kind, but he has some bad _____.   [11.6]

5. (*chicken, chicken*) The poor family used to keep some _____ for eggs. Last

    Saturday, however, they ran out of food and got very hungry. Since then, they have had

    _____ at several meals.   [11.5]

11.10 Chapter Check: Finish sentence B. It should have about the same meaning as sentence A.

1. A.   Would you like a cup of tea?

    B.   Would you like _____ tea?   [11.4b]

2. A.   I would like some pie, please.

    B.   I would like a _____, please.   [11.4c]

3. A. The world *cloth* refers to the material that most clothes are made of.

    B. The word *cloth* refers to the material that _____ is

        made of.   [11.7a]

4. A. Poor Ralph has no friends.

    B. Poor Ralph doesn't _____.   [11.4b]

11.11 Chapter Check: In each blank write *a*, *an*, or *some*.

1. We might have _____ bad weather tonight.   [11.2, 11.4]

2. The American Midwest has _____ interesting climate.   [11.2, 11.4]

3. There is _____ serious overpopulation problem in that country.   [11.2, 11.4]

4. The police found _____ evidence that _____ crime had been

    committed.   [11.2, 11.4, 11.6]

5. Waiter, I think I would like _____ watermelon for dessert.   [11.5]

11.12 Warm-up: This memory game is fun to play and good for noun phrase practice. Pretend that you're going to the grocery store. Mention something that you are going to get. The next student repeats what you said and adds something else, and so on. Example:

> *I'm going to the grocery store. I'm going to get a gallon of milk.*
> *I'm going to the grocery store. I'm going to get a gallon of milk and a dozen eggs.*
> *I'm going to the grocery store. I'm going to get a gallon of milk, a dozen eggs, and some peanut butter.*

11.13 Communication: Form small groups and pretend that you are in Mike's Cafe. Use Mike's Cafe menu (page 134), and take turns playing the roles of waiters and customers. When you are the waiter, quickly write down each customer's order. When the role-play is over, the teacher may ask you what some of the customers ordered.

11.14 Sentence Writing: Answer these questions about Mike's Cafe menu (page 134) with complete sentences.

1. How much does an ear of corn cost?
2. How much does Mike charge for a pie?
3. If you want pop to drink, but you want to spend only 60 cents, what do you say?
4. What kind of sandwich can you get for exactly $2.45?

11.15 Sentence Writing: You are at Mike's Cafe with a friend and you're very hungry. Look at the menu and then write down both of your orders.

> MIKE: What would you folks like today?
> YOU: I would like . . .
> YOUR FRIEND: And I want . . .

11.16 Sentence Writing: Look at these sentences:

A squirrel is a mammal.
Squirrels are mammals.

These sentences have about the same meaning; they talk about a class of things (squirrels). This noun is a count noun, as you can see, and we use both forms—singular and plural—to make a generalization about this class. In the following exercise you will read about tiny animals that have only one cell and can be seen only with a microscope. *Rewrite each sentence, changing singular subjects to plural and plural subjects to singular.* Make all other necessary changes. Notice that the meaning does not change. Example:

A protozoan is a one-celled animal.
Protozoans are one-celled animals.

1.   An amoeba is a protozoan.
2.   Amoebas are very simple organisms.
3.   A flagellate is also classified as a protozoan.
4.   Flagellates are more complex than amoebas.

11.17 Paragraph Writing: Imagine that you and a friend from another school are going to meet in Colorado for a camping trip. You and your friend must make careful plans so that you will have what you need in the wilderness. Write a letter to your friend. Tell him or her what equipment you have and what you don't have. Offer to bring certain things for the trip and ask your friend to bring other things.

11.18 Reflecting: Read the next episode of the mystery story. Examine the noun phrases. There are many count and noncount nouns—and several that can be either count or noncount. In the second half of the passage, Farmer uses the noun **crime** first as a count noun and then as a noncount noun. Do you understand the difference between the two uses of the noun?

I waited until it was dark and drove to Dr. Weber's house. I was tired. "What am I doing here?" I asked myself aloud. "I should be at home drinking beer and eating pizza."

I got my burglary equipment out of the glove compartment. There was a small flashlight, gloves, a roll of masking tape, and a rock the size of my fist. I left the keys in the car and the door unlocked.

The yard was dark. I went around to the back of the house, trying not to step on any roses or any big dogs.

The back door was one of those doors with several small panes of glass. I covered one of the panes with masking tape and then hit it with the rock. The glass broke but didn't make any noise. I pulled away the tape and the shards of glass and reached in to unlock the door from the inside.

It was already unlocked.

"This isn't my day," I groaned.

Inside Weber's house I found a file marked "Daniels." I took it with me. I left a 10-dollar bill on the table to pay for the window I broke to get in.

There was a police car parked right behind my car. Lieutenant Farmer was sitting on the hood of my car smoking a cigarette.

"I want to report a burglary," I said.

"Burglary is a crime," Farmer said. "Crime doesn't pay."

"You're full of wisdom tonight," I said. "Get off my car."

"Did you find anything?"

"No evidence," I said. "I did find a lot of insurance policies. He loves insurance. He has his bathtub insured."

"Maybe he's afraid," Farmer said.

"You will be, too, if you don't get off my car."

Farmer climbed down. He put out his cigarette on the hood of my car. "I got your car dirty," he said. "But I'm sure you have insurance."

11.19 Real-World Work

THINK/PRACTICE

1. We usually identify something by using expressions like these: "This/That is a wrench." "These/Those are wrenches." "This/That is salad dressing." Notice that we don't usually use the word *some* when we are telling what something is. Today, while you are walking around, practice expressions like these. Be sure to use *a* or *an* with singular count nouns.

2. As you are walking around today, think of the good things and bad things about your hometown, your country, and the town and country where you are living now. Some of these things will be noncount; others will be count. Pay careful attention to determiners (*a* or *an*, *some*, and quantity expressions) and singular versus plural. Example:

    My hometown has great weather, beautiful scenery, several fine beaches, and a good art museum.

LOOK/LISTEN

In a newspaper, magazine, or book, look for nouns that you think can be either count or noncount. Cut out or copy the paragraph in which the noun is used. Indicate whether it refers to something that is tangible or intangible, and whether it is used as a count or noncount noun. Then try to write another sentence in which the word is used in its other sense. Your teacher may want you to bring one or more of the examples you have found to class.

USE

When we ask for something, we use *a* or *an* with singular count nouns, and we use *some* with plural and noncount nouns: "I would like an ice cream cone." "I need some paper." "Could you get some napkins out?" Practice telling yourself what you want and need. Go to a store that sells some of the things you need, and tell the clerk what you would like. Try to use *a* or *an* and *some* correctly.

12

Noun Modifiers

REVIEW

Some of the underlined nouns in the following paragraph should be plural, and some need **a** or **an**. Others are noncount and should not be changed. Make all the necessary changes in the paragraph. *Do not change any verbs*; make the subjects agree with the verbs.

Scientist have been studying sleep for many year. They have learned, for example, that three-month-old child sleep around 14 hour a day. Typical adult, however, sleeps about 7.5 hour. Another study has shown that when baby are asleep, they dream about 40 percent of the time. Adult, on the other hand, dream only about 20 percent of the time. Dream occur during several period of rapid eye movement, or REM; each of these period lasts about 20 minute.

PREVIEW

Both count and noncount nouns can be modified by various kinds of words:

1. adjectives that come before the noun (A *typical* adult . . .),
2. adjectives that come after a linking verb (When babies are *asleep* . . .),
3. other nouns (. . . *eye* movement . . . three-*month*-old children . . .),
4. quantifiers (. . . *many* years . . . *several* periods . . .), and
5. forms of *other* (*Another* study . . .).

In this chapter we will work with these noun modifiers.

Stretch and Tank are student athletes at the small college where Doris Jones is Dean of Students. Stretch plays basketball, while Tank is on the football team.

<table>
<tr><td colspan="3" align="center">12.1   Adjectives</td></tr>
<tr><td>Complete these model sentences.</td><td>Check.</td><td>Complete these rules.</td></tr>
<tr>
<td>a. First, comment about Stretch's and Tank's height.

Stretch is very _____.

Tank is quite _____.</td>
<td>

tall

short</td>
<td>Adjectives, such as _____ and

_____, can go after the verb be and certain other verbs. They modify the

_____ of the sentence. These are called predicate adjectives.</td>
</tr>
<tr>
<td>b. Second, consider whether they are nice or mean.

Stretch seems very _____.

Tank looks rather _____.</td>
<td>

nice

mean</td>
<td>Other verbs besides be that take predicate adjectives are become, get, seem, appear, and sensation verbs such as taste, feel, smell,

and _____. An adjective can be expressed with more force or precision if we use an intensifier before it. The most common intensifier before an adjective is

_____. Here are some other common intensifiers ranging from weak to strong:

WEAK   STRONG

fairly
somewhat }   rather   quite   } extremely
terribly
awfully</td>
</tr>
<tr>
<td>c. Stretch is _____ _____ man.

Tank is _____ _____ man.</td>
<td>a tall/nice

a short/mean</td>
<td>Most adjectives can also come before nouns. If an article (a or an) is required, it comes

_____ the adjective.</td>
</tr>
</table>

Oral Practice 1:   Use these adjectives to describe the members of your class:

tall	studious	nice
short	intelligent	cheerful
young	energetic	friendly
mature	interesting	quiet

You can use other adjectives, of course, but avoid negative ones; you wouldn't want to insult a classmate. Example:

Maryam is intelligent.

Continue, but now add an intensifier (*extremely, very, quite, rather, somewhat, fairly,* and so on). Example:

Maryam is quite intelligent.

Continue, but now use another linking verb. Example:

Maryam seems quite intelligent.

Continue, but now use the be + adjective + noun structure.

Maryam is a quite intelligent woman from Iran.

Written Practice 1:   Complete these sentences. The sentences can be about your class-mates, other friends, family members, or famous people. In sentence A, use a predicate adjective (see Rule Builder 12.1a and b); in sentence B, use the adjective + noun structure (see Rule Builder 12.1c). Use a variety of intensifiers. Example:

> A.   *Boris Becker is extremely strong.*
> B.   *Boris Becker is an extremely strong tennis player.*

1. A. _____ is _____.

    B. _____.

2. A. _____ seems _____.

    B. _____ seems to be _____.

3. A. _____ looks _____.

    B. _____ looks like

    _____.

4. A. _____ and _____ are

    _____.

    B. _____

    _____.

12.2	Adjectives that Can Come Only after a Linking Verb; Adjectives that Can Come Only before Nouns		
Complete these sentences with adjectives that begin with the syllable *a-*. The first one is done for you.	Check.	Complete these rules.	

a. A frightened man is *afraid*. **Two very similar things are** _____. **The opposite of dead is** _____. **If a person feels bad after doing something wrong or doing something** **poorly, he or she is** _____. **After you stop sleeping, you are** _____. **The opposite of awake is** _____. **If no one is with you, you are** _____.	afraid alike alive ashamed awake asleep alone	Most adjectives can be used in two positions without changing the form: 1. after a linking verb: **Bill is very *happy;*** or 2. before a noun: **The *happy* kids went home.** But some adjectives cannot come before nouns. Many of these are adjectives that begin with the syllable _____. Some examples are _____, _____, and _____.
b. If a reason is the most important one, **it can be called the** _____ **reason.** **If you had never seen a certain person before, you might call him or** **her a** _____ **stranger.** **If only one person survived an accident, that person would be** **called the** _____ **survivor.**	main/ principal/ prime/chief total only/sole	Some adjectives must always come before nouns. They can never come after the verb *be.* Some examples are _____, _____, and _____. Other examples are ***utter*** and ***mere***: **She is an *utter* fool.** **That is *utter* nonsense.** **He is a *mere* child.** **We lost by a *mere* three points.** Notice that ***mere*** is preceded by ***a*** when it is used before a number. Normally, a number and a noun, like *three points*, have no article. With the word ***mere***, however, we say, ''a mere three points.''

Oral Practice 2A: Tell the class something you are afraid of.

Oral Practice 2B: Think of two or more things that are alike.

Oral Practice 2C: When should a person feel ashamed? Example:

A person should feel ashamed when he cheats on a test.

Oral Practice 2D: Think of someone or something that is unique in some way (that is, the only one of its type). Example:

Benchley Hall is the only tall building on campus.

Oral Practice 2E: What is the chief crop or product of your country or region?

Oral Practice 2F: What was the main reason you chose to come to this school? What were your principal concerns when you first arrived at this school?

Written Practice 2:   Complete each sentence with an appropriate adjective from Rule Builder 12.2.

1. The boy did not show his school report card to his parents because he was

    _____ of his grades.

2. The _____ idea of a paragraph is often presented in the topic sentence.

3. My brother was _____ to go on the roller coaster, but we talked him into

    doing it.

4. I don't mind being _____ on weekend nights if I have a good book to read.

5. The angry customer ended up calling the clerk an _____ fool.

6. They won't call off the game because of the rain; this is a _____ sprinkle.

7. It's a miracle that all the people in the car are _____ after that terrible crash.

8. Jim's coming to the party was a _____ surprise for me.

12.3 Modifying Nouns with Nouns		
Complete this model sentence.	Check.	Complete these rules.
Stretch and Tank are both 21 years old. Their apartment has four rooms. Their roommate repairs computers for a living. **Stretch and Tank are 21-** _____ **students who share** ____ _____ _____ **apartment with** ____ _____ **repairman.**	 year-old a four room a computer	Sometimes nouns are used like adjectives; that is, sometimes nouns modify other nouns. We usually keep such a noun in its base form. So even if a noun has a plural meaning, when it is used to modify another noun, it does not end in ____ _____. For example, the science of computers is called **computer science**. A building with three stories is **a three-story building.** If the modifying noun comes with a number, the number and the modifier are connected with a **hyphen.** If an article is needed with a noun which is modified by a another noun, the article goes _____ the modifying noun. For example, if a vacation lasts three weeks, we call it _____ _____ **vacation**.

Oral Practice 3A: Many of the features you might want in a house, apartment, or rented room have names that are compounds. A compound is a structure in which one noun modifies another. Sometimes the expressions are so common that they have become single words—for example, *bathroom*. With your classmates, try to make a list of desirable features in a house. Examples:

> *two bathrooms*
> *storm windows*

Oral Practice 3B: The names of stores, shops, departments, and offices are often compounds. With your classmates, see how many you can think of. Examples:

> *grocery store*
> *philosophy department*
> *post office*

Written Practice 3A: Complete these sentences.

1.   A person who paints houses is called _____ painter.

2.   The office building has seven stories; in other words, it is _____

   _____ building.

3.   Someone who was born in January, 1988, is _____ child now.

4.   A building where chickens are kept is called ＿＿＿＿＿＿＿ house.

5.   A map of the campus can be called ＿＿＿＿＿＿＿ map.

Written Practice 3B: Rewrite each sentence, changing the underlined words into a compound.

1.   All the <u>tickets for the concert</u> have been sold.
2.   <u>Costs for insurance</u> have been going up dramatically.
3.   I really don't care for <u>television in the daytime</u>.
4.   Every culture has its own <u>traditions for weddings</u>.
5.   The Rockies are the highest <u>range of mountains</u> in the U.S.
6.   Call 555-2410 to get <u>information about movies</u>.
7.   We need <u>an apartment with two bedrooms</u>.
8.   The computer center is offering <u>a course lasting four weeks</u> for beginners.

12.4 Quantifiers		
Underline the correct quantifier in each model sentence.	Check.	Complete these rules.
(*Many/Much*) **customers think Mike's is a great place to eat because it doesn't take** (*many/much*) **time to get served.**	Many much	Some quantifiers can be used with both count and noncount nouns. Some examples are *a lot of* and *some*.
I have (*a few/a little*) **money; let's stop at the Cookie Shoppe and have** (*a few/a little*) **cookies.**	a little a few	Other quantifiers can be used only with **count** nouns, such as *customers* and ＿＿＿＿＿＿＿.
Universities libraries usually have (*a large number of/a great deal of*) **books and other materials; consequently, one can find** (*a large number of/a great deal of*) **information there.**	a large number of a great deal of	Some of these are: *many*, ＿＿＿ ＿＿＿＿＿, ＿＿＿ ＿＿＿＿＿ ＿＿＿＿＿ ＿＿, and ＿＿＿＿＿＿＿.
I have used our university's library (*several/quite a bit of*) **times. The librarians there have given me** (*several/quite a bit of*) **help.**	several quite a bit of	Still other quantifiers can be used *only* with **noncount** nouns, such as *money* and ＿＿＿＿＿＿＿. Some of these are ＿＿＿＿＿＿＿, ＿＿＿ ＿＿＿＿＿＿＿, ＿＿＿＿ ＿＿＿＿＿＿＿ ＿＿＿＿＿ ＿＿, and *quite a bit of*.

> NOTE: Look at these sentences:
> > **Did you spend much time in Paris when you were in France?**
> > **They don't have much money, but they seem very happy.**
> > **He wasted a lot of time.** or **He wasted a great deal of time.**
>
> In questions and negative statements, it is normal to use ***much*** before a noun. In positive statements, use ***a lot of*** or, more formally, ***a great deal of*** instead of *much*.

Oral Practice 4A: Tell the class about some things that you have a small quantity of. Use ***a few*** with count nouns and ***a little*** with noncount nouns. Examples:

I own a few art books.   *I have a little money in the bank.*

Oral Practice 4B: Now tell the class what you have ***several*** or ***quite a bit of***.

Oral Practice 4C: Ask your classmates ***how much*** or ***many*** of something they have. Example:

How many courses are you taking this semester?

Written Practice 4A: Complete these sentences with *much* or *many* and a noun.

1. I am not a patient person; that is, I don't have _____.

2. The performers were very disappointed because there were not _____

    _____ in the audience.

3. We must hurry; we don't have _____.

4. He's supposed to be my advisor, but he doesn't give me _____

    _____.

5. Unless you study hard, you won't make _____ in English.

6. To get a passing grade on the composition, the student must write a well-developed

    essay without _____.

Written Practice 4B: Complete these sentences with *a great deal of* or *a large number of* and a noun.

1. My sister is a very patient person; in other words, she has _____

    _____.

2. The next night there were _____ in the audience,

    and the performers felt much better.

3. We don't have to hurry. The movie doesn't start until 9:30, so we have

    _____.

4. Unlike my advisor, my father gives me _____.

5. If you study hard, you can make _____ in

    English in one semester.

6. My grade on the first composition was low because I made _____

    _____.

12.5 Negative Quantifiers		
Complete these model sentences.	Check.	Complete these sentences.
a. Tank was lonely as a child because he didn't have any friends. *or* . . . **because he had _____ friends.** **_____ neighborhood children came to Tank's house to play.**	no No	With objects, use one of these negative structures: *not* . . . + _____ + **noun** or _____ + **noun** With subjects, use this structure: _____ + **noun**
b. Because Tank's family was poor, he **didn't have _____ TV.** *or* . . . **he had _____ TV.**	 a no	When the expected quantity is one (for example, you would not expect a poor family to have more than one TV), use one of these structures: *not* . . . + _____ + **singular count noun** or _____ + **singular count noun**
c. Tank wasn't successful in school as a child because he didn't do any homework. *or* . . . **because he did _____ homework.**	 no	The quantifier *no* can also be used with **noncount** nouns, such as _____.
d. Now Tank is a football star in college, but he still doesn't have many friends. *or* . . . **he still has very _____ friends.** *or* . . . **has only ____ _____ friends.**	 few a few	Another way to express the negative idea *not many* is to use these structures: **(very)** _____ + **plural count noun** _____ _____ *few* + **plural count noun**

| e. Tank still doesn't do much homework, and because he is a student, he still doesn't have much money.
or Tank still does very

_____ homework, and . . .

he still has only _____ _____ money. | little

a little | Another way to express the negative idea **not much** is to use these structures:

(very) _____ + noncount noun

_____ _____ *little* + noncount noun |

> NOTE: Notice the important difference between *few* and *a few* and between *little* and *a little*. *Few* and *little* emphasize the lack or absence of something. Example:
> **I'm tired. I had *little* sleep last night.**
> On the other hand, the expressions *a few* and *a little* (Rule Builder 12.4) emphasize the presence of something. Example:
> **Now I feel better. I got *a little* sleep after class.**

Oral Practice 5A: Mention some things that you don't have or some things that are not in this classroom. Use two structures for each idea. Examples:

I don't have a car. I have no car.
I don't have any money in my pocket. I have no money in my pocket.
There aren't any coat hooks in this room. There are no coat hooks.

Oral Practice 5B: With a partner, go through the sentences in Written Practice 4A. How could each of these ideas be expressed with *very few* or *very little*? Example:

I am not a patient person; that is, I have very little patience.

Oral Practice 5C: Tell the class something that you have very few or very little of.

Written Practice 5A: Answer the following questions in complete negative sentences. Use *not* in some of your answers and *no* in the others.

1. Do you have a car?
2. Do you have any extra lenses for your camera?
3. Does the planet Mars have any rings?
4. Are there any living organisms on Mars?
5. Do you have some flour I can borrow? I want to bake you a cake.
6. Do you have any matches?

Written Practice 5B: Complete these sentences with *few*, *a few*, *little*, or *a little*.

1. Oscar wanted to buy a newer car, so he had to borrow _____ money from the bank.

2. The bank didn't want to give him a loan because he had _____ money in his savings account.

3. He was able to borrow _____ dollars from a friend.

4. I could finish all my assignments if I had _____ more time.

5. During a basketball game there are _____ parking spaces available on campus.

6. I know Colonel Sanders; he came to our house _____ times.

7. He can't win the election; _____ people trust him.

8. Don't worry; _____ things can go wrong if you know what you're doing.

Written Practice 5C: Complete these sentences with *very little* or *very few* and a noun.

1. I am not a patient person; that is, I have _____.

2. The performers were very disappointed because there were _____
   _____ in the audience.

3. We must hurry; we have _____.

4. He's supposed to be my advisor, but he gives me _____
   _____.

5. Unless you study hard, you will make _____ in English.

6. To get a passing grade on the composition, the student must write a well-developed essay with _____.

Written Practice 5D: Rewrite each sentence using the word *only*. The meaning will not change.

> *The forest doesn't have much time left.*
> *The forest has only a little time left.*

1. Developers want to cut it down; they won't leave many trees.
2. Not many of the residents of this area are in favor of this plan.
3. Not much concern has been expressed about the project outside the area, though.
4. The city council called a special meeting about the project last week, but not many people showed up.

12.6 The Forms of *Other*		
Complete these model sentences. Write only one word in each blank.	Check.	Complete these rules.
a. **Mike has ordered a new dishwasher for his cafe. _____ equipment that he wants includes a new refrigerator and a microwave oven. Some people love hamburgers; _____ people hate them.** *or* **Some people love hamburgers; _____ hate them.**	Other other others	***Other*** is used with noncount nouns, such as _____, and plural nouns, such as *people*. If the plural noun is left out, the correct form of *other* is _____.
b. **There are several customers at the counter in Mike's Cafe. One customer has ordered some bread and cheese, and _____ customer has ordered a hamburger and some coffee.** *or* **One customer has ordered bread and cheese, and _____ has ordered a hamburger and some coffee.**	another another	When ***other*** is used with a noun that requires *a* or *an*, *an* and *other* are combined, forming the word _____. If the meaning is clear, the noun can be left out.
c. **Charley has eaten his hamburger, but he's still hungry. He says, ''I'd like _____ hamburger and _____ coffee.''**	another some more	Another meaning of ***another*** is ''one more.'' However, if we want more of something that is noncount, such as *coffee*, we say, _____ _____. (We could say, ''another *cup* of coffee.'')
d. **The people who eat at Mike's enjoy talking to _____ other.** *or* . . . **to one _____.**	each another	When Person *X* does something to Person *Y*, and Person *Y* does the same thing to Person *X*, we use one of these expressions: _____ _____ or _____ _____.
e. **Two of Mike's customers, Elmer and Biff, are a little crazy. Elmer talks to himself and Biff does the same thing. They're usually together, but they never talk to _____ other; they are always talking to _____.**	each themselves	Notice the difference between the meaning of ***themselves*** and ***each other*** in model sentence **e**.

Oral Practice 6A: Tell the class where some of your friends are from. Begin by saying, ''One of my friends . . . '' or ''Some of my friends . . . '' and then use **another** and **other(s)** correctly.

Oral Practice 6B: Here are the results of the World Cup championship soccer games from 1950 to 1990. Make sentences using the expression **each other** and the verbs *play, face, oppose, confront, compete against,* and *go up against.* Some of the sentences should be negative; use the adverb *never.*

Year	Country	Score	Country	Score
1950	Uruguay	2	Brazil	1
1954	West Germany	3	Hungary	2
1958	Brazil	5	Sweden	2
1962	Brazil	3	Czechoslovakia	1
1966	England	4	West Germany	2
1970	Brazil	4	Italy	1
1974	West Germany	2	Netherlands	1
1978	Argentina	3	Netherlands	1
1982	Italy	3	West Germany	1
1986	Argentina	3	West Germany	2
1990	West Germany	1	Argentina	0

Written Practice 6:   Complete these sentences with **other**, **others**, or **another**.

1. Do you have any _____ running shoes? I don't like any of these.

2. I've seen only one picture of your family. Show me some _____.

3. I've already had one piece of pie, but I could probably eat _____.

4. Some people think you should go to school for 12 years. _____ people think you need to go for only five or six years.

5. She might be absent because she's sick. _____ possible reason is that her car broke down.

6. Some of the books in the store escaped damage from the fire; _____ were damaged to some extent; and the rest were completely destroyed.

7. My Korean pen pal and I have written to one _____ for nearly 10 years now.

8. Most of my classmates were at Saturday night's party along with several _____ people that I didn't know.

9. Our family has an unusual New Year's tradition; we always give each _____ humorous gifts.

10. Oaks and hickories are the most common trees in this forest; some _____ are redbuds, walnuts, and cedars.

NOTE: Sometimes one noun may have more than one modifier. This is the normal order:

determiner
or   } + *other* + adjective(s) + modifying noun(s) + noun
quantifier

Example: ***any***   ***other   white***   ***tennis***   ***shoes***

12.7 Chapter Check: Complete these sentences with your choice of the two quantifiers and the correct form of the noun given. If you are unsure of an answer, check the indicated model sentence and rule.

1. (*much/many, mistake*) I didn't make _____ on

    the test.   [12.2a, 12.4]

2. (*much/many, news*) I didn't hear _____ good _____ on the radio this

    morning.   [12.2, 12.4]

3. (*several/quite a bit of, assignments*) I have _____ to do

    for tomorrow.   [12.2a, 12.4]

4. (*much/many, work*) Yesterday I didn't have _____ to do;

    (*a few/a little, page*) I just had to read _____.   [12.4]

12.8 Chapter Check: Complete these sentences with modifiers that make sense.

1. My _____ teacher seems very _____.   [12.1b]

2. I would not want to tell my parents I failed a course because I would feel too

    _____.   [12.2a]

3. When my friend called me at midnight last night, the first thing she said was,

    "Were you _____?"   [12.2a]

4. I hope to have some fun while I'm at this school, but my _____ purpose for

    being here is to study and get my degree.   [12.2b]

5. _____ reason I came here to study was because I wanted to make friends from

    _____ cultures.   [12.6a & b]

6. Only _____ time remains before my next _____ test.   [12.5e]

12.9 Chapter Check: Finish sentence B. It should have about the same meaning as sentence A.

1. A. The rate of unemployment in my country has been stable for several years.

    B. The _____ rate in my country has been stable for

    several years.   [12.3]

2.   A.   My little sisters always used to tease one another.

     B.   My little sisters always used to tease each _____.   [12.6d]

3.   A.   Use of videotapes in classrooms has increased dramatically in recent years.

     B.   _____ use in classrooms has increased dramatically in

          recent years.   [12.3]

4.   A.   Video technology is especially popular among teachers of languages.

     B.   Video technology is especially popular among _____

          teachers.   [12.3]

5.   A.   I have to type a paper that is 25 pages long before tomorrow afternoon.

     B.   I have to type _____ paper before tomorrow afternoon.   [12.3]

6.   A.   Unfortunately, I have to get a lot of information from the library before I can start

          typing.

     B.   Unfortunately, I have to get a great _____ information from the library be-

          fore I can start typing.   [12.4]

12.10 Warm-up: Ask questions about the contents of your classmates' wallets, purses, or
book bags. Answer in complete sentences. Use a variety of quantifiers in your answers.
Examples:

Do you have an eraser?	*Yes, I have an eraser.*
Do you have any food?	*No, I have no food.*
Do you have any quarters?	*Yes, I have several quarters.*

12.11 Communication: Interview three classmates from three different places. Ask your
classmates questions to get the information requested. Ask **how much** and **how many** questions. The answers will be quantifiers such as **a little**, **a lot**, **not many**, and so on. Record the
information in the chart.

PLACE:	_____	_____	_____
Rain?	_____	_____	_____
Significant snowstorms?	_____	_____	_____
Major rivers?	_____	_____	_____
Family farms?	_____	_____	_____
Oil?	_____	_____	_____
Very large universities?	_____	_____	_____
Quite beautiful scenery?	_____	_____	_____

12.12 Report Writing: Write a report about the information you received in 12.11 Communication. Begin in this way: ''In class today I interviewed people from Country A, Country
B, and Country C, and learned some interesting facts. Country A and Country B have a great
deal of rain, but Country C has very little.'' (Of course, write the names of the countries and
not Country A, B and C.)

12.13 Sentence Writing: Write four *how much* and *how many* questions that people ask about your country and write the answers that you give. Don't use the same questions that you used in 12.11 Communication.

12.14 Sentence Writing: Think of an excuse you can give to refuse the following requests politely. Use *very few* or *very little*. Then give an answer that means, "Yes, that's okay," by using *a few* or *a little*. Example:

> *Do you want to see a movie?*
> *a. Sorry, I have very little time tonight.*
> *b. Yes, I have a little time for fun tonight.*

1. Do you want to buy my old typewriter? (Use the word *cash*.)
2. Do you want to have coffee with us? (Use the word *time*.)
3. Do you have the tools I need to fix my car?
4. Do you have enough room to store some furniture for me?
5. Could you bring some glasses for our party?
6. Do you have any old newspapers that we could take to the recycling center?

12.15 Sentence Writing: Look back at the World Cup soccer results (Oral Practice 6B.) Write five sentences about those games. Each sentence should contain the expression *each other* or *one another*. Two of the sentences should be negative. Example:

> *When Uruguay and Brazil faced each other for the 1950 World Cup, Uruguay won 2 to 1.*

12.16 Paragraph Writing: Look on or around the desk or table where you are working now. Describe several of the things that you see. Make your descriptions more precise by using noun modifiers. Example:

> *I have several pieces of equipment in a red wire basket on my desk.*
> *For example, there is a small pair of good Swedish scissors with orange plastic handles.*

12.17 Reflecting: Read the next episode of the mystery story. Examine the way adjectives and other noun modifiers are used. Find the adjectives that have the *-er* ending. As you probably know, these are comparative forms. You will practice using comparative structures in chapter 16.

Farmer decided he would rather take me out for a few stiff drinks than throw me in a cold jail cell for the night. We went downtown to a classy new bar that I didn't know, filled with young business executive types that spent more on silk socks than I make in six months. I held the door for him.

''You're older,'' I explained.

''I'm also not as ugly as you are,'' he said.

''But that's not why I'm holding the door for you,'' I said.

We went in. I was punched in the nose by heavy smoke and perfume-filled air. Sophisticated jazz music rasped out of thousand-dollar speakers. Everyone was dressed in eight-hundred-dollar suits. Otherwise, it was the same as every other bar I know.

''Oh no,'' I said.

''What's the matter?''

''I was supposed to take Linda to dinner tonight.''

''And you forgot,'' Farmer said. ''Why don't you call her?''

''Not tonight. She'll be very upset. She'll be madder than a wet cat.''

''She can get mad, all right,'' Farmer said.

''I'll call her tomorrow. She'll be much calmer then.''

''By tomorrow she'll have a smarter boyfriend,'' Farmer said.

12.18 Real-World Work

THINK/PRACTICE

As you are standing, walking, or riding around today, look at the people and things near you. Make up sentences about them with more than one noun modifier before the nouns. Example:

Over there are several green trash cans.

LOOK/LISTEN

Find an interesting story in a newspaper or magazine. Read it. Then go through the story again and underline nouns. Look at the words that come before the nouns. Can you find examples of all the types of noun modifiers discussed in this chapter—quantifiers, forms of *other*, adjectives, and nouns that modify other nouns? Find some nouns that are preceded by several modifiers. Do these modifiers follow the order outlined in the note on page 155?

USE

1. When someone asks you if you have time to do something, think of the impression you give if you say, ''I have **a little** time.'' This will imply that you want to do it. If you say, ''I have **little** time,'' though, the person will think you don't have *enough* time. Remember that **a few** and **few** also give positive and negative impressions. Look out for these words!

2. Most Americans love to talk about the weather. Try to get into a weather conversation today. Ask an American acquaintance some weather questions about his or her part of the country. He or she will probably ask about your country's climate. Be careful with the count and noncount nouns. Use articles, quantifiers, and other noun modifiers correctly.

3. In your journal writing this week, focus on descriptions of people and things you see around you.

Pronouns

REVIEW

In the column on the left you will find determiners and noun modifiers. Write them in the correct order in the blanks in the car advertisement on the right.

BEST	*THE*	*FAMILY*	
new	*our*	*five-passenger*	
finest	*road*	*the*	
six-cylinder	*powerful*	*its*	
reliable		*power*	
velour		*beautiful*	
other	*fine*	*many*	
exciting	*test*	*a/an*	

_____ **CAR IN THE WORLD**

We believe that _____

Stallion is _____

car on the market today.

_____

engine provides quick response and gives you

plenty of power in reserve. The Stallion also

features _____ windows,

_____ upholstery, and

_____ features.

Come in today for _____

drive.

PREVIEW

Read the following paragraph.

> My husband and I saw the ad for the new Stallion in a newspaper and decided to check it out. We liked everything about it. When we took it for a test drive, everyone seemed to stop and take a look at us and our fancy car. When we got back to the showroom, there was only one difficult decision. The dealer had two Stallions in stock, and we couldn't decide whether to take the blue one or the red one. We made the decision so quickly that we had to laugh at ourselves on the way home.

The underlined words in the paragraph are pronouns, words that take the place of nouns or noun phrases. Tell what these pronouns take the place of. The first one has been done for you.

1. I   *the writer of the paragraph*   4. us   _____

2. it _____   5. one _____

3. we _____   6. ourselves _____

Pronouns such as *I*, *we*, and *it* are called **personal pronouns**. You have known these words since your earliest weeks as an English student. We will briefly review them in this chapter. *Ourselves* is a **reflexive pronoun**. The pronoun *one* in the expressions *the blue one* and *the red one* takes the place of simple nouns and can be used with determiners and modifiers. Finally, the words **everything** and **everyone** in the second and third sentences of the paragraph are usually called **indefinite pronouns.**

13.1 Subject and Object Personal Pronouns		
Complete these model sentences.	Check.	Complete these rules.
Bernard's best friend is named Mary. He often walks home from school **with _____. or She often walks** **home with _____.** **_____ live in the same building.**	her him They	When the meaning is clear, you can replace a noun with a personal pronoun, such as **he**, _____, _____, _____, and _____. These are the subject and object personal pronouns: **SINGULAR** **PLURAL** **Subject Object Subject Object** *I* me we us *you* ___ ___ ___ ___ him ___ ___ *she* ___ ___ ___ ___ it ___ ___ Remember that after a preposition, such as *with*, *we* use the **object** form of the pronoun.

Oral Practice 1A: Tell the class about a friend or some friends that you have. Tell what he/she/they is/are studying. Then tell what you enjoy doing with this friend or these friends. Example:

> *I have two friends from Bolivia. They are both studying chemical engineering. I enjoy playing cards with them.*

Oral Practice 1B: Mention something you recently bought. Why did you buy it/them? How much did it/they cost? Give some more interesting information about it/them. Example:

> *I recently bought some new sunglasses. They have red frames and blue lenses. They cost over thirty dollars. I bought them because they looked good on me.*

Written Practice 1:   Complete this paragraph using pronouns.

My mother is a fanatical letter-writer. _____ writes letters all the time. She always sends _____ a card on my birthday. _____ sends cards on holidays; _____ even sends _____ for no reason at all! My brothers and sisters and I joke about this habit of hers, but _____ enjoy _____ a lot. Our mother makes us laugh sometimes, but we adore _____ because _____ is the most thoughtful person that _____ know.

13.2 Reflexive Pronouns		
Complete these model sentences.	Check.	Complete these rules.

a. Bernard often looks at reflections of himself in shop windows when he walks to school. One day his friend Mary decided to ask him about this habit.
 	
Mary: Why do you always look at
 	
_____ in the windows?
Bernard: I'm not looking at
 	
_____. I'm looking at the things in the stores.
	
	yourself
	
	myself
		A **reflexive pronoun** is used for the object when the subject of a verb and the object refer
		
		to the _____ person or animal.
		
		Subject Pronoun **Reflexive Pronoun**
		   I *__myself__*
		  we _____
		you (singular) _____
		you (plural) _____
		  he _____
		  she _____
		  it _____
		  they _____

b. Since he was six years old, Bernard has fixed his own brown bag lunches. He is proud that he can do this all
 	
by _____.
       or
He is proud that he can do this
 	
_____.
	
	himself
	
	himself
		We can express the meaning ''without assistance'' with the following expression:
		
		   _____ + **a reflexive pronoun**
		For more emphasis, this expression is often
		
		preceded by the word _____.
		When (**all**) **by** + reflexive has this meaning, (**all**) **by** can be left out.

c. Mary would like to do homework with Bernard, but Bernard prefers to **study _____ himself.**	 by	The expression _____ + reflexive can also mean ''alone.'' When it has this meaning, **by** cannot be left out.
d. Last week Bernard received an award for academic excellence. The **principal _____ presented the award.**	 himself	You can emphasize a noun by putting the appropriate reflexive pronoun _____ it. This often indicates that it is surprising that this person or thing was involved.

Oral Practice 2:   Think of something that you or someone else did or does or can do without any help. Use the expression **all by myself** (**herself**, and so on). Then repeat the sentence without **all by**. Which of the two statements puts more emphasis on the fact that it was done without the help of anyone else? Sometimes very young children can do surprising things by themselves. Think of something you have seen a child do alone. How would you emphasize how surprised you were to see this?

Written Practice 2A: Complete these sentences about the things some people or animals do to or for themselves.

1. No one celebrates Tony's birthday, so every year he buys _____ a huge present.

2. She owns her own company and gives _____ a raise every year.

3. I write _____ little reminder notes every day.

4. Do you realize you often talk to _____ while you work?

5. Cats clean _____ with their tongues.

6. My classmate Mindy and I have a special study technique. We always write a practice
    test for _____ before we take a real test.

Written Practice 2B: Review Rule Builder 12.6e before doing this exercise. Then finish sentence B. It should have about the same meaning as sentence A. In each sentence, use either **themselves** or **each other**, whichever is appropriate.

1. A. Harry talks to himself, and so does his brother Harvey.

    B. Harry and Harvey _____.

2. A. Monica gave her husband, Ted, a gift on their wedding anniversary. Ted did the
        same for her.

    B. Monica and Ted _____

        _____.

3. A. My little brother can dress himself, and my little sister can dress herself, too.

    B. Both my little brother and my _____

        _____.

4. A. Ben enjoyed himself at the party last night, and his new girlfriend enjoyed herself,
        too.

    B. Ben and his new girlfriend _____

        _____.

5. A. Now Ben spends most days with his girlfriend.

    B. Now Ben and his new girlfriend _____ with _____

        _____.

6. A. An unhappy person usually does not love himself or herself.

    B. Most unhappy people do not _____.

7. A. Billy helped himself to the cookies, and so did Timmy.

    B. Billy and Timmy _____.

8. A. When their mother came home, Billy accused Timmy of taking the cookies, and
        Timmy accused Billy.

    B. When their mother came home, Billy and Timmy _____

        _____.

13.3 Indefinite Pronouns		
Complete these model sentences.	Check.	Complete these rules.
a. Not everyone in Bernard's apartment building (speak) _____ **English as a native language.**	speaks	As you learned in chapter 6, indefinite pronouns, such as _____, are singular.
b. Someone on Bernard's floor (be) _____ **a native speaker of Urdu, and** _____ **people on the twenty-first floor** (speak) _____ **Hungarian.**	is some speak	*Somebody, something*, and _____ refer to only one person or thing. If you want to refer to more than one, use *some* or some other quantifier + a noun.
c. Surprisingly, there isn't anyone from a Spanish-speaking country on Bernard's floor. *or* **. . . there is** _____ **from . . .** *or* _____ **from a Spanish-speaking country lives on Bernard's floor.**	nobody/ no one Nobody/ No one	*Anyone* (or *anybody* or *anything*) is used in questions and in _____ statements. The expression *not . . . anyone* (*anybody/anything*) can be replaced with *no one* (_____/*nothing*). Notice that *no one* is written as two words. If the indefinite pronoun is the subject of a negative statement, use *nobody* or _____ or *nothing*.
d. Of course, Bernard's apartment building has no restrictions based on race, religion, or national origin. _____ **can rent one of these apartments.**	Anyone/ Anybody	Besides being used in questions and negative statements, *anyone* or _____ is often used as the subject before these modal verbs: _____ or *could*.

Oral Practice 3A: Tell the class something that **everyone, anyone, no one,** or **someone** can do.

Oral Practice 3B: Try to find someone in class who likes or likes to do, can do, has done, or did a certain thing. Examples:

Does anyone in class like black coffee?
Has anybody here seen the new Woody Allen movie?
Did anyone go to the 1988 Olympics in Seoul?

Written Practice 3:   Complete each sentence with an appropriate indefinite pronoun.

1. Not _____ in the U.S. has English as a native language.

2. This situation is _____ that many English speakers rarely think of.

3. _____ is aware that a lot of U.S. citizens speak Spanish as a native language.

4. Every time that _____ has suggested bilingual education, public reactions have been strong—either for or against the idea.

5. Does _____ think about the fact that German was once one of America's most-spoken languages?

6. I made a mess. Do you have _____ to wipe this coffee up with?

7. _____ is going on in the apartment upstairs.

8. I don't have _____ at all like that!

9. _____ left the car window open.

10. I don't know _____ who can do that.

11. Does _____ have a match?

12. _____ else showed up for the meeting, so we left.

13. Surely _____ in the world wants to be happy.

14. I can't decide what to eat; _____ looks very good.

15. He is very hard to please; _____ satisfies him.

13.4 The Pronoun *One*		
Complete these model sentences.	Check.	Complete these rules.
a. The pictures on the left are originals; **the _____ on the right are forgeries.** **For example, that painting is by** **Picasso; _____ _____** **was painted after his death by an imitator.** **Those paintings are genuine** **Mondrians; _____ are fakes.** **These counterfeit paintings are worth nothing; those genuine** **_____ are worth a fortune.**	ones this one these ones	The pronoun **one** can take the place of a **count noun**. We use it often when we compare things instead of repeating the same noun, or when we choose between things. Like count nouns, the word **one** can be singular or _____. It can also be used with determiners, such as _____ or **this**, and can be modified with adjectives or adjective phrases. Thus you will find expressions like these: **the huge green ones** **the ones on the right.** Although you can use **one** after **this** or **that**, do not use **ones** immediately after the plural forms, **these** or _____. Use **ones**, however, if *these* or *those* is followed by an _____, such as *genuine*.
b. Picasso painted his work with oil paints; the imitator painted **_____ with acrylics.**	his	Do not use the pronoun **one** after possessives, such as *John's, your,* or _____.

Oral Practice 4A: Look at the library picture in chapter 7 (7.10 Warm-up). Make sentences that point out differences between two or more members of these categories:

> *librarians*
> *maintenance workers*
> *students (young men, young women)*
> *professors*

Use the pronoun **one** or **ones** in your sentences. Example:

> *The young woman with dark hair is sleeping; the one with blond hair is listening to music.*

Oral Practice 4B: Look at the family scene in chapter 7 (7.18 Paragraph Writing). Using the pronoun ***one*** or ***ones***, make sentences about two or more members of these categories:

> *men*
> *women*
> *girls*
> *boys*
> *cats*

Written Practice 4:   Rewrite each of these sentences, taking out the repeated noun and making other necessary changes. In some sentences you will be able to use *one* or *ones*; in others you will not. Example:

> *His battery is working fine; my battery has a problem.*
> *His battery is working fine; mine has a problem.*

1.   The book over there is a first edition of *Alice in Wonderland*; this is a later edition.
2.   On the left are old models; on the right you see the new models.
3.   Our cats are all at home; that must be his cat.
4.   Do you prefer those gloves or these gloves?
5.   I like these brown gloves quite a bit, but I think I like those black gloves better.

13.5 Chapter Check: Rewrite these sentences replacing the underlined nouns and noun phrases with pronouns. If you are unsure of an answer, check the indicated model sentence and rule.

1.   Yesterday I decided to replace the old tires on my car. I had had the tires for three years, and they were nearly worn out.   [13.1]
2.   I went to several stores. The first store didn't have any tires in the right size.   [13.4a]
3.   The second store had the right tires, but everyone was too busy to put the tires on imme-
     diately.   [13.4a, 13.1]
4.   I finally had some luck at the third store. I had my choice of two kinds of tires. One kind was considerably cheaper, but I finally decided on the more expensive tires.   [13.4a]
5.   The new tires were put on immediately, and in half an hour I was back at work.   [13.1]

13.6 Chapter Check: Finish sentence B. It should have about the same meaning as sentence A.

1.   A. There wasn't anyone in the office when we entered.

     B. _____ was in the office when we entered.   [13.3c]

2.   A. All the people in the town seem to like the new mayor.

     B. _____ in the town seems to like the new mayor.   [13.3a]

3.   A. The little girl fixed her bike without any help.

     B. The little girl fixed her bike all _____.   [13.2b]

4. A. Many of the people stayed to watch the fire even though they had been told to go home.

    B. Even though the people had been told to go home, many of _____ stayed to watch the fire.

                                                                            [13.1]

5. A. I went to the lecture, but unfortunately I learned nothing new.

    B. I went to the lecture, but unfortunately I didn't _____

   _____.

                                                                            [13.3c]

> NOTE: For 13.7 Warm-up and 13.8 Communication, you will need pictures of products from magazines or catalogues.

13.7 Warm-up: In 13.8 Communication, you will ask your classmates to choose between two or three products that you show them. As a warm-up, show the pictures of the products to the class and introduce them as in this example:

> *I'm going to ask you which of these two watches you prefer. This one is gold. It has a black face without numbers. This other one is silver. It has a white face and Roman numerals.*

13.8 Communication: In this activity, you will work in groups of five to eight people. Ask the other members of the group to tell you which of the two or three products from 13.7 Warm-up they prefer. They should answer without pointing; they should tell which one they like best by using ***the one*** and a modifier. Examples:

> *I prefer the silver one.*
> *I like the one with the black face best.*

Have a pencil in your hand and mark down the votes. Later, you can show the whole class the pictures and report on the results of your poll. Example:

> *I showed five people these two watches. Three of them preferred the gold one, and two preferred the silver one.*
>   *or*
> *Nobody picked the silver one; everyone liked the gold one best.*

13.9 Sentence Writing: Rewrite these sentences, adding reflexive pronouns to show that it is surprising that these people did these things.

1. The company president called me to apologize for the mistake.
2. The children made the decision about the new playground equipment.
3. I couldn't believe that the queen answered the phone.

13.10 Sentence Writing: We often use the passive voice because we don't know or don't want to tell who did something. In informal English, instead of using the passive, we often use **somebody** or **someone** as the subject of the sentence. Rewrite these sentences changing more formal sentences to less formal ones and vice versa. Example:

The window was broken during the night.
Someone broke the window during the night.

1. I was told that he never ate pork.
2. Somebody predicted a snowstorm for tonight.
3. The angry demonstrator was allowed to speak to the TV audience.
4. A gift was left on my front porch.
5. Someone wove this material by hand.

13.11 Paragraph Writing: Look at the family scene in chapter 7 (7.18 Paragraph Writing). Imagine that you know this family. You might imagine that this is your family when you were a child, or maybe it is a family that you have visited recently. Give names to the people. Pretend that you are sending this picture to a friend. In your paragraph, tell your friend who the people are and tell something about them.

Try to use the pronoun **one** and personal pronouns correctly. Remember that you cannot use a pronoun until you have first referred to the person with a noun. Remember that **one** refers to one of a group or a pair. Examples:

In the picture you see two <u>men</u>. *The* <u>one</u> *with glasses is my grandfather . . .*
The family has four <u>girls</u>. *The* <u>one</u> *feeding the cat is named . . .*

Here are some other expressions with **one** that you may want to use:

the one drinking milk
the one listening to music
the one in the sweater
the older one
the one flying a paper airplane

Remember that the personal pronouns (*she, he, them* and so on) refer to particular people. Example:

. . . is <u>my dear grandfather</u>. <u>He</u> *was a professor of history . . .*

13.12 Paragraph Writing: Think of an incident that involved several members of your family—perhaps something humorous or something exciting. Relate the incident in a paragraph.

13.13 Paragraph Writing: This short paragraph contains many confusing pronoun usages; the reader might be confused about which noun the pronouns refer to. Find any unclear pronoun usages and rewrite the paragraph to resolve them.

> August and September can be very long months in Kansas. It is a hard month mostly due to high temperatures. They can also bring cool nights. People are unsure whether to use their air conditioners or open the windows and use fans. The nights are too cool for air conditioners, and they are worried about energy costs. Most of them decide to use fans unless there is an exceptionally hot week. September can turn cold at the end, and so people hardly ever use them.

13.14 Reflecting: Read the next episode of the mystery story. Then examine the use of pronouns, especially personal pronouns such as ***her***, and reflexive pronouns such as ***myself***. The pronoun ***one*** is also used once, and there is one indefinite pronoun. Can you find those two occurrences?

> On Wednesday I crawled out of bed at noon and looked at myself in the mirror. My eyes were red. I had gone out for a few drinks with Farmer Tuesday night. I decided to shave, but I didn't have any razors. I dug around in the wastebasket until I found an old one. It was dull. I cut myself on the chin five times.
>
> When I had finished, I looked like I had been in a fight with the cat. "You handsome devil," I told myself. After breakfast I remembered suddenly my promise to Linda to take her out to dinner the night before. I had forgotten all about it because of my case. I called her.
>
> "Hello?" she said.
>
> "It's me," I said. She hung up. I called again.
>
> "I'm sorry about last night," I said. "I had an emergency."
>
> "What was her name?"
>
> "Lieutenant Farmer. *His* name. Anyway, I thought we could treat ourselves to a night on the town tonight."
>
> She hung up.
>
> "She'll call back," I said. "No one stays mad at me for long."

13.15 Real-World Work

THINK/PRACTICE

Wherever you are, look around and notice two or more people or things from the same category—for example, three little girls, two large trees, two cars. Make sentences about them. Examples:

Those three little girls are jumping rope.
They seem to be having fun.
The one with the red dress is jumping now.

LOOK/LISTEN

Pronouns take the place of nouns. To read well, you must know what each pronoun in a text is taking the place of. Choose a passage in a book or magazine. Mark all of the personal pronouns (*she, it, them,* and so on). Draw a connecting line between each pronoun and the noun it refers to. Your teacher may want you to bring a copy of your passage to class so that you and a classmate can work together on figuring out the references.

USE

1. When you write, be sure that the reader will clearly understand which noun each pronoun refers to. Pronouns are important because repeating the same noun several times would make your writing repetitive and probably boring, but pronouns must be used clearly and carefully.

2. Learners of English often have trouble with the use of *one* as a pronoun. Some people avoid using it and unnecessarily repeat a noun. If you do this, practice using *one* when you can. For example, imagine that you have been in a clothing store looking at shirts with a salesman for half an hour. It would sound a little funny to say, "I think I'll take this shirt." It would sound much more natural to say.

   I think I'll take this one.

Other people sometimes leave out nouns after adjectives but fail to replace them with *one.* They may say, for example, "I like this blue." The correct version is,

   I like this blue one.

Finally, some ESL students overuse *one.* They use *one* after *these, those, my, your,* and so on. Remember, you can't use *one* after *these, those,* or possessives.

Do you fall into any of these categories? If so, practice using *one* correctly while the information you've learned about its usage is fresh in your mind.

14

Objects

REVIEW

Fill in the blanks with pronouns and verbs. Put just one word in each blank.

     My Aunt Elsa and Uncle Floyd have the strangest marriage I know of. _____ _____ complete opposites. When they were married, she wanted to invite hundreds of people to the wedding, but _____ wanted only a few close friends to come. Uncle Floyd wanted a pet, so _____ went out and bought a cat. Elsa had different ideas; that same day _____ brought a dog home. _____ disagree about everything. Floyd and Elsa have four children, who, fortunately, _____ normal.

     Floyd recently visited my family. I enjoyed being around _____, and he must have liked _____, too, for he gave _____ a present—a book about the Midwest. He had gifts for the rest of the family, too; he gave _____ sweaters that Elsa had knitted. We sent a batch of cookies back with Floyd to give to _____.

PREVIEW

All of the pronouns in the second paragraph of the preceding passage are called **objects** in grammar. An object *receives* the action of a verb or comes after a preposition. Look at the following faulty sentences. Do you know what is wrong in each of them? Can you fix them?

I will explain you the situation.
Pete doesn't like very much some of his classes.
I asked the boy to give me the rock, but he wouldn't give me it.
Before you buy a new computer program, you should try out it.

The errors in the preceding sentences all involve **word order**. The emphasis in this chapter will be on **word order rules for objects**.

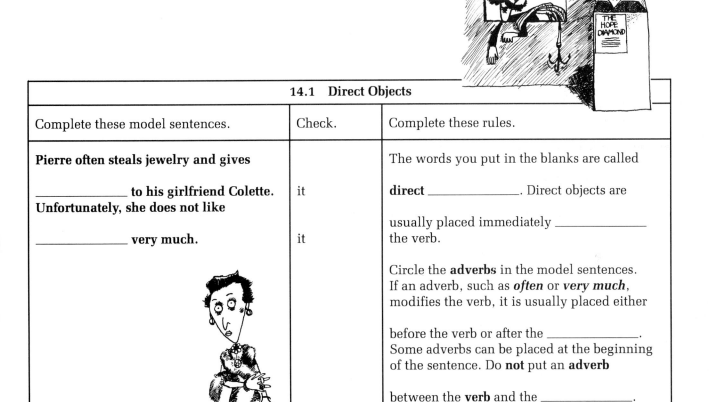

14.1   Direct Objects

Complete these model sentences.	Check.	Complete these rules.
Pierre often steals jewelry and gives _____ **to his girlfriend Colette. Unfortunately, she does not like** _____ **very much.**	it it	The words you put in the blanks are called **direct** _____. Direct objects are usually placed immediately _____ the verb. Circle the **adverbs** in the model sentences. If an adverb, such as **often** or **very much**, modifies the verb, it is usually placed either before the verb or after the _____. Some adverbs can be placed at the beginning of the sentence. Do **not** put an **adverb** between the **verb** and the _____.

Oral Practice 1:   Tell the class something you like very much, want very badly, or do very often. Example:

I play tennis very often.

> NOTE: In Written Practice 1, you will add frequency adverbs to sentences. In Rule Builder 7.4, you learned that the most common place for frequency adverbs is before the main verb. This is true for **never**, **always**, **often**, and **usually**. **Sometimes** and **occasionally** can go before the verb, but the most common place for these two adverbs is before the subject. Frequency adverbials with more than one word usually go after the object.

Written Practice 1:   Rewrite these sentences, adding the words in parentheses. Try to follow the rules in the note above.

1. Pierre gives the jewelry to Colette. (*usually*)
2. He forgets his tools. (*never*)
3. He drops the jewelry. (*sometimes*)
4. He hides it in his bag. (*always*)
5. He surprises museum guards. (*often*)
6. I tried to call up my old friend Susan last night. (*several times*)
7. I got a busy signal. (*every time*)
8. When she has a lot of work to do, she takes the phone off the hook. (*occasionally*)
9. Does Higgins wear a business suit? (*always*)
10. When do stores cut the prices for summer clothes? (*usually*)

14.2 Indirect Objects		
Complete these model sentence.	Check.	Complete these rules.
a. Pierre steals _____ _____ **Colette.**	jewelry for	In sentence **a**, the jewelry is what Pierre actually grabs; it receives the action of the verb **directly**. We call *jewelry* a _____ object. Pierre takes the jewelry for Colette; she benefits **indirectly** from the act of stealing. *Colette* is the _____ object. To show that she benefits, use the preposition _____.
b. After he steals the jewelry, he gives _____ _____ **Colette.**	 it to	In sentence **b**, *Colette* is again the _____ object. This kind of indirect object is sometimes called the **dative**, which comes from the Latin word for *give*. Indirect objects of this type receive things that people give, send, and so on. Use the preposition _____.

Oral Practice 2:   Giving presents to friends and family members is an important part of certain holidays in American life. Are there holidays in your culture when this custom is important? Describe the things you might give to members of your family. What other things might you do for people at these times?

Written Practice 2:   Complete these sentences.

1.   When Pierre borrows Colette's car, he always returns _____ her.

2.   If Colette sees an article about jewels in the newspaper, she cuts it out and sends

_____.

3.   When the police asked about the jewels, Pierre said he had given

_____.

4.   It has been nearly three weeks since I wrote a _____ my parents.

5.   I don't understand number 3; could you explain _____ me?

6.   Mrs. McGill is baking _____ Mr. McGill, who will celebrate his

sixtieth birthday tonight.

14.3 Indirect Object + Direct Object; Verbs that Allow this Structure; Verbs that Don't Allow this Structure.		
Complete these model sentences.	Check.	Complete these rules.
a. Pierre gives the jewelry to Colette. *or* **Pierre gives _____ jewelry.**	Colette	With some verbs, such as *give*, we can put the **indirect object** _____ the **direct object**. When we do this, we do not use a preposition.
b. Colette always explains her feelings **about jewelry _____ him.**	to	Some verbs do not allow the indirect object to come first. An example of this type of verb is _____. The verbs that allow the indirect object to come first are usually common one-syllable (often irregular) verbs. The verbs that do not allow this structure are usually two- or three-syllable verbs.

Here is a list of verbs that take two objects. Following the rule in 14.3b, put them in the right lists.
The verbs marked with asterisks (*)—*offer*, *cash* and *say*—are exceptions to this rule.

mention	show	make	describe	sell	translate	admit
buy	bring	send	recommend	report	charge	write
get	reveal	tell	introduce	give	cost	declare
teach	hand	open	ask	offer*	cash*	say*
lend	pay					

These are verbs that allow the indirect object to come first. Example: **She *showed* him the book**	These are verbs that do **not** allow the indirect object to come first. Example: **She *mentioned* the book to him.**
_____ _____ _____ _____ _____ _____ _____ _____ _____ _____ _____ _____ _____ _____ _____	_____ _____ _____ _____ _____ _____ _____ _____ _____ _____

NOTE: With the verbs *charge*, *cost* and *ask*, always use this word order: *indirect object + direct object*. Example:
> *He asked me several questions.*

Oral Practice 3:   A friend of yours is planning to come to this university to study. This friend has written you a letter asking for help. Tell your classmates some things that you might do for him or her. For example, what might you write, tell, mention, ask, describe, translate, recommend, send, offer, give, lend, explain, and so on?

Written Practice 3: Underline the **indirect** objects in these sentences. Then rewrite the sentences, changing the indirect object to a pronoun. *Wherever possible, put this pronoun before the direct object.* Examples:

> *I sent a card to <u>my mother.</u>*
> *I sent her a card.*
> *Please introduce me to <u>your wife.</u>*
> *Please introduce me to her.*

1. He offered a great job to his son-in-law.
2. William mentioned my letter to his father.
3. They told that story to Martha.
4. I made a promise to my family.
5. Andy admitted his mistakes to his parents.
6. I need to get some stamps for my roommate.
7. You should open the door for that elderly man.
8. The accident taught an important lesson to Bob.

14.4 **Direct Object Pronoun** + *To/For* + **Indirect Object**		
Complete these model sentences.	Check.	Complete these rules.
When Pierre steals jewelry, he gives _____ _____ _____. **Although Colette doesn't want the jewelry Pierre steals, he always gives** _____ _____ _____.	it to Colette it to her	First, circle the objects in the model sentences that are **pronouns**. When the **direct** object is a **pronoun**, it must come _____ the indirect object, and the indirect object must be preceded by _____ or _____.

Oral Practice 4: You have just won a VCR in a contest. What are some things that you are going to do or are not going to do with it? Use one of these verbs in each sentence:

mention	sell	lend
describe	give	send
show		

Written Practice 4: Complete these sentences with direct and indirect object pronouns.

1. Whenever my friend Forest hears a joke, he always tells _____.
2. Whenever Pete's wife gets a good grade, she always shows _____.
3. Whenever my sister gets her picture taken, she gets an extra copy and mails _____.
4. Last night Eduardo's friend Laura heard a great piece of music on the radio. This morning she described _____.

5. Whenever my father buys a new car, he brings his old one over to my place and sells

    _____.

6. I wanted a certain album for my birthday, and my children bought _____.

7. Gerald heard about the scandal. Whe he saw Betty, he mentioned _____.

14.5 Position of Objects of Prepositions and Objects of Phrasal Verbs		
Complete these model sentences.	Check.	Complete these rules.
a. Pierre broke into a museum, but the **police caught _____.**	him	**REMEMBER**: In this sentence *him* is a _____ object.
b. Pierre confessed his crimes **_____ the police.** **Pierre doesn't speak English, so a** **French student translated his** **confession _____ them.**	to for	**REMEMBER**: In these two sentences, *the* *police* and *them* are _____ objects. ***To*** and ***for*** are _____.
c. They sent Pierre _____ jail. **From jail he sent a note _____** **his mother.**	to to	Objects of ***to*** and ***for*** are not always indirect objects. In model sentence **c**, is *jail* an indirect object? _____. Is *mother*? _____.
d. Colette came _____ the jail. **She wanted to cheer _____** **Pierre.** *or* **She wanted to _____** **Pierre _____.**	to up cheer up	In the first sentence, *to* is a preposition and *jail* is the object of the preposition. But *up*, in the second sentence, is not really a preposition. It is part of the verb *cheer up*. We call verbs like this **phrasal verbs**. Many phrasal verbs can have objects; that is, they are **transitive**. The object of *cheer up* is _____. With most transitive phrasal verbs, the object can go either before or _____ the second word of the verb.
e. Colette came to see Pierre. She **wanted to cheer _____ _____.**	 him up	If the object of a separable phrasal verb is a **pronoun**, the object pronoun *must* come _____ the second word of the verb.

Oral Practice 5A: Use one of the following pairs of verbs in a sentence like this example:

I put on my blue sweater, but then I changed my mind and took it off.

turn on—turn off	pick up—put down
turn up—turn down	hire—lay off
hand out—hand in	order—send back
put on—take off	look over—give back

Written Practice 5:   Rewrite these sentences, changing the underlined words to pronouns.

1. After the phone call, the police locked up Pierre.
2. Pierre walked around the cell slowly; he was checking out the cell.
3. He found an old magazine on a shelf; he tore up the magazine and set it on fire.
4. Pierre yelled, "Fire!" and the guard rushed in to put out the fire; Pierre rushed out.
5. It was a clever trick. By the time the guard had figured out the trick, it was too late.
6. "Crime doesn't pay," thought Pierre as he was running to the train station. "Maybe I should give up crime."

Oral Practice 5B: Close your book and tell the story of Pierre's arrest and escape.

14.6 Chapter Check: Complete these sentences. If you are unsure of an answer, check the indicated model sentence and rule.

1. Enrique will never be very good at English because he (*speak + always*)

   _____ Spanish.   [14.1]

2. Mieko likes to sew; she is always making something _____

   someone.   [14.2a]

3. Maria would like to see this story; you should show _____.   [14.4]

4. You have just taken some flowers to your sick classmate, Naser. Another classmate,

   Mehdi, asks, "Did you take anything to Naser?" This is your answer:

   Yes, I took _____.   [14.3a]

   Your classmate replies: That probably cheered _____.   [14.5e]

14.7 Chapter Check: Finish sentence B. It should have about the same meaning as sentence A.

1. A. In the U.S., traditionally a man requests a woman's company for a date and then
      goes to her home and gets her.

   B. In the U.S., traditionally a man asks a woman out and then picks _____

      at home.   [14.5e]

2. A. Another tradition is for the man to send flowers to the woman.

    B. Another tradition is for _____

    flowers.   [14.3a]

3. A. Sometimes it is difficult to choose presents for older people.

    B. Sometimes it is _____ out presents for older

    people.   [14.5d]

4. A. Last year I finally bought my parents a gift certificate.

    B. Last year I finally _____ my

    parents.   [14.2a]

5. A. What can we do for Ted to make him happier?

    B. What can we do for Ted to cheer _____?   [14.5e]

6. A. Telephone me if you have any questions.

    B. _____ up _____ have any questions.   [14.5e]

14.8 Warm-up: Think of what you do to or for your friends. With your classmates, make a list of things that one friend does to or for another.

14.9 Communication: Think of a friend who lives in another country or another state. Then form a group with three of your classmates. Ask each other about your distant friends. Ask each other **how often** you do the things listed. Try to use complete sentences in asking and answering. Write the answers in the blanks (for example, **every day, once a week, never**).

Classmate's name	_____	_____	_____
Friend's name	_____	_____	_____
Think about	_____	_____	_____
Call up	_____	_____	_____
Write letters	_____	_____	_____
Send presents	_____	_____	_____

Now tell the class about the long-distance friendship of one of the people you interviewed.

14.10 Sentence Writing: Complete these sentences with the correct particles. Check yourself by looking up the phrasal verbs in Appendix 3. Then rewrite the sentence, putting the particle after the object. Finally, write the sentence again, this time replacing the object noun with a pronoun. Example:

Sam put __on__ his favorite shirt.
Sam put his favorite shirt on.
Sam put it on.

1. He tucked _____ his shirttail.

2. He put _____ his shoes.

3. He laced _____ his shoes.

4. He cleared _____ the table.

5. He cleaned _____ the mess in the kitchen.

6. He zipped _____ his coat.

14.11 Sentence Writing: *Put* is the first word in several phrasal verbs. Use your dictionary or Appendix 3 to find the phrasal verbs beginning with *put* that have the same meanings of the expressions given. Write a sentence using each phrasal verb. Write the sentence again using the other possible word order. Example:

> *''to get dressed'' = ''to put (clothing) on''*
> *When Harry put on the funny hat, everyone laughed.*
> *When Harry put the funny hat on, everyone laughed.*

1. ''to return (something) to a proper place'' = _____

2. ''to save (money, etc.) for a special purpose'' = _____

3. ''extinguish'' = _____

14.12 Sentence Completion: The prepositions *at*, *on*, and *in* can cause problems for learners of English. These prepositions are used both in phrases of **time** and phrases of **place**. In both cases, going from *at* to *on* to *in* means going from more specific to more general.
  At is usually the most specific; we use *at* for times of the clock and for addresses.

> *at 7:30*   *at 344 North Elm*

On is less specific; we use *on* for days and dates, and for streets.

> *on Thursday*   *on North Elm Street*
> *on March 29*

In is the most general; we use *in* for months, years, and decades, and for cities, states, countries, and continents.

> *in March*   *in Detroit*
> *in 1955*   *in Michigan*
> *in the 1990s*   *in the United States*
>   *in North America*

Now try to use the correct preposition—*at*, *on*, or *in*—in each of these sentences.

1. We finally got home _____ midnight.

2. We are going to have our first test _____ September 9.

3. I arrived in this country _____ August, 1988.

4. Our new apartment is _____ 3124 East 24th Avenue.

5. We used to live in a place _____ Lincoln Boulevard.

6. Before that we lived _____ Japan for several years.

7. Devil's Tower is located _____ Wyoming.

8. Halloween is celebrated _____ October 31.

9. Thanksgiving, another American holiday, occurs _____ November.

10. The local news is broadcast on TV every evening _____ 6:00.

11. Many theaters are located _____ Broadway, a New York City street.

12. The Declaration of Independence was signed _____ Philadelphia, Pennsylvania _____ 1776.

13. The British prime minister's residence is _____ 10 Downing Street.

14. In most parts of the U.S., the hottest weather occurs _____ July.

NOTE: Very often in English a particular preposition is used after a certain word; sometimes a particular preposition is used before a certain word. Many common preposition combinations can be found in Appendix 2.

14.13 Paragraph Completion: Complete this paragraph with the correct prepositions. After finishing, check your answers by referring to Appendix 2.

My grandfather was typical of many Europeans who felt the need to abandon their homes and begin new lives in the United States. He was born in Germany in the 1880s. As a young man, he *went* _____ a good university near his hometown and *found pleasure* _____ the life of a student. However, severe economic problems forced him to *drop out* _____ school and attempt to *get into* the job market. After months of frustration and suffering, and after *thinking* _____ the various alternatives, he decided to emigrate to America. Although he *was without* experience, he did not *have any doubts* _____ his ability to *live through* almost any kind of hardship. After disembarking in New York, he kept moving until he *arrived* _____ Chicago. There he found a job and *was introduced* _____ the woman (another German immigrant) who would become my grandmother. After a couple of years of working and saving, he *got married* _____ his sweetheart, and they moved to Kansas, where he found a spot that *looked* _____ the area where he had grown up, and began to farm. They had nine healthy children and lived a long and happy life.

14.14 Paragraph Writing: Rewrite the paragraph in 14.13 Paragraph Completion, replacing all of the expressions in the blanks with **transitive verbs**—verbs that do not require prepositions before their objects. Use the verbs in the following list in your rewrite.

attend	enjoy	leave	reach
consider	enter	marry	resemble
doubt	lack	meet	survive

14.15 Sentence Writing: Write questions to ask your classmates beginning with ''To whom . . . ?'' or ''For whom . . . ?'' Use some of these verbs: *explain, lend, owe, admit, translate, give.* Then rewrite each question using the more informal structure beginning with ''Who . . . ?'' Example:

> *To whom do you occasionally give advice?*
> *Who do you occasionally give advice to?*

14.16 Paragraph Writing: Write a paragraph about the long-distance friendships of the classmates you interviewed in 14.9 Communication.

14.17 Reflecting: After reading this episode of the mystery story, examine the passage for objects—direct objects, indirect objects, and objects of prepositions. Look at the sentences that have both direct and indirect objects. Could any of these have a different word order?

> When I went to my office Wednesday afternoon, Deanne Miller was waiting for me. She was wearing a different business suit. She looked worried.
> I offered her the chair. ''Would you like some coffee?'' I asked.
> ''When did you make it?'' she asked me.
> ''Just yesterday,'' I told her.
> ''Yes, I'll have some.''
> I found a clean cup for her and gave it to her. She sipped it slowly.
> ''What's bothering you?'' I asked.
> ''Someone called me last night. It scared me.''
> ''Who was it?''
> ''A woman. I didn't recognize her voice. She asked me where my husband was.''
> ''What exactly did she say to you?''
> ''She said, 'Where are you hiding your husband? Tell him he can't hide forever.' '' Deanne Miller's hand was shaking. She put her cup on my desk.
> ''That's interesting,'' I said.

14.18 Real-World Work

THINK/PRACTICE

The rules for direct and indirect object placement are fairly easy to understand, but, like most language rules, they are difficult to remember. Sometimes statements of rules are a good starting point for learning a structure. Reread the rules in Rule Builders 14.3 and 14.4. Then, as you are walking or riding around today, make up as many sentences as you can that use these structures. Examples:

> *I should get my roommate a birthday present.*
> *I should get her a birthday present.*
> *My roommate explained the problem to me.*
> *My roommate explained it to me.*
> *I gave the teacher my homework.*
> *I gave it to my teacher.*

Practice the structures until you can produce them without thinking about the rules. You will be able to say the right thing quickly, the way a native speaker would, and you'll no longer have to think of the rules.

LOOK/LISTEN

Look and listen for phrasal verbs. They are very common, especially in informal English. Write down phrasal verbs that you want to remember, and if you hear any that you don't understand, be sure to ask your teacher for an explanation.

USE

You probably have some questions about some of the courses you are taking this semester. Perhaps you want one of your teachers to *explain* or *describe* or *recommend* something *to you*, or *to show, tell,* or *give you* something. Remember that you will probably say, "Could you please show me . . . /tell me . . . /give me . . ." but that you cannot use this structure with the longer verbs. You will have to say, "Could you please explain/describe/ recommend (something) to me."

Noun Phrase Review I

15.1 Part Three Check: Fill in the blanks with the correct form of the word given. Add **a** or **an** or **some** wherever necessary. If you are unsure of an answer, check the indicated model sentence and rule.

1. (*plan*) The two friends have made _____ to visit Colorado. [11.2a]

2. (*scenery*) They have heard about the beauty of the _____ there. [11.2b]

3. (*money, food*) They hope to save _____ by taking along _____

   to eat. [11.1]

4. (*warm clothing*) Friends have told them to take _____. [11.7a]

5. (*good time*) I'm sure they will have _____ there. [11.6, 11.4a]

6. (*glass*) We surprised the bartender by ordering three _____

   of milk. [11.3b]

7. (*extra bedroom*) We don't have _____,

   but you can sleep on our sofa. [12.5b, 11.4a]

15.2 Part Three Check: Finish sentence B. It should have about the same meaning as sentence A.

1. A. I should buy a present for my father.

   B. _____ a present. [14.3a]

2. A. In most libraries, after you look at a book, you should not return it to its original
    place yourself. You should let a librarian do this.

    B. In most libraries, after you look at a book, you should not put _____ your-
    self. You should let a librarian do this.   [14.5e]

3. A. I offered the old woman some money, but she would not accept it.

    B. I offered some money _____, but she would not accept
    it.   [14.2a]

4. A. Often I take a walk before going to bed.

    B. I _____ before going to bed.   [14.1]

5. A. Every knife in the kitchen was dull.

    B. All the _____.   [11.3d]

6. A. A woman who was 102 years old recently received a B.A. degree.

    B. A _____ woman recently received a B.A. degree.   [12.3]

15.3 Part Three Check: Rewrite these sentences, replacing the underlined noun phrases
with pronouns and making all other necessary changes.

1. We should tell Mrs. Benson about the change in plans.   [13.1]
2. I told the girls that we would be late.   [13.1]
3. Please give me the tickets.   [13.1,14.4]
4. The funny get-well card should cheer up Mr. Bradley.   [13.1,14.5e]
5. The crowd began to throw cans and bottles onto the field.   [13.1,6.6c]
6. You should try to explain the problem to your teacher.   [13.1,14.3b]
7. Please send me my grades by mail.   [13.1,14.4]

Self-Test

This self-test will help you review count versus noncount nouns and irregular plurals. Cover
the answers on the right, and write **some** and the correct form of the noun given—singular for
noncount nouns, and plural for count nouns. Mark the ones you miss and keep working with
them until you know them.

1. tooth   _**some teeth**_   some teeth

2. furniture   _____   some furniture

3. homework   _____   some homework

4. embargo   _____   some embargoes

5. slang   _____   some slang

6. landlady   _____   some landladies

7. evidence   _____   some evidence

8. mail   _____   some mail

9. wife   _____   some wives

10.	progress	_____	some progress
11.	equipment	_____	some equipment
12.	clothing	_____	some clothing
13.	traffic	_____	some traffic
14.	information	_____	some information
15.	hypothesis	_____	some hypothes<u>es</u>
16.	luggage	_____	some luggage
17.	policeman	_____	some police<u>men</u>
18.	knowledge	_____	some knowledge
19.	branch	_____	some branch<u>es</u>
20.	idea	_____	some ideas
21.	machinery	_____	some machinery
22.	foot	_____	some f<u>eet</u>
23.	news	_____	some news
24.	thief	_____	some thiev<u>es</u>
25.	kiss	_____	some kiss<u>es</u>
26.	box	_____	some box<u>es</u>
27.	human being	_____	some human beings
28.	luck	_____	some luck
29.	machine	_____	some machines
30.	advice	_____	some advice
31.	woman	_____	some wom<u>en</u>
32.	mistake	_____	some mistakes
33.	child	_____	some child<u>ren</u>
34.	music	_____	some music
35.	dish	_____	some dish<u>es</u>
36.	quiz	_____	some qui<u>zz</u>es

15.4 Sentence Writing: Write five sentences about something you have and something related that you don't have. Use **not** in some sentences, **no** in others. Examples:

I have three sisters, but I have <u>no</u> brothers.
I have a motorbike, but I do <u>not</u> have a car.

15.5 Sentence Completion: Complete these sentences with the appropriate reflexive pronouns. The first one has been done for you.

1. Sometimes I get very mad at _____*myself*_____.

2. Children, I hope you enjoy _____ at the party.

3. We should promise _____ never to be late to class.

4. Harry has been feeling very sorry for _____ since his girlfriend left him.

5. The two children introduced _____ to everyone in the room.

15.6 Sentence Writing: Write sentences placing these things in the proper categories:

turtleneck	pick	divan
brooch	wrench	highboy
parka	pipette	oboe
	lathe	

These are the categories you can choose from:

lab equipment	machinery	tools
jewelry	furniture	musical instruments
	clothing	

With some of the categories you will have to use the expression *a kind of* or *a piece of*. Be sure to use your dictionary or ask a native English speaker whenever necessary. Examples:

A turtleneck is a piece of clothing.
A pick is a tool.

15.7 Paragraph Writing: Rewrite the following passage, replacing all the underlined count nouns with noncount nouns with about the same meaning. Underline the substituted noncount nouns in the new version. Make all other necessary changes. Here are some noncount nouns you might want to use:

baggage	homework	poetry
clothing	mail	time
furniture	money	trouble
vocabulary		

Julio is a foreign student in the U.S. His first week in this country consisted of nothing but problems. The airline which brought him here lost his bags, so the only clothes he had to wear for several days were those which he arrived in. His scholarship check was late, so he had to live for over a week on only a few dollars. When he arrived at the apartment which he had leased by mail, he found that he had no chairs, tables, or beds. His first weeks at school were awful. There were not enough hours in the day to do all the assignments, and he did not know enough English words to understand his textbooks, especially the book of poems he had to read for his English course. Worst of all, he received very few letters from home during his first month here. Fortunately, everything soon got better, and now Julio is happy here.

If you have replaced the underlined count nouns with noncount nouns, you should have also changed two verbs, two quantity expressions, and one demonstrative (*this, that, these, those*). Read the paragraph you have written, and see if you have made these changes.

15.8 Letter Writing: Read the following letter and write a response.

Dear _____, (your name)

I am an American living in this city. I own two small restaurants. For a long time I have wanted to open a new restaurant in this town. This restaurant will serve international foods, the kinds of everyday things international students eat at home.

To open a restaurant like this, I need a lot of information about the kinds of things you eat with your family in your country. Could you please write and tell me several things which people in your country enjoy eating? I need to know the names of the foods, and I also need to know about how much of each food one person might eat in a typical meal. This would help me a lot in creating a menu for my restaurant.

Thank you very much for your time. I hope to hear from you soon.

Sincerely,

Jack Smith

P.S. I hope to see you at the restaurant!

15.9 Sentence Writing: Fill in the blank in sentence A. Then use the verb given to write sentence B, which should have about the same meaning as sentence A. Some of the verbs in the exercise are followed by prepositions; others are not. Check your answers with Appendix 2.

1. A. We went _____ a concert last Saturday.

    B. (*attend*) _____.

2. A. There we listened _____ some excellent music from India.

    B. (*hear*) _____.

3. A. One of the musicians looked _____ Ravi Shankar.

    B. (*resemble*) _____.

4. A. The audience was pleased _____ the performance.

    B. (*appreciate*) _____.

5. A. After the concert, some friends and I went to a cafe and talked _____ the performance.

    B. (*discuss*) _____

    _____.

16

Degree

REVIEW

Let's begin this chapter by reviewing *how* + **adjective** questions.

1. You want to know the height of Mount Everest, so you ask,

    _____

2. You want to know the width of the Mississippi River, so you ask,

    _____

3. You want to know your friend's height, so you ask him or her,

    _____

PREVIEW

We use adjectives to modify nouns—that is, to tell about the qualities of people and things. For example, we may simply want to say that someone is interesting, or something is important. However, we might also want to say something about the *degree* of this quality. We occasionally want to say that something is

> *more important than* something else
> *less important than* something else
> *as important as* something else
> *so important that* I can't forget it
> *important enough* to remember
> *too important* to forget

This chapter will emphasize adjectives, which are often used with statements of degree. You will also see how the concepts of degree apply to adverbs, verbs, and nouns.

Try to complete these sentences with the correct choice.

1. John is nearly _____ as Jim.

    a. tall   c. taller

    b. so tall   d. as tall

2. The test was _____ that over half of the class failed.

    a. very hard   c. so hard

    b. hard so   d. too hard

3. You'll have to wait until next semester to take that course. It's _____ add it
    this semester.

    a. late to   c. too late for

    b. too late to   d. so late for

4. Everyone who works there is rude, but Mr. Fenster is _____ anyone else.

    a. worse than   c. worst than

    b. the worse of   d. the worst of

16.1   Comparative Adjectives and Adverbs

Complete these model sentences.	Check.	Complete these rules.
a. Stretch is much (*tall*) _____	taller	To make the **comparative** form of a one-
_____ **Tank.**	than	syllable adjective or adverb, add _____. To show that the difference between the two
Stretch is a little (*old*) _____	older	things or people is very great, you can use the
_____ **Tank.**	than	**intensifier** _____ before the comparative adjective or adverb. If the
Stretch can run (*fast*) _____	faster	difference is slight, you can use the expression
and jump much (*high*) _____	higher	*a* _____. To introduce the second member of the comparison, use the word
_____ **Tank.**	than	_____.

16.1 Comparative Adjectives and Adverbs (Continued)		
Complete these model sentences.	Check.	Complete these rules.
b. Stretch is much (*happy*) _____ _____ **Tank.**	happier than	To make the comparative form of an adjective or adverb with one or two syllables ending in a consonant + **y**, change the **y** to _____ and add _____. When the adjective or adverb ends in -*ly*, sometimes this is not the case. See rules **e** and **f**.
c. After the football team lost its last game, Tank was even (*sad*) _____ **than he usually is.**	 sadder	To form the comparative of one-syllable adjectives that end with **consonant + vowel + consonant,** double the consonant before adding _____. Review the related rule about verbs: Rule Builder 8.1b.
d. Stretch is _____ _____ **basketball player** _____ **Tank, but Tank plays football** _____ _____ **Stretch. Tank is** _____ **at basketball** _____ **Stretch, and Stretch is** _____ **at football** _____ **Tank.**	a better than better than, worse than worse than	The comparative forms of the adjectives **good** and **bad** are _____ and _____. The comparative forms of the adverbs **well** and **badly** are also _____ and _____.
e. School work is very easy for Stretch but very difficult for Tank because Stretch is much _____ **intelligent** _____ **Tank. In other words, Tank is** _____ **intelligent** _____ **Stretch. Stretch understands new concepts much** _____ **quickly** _____ **Tank.**	 more than less than more than	To make the comparative forms of most adjectives and adverbs with two or more syllables, put _____ or its opposite, _____, before the adjective.

f. Stretch is a much (*friendly*) _____ **person** _____ **Tank.** *or* **Stretch is a much** _____ **friendly person** _____ **Tank.**	friendlier than more than	Some adjectives can be made comparative in two different ways—by adding _____ to the adjective or by putting _____ before it. The adjectives **handsome**, **stupid**, and **quiet** are like this, as well as several others that end in **-ly**, and **-le**. Here are some examples: **kindly—kindlier** *or* **more** **kindly** **noble—**_____ *or* _____ _____
g. Most people like Stretch _____ **than they like Tank.**	more	**More** and **less** can be used without an adjective or adverb. In model sentence **g**, **more** modifies the _____.

Oral Practice 1:   Think of two people you know or know about. Make sentences of comparison. Examples:

> *My father is a little older than my mother.*
> *Elvis Presley was even more popular than Michael Jackson is.*
> *My brother works more carefully than I do.*
> *I like sports more than my brother does.*

Written Practice 1:   Use the adjectives and adverbs given to make comparisons. Use *much* or *a little*.

1. (*lazy*) My uncle is _____ my father.

2. (*energetic*) Professor Jones _____ his students.

3. (*careful*) Zack _____ driver _____ I am.

4. (*good*) Joe _____ pianist _____ his sister.

5. (*alert*) Drivers need to be _____ in the rush hour _____ at other times.

6. (*bad*) Last night's lecture was _____ last Thursday's.

7. (*slowly*) My roommate reads _____ I do.

8. (*carefully*) My mother drives _____ my father.

9. (*often*) I watch TV _____.

10. (*badly*) _____ hurts _____ a toothache.

11. (*fast*) A train can go _____.

12. (*loudly*) My neighbor plays his stereo _____.

13. For dessert, I like _____ than _____.

14. I'm worried about Julio. He is smoking _____ he used to.

16.2 Repeated and Double Comparatives		
Complete these model sentences.	Check.	Complete these rules.
a. I don't know what's wrong with Tank. He's getting meaner and _____. **At the same time, Stretch seems to be getting more and** _____ **friendly.**	meaner more	To show that a quality or quantity is increasing, you can repeat a comparative. In comparatives that use ***more*** or ***less***, only _____ or _____ is repeated, not the adjective or adverb.
b. The meaner Tank is, _____ _____ **unpopular he becomes.** **In other words,** _____ **meaner Tank is,** _____ **popular he becomes.**	the more the the less	To show that an increase or decrease in one quality or quantity causes an increase or decrease in another, you can use the double comparative structure. Both clauses begin with the word _____. If ***more*** modifies an adjective or adverb, put the adjective or adverb immediately _____ ***more***. REMEMBER: If the adjective or adverb has only one syllable, for example, _____, don't use *more*; add _____ to the end of the adjective or adverb.

Oral Practice 2A: Think of something that is slowly changing. Express the idea with a repeated comparative. Example:

> *The pollution problem is getting more and more serious.*
> *Now that summer is over, the nights are getting cooler and cooler.*

Oral Practice 2B: Mention one change that leads to another. Use the double comparative structure. Example:

> *It seems that the more I study my calculus book, the less I understand.*
> *The warmer the weather is, the harder it is to study.*

Written Practice 2:   Using both structures discussed in Rule Builder 16.2, write two sentences to describe the relationship between these situations. Example:

> *Harry kept driving faster. I got very nervous.*
> *Harry drove faster and faster. The faster he drove, the more nervous I got.*

1.   The party kept getting louder. My mother got very annoyed.
2.   As the engine design continued to get more complex, the chances for problems became greater.

3.   I kept thinking more about the situation. It became less and less clear.

4.   As Milly thought more about her family, she felt more homesick.

16.3 Equality and Inequality		
Complete these model sentences.	Check.	Complete these rules.
a. Stretch has a brother who is the same height as Stretch. In other words,		To show that a quality or quantity of two things is equal, use this structure:
Stretch's brother is just _____	as	*(just)* _____ + **adjective/adverb** + _____
tall _____ Stretch.	as	You can show that one thing is just a little less in a quality or quantity with this structure:
Also, he can jump nearly _____	as	_____ (or *almost*) *as . . . as*
high _____ Stretch.	as	
b. Tank, on the other hand, is		To show that a quality or quantity in two things is unequal or not the same, use this structure:
_____ nearly _____ tall	not, as	
_____ Stretch.	as	*not* _____ + **adjective/adverb** + _____
He cannot jump _____	nearly	This expression never means ''more''; it
_____ _____ _____ Stretch.	as high as	always means _____. The word *less* is not usually used with one-syllable adjectives or adverbs; to express that meaning, use *not* + *as . . . as*. To show that the difference is great, use the adverb _____.
c. As we have seen, Tank is less intelligent than Stretch. That is to say,		The expression *as . . . as* is also used with adjectives and adverbs that have two or more syllables. Therefore, with these adjectives and adverbs there are two ways to express the idea of inequality:
Tank is not _____ _____	as intelligent	
_____ _____.	as Stretch	*less* + adjective/adverb + _____
Tank does not understand new		*or*
concepts _____ quickly _____ Stretch.	as, as	*not* _____ + adjective/adverb + _____

Oral Practice 3A: Use the *as . . . as* structures to make sentences comparing your hometown and this city or this school and your previous school.

Oral Practice 3B: Mention something that two members of your family do differently. Use *more*. Example:

My little sister plays much more quietly than my little brother.

Then paraphrase what you have said using ***not as . . . as.*** Example:

In other words, my little brother does not play nearly as quietly as my little sister.

Written Practice 3:   Complete these sentences of inequality. Use *not as . . . as.* The first one has been done for you.

1. (*age*) In many cultures most wives _____ *are not as old as* _____ their husbands.

2. (*height*) The Empire State Building _____ the Trade Center.

3. (*reliability*) This pen _____ that other one.

4. (*weight*) An apple _____ a grapefruit.

5. (*popularity*) Michael Jackson _____ Elvis Presley was.

6. (*interest*) This newspaper _____ the one from my hometown.

7. (*speed*) _____ cannot run _____ _____

    _____.

8. (*quickness*) Sometimes I don't understand new English structures _____

    _____.

9. (*cheerfulness*) _____ doesn't answer the telephone _____

    _____.

10. (*patience*) Last year my _____ teacher did not answer questions

    _____.

16.4 Comparing Quantities		
Complete these model sentences.	Check.	Complete these rules.
a. Stretch is a member of a wealthy **family. He has much** _____ **money** _____ **Tank.** **Tank does not have nearly** _____ _____ **money** _____ **Stretch.** **That is to say, he has much** _____ **money** _____ **Stretch.**	more than as much as less, than	In comparisons of quantity, use **more, as** **much . . . as,** and **less** with _____ nouns, such as *money*. Review chapter 11 on count and noncount nouns. Just as with adjectives and adverbs, **a little, a lot,** or _____ can be used before **more** and **less** + noncount nouns. Just as with adjectives and adverbs, **just** and _____ can be used with **as . . . as** + count or noncount nouns.
b. Because he is nice, Stretch has _____ **friends** _____ **Tank.** **Because he is rather mean, Tank does** **not have** _____ _____ **friends** _____ **Stretch.** **That is to say, he has** _____ **friends** _____ **Stretch.**	more, than as many as fewer than	In comparisons of quantity, use **more, as** **many . . . as,** and _____ with count nouns, such as _____. These expressions are common with count nouns: **many more, a lot more, a few more, a** **lot fewer.**

Oral Practice 4:   Three executives recently filled out questionnaires about their personal lives. Use their answers to make comparisons.

Question	Janet Walker	R.D. Sutcliff	Peter Carlson
How much money do you make per year?	$50,000	$75,000	$45,000
How many cars do you own?	3	3	2
How many cups of coffee do you drink per day?	0	5	5–10
How much free time do you have?	some	none	very little
How many people are there in your immediate family?	3	7	1
How much stress do you feel in your work?	some	a lot	a lot
How many times per year do you visit a doctor?	3	4	4

Written Practice 4:   Write six sentences about the executives. Use each of these expressions at least once: *more*, *less*, *fewer*, *as many*, *as much*, *not as many*, *not as much*. Try to make two comparisons in some of your sentences. Example:

Janet Walker earns more money than Peter Carlson but less than R. D. Sutcliff.

16.5 The Second Member of a Comparison		
Complete these model sentences.	Check.	Complete these rules.
a. Stretch doesn't like football as much _____ **basketball.** **In fact, Stretch likes basketball even** **more** _____ **Tank likes** **football.**	as (he likes) than	In comparative sentences with *as . . . as* or *than*, the second clause is often shortened because it uses many of the same words as the first clause. Which word in the following sentence can be left out? **Stretch is taller than Tank is.** _____ Similarly, in the first model sentence, we can leave out the words *he likes* without confusion. But in the second sentence, nothing can be left out of the second clause because both the subject and the object change.
b. Most people like Stretch more than _____ _____ _____.	they like Tank	Is it a good idea to leave out the words *they* *like* in model sentence **b**? _____ If we do, the sentence has two meanings. It can mean that most people like Stretch more than they like Tank, or that most people like Stretch more than _____ likes Stretch.
c. Tank said sadly, "Stretch's grades are **always better than** _____ **grades."** *or* **"Stretch's grades are always better** **than** _____."	my mine	When we compare two things of the same kind that are modified by possessives, like *my*, we can leave out the second noun and use a possessive pronoun, such as _____.
d. The tickets to Stretch's basketball **games are not as expensive as** _____ _____ **to Tank's** **football games.**	the ones or those	When we compare two things from a category, we often use the pronoun *one* in place of the second noun. *One* or *ones* can only replace a count noun. (Review Rule Builder 13.4.) If the noun is plural, you can replace it with *the ones* or _____.
e. The equipment used in football is **more expensive than** _____ **used in basketball.**	that	*Equipment* is a _____ noun, so it cannot be replaced by *one*. Use _____ instead.

Oral Practice 5A: Think of something that you really like. Then make two comparative sentences like these:

> *I like pizza more than tacos.*
> *I like pizza more than my roommate does.*

Do you see why it's a good idea to use the auxiliary verb *does* in the second example?

Oral Practice 5B: Now think of something that you don't like very much.

> *I don't like tacos as much as pizza.*
> *I don't like tacos as much as my roommate does.*

Oral Practice 5C: Everyone who has a backpack or book bag should put it on his or her desk. Now make comparisons. Try to use **one**, as well as possessives, in some of the sentences. Examples:

> *Kapula's pack is larger than Tuan's.*
> *That blue bag has more in it than this yellow one.*
> *I like Amir's backpack more than mine.*

Written Practice 5:   Complete these sentences. They should all contain comparisons.

1.   My country has more _____.

2.   I didn't hear as much noise last night _____

     _____.

3.   The weather here is _____.

4.   The books that I had to buy this semester cost _____

     _____.

5.   The trains in _____

     _____.

6.   The scenery in _____ is not as _____.

7.   I enjoy the music of _____

     _____.

16.6 *Too* and *Enough*		
Complete these model sentences.	Check.	Complete these rules.
a. Stretch is too tall _____ drive Tank's car.	to	Stretch can't drive Tank's car because he is extremely tall and Tank's car is very small. You can express that idea with this structure: _____ + **adjective/adverb** + **an infinitive** The infinitive is *to* + the _____ form of the verb.

b. In other words, Tank's car is too small for Stretch _____ _____. Tank is _____ poor to buy a bigger car. In other words, a bigger car is _____ expensive _____ _____ to buy.	to drive too too, for Tank	As we have seen, Stretch can't drive Tank's car. Here is another way to explain why he can't: **Stretch can't drive Tank's car.** **Tank's car is too small _____ Stretch to drive.** The object of the first sentence (_____ _____) is the subject of the second sentence. But *Tank's car* is still the object of *drive* in the second sentence. Don't put *it* after *drive*.
c. Stretch is 18 years old, so he's old _____ to vote. Tank won't be 18 for several months. He's too young to vote; in other words, he's not ____ _____ _____ _____.	enough old enough to vote	If someone is not *too* young to do something, he/she is _____ *enough* to do it. Notice that *enough* comes _____ the adjective (or adverb). *Too* and *enough* can be used with adjective opposites such as *young* and *old*, to make sentences that have about the same meaning.
d. Stretch has _____ money and _____ friends _____ have a good time on weekends, but he doesn't have _____ time.	enough enough, to enough	You can use *enough* with nouns to refer to quantity. The word order is different, though; *enough* usually comes _____ nouns.
e. Tank doesn't have wonderful weekends either, because he has too _____ homework, too _____ football practice sessions, too _____ friends, and too _____ money.	much many few little	You can also use *too* with nouns to refer to quantity, but you must put a quantifier after *too*. With count nouns use *many* or _____; with noncount nouns use _____ or _____.

Oral Practice 6A: Tell the class some things that 16-year-olds are not old enough or are too young to do legally in your country. What about 18-year-olds?

Oral Practice 6B: Think of something that is too difficult, dangerous, expensive, and so on for you to do. Tell the class what it is. Example:

> *The teacher's desk is too heavy for me to lift.*
> *Florida is too far away for me to visit between semesters.*

Oral Practice 6C: Tell the class something that you do not have enough of. Tell what is impossible because you don't have enough of it. Then express the same idea using *too.* Example:

> *I don't have enough experience to be a clothing salesperson.*
> *I have too little experience to be a clothing salesperson.*

Written Practice 6:   In the United States, a person must be 35 years old before he or she is eligible to be president. Helen Foreman is 35. Ramon Espinoza is 63. Frank Vitelli is 34. Barbara Wilson is 25. Using these facts, complete these sentences. Use *old* or *young* in each sentence.

1.   _____ is just barely _____ to be president.

2.   _____ is not quite _____
     _____.

3.   _____ is much _____
     _____.

4.   Last year _____ was _____
     _____, but this year she is _____.

5.   In 10 years _____
     _____.

6.   Of the four, only _____ was not too _____
     _____ in 1988.

7.   Next year _____ will become _____
     _____, but this year he is _____.

16.7 Expressing Cause and Effect with *So* and *Such*		
Complete these model sentences.	Check.	Complete these rules.
a. Stretch is very tall. How tall? He is _____ **tall that he can touch the ceiling.**	so	If you want to show that someone is *very* tall, for example, and because of this, he or she can do something special, you can use this structure: _____ + **adjective/adverb** + _____ + **clause** *That* is often omitted, especially in speaking.

b. Stretch has a lot of money. How much? He has _____ much money that he never has to look at price tags.	so	Use **so** with these quantity words: *few, little,* **many**, and _____. The structure is: ____ + $\left\{\begin{array}{l}\textit{few}\\\textit{little}\\\textit{many}\\\textit{much}\end{array}\right\}$ + noun _____ + clause Use **many** and _____ with count nouns; use _____ and _____ with noncount nouns.
c. Tank is a very mean guy. How mean is he? He is _____ a mean guy that everyone is afraid of him.	such	Before an adjective + noun, don't use *so.* Instead, use _____. If the noun is a singular count noun, put **a** or **an** after _____.

Oral Practice 7A: Think of famous people who have or had some notable qualities. Make *so . . . that* sentences about them. Example:

Aristotle Onassis was so rich that he could buy anything he wanted.

Oral Practice 7B   What was the best or worst meal, movie, book, TV show, party, or class that you've experienced recently? How good or bad was it? Use *so* or *such* in your answer. Example:

The best book I've read recently was The Maltese Falcon. It was such an exciting story that I stayed up until 3:00 A.M. to finish it.

Oral Practice 7C: Describe the amount or number you or other people have of some of the following things. Use *so* + *much/many/few/little.*

patience	free time
curiosity	confidence
debts	plans
work	household appliances

Example:

I have so little free time that I never go to the movies.

Written Practice 7:   Finish sentences B and C. They should have about the same meaning as sentence A.

1. A.   My roommate is smart enough to pass all his tests without studying.

    B.   My roommate is so _____ he can pass all his tests without studying.

    C.   My roommate is _____ smart guy _____

    _____.

2. A.   Stan is a very good musician. In fact, he is getting a full scholarship from his university.

    B.   Stan is a musician. He is so _____

    _____.

    C.   Stan is _____ musician _____

    _____.

3. A.   Tank is very rude; as a result, almost nobody likes him.

    B.   Tank is _____ rude that _____.

    C.   Tank is such _____.

4. A.   Stretch is very tall; because of this, he has to duck when he goes through most doors.

    B.   Stretch is so _____

    _____.

    C.   _____ tall man _____

    _____.

Read the following information about Rhode Island and Alaska, and then do 16.8 and 16.9 Chapter Checks.

Statistics	Rhode Island	Alaska
Total area	1,214 square miles	586,412 square miles
Inland water	165 square miles	19,980 square miles
Population (1980)	947,154	400,481
Number of electoral votes	4	3
Date of statehood	May 29, 1790	January 3, 1959
Climate		
Average annual snowfall	40 inches	106 inches
Average annual rainfall	43 inches	55 inches
Geography	Sandy lowlands (east)	Very mountainous
	Gently rolling hills (west)	

16.8 Chapter Check: Complete these sentences. If you are unsure of an answer, check the indicated model sentence and rule.

1.   Alaska is much _____ Rhode Island.   [16.1a]

2.   (Use *small*.) However, the population of Alaska is _____ that of

Rhode Island.   [16.1a]

3.   Alaska has much _____ inland water _____ Rhode Island.   [16.4a]

4.   Alaska has _____ electoral votes _____ Rhode Island.   [16.4b]

5.   (Use *cold*.) In January, Rhode Island is almost as _____ Alaska.   [16.3a]

6.   (Use *cool*.) However, Rhode Island is not _____ as Alaska in July.   [16.3b]

7.   Alaska is _____ mountainous _____ it is difficult to reach some parts

of the state.   [16.7a]

8.   In an average year, Alaska has _____ snow _____ Rhode Island

_____ rain.   [16.5a]

9.   (Use the adverb *long*.) Rhode Island has been a state much _____

_____.   [16.1a]

10.   Alaska is _____ mountainous and sparsely populated state that many people

would not want to live there.   [16.7c]

11.   (Use *cold*.) Many people fear that Alaska is _____ for them to be comfortable

there.   [16.6a]

16.9 Chapter Check: Finish sentence B. It should have about the same meaning as sentence A.

1.   A.   Rhode Island is much smaller than Alaska.

B.   Rhode Island is not nearly _____.   [16.3b]

2.   A.   The population of Rhode Island is greater than that of Alaska.

B.   _____ people live in Rhode Island _____ in Alaska.   [16.4b]

3.   A.   Alaska has a little more rain than Rhode Island but a lot more snow.

B.   Rhode Island has almost _____ Alaska, but not

nearly _____.   [16.4a]

4.   A.   There are more cool summer days in Alaska than in Rhode Island.

B.   There are _____ cool summer days in Rhode Island _____

_____.   [16.4b]

5.   A.   Rhode Island has been a state much longer than Alaska.

B.   Alaska has not been a state as _____.   [16.3b]

6. A. There is not nearly as much wilderness in Rhode Island as there is in Alaska.

   B. Alaska has _____

   _____. [16.4a]

7. A. Alaska's climate is too harsh for many crops to be grown.

   B. Alaska has _____ that not many crops can

   be grown. [16.7c]

8. A. Alaska's oil and natural gas deposits are so great that there is no state income tax.

   B. Alaska's oil and natural gas deposits _____ enough _____

   _____. [16.6c]

16.10 Research: Prepare for 16.12 Communication by getting the following information about your native country or the state where you live now in this country: the area in square miles, the population, and the number of cities with more than 500,000 people. Finally, be sure you know how much oil is produced in your country or state: none, a small amount, a fairly large amount, or a great deal.

16.11 Warm-up: Compare the following information about three vans. Which van would you buy? Why?

Van	Price (U.S. dollars)	Gas Mileage (city miles p/gallon)	Length (inches)	Storage Space (cubic feet)	Acceleration (0–60 in seconds)
A	$19,000	15 mpg	191	271	13.3
B	$17,000	18 mpg	170	250	13.5
C	$20,000	14.5 mpg	190	300	18.5

16.12 Communication: Form groups of three or four. Ask each other questions to get the information needed in the following chart. Student A should interview student B; student B should interview student C; and so on. Then everyone should be prepared to compare the three or four countries involved.

Country   _____   _____   _____   _____

Area   _____   _____   _____   _____

Population   _____   _____   _____   _____

Large cities   _____   _____   _____   _____

Oil   _____   _____   _____   _____

16.13 Sentence Completion: Finish these sentences about Alaska and Rhode Island. Make sure they are true according to the information in the chart for 16.8 and 16.9 Chapter Checks.

1. Rhode Island has more _____.

2. In Alaska there is _____.

3.   The population of Rhode Island _____.

4.   The hills of Rhode Island are not _____.

5.   In 1980 Rhode Island had over twice as many _____.

16.14 Sentence Writing: Write five sentences comparing the vans in 16.11 Warm-up. Try to make two comparisons in some of your sentences. Example:

Van A is more expensive than B, but it is not as expensive as C.

Use these modifiers in some of your sentences: **much**, **a little**, **almost**, **nearly**, **not nearly**.

16.15 Paragraph Writing: Write a paragraph comparing the three or four countries that you discussed in 16.12 Communication. Try to use all of these expressions: **more**, **less**, **fewer**, **as . . . as.**

16.16 Sentence Writing: Write **so . . . that** sentences like this one:

Stretch is <u>so tall that</u> he hits his head on the ceiling.

1.   Think of a time when you were very tired. How tired were you?
2.   Think of someone who is very rich. How rich is this person?
3.   Think of a test you took that was very difficult. How difficult was it?
4.   Think of a day when it was very hot. How hot was it?
5.   Think of a time when you were very angry at someone. How angry were you?

Now rewrite sentences 2, 3, and 4, using **such**:

Stretch is <u>such a tall person</u> that he hits his head on the ceiling.

16.17 Sentence Writing: Finish sentence B. It should have about the same meaning as sentence A.

1.   A.   As it gets hotter, I feel worse and worse.

     B.   _____ hotter it gets, _____.

2.   A.   As we went deeper into the jungle, I became more and more apprehensive.

     B.   _____, the more _____

     _____.

3.   A.   As an office gets larger, a manager knows fewer and fewer employees.

     B.   _____ larger _____, _____

     _____.

4.   A.   As the music got louder, the audience screamed more and more loudly.

     B.   _____, the more _____

     _____.

16.18 Paragraph Writing: Imagine that you have a job and take home $1000 a month. Following is a list of necessary expenditures—rent, groceries, and so on—and a list of things you would like to buy. Which of these things do you want more than others? Which of the things do you have enough money to buy in the next six months? Which things are too expensive for you to buy soon? Discuss how each purchase will affect your other choices. Example:

If I buy a new desk chair this month, I won't have enough money to get a new camera lens until next month.

Necessities	Monthly Cost	Things I Want	Cost
Rent	$325	Used washing machine	$ 125
Groceries	$150	Cassette tape recorder	$ 100
Utilities	$130	Computer	$1500
Telephone	$ 25	Lens for camera	$ 120
Gasoline	$ 40	New desk chair	$ 100
Car insurance	$ 60		
Miscellaneous	$100		

16.19 Sentence Completion: Prepositions are important in making comparisons. Supply the correct prepositions in these sentences, in which the Japanese and English languages are compared. Refer to Appendix 2 if necessary.

1.   Japanese differs _____ English in that it has few different vowel sounds.

2.   Compared _____ English, Japanese does not have very many consonant

     clusters—such as [sks] in the word *asks.*

Sentence 3 expresses one difference and one similarity. You should be able to see which is the difference and which is the similarity. Use **unlike** to introduce the difference and **like** to introduce the similarity.

3.   _____ English, Japanese expresses tense by changing the form of the verb. But

     _____ English, Japanese does not have auxiliary verbs.

4.   Another difference _____ the two languages is that Japanese has no relative

     pronouns.

16.20 Sentence Completion: Many people, both native and non-native speakers of English, have trouble with **as** and **like**. Here are several points to review before doing this exercise.

As can be a conjunction as well as a preposition. Example:

As I told you before, Ms. Bolinsky is not a professional singer.

In informal speaking and writing, you may observe native speakers using **like** as a conjunction. For academic writing, you should try to get into the habit of using **as** to introduce clauses, rather than **like**.

Here is an example of the preposition **as**:

> The word <u>after</u> can be used as a preposition.

That sentence means, ''*After* can be used with the function of a preposition.'' The preposition **as** can also mean ''in the capacity of'' or ''in the role of.'' Examples:

> *Mick was hired as a night guard for the factory.*
> *I'm going to the Halloween party as Frankenstein's monster.*

Like, as a preposition, means ''similar to.'' Example:

> *You look like my sister.*

Remember from Rule Builder 16.3 that **as . . . as** is used to express equality. Example:

> *I worked just as long as you did.*

Complete these sentences with **as** or **like**.

1. _____ you know, the TOEFL will be given this Saturday.

2. I like Mr. Johnson _____ a person but not _____ a teacher.

3. _____ many students, Mieko has trouble with verb tenses.

4. Sam eats _____ much _____ a horse.

5. Sam eats _____ a horse.

6. Cary does her homework every night _____ a good student should.

7. Do you think Doris looks _____ her mother?

8. My little daughter can climb trees _____ a monkey.

9. My father worked for years _____ an underpaid bank teller.

10. _____ the teacher said, we should get plenty of rest before the exam.

16.21 Reflecting: Read the next episode of the mystery story. Then examine the passage for structures of comparison. Can you also find two places where *enough* is used?

> I talked to Deanne Miller about her threatening phone call for awhile. I asked her if she had enough time to come with me while I got something to eat. We walked downtown together. She was a walker; we went so quickly that I worked up a sweat. I took off my jacket. It was a nice spring day. I decided I needed more time to take walks now that spring was here.
>
> The closest restaurant to my office was a little cafe. Mrs. Miller looked at the place from outside with a frown.
>
> ''It's not as bad as it looks,'' I promised her. ''And there are fewer people here than in the other places.''
>
> I ordered more than she did; she obviously wasn't as hungry.
>
> ''Somebody thinks you helped your husband disappear,'' I said.
>
> ''Crazy,'' she said.
>
> ''Maybe the woman who called you knows more than we do,'' I said. ''But who is she?''
>
> ''I don't know,'' she said. ''But it's scary.''
> (Continued p. 210)

"There are scarier things, " I said. "I'm a little confused."

"Why?" Deanne Miller asked.

"Well, somebody made your husband disappear. I think we can assume that this person isn't very nice. Now somebody *else* called and threatened you. That couldn't be the same person. Whoever took your husband doesn't need to threaten you."

"Now I'm just as confused as you are," she said.

"It means your husband has more enemies than we thought."

I checked my wallet. I had barely enough cash to pay for our lunches.

16.22 Real-World Work

THINK/PRACTICE

As you walk around, make up sentences comparing the things and people you see.

LOOK/LISTEN

1. Advertisements are a good source of comparative structures. Find a magazine with a lot of full-page ads. See how many comparative and equative structures you can find in 10 minutes. Look for repeated and double comparatives, too. Keep your eye out for the other structures you've been working on in this chapter: *too* and *enough* + **infinitive** and *so/such . . . that.*

2. Look at the Help Wanted ads in your local newspaper. Look at the qualifications that employers require and prefer for each position. Think of the qualifications that you have and don't have, using *enough:* "I don't have enough teaching experience for that job," or, "I have driven a car long enough to be a taxi driver."

USE

1. Get into a conversation with someone who has come here from a different place (not your country). Discuss how your native countries are different from the United States.

2. Find out what people of college age are old enough to do and too young to do in the U.S. and other countries. Your teacher may want you to report your findings to the class. Here are some areas you might want to consider: driving a car, voting, joining the military, drinking alcohol, and getting married. You can probably think of other related topics.

17

Definite Determiners

REVIEW

Write *a* or *an*, the indefinite article, in the blanks wherever necessary.

_____ terrible disease struck Europe in the Middle Ages. People fled cities to avoid the plague, and throughout the continent this had _____ important effect on _____ language, economics, and politics. _____ essential task was to burn all objects infected by the plague.

PREVIEW

The **definite article** in English is *the*. In the following paragraph, add *the* to noun phrases that refer to specific people or things.

"_____ awful plague I just told you about was terrible for Europe," our teacher said. "_____ disease in general has always been a problem for humankind. Descartes, who is often called _____ father of modern philosophy, once said that _____ health was always necessary before _____ people could be happy. For _____ people of Europe during _____ period we are discussing, _____ happiness was difficult to find."

The is just one of the words that can begin a **definite** noun phrase. Others are the **demonstratives**—*this*, *that*, *these*, and *those*—and the **possessives**—*my*, *your*, *their*, *Helen's*, and so on. Circle the **definite determiners** in the following sentences. There are four definite determiners in the two sentences.

The two astronauts landed on the moon.
That experience will always live in their memories.

Three astronauts, Maria, Skip, and Leo, are scheduled to blast off for the moon in a few hours. It's time to start getting ready.

17.1 Possessive Nouns and Pronouns		
Complete these model sentences.	Check.	Complete these rules.
a. Skip and Leo are in the male **astronaut _____ dressing room, that** **is, the men _____ locker room.**	s' 's	Definite determiners like *the astronauts'* and *the men's* are called possessives. To make a possessive from a plural noun, such as _____, simply add an apostrophe ('). But if the plural form does not end in -s, add _____. Example: _____.
b. Skip _____ locker is on the left.	's	To make a possessive from a singular noun, such as *Skip* or *friend*, add _____.
c. Leo _____ is on the right.	's	In this sentence, the noun after the possessive *Leo's* has been left out. This can be done because we know from the context that it is *Leo's* _____ that is on the right.

d. Skip: Is this _____ helmet, Leo? Leo: No, I think that's _____. Skip: I don't think so. I don't think _____ helmet has a picture of your wife in it. Leo: Oh, yeah, you're right. That's _____.	your yours my mine	Possessives can also be made from pronouns. Sometimes the form that is used with a noun is different from the form that is used when the noun is left out.

Subject	Possessive + Noun	Possessive without Noun
I	*my*	*mine*
we	_____	_____
you	_____	_____
he	_____	_____
she	_____	_____
it	_____	_____
they	_____	_____

> NOTE: Nouns or names that end in *s* in the singular may be made possessive with or without an *s* after the apostrophe.
> Example:
> **the waitress' salary** *or* **the waitress's salary**

Oral Practice 1A: Point out the differences between some of the things that belong to people in your classroom. Example:

> *Fahad's sweater is red, but mine is gray.*
> *Teresa's hair is longer than Irma's.*

Oral Practice 1B: The word ***own*** (often the expression ***very own***) is sometimes used after a possessive. Example:

> *Morris has his very own darkroom.*
>   *or*
> *Morris has a darkroom of his very own.*

This indicates that it is unusual or very special for an individual to own such a thing. Mention something that you have or that someone you know has that falls into this category.

Written Practice 1A: Give the possessive form of each of these nouns and write an appropriate noun after it. The first one has been done for you.

1. the wind   *the wind's force*

2. their children   _____

3. the babies   _____

4. the Joneses   _____

5. the president   _____

6. that book   _____

7. the reporters   _____

8. the women   _____

9. my parents   _____

10. her students   _____

Written Practice 1B: Complete each of these sentences with a possessive.

1. I think I hear _____ phone ringing, Sam.

2. You're taking calculus from Professor Wilson? I hear _____ tests are awful.

3. We have two cats, so _____ apartment is very crowded.

4. Maggie isn't coming; _____ car won't start.

5. I don't want this book; _____ cover is torn.

6. The Jacksons live on the corner. _____ house is light blue.

7. My new car stereo is similar to Jennifer's. The main difference is that _____ has auto reverse, and _____ doesn't.

8. Our house is very different from the Smiths' house. _____ is nearly 75 years old and very large; _____ is small and rather new.

17.2 Demonstratives: *This, That, These*, and *Those*		
The astronauts are eating their last meal in the spacecraft before the moon landing.		
Complete these model sentences.	Check.	Complete these rules.
a. Maria: _____ meal is better than the one we had last night, isn't it?	This	***This, that, these,*** and ***those*** are another kind of definite determiner. They are called **demonstratives.** _____ is used to refer to a person or a thing that is near in space or time.
b. Skip: I'll say! _____ meal was terrible.	That	To refer to something that is farther away in space or time, use the demonstrative _____.
c. Maria: _____ peas taste almost fresh. The beans we had last night were like rubber.	These	The plural form of ***this*** is _____.
d. Skip: Yes, weren't _____ beans awful?	those	The plural form of ***that*** is _____.

Oral Practice 2:   Point out a difference between two things, one which is near in space or time and the other which is distant. Examples:

> *Those windows are closed, but these windows are open.*
> *This chapter is easier than those chapters on verb tenses.*

Written Practice 2:   Complete these sentences with demonstratives.

1. Where are _____ books I left here yesterday?

2. _____ cookies are great, Mom! I think I'll have a few more.

3. _____ car gets 25 miles per gallon; _____ one gets only 15.

4. There goes _____ strange man I told you about.

5. _____ shoes are too tight! Can I try on _____ pair over there?

6. Shovel _____ dirt right here into _____ hole over there.

7. Who is _____ girl standing at the bus stop?

8. _____ boys on the corner were throwing snowballs at my car.

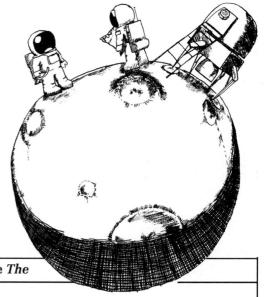

	17.3 **The Definite Article** *The*		
Complete these model sentences by writing ***the*** in the blanks if it is needed.	Check.	Complete these rules.	
a. Skip has stayed in lunar orbit, while Leo and Maria have gone down to _____ **moon in a special landing craft.**	the	When you think your reader or listener will know specifically which thing you are referring to, put _____ before a noun. Something can be specific or unique for you and your listener or reader for various reasons. (a) It may be something that is unique for everybody, for example, the _____ .	

17.3 The Definite Article *The* (Continued)		
b. **The astronauts have been wondering** **if _____ surface of the moon will support them.**	the	(b) It may be unique because it is defined clearly as a specific thing in the sentence. What phrase in model sentence **b** makes it clear what surface is being referred to? _____ _____ _____?
c. **Leo has opened _____ hatch and climbed down.**	the	(c) It may be unique in a given location or situation. In model sentence **c** we know from the context that Leo has opened the hatch of the _____ _____.
d. **Maria, who has a map, has followed him. Leo is looking around, and** **Maria is looking at _____ map and trying to get oriented.**	the	(d) It may be unique because you have already mentioned it.
e. **Maria: Isn't _____ space exploration exciting, Leo?**	no article	With noncount nouns that refer to something in general, don't use _____. Use *the* with a noncount noun only when you are referring to a specific case. Look at the following sentences, and write *the* in the sentence which refers to a specific instance: _____ **exploration has always appealed to adventuresome people.** _____ **exploration of the moon is still in its early stages.**
f. **Leo: Yes, it certainly isn't ____ same as exploring on earth.**	the	Always use *the* with the word _____.

NOTE: If *of* follows a noun, we usually use *the* before the noun. This isn't true with other prepositions. Compare these two sentences:

*I just read a book about **the** energy needs **of** China.*
*I just read a book about energy needs **in** China.*

Oral Practice 3A: With your classmates, describe the classroom by taking turns making sentences like this:

In the front of the room is a table.

The next student must begin with a prepositional phrase using the last noun from the previous sentence. Example:

Behind the table is a chair.

Oral Practice 3B: One way we can make something definite is by using an ordinal number—*first, second, third, fourth,* and so on—or the expressions *the next* and *the last.* Think about something difficult that you have done several or many times. Tell about the different experiences you had those different times. Example:

I like to water-ski. But I remember the first time I tried it; I fell almost immediately. The same thing happened the second and third time. But the next time, my fourth try, I stayed up and went all around the lake.

Oral Practice 3C: With your classmates, think of things that are found in your town or area. Example:

the river
the downtown mall

Written Practice 3: Write *the* in the blanks where needed.

_____ first hunters in North America who turned to farming to supplement their food supply lived in _____ area east of _____ Rocky Mountains. _____ remarkable discovery that _____ plants could be controlled in a garden began a revolution in Indian life. _____ first farmers hunted and lived in _____ caves and probably began _____ development of _____ science of _____ gardening by taming a few wild edible plants.

_____ excavations of _____ archeologists have reconstructed _____ development of early farming. _____ most important discovery was that _____ tobacco and _____ corn were _____ latest plants to be cultivated—many centuries after _____ cultivation of other plants. It has also been found that only after _____ beginning of corn cultivation did these farmers begin to have _____ pottery.

17.4 *The with Other and Rest*		
Complete these model sentences.	Check.	Complete these rules.
a. Two of the three astronauts went **down to the moon.** ____ _____ ____ **stayed in the space capsule.**	The other one	When we refer to the only remaining number of a group, we use the article ____ with **other**. *The other* is usually used with a noun or the indefinite pronoun ____.
b. One of the astronauts stayed in the **capsule.** ____ _____ **astronauts went down to the moon.** **or** ____ _____ ____ **went down to the moon.** **or** ____ _____ **went down to the moon.**	**The other** **The other ones** **The others**	In these sentences we use the article _____ because we are referring to ____ of the remaining members of the group. When **other** refers to more than one person or thing, we add *-s* to **other** only when it is *not* followed by a noun, a number, or the indefinite pronoun _____.

c. While they were on the moon, the astronauts collected hundreds of rocks. They selected about 100 to
 	
 bring back to earth; they left ____
 	
 _____ **on the moon. They also collected some soil; they selected a small amount to bring back and left**
 	
 ____ _____.
	the
	
	 others/rest
	
	 the rest
		If there are more than two things remaining, *the others* can be replaced with *the rest*. With
		
		 noncount nouns, such as _____, *the rest* is more commonly used than *the other*. When a noun follows *the rest, of* must be used:
		           The rest of the rocks were . . .
		           The rest of the soil was . . .
		The rest is also used with singular count nouns:
		           I can't eat the rest of this apple.

Oral Practice 4:   First, make a sentence based on this structure:

	have	*two*	*roommates*
I	*own*	*three*	*sisters*
My father	*know*	*a few*	*books for this course*
Bill Cosby	*bought*	*several*	*houses*
etc.	*etc.*	*many*	*cameras*
		etc.	*children*
			etc.

Example:

I have two roommates.

Then add one or more sentences using a form of *other*. Example:

One is from Bolivia, and the other is from Indonesia.

Written Practice 4:   Complete these sentences with forms of *other* or *rest*. Use ***the*** wherever necessary.

1. There are at least two American towns named Portland. One is the largest city in Maine; _____ is the largest city in Oregon.

2. The people who came to the festival ate only about half the food. _____ was given to charity.

3. One of Tim's three brothers still lives at home; _____ have gone off to college.

4. In the early years of American history, there were two presidents named Adams. One was the father of _____.

5. Every atom has three kinds of particles. One kind, electrons, circles _____, protons and neutrons, which make up the nucleus.

6. I can't eat _____ of this sandwich. Would you like it?

7. Only one person lost his life in the accident; _____ were saved by their seat belts.

8. There are three candidates for the office. One belongs to the Democratic Party; _____ say they are independents.

9. I could only solve the first three problems. _____ six seemed impossible to me.

10. Only three students from our class are going on the field trip. _____ say they are too busy.

17.5 Superlatives		
Complete these model sentences.	Check.	Complete these rules.
a. Stretch is taller than any other student in the school. In other words, **he is _____ tallest student in the school.** **He is our _____ student.**	the tallest	English has a special form for extremes; it is called the **superlative** form. To make the superlative form of a one-syllable adjective, such as _____, add ____. If a one-syllable adjective ends in **consonant + vowel + consonant,** double the final consonant. For example, the superlative of *thin* is _____. Before a superlative adjective, we usually put a definite determiner, such as _____ or _____.
b. Stretch is happier than most students in the school. In other words, he is **one of ____ _____ students in the school. He is also one of our** **(*friendly*) _____ students.**	the happiest friendliest or most friendly	To make the superlative form of a two-syllable adjective ending in **y**, change the ____ to ____ and add ____. Adjectives that end in **ly** and certain other adjectives have two possible superlative forms. See the rules for forming comparatives in Rule Builder 16.1.
c. Stretch is also more intelligent than most students in the school. In other **words, he is one of ____ _____** **_____ students in the school. On the other hand, Tank is one of** **____ _____ intelligent students in the school.**	the most intelligent the least	To make the superlative form of most adjectives with two or more syllables, use the words ____ _____. The opposite of *the most* is ____ _____.
d. Tank is a very good football player; **in fact, he is probably _____** **_____ football player on the team.** **Unfortunately, he is probably** **____ _____ student on the team.**	the best the worst	The superlative of ***good*** is ____ _____, and the superlative of ***bad*** is ____ _____. Do you remember the **comparative** forms of these words? _____ and _____.

e. **Of all the student-athletes at our** **school, I like Stretch** ____ **_____, and I like Tank** ____ **_____.**	the most the least	*The most* and *the least* can be used to modify verbs. In these model sentences, *the most* and *the least* modify the verb _____. When these expressions are used alone to modify verbs, *the* can be left out: **Of all the student-athletes, I like Stretch most.**
f. **Stretch comes from a rich family; Tank comes from a very poor one. Of all the people I know at our school,** **Stretch has** _____ _____ **money, and Tank has** _____ **_____.**	the most the least	*The most* and *the least* can also modify nouns. Use *the least*, however, only with noncount nouns, such as _____.
g. **Stretch is very popular, while poor Tank has almost no friends. In fact, of all the people I know at our school,** **Stretch has** ____ _____ **friends, and Tank has** ____ **_____.**	the most the fewest	Instead of *the least*, use **the** _____ to modify _____ nouns, such as *friends*.

Oral Practice 5A: Think of something or someone that you know is Number 1 (the tallest building, the fastest animal, and so on). Ask your classmates if they know what it is. Here are some adjectives that may help you: *good*, *long*, *high*, *old*, *large*, *famous*, and *popular*. Example:

> *What is the tallest building in the world?*

Oral Practice 5B: Make up a problem with three terms for your classmates to solve. Example:

> *This is about three people: Jack, Jim, and Jerry. If Jim runs faster than Jack, and Jerry runs faster than Jim, who runs the fastest?*

Written Practice 5:   Complete sentences B and C so that they have about the same meaning as sentence A.

1.   A.   Alaska is larger than any other state in the U.S., and Rhode Island is smaller than any other state.

    B.   Alaska is the _____ state in the U.S., and Rhode Island is

       _____.

    C.   Of all the states in the U.S., Alaska has _____ land and Rhode Island

       _____.

2.   A.   California is more populous than any other state in the U.S. Alaska is less populous than any other state.

    B.   California is _____ state in the U.S. and Alaska

       _____.

    C.   Of all the states, California has _____ people and

       Alaska _____.

3.   A.   Yellowstone is larger and older than any of the other U.S. national parks.

    B.   Yellowstone _____ park in the U.S.

    C.   Of all the U.S. national parks, _____

       _____.

4.   A.   The Mississippi is longer than any other river in the U.S.

    B.   The Mississippi _____ river in the U.S.

    C.   Of all the rivers in the U.S., _____.

5.   A.   Lake Superior is larger than any other lake in the U.S.

    B.   Lake Superior _____ lake in the U.S.

    C.   Of all the lakes in the U.S., _____.

17.6 *The* with Place Names		
Complete these model sentences.	Check.	Complete these rules.
_____ Alaska is the largest state in the U.S.	no article	As you saw in Written Practice 5, some place names require the definite article *the*, while others do not. Most place names do not require *the*—for example, the names of continents, countries, states, and cities. Here are the important *exceptions* to this rule:
_____ Mississippi is the longest river.	The	• The names of most bodies of water (oceans, seas, channels, canals, gulfs, and _____) require _____, but do not use *the* with names of lakes.
_____ Lake Superior is the largest lake.	no article	• The names of deserts and peninsulas require *the*. • The points of the compass used as geographical names require *the*—for example, *the West, the Middle East*. • Buildings: Use *the* with names that include the words *Building*, *Tower*, *Center*, or *Hotel*. Do not use *the* with names that include the words *Hall* or *Hospital*. The names of most buildings on college campuses do not include *the*. • Place names that are plural or that contain the preposition *of* require *the*.

Oral/Written Practice 6A: With your classmates, think of place names in the following categories. Make lists in your book for future reference. Be sure to use *the* where needed.

1. Continents: _**North America,**_ _____

    _____

2. Major Rivers of the World: _**the Mississippi,**_ _____

    _____

3. Major Lakes of the World: _**Lake Superior,**_ _____

    _____

4. Major Deserts of the World: _**the Sahara,**_ _____

    _____

5. Names with Plurals: _**the United States,**_ _____

    _____

6. Names with *of:* _**the University of Kansas,**_ _____

    _____

7. Names of Buildings: _**the Empire State Building, Carnegie Hall,**_ _____

    _____

Oral Practice 6B: Mention some famous places in your native country.

NOTE: One very confusing aspect of English article use involves places where people commonly go. Some of these places require *the*; with others no article is used. Here are two examples from American English:

> **My brother is at *the university*.**
> **My brother is at *college*.**

The	*No the*
the store	*bed*
the supermarket	*church*
the hospital	*school, college*
the university	*work*
the post office	*town*
the bank	*jail, prison*
the police station	*breakfast, lunch, dinner,* etc.

Practice using these place names in sentences beginning with

> **She is going to . . .**   **She is at/in . . .**

Home and *downtown* are two other very common places that people go. Do *not* use *the* when talking about going to or being at these places. These place names are special because you don't need to use a preposition with them either. Look at these sentences:

> **She is going downtown.**   **She will be downtown soon.**
> **She is going home.**   **She will be home soon.**
>   or **She will be at home soon.**

Do **not** use *to* before these words. Do **not** use *at* or *in* with *downtown*. However, you can use *at* with **home**.

17.7 *The* with Nationality Names		
Complete these model sentences.	Check.	Complete these rules.

a. Ben lives in the House for International Living. Students from many countries live there. Ben has learned a lot about other cultures since he moved into this house. For example, he has learned that, in general, _____ French and _____ Japanese are much more serious about food than _____ Americans.	the, the
	
	no article
	or *the*
		If a nationality **adjective** ends in *ch* or *sh*, *the* is used with this adjective to refer to the national group in general.
		
		    Example:_____ _____
		If this expression is the subject of a sentence, use a **plural** verb.
		    If a nationality adjective ends in *ese*, *the* is used with this adjective to refer to the group in general.
		
		    Example: _____ _____
		Again, use a **plural verb**.
		    If a nationality adjective ends in *an* (the most common ending) or anything else besides *ch*, *sh*, or *ese*, this form can also be used as a regular count noun. When we refer to the whole group, we must add
		
		_____ to the noun. *The* can be used, but it is not needed.
		
		    Example: _____

b. Right now in the house, there are two students from Guatemala, one from Thailand, two from Japan, one from China, and one from Sweden. That is, there are two _____, a _____, two _____, a _____, and _____ _____.	Guatemalans Thai Japanese Chinese, a Swede	Remember: Nationality names that do **NOT** end in *sh*, *ch*, or *ese* are regular count nouns. To refer to one individual from one of these nationality groups, put _____ before the noun; to refer to more than one, add _____ to the noun. Nationality names that end in *ese* can be used as count nouns, but when you refer to more than one person do not add _____. Most nationality adjectives that end in *sh* and *ch* have special noun forms; for example, the noun form of *Swedish* is _____.

Oral Practice 7A: If you have an international classroom, work with your classmates to make a list of the correct way to refer to each nationality group in general, to one individual in the group, and to several individuals in the group. Example:

Country	Nationality Group in General	Individual in Group	Several Individuals in Group
Japan	the Japanese	a Japanese	several Japanese
Germany	(the) Germans	a German	several Germans
Denmark	the Danish	a Dane	several Danes

Oral Practice 7B: Describe the make-up (in terms of nationalities) of your class or your international club.

Oral Practice 7C: Work with your classmates to think of nationalities in the three groups of nationality names—those like *Guatemalan*, *Chinese*, and *Danish*.

Written Practice 7:   Fill in the blanks with the correct form of the nationality word. Use a dictionary if necessary. Use articles (***a/an, the***) wherever necessary. The first one has been done for you.

1.   (*England, America*) ***The English*** drink more tea than ***Americans*** do.

2.   (*France*) _____ are famous for their good wines.

3.   (*Algeria, Egypt*) There is only one _____ in our class, but there are many _____.

4.   (*Malaysia*) _____ are known for their hospitality.

5.   (*Thailand*) I recently met _____ at a school party; she seemed very nice.

6.   (*Syria, Iraq*) Since coming here, I have met several _____ and many _____.

7.   (*Venezuela*) _____ often dislike Ohio winters.

8.   (*the Netherlands*) _____ are noted for their tolerance.

9.   (*Lebanon*) _____ have suffered a great deal for many years.

10. (*Greece*) _____ have a long, well-documented history.

17.8 Chapter Check: Complete these sentences. *Some blanks should remain empty.* If you have trouble, check the indicated model sentences and rules.

1. Two men who were born nearly 300 years ago had names that are still famous today.

   One of them invented the thermometer that is widely used in _____ U.S.A. and

   _____ Britain, and _____ developed the thermometer that

   is used in most of _____ rest _____ world.   [17.6, 17.4a,17.4c,17.3a]

2. _____ first was named Gabriel Daniel Fahrenheit.   [17.3b]

3. Fahrenheit was born in _____ Poland in 1686. _____ parents died when

   he was 15, and he went to _____ Amsterdam.   [17.6,17.1d]

4. In _____ Amsterdam he became a manufacturer of _____ scientific

   instruments and developed _____ Fahrenheit thermometer.   [17.6,17.3e,17.3b]

5. _____ man was named Anders Celsius, _____

   Swede.   [17.4a, 17.7b]

6. On _____ thermometer which he invented, _____ boiling point of _____

   water was established as 0 degrees and _____ freezing point

   as 100.   [17.3b, 17.3e]

7. _____ scale was reversed shortly after _____ death in 1742.   [17.3d, 17.1d]

8. Even though they were alive at _____ same time, they apparently did not know one

   another.   [17.3f]

9. _____ two men lived long ago, but _____ names are still among the _____

   famous in _____ world.   [17.3d, 17.1d, 17.5c, 17.3a]

17.9 Warm-up: Look at the pictures in 17.10 Communication. Look at each picture and discuss what you see. Examples:

> In the first picture, I see a monster and a couple of kids. The kids look terrified. They are dropping all their things. But now that I look at the picture more carefully, I see that the monster looks scared, too.

17.10 Communication: The following pictures tell a story, but they are not in the right order. Study them and, with the help of your partner(s), figure out the proper sequence. You can write the proper number of each picture in the space provided. The first and last pictures have already been numbered. Your pair or small group should then work together on writing down the story, with one student acting as the secretary. The group should then proofread the story carefully, checking especially for places where **the** has been left out and making sure that any demonstratives and possessives are correct.

17.11 Sentence Writing: Write three **whose** questions that someone might ask you, and write your answers. Example:

Whose car shall we take tonight?
Let's take mine.

17.12 Sentence Completion: A few quantifiers always include the preposition *of*—for example, *a lot of*, *a great deal of*, *a [large] number of*, *hundreds of*— but most do not—*some*, *several*, *a few*, *a little*, *much*, *many*, *most*, *all*, *one*, *two*, *a hundred*, *three million*, and so on. Examples:

> *Bill has a lot of friends.*
> *Bill has many friends.*

However, to refer to part of a definite whole, you can use these structures:

> quantifier   +   *of*   +   definite determiner + noun
> quantifier   +   *of*   +   personal pronoun

Examples:

> *Many of Bill's friends are international students.*
> *Many of them live in Bill's scholarship hall.*

In this exercise, write *of* in the blanks wherever necessary.

1. Many _____ foreign students suffer from culture shock in the U.S. Some _____ them are forced to give up and go back home, but most _____ them adapt quite well.

2. I like most _____ vegetables; some _____ my favorite vegetables are asparagus, broccoli, and cauliflower.

3. Not all _____ Americans liked Ronald Reagan's policies, but even many _____ his opponents liked the man himself.

4. Most _____ the shoes in that store are very expensive.

5. There are many _____ opinions about that theory.

6. One _____ Bill's friends is from Bolivia.

7. Agriculture is very important in most _____ the countries in that area.

8. I wasted a lot _____ time trying to fix my radio.

9. Nearly a thousand _____ people came to the concert, but only about 200 _____ them were there at the end.

10. Ming invited over a hundred _____ his friends and acquaintances to his twenty-first birthday party.

17.13 Sentence Completion: Complete the following sentences. Use each of these quantifiers at least once: *most*, *many*, *much*, *a lot of*, *several*, *some*, *a few*, *a little*. The first one has been done for you.

1. <u>*Most of*</u> the tourists <u>*have left*</u> , but <u>*a few of them*</u> are still in the square.

2. _____ Professor Williams's assignments are _____, but

     _____.

3. We _____ the pizza, but we left _____ for you.

4. _____ of the town's buildings were destroyed by the hurricane, but

     _____.

5. _____ in the House for International Living come

     from _____, and _____.

17.14 Sentence Writing: The Guinness Book of World Records is a great source of superlatives. According to the 1987 edition of that book, these are the record-holding buildings in their categories. Write a sentence about each building. Remember that **the** is normally used for superlatives and for the names of buildings. Example:

>   *tall—office building—Sears Tower—Chicago*
>   *The tallest office building in the world is the Sears Tower in Chicago.*

1. large—office buildings—twin towers of World Trade Center—New York City
2. old—wooden buildings—Pagoda, Chumanar Gate, Temple of Horyu—Nara, Japan
3. large—embassy—USSR Embassy—Beijing, China.

17.15 Sentence Writing: Following is a list of the worst hurricanes in the United States for the years 1900–1986. One important thing to understand about **intensity** is that the lower the pressure is, the calmer the eye of the hurricane is, and, therefore, the more intense the hurricane is.

Destructiveness				Deadliness				Intensity			
Year	Name	Place	Cost, U.S. (billions)	Year	Name	Place	Deaths	Year	Name	Place	Pressure (inches)
1938	(no name)	New England	$2.6	1900	(no name)	Texas	6,000	1919	(no name)	Florida	27.37
1955	Diane	Northeast U.S.	$3.1	1919	(no name)	Florida	600 +	1928	(no name)	Florida	27.43
1965	Betsy	Fla./La.	$4.7	1928	(no name)	Florida	1,836	1935	(no name)	Florida	26.35
1969	Camille	Miss./La.	$3.8	1935	(no name)	Florida	408	1960	Donna	Florida	27.46
1972	Agnes	Florida	$4.8	1938	(no name)	New Eng.	600	1969	Camille	La./Miss.	26.84

Write five sentences about these hurricanes. You know you can use the superlative for the worst hurricane in each category. Example:

>   *The most destructive hurricane in the U.S. from 1900–1986 was Agnes in 1972.*

Did you know that you can use it for the second worst, the third worst, and so on? Use this structure in at least three of your sentences. Example:

> *The fourth most intense hurricane during this period was the one that hit Florida in 1928.*

17.16 Report Writing: In police reports and some other kinds of reports, determiners and pronouns are often left out. Rewrite this report, supplying all of the missing articles, possessives, and pronouns.

> At 1:45 P.M. on Tuesday, May 28th, man in early twenties pulled into parking lot on east side of main post office. Called to woman who was leaving post office by east door. Said he was looking for police department. As woman approached car to give man directions, man pulled gun and demanded woman's purse. Woman threw purse into man's face and grabbed gun. Man drove off in car, blue 1978 Chevrolet.

17.17 Sentence Writing: In American newspaper headlines, determiners—such as *the* and **possessives**—and pronouns are often left out. Also, the present tense is used instead of the present perfect or the past tense. Read these headlines, and then write what really happened. Example:

> *Planning Committee publishes recommendations*
> *The planning committee (has) published its recommendations.*

1.   University announces courses for fall semester
2.   Mayor's wife loses control of car; breaks one leg, lacerates other; blames self
3.   Royal couple decides to bring dog on trip to U.S.
4.   Chairman of math department resigns; wants more time with family
5.   Swimmer wins first gold medal for U.S. in '88 Olympics

17.18 Sentence Writing: Answer the following questions with complete sentences. If the question is followed by a word in parentheses, use that word in your answer. Be careful to use *the* whenever necessary; be careful not to use *the* when the noun has a generic reference.

1.   Where does all our energy ultimately come from?
2.   How many people live in the U.S.? (*population*)
3.   What do most people listen to on their car radios?
4.   What part of the U.S. is California in?
5.   What do most automobiles use for fuel?
6.   What political party did John Kennedy belong to? (*Democratic*)
7.   Which chapter of this book deals with tag questions? (*first*)
8.   What kinds of books do you like to read?

17.19 Paragraph Writing: Write a paragraph or a short essay on national stereotypes—that is, simplified beliefs, both positive and negative, about people from certain countries. Think of beliefs that people in this country or in your native country have concerning three or four national groups. You might want to interview some Americans; you will probably be surprised at some of their stereotypes. In your paragraph or essay, tell how much truth you think these stereotypes contain. You might compare the stereotypes with the experiences that you have had with people from these countries.

Before writing, review Rule Builder 17.7. Identify the members of these national groups correctly.

17.20 Reflecting: Read the next episode of the mystery story. Then find all the possessives—nouns and pronouns—in the passage. Finally, examine the many occurrences of the article *the.* Can you explain why *the* is used in each of those cases?

> After lunch Deanne Miller and I walked back to the office. We stopped in front of her car, which was parked on the street in front of the building.
>
> "I talked to your husband's boss," I said. "She said your husband never showed up at the office the day he disappeared."
>
> "He told me he was going to check on something before he went to the office," she said. "Something about the Weber case. But he didn't say exactly what it was."
>
> I held the car door for her and she climbed in.
>
> "I don't think you should worry too much about that phone call you got," I said. "But it is interesting. We're going to find out who that woman was."
>
> "How?" she asked.
>
> I smiled mysteriously. "Leave that to me. That's what you're paying me for."
>
> I took the elevator up to the fifth floor and got the tape recorder out of my desk drawer. I set it beside the telephone. Then I took out the file Farmer had given me, the file of Carl Miller's notes from the insurance company, the other file I had stolen from Weber's house, a phone book, and a pencil.
>
> I read through the first file and copied down all the women's names I found. Then I did the same for the other files.
>
> Then I went to work. If I could get a recording of all of the voices of women involved in the case, perhaps Mrs. Miller would be able to recognize the one who called her.

17.21 Real-World Work

THINK/PRACTICE

1. Think of a sport or activity which is competitive. Think of the kinds of collections of things that people have. Then think of someone you know who is very good at the sport, or who has a large collection, and make sentences like these:

   Ben is the best badminton player that I know.
   Charlotte has the largest collection of records of all the people I know.

2. As you walk or ride around today, think of all the places where you have been recently and where you need to go soon. Remember: Some of these places require ***the***; others don't. Examples:

   I was <u>at the hospital</u> two weeks ago.
   I need to go <u>to class</u> in about 30 minutes.

LOOK/LISTEN

1. Look at the headlines in today's newspaper. Try to restate them in normal English.
2. Find a copy of *The Guinness Book of World Records*. Find some interesting facts in an area that interests you. Your teacher may want you to report on some interesting records that you've learned about.

USE

1. Sometimes while a person is reading a newspaper, another person asks, ''What's the news?'' The person who is reading the paper usually glances at the headlines to get the information asked for. He or she does not read the headlines to the other person but rather translates them into normal English. Have a friend ask you that question. When you answer, be careful to add missing determiners and endings.
2. You will probably learn some things from *The Guinness Book of World Records* that would be fun to tell a friend about. Use superlatives to tell your friend about some particularly weird or amazing facts that you learned from that book.

18

Adjective Phrases and Clauses

WHO WAS THAT NOUN I SAW YOU WITH LAST NIGHT?

ADJECTIVE CLAUSE

REVIEW

In chapter 12 we worked with adjectives, words which modify nouns. In chapter 16, we used the structure **so + adjective + a result.** Let's begin this chapter with a review of that structure.

Finish sentence B. It should have about the same meaning as sentence A.

1. A. Because Rosie, my elephant, is very big, I had to enlarge the bathroom door.

   B. Rosie, my elephant, is so _____

   _____

2. A. My pet elephant is very heavy; as a result, she broke the bathroom scales.

   B. My pet elephant is so _____

   _____

PREVIEW

In this chapter the focus will be on **adjective phrases** and **adjective clauses**, which also modify nouns. We will deal with expressions like those underlined in the following sentences:

The man <u>repairing the table</u> has worked at this university for years.
The table <u>on which he is working</u> collapsed yesterday afternoon.
The university <u>where he works</u> is located in the Midwest.

18.1 Relative Pronouns as Subjects of Adjective Clauses		
Turn back to chapter 7, and study the library picture (7.10 Warm-up). Then complete these model sentences, which are based on that picture.	Check.	Complete these rules.
a. The student _____ must take a test tomorrow is studying very hard.	who/that	The **subject relative pronouns** which refer to people are _____ and _____. *Who* is more common.
b. One professor is reading books **_____ are about aviation.**	that/which	The **subject relative pronouns** which refer to things are _____ and _____. *That* is more common.
c. The maintenance worker **_____ _____ repairing the table wears glasses.** *or* **The maintenance worker** **_____ the table . . .** **The light bulb _____ _____ in the middle of the room is burnt out.** *or* **The light bulb _____ _____** **_____ of the room . . .** **The librarian _____ _____ responsible for the reference books wears glasses.** *or* **The librarian _____ for the reference books . . .**	who/that is repairing that/which is in the middle who/that is responsible	If a relative pronoun is followed by a form of the verb *be*, it is usually possible to take out both the _____ _____ and the form of _____. When you do this, you no longer have an adjective clause; you have an adjective phrase. **REMEMBER:** When you shorten a subject-focus adjective clause, you must take out both the relative pronoun and the verb *be*. Leaving out only one of these two words is a common error.
d. The girl _____ has the Walkman® is listening to music. *or* **The girl _____ the Walkman . . .** **The table _____ has a broken leg is being fixed.** *or* **The table _____ a broken leg . . .**	who/that with that/which with	If a relative pronoun is followed by a form of the verb _____ indicating that something belongs to someone or something, it is usually possible to replace the relative pronoun and the verb with the preposition _____.

18.1 Relative Pronouns as Subjects of Adjective Clauses (Continued)		
e. **The librarian** _____ **doesn't have glasses is by the card catalog.**	who/that	If ***have*** is negative, the preposition which can often be used is _____.
or **The librarian** _____ **glasses . . .**	without	

Oral Practice 1A: Tell the class about one of your friends or possessions that can do something interesting. Example:

> *I have a friend who likes to stand on his head.*
> *I have an alarm clock that can talk.*

Oral Practice 1B: Tell the class about something you own—or would like to own—that has a special feature. Use an adjective clause. Then repeat the sentence using ***with***. Example:

> *I would like to get a watch that has an alarm.*
> *I would like to get a watch with an alarm.*

Oral Practice 1C: Form small groups or pairs. Ask one of the members of your group if he or she has met another person in the class. The group member who is asked the question should pretend not to know the person. Then identify the person with an adjective phrase or clause. Example:

> *Have you met Dani?*
> *Who's Dani?*
> *He's the guy wearing the blue sweater.*

Oral Practice 1D: Ask another student to tell you the name of someone else in the class. Use an adjective clause with ***who has*** to identify the person. Example:

> *What's the name of the student who has a green backpack?*

The student who answers should change ***who has*** to ***with***. Example:

> *The student with a green backpack is Jane.*

Written Practice 1:   Complete these sentences by writing one word in each blank.

1. The maintenance worker _____ is repairing the table is wearing a plaid shirt.
2. The telephone _____ is in back of the room has a telephone book hanging from it.
3. The man _____ a beard has a rather strange look in his eye.
4. The girl _____ dark hair is sleeping.

5. The desk _____ is located in the back is the reference desk.

6. The professor _____ is using the card catalog teaches English.

7. The maintenance worker _____ a hat is changing the light bulb.

18.2 Relative Pronouns as Objects		
Complete these model sentences.	Check.	Complete these rules.
a. One of the professors _____ we see in the library teaches the history of aviation. *or* **One of the professors _____** **_____ in the library teaches the history of aviation.**	whom/who/ that we see	In formal English, the **object relative pronoun** which refers to people is _____. In more informal English, we can use _____ or _____. Often, especially in speaking, we omit the object relative pronoun. It's often okay to leave out a relative pronoun when it is the object of the adjective clause.
b. All the books _____ he is reading are about aviation. *or* **All the books _____ _____ reading are about aviation.**	that/which he is	The **object relative pronouns** which refer to things are _____ and _____. We often _____ these _____, too.

Oral Practice 2:   Tell the class an interesting fact about someone you know or something you own. Begin your sentence with a structure like this:

A woman (that) I know . . . or A book (that) I have . . .

Written Practice 2:   Complete these sentences.

Let me tell you about some good luck _____ I had recently. At an auction, I found a beautiful old desk _____ I wanted very much. It belonged to a man _____ I had met at a party the week before. He told me the desk had once been used by a relative _____ he had never met. The relative had worked for a newspaper in a small town _____ I had never heard of. The desk was not one of the pieces _____ the antique experts wanted, so I was able to get it at a good price. When I cleaned out the desk, in the back, I found an old newspaper _____ the previous owners had not seen. The huge headline _____ I saw when I unfolded the paper said, ''President Lincoln Assassinated''!

18.3 Relative Pronouns as Objects of Prepositions		
Complete these model sentences. Then underline the adjective clauses and circle the subjects of these clauses. Finally, draw a box around the direct objects in the clauses.	Check.	Complete these rules.
a. The librarian to _____ I gave the book was very polite. **The phone on _____ the maintenance worker is talking is in the back of the room.**	whom which	When the relative pronoun is the object of a preposition, in the most formal situations we put the preposition before the relative pronoun at the beginning of the adjective clause. The relative pronoun after a preposition is always _____ for people and _____ for things.
b. The librarian that I gave the book **_____ was very polite.** *or* **The librarian I _____** **_____ _____ _____ was very polite.** **The phone that the maintenance** **worker is talking _____ is in the back of the room.** *or* **The phone the maintenance** **worker _____ _____** **_____ is in the back of the room.**	 to gave the book to on is talking on	In less formal English, we can put the preposition at the _____ of the clause. The relative pronoun at the beginning of the clause is usually _____ for both people and things, although *who, whom,* and *which* may be used. Often, especially in conversational English, we _____ _____ the relative pronoun *that* when it is the object of a preposition.

Oral Practice 3:   Tell the class something about the last present you gave to someone, and then tell the class something about the person you gave it to. For example, you might say,

> *The last present I gave to someone was a . . .*
> *The person to whom I gave it . . .*   or   *The person I gave it to . . .*

Written Practice 3A: Complete these sentences by writing one word in each blank. Then underline the adjective clauses.

1. The teacher to _____ I gave my homework took it on vacation with her.
2. The woman I ate dinner _____ last night is a social worker.
3. The bed _____ he was lying _____ creaked all night long.

4. The book he told me _____ is one of the best novels I have ever read.

5. Could you please tell me about the test _____ we have to study _____?

6. The young man to _____ the President was referring formerly lived in this town.

    (informal) The guy the President was referring _____ used to live here.

Written Practice 3B: Finish sentences B and C. They should have about the same meaning as sentence A.

1. A. I am interested in a medical career.

    B. Medicine is a career I _____.

    C. Medicine is a career in _____.

2. A. Clark finally found the article. He had been looking for it all day.

    B. Clark finally found the article for _____

        _____.

    C. Clark finally found the article he _____

        _____.

3. A. The murder was committed with a gun, but the police have been unable to find it.

    B. The police have been unable to find the gun that _____

        _____.

    C. The police have been unable to find the gun _____

        _____ was committed.

4. A. You will receive a list of people. You should send newsletters to the people on that list.

    B. You will receive a list of the people that you _____

        _____.

    C. You will receive a list of the people _____

        newsletters.

5. A. We can depend on Benson.

    B. Benson is a person _____ depend.

    C. Benson is a person we _____.

18.4 Adjective Clauses of Place		
Complete these model sentences.	Check.	Complete this rule.
The room _____ _____ **the people are working is usually very crowded.**	in which	When we refer to a place, ***in/at/on/to*** + ***which*** can be replaced by _____. This structure can also be used:
or **The room** _____ **the people are working . . .**	where	**The room (that) the people are working in is . . .**
The desk _____ _____ **the reference librarian is working is in a corner of the room.**	at which	**The table (that) the reference librarian is working at is . . .**
or **The desk** _____ **the reference librarian is working . . .**	where	

Oral Practice 4:   Identify the following things to the class: the town where you were born, the place where you go out to eat most often, and the store where you can spend the most time without getting bored. Example:

Tokyo is the town where I was born.

Written Practice 4:   Finish sentences B and C. They should have about the same meaning as sentence A. Use *where* in all of the C sentences.

1. A.   There are tables in the back of the restaurant. You can smoke at those tables.

    B.   The tables at _____ are in the back of the restaurant.

    C.   The tables _*where*_____ are in the back of the restaurant.

2. A.   He planted his flowers in a garden that is not far from the orchard.

    B.   _____ which he planted his flowers is not far from the orchard.

    C.   _____ is not far from the orchard.

3. A.   The room that Van Gogh painted most of his pictures in is a great tourist attraction.

    B.   _____ in _____

    _____ is a great tourist attraction.

    C.   _____

    _____ is a great tourist attraction.

4.   A.   The game will be played in an arena that holds over 30,000 people.

B.   The arena in _____

_____.

C.   _____

_____.

18.5 Chapter Check: Complete these sentences *by writing one word in each blank*. If you have any trouble, check the indicated model sentences and rules.

1.   A parasite is a plant or animal _____ lives in or on some other living thing and

gets food from it.   [18.1b]

2.   The plant or animal _____ _____ a parasite lives is called a host.   [18.3a]

3.   An example of a parasite is the tick. A tick crawls up a small plant _____

it waits for a host to walk by.   [18.4]

4.   It clings to a warm-blooded animal _____ brushes against the plant, and then the

tick gorges itself on the animal's blood.   [18.1b]

5.   A person _____ _____ a tick has lived may become a victim of Rocky Mountain

spotted fever or Lyme disease.   [18.3a]

18.6 Chapter Check: Finish sentence B. It should have about the same meaning as sentence A.

1.   A.   The plant or animal on which a parasite lives is called a host.

B.   The plant or animal that _____

_____.   [18.3b]

2.   A.   A tick crawls up on a small plant, where it waits for a host to pass by.

B.   A tick crawls up on a small plant on _____

_____.   [18.3a]

3.   A.   A person with Rocky Mountain spotted fever may become very ill.

B.   A person who _____

may become very ill.   [18.1d]

4.   A.   Rocky Mountain spotted fever is a disease characterized by fever and muscular

pain.

B.   Rocky Mountain spotted fever is a disease that _____

by fever and muscular pain.   [18.1c]

18.7 Warm-up: Think of one person in your class. Your classmates will try to guess who that person is after you give a clue with an adjective clause or phrase. Example:

I'm thinking of a woman who comes from Malaysia.
I'm thinking of a guy wearing black jeans.

Now think of a sport. Again, give your classmates a clue with an adjective clause or phrase. Example:

I'm thinking of a sport in which a player must hit a ball with a stick.

18.8 Communication: This activity is a guessing game. First, form pairs. The teacher will give each pair the name of a person, a place, or a thing. With your partner, make a list of special facts about this person, place, or thing. Example:

> **Eisenhower**
> *He was President of the United States.*
> *He became famous during World War II.*
> *People called him Ike.*

With your partner, using your list of facts, practice making statements that begin this way: ''We're thinking of . . . '' Examples:

> *We're thinking of a man who was President of the United States.*
> *We're thinking of a man that became famous during World War II.*
> *We're thinking of the man people called Ike.*

Each pair will then let the rest of the class guess their person, place, or thing. Give one clue. Call on one person who has raised his or her hand, and let that person guess. If that person guesses wrong, give another clue, and so on.

18.9 Sentence Writing: The more words that a newspaper classified ad has, the more it costs. Because of this, people who put ads in newspapers do not write complete sentences. Most determiners and verbs are left out, and adjective clauses and phrases are incomplete. Read each of these For Rent ads and write a sentence *with an adjective clause* telling what the person is offering. Then rewrite the sentence, reducing the adjective clause to *an adjective phrase* if possible. Example:

Downtown apartment 10th and Ohio.
Wood paneling.   Nice carpet.   Call
Bryan 321-4403.

Bryan is offering a downtown apartment which is located at 10th and Ohio and has wood paneling and a nice carpet.

Bryan is offering a downtown apartment at 10th and Ohio with wood paneling and a nice carpet.

Here are some abbreviations that you will need to know:

A/C	= air conditioning	br	= bedroom
apt	= apartment	mo	= month

Quiet room in very big house. Off-street parking. $280/mo. Call 391-4309. Bob.

---

1 br. apt. Near campus. Free cable TV. A/C. Call Helen 842-8999.

Small, clean house. 2 blocks from shopping center. 4 rooms. Nice yard. Sara 442-8771.

18.10 Sentence Writing: Look back at the family scene in chapter 7 (Paragraph Writing 7.18). Pretend that you know these people. Perhaps they are members of your family or members of a family with whom you had dinner recently. Identify **six** of the people (and cats, if you want) by saying *what he or she is doing*. In some of these sentences, use **adjective clauses**. In others, make **adjective phrases** by omitting *who is*. Examples:

The little girl who is giving her food to a cat is Carla.
or *The little girl giving her food to a cat is Carla.*

18.11 Sentence Writing: Clarify the meanings of the underlined nouns by modifying them with adjective clauses. If possible, reduce the adjective clauses to adjective phrases as explained in Rule Builder 18.1. Example:

I can't eat the food.
I can't eat the food that is served at that restaurant.
I can't eat the food served at that restaurant.

1. Students often receive very poor grades.
2. I have never met a person.
3. People are in constant danger.
4. I don't like sports.
5. Television programs should be taken off the air.
6. I especially enjoy reading books.
7. An automobile is necessary for a person.

18.12 Sentence Writing: Definitions often have adjective clauses. Define six of the following words using adjective clauses. Then, if possible, reduce the adjective clause to a phrase. Use your dictionary if necessary. Examples:

A convertible is an automobile that has a removable top.
A convertible is an automobile with a removable top.

a peninsula	Delaware	a cardiologist
a chaise longue	an adjective	a launch pad
a mechanic	a Nissan	Luxembourg
a pediatrician	a bureaucrat	a Jack-in-the-Pulpit

18.13 Paragraph Writing: The following paragraph is grammatically correct, but it has too many simple sentences, not enough sentence variety. Rewrite the paragraph, changing all the underlined sentences to adjective clauses.

There are many steps in making wood into paper. First, logs are taken to a mill. There the bark is taken off. The wood is then cut into chips. These chips are cooked with a chemical until the wood fibers, or pulp, separate. On a bronze screen the wet pulp is formed into a sheet. This sheet goes between rollers. The rollers squeeze out some of the moisture. The sheet then passes over a series of heat rollers. The heat rollers dry it out. Finally, the finished paper is wound onto a big roll.

18.14 Paragraph Writing: You have been asked to write a paragraph describing a small Midwestern town for a book on travel in the U.S. Using the picture as a guide, describe the main street of Amsterdam, Missouri. Give the reader interesting information about each of the buildings. Use adjective clauses. This is how your paragraph should begin:

As you leave Highway 69, you drive down the Main Street of Amsterdam, Missouri. On your left, the first building you see is a bank *which robbers held up six times in 1927.* Next to the bank, you . . .

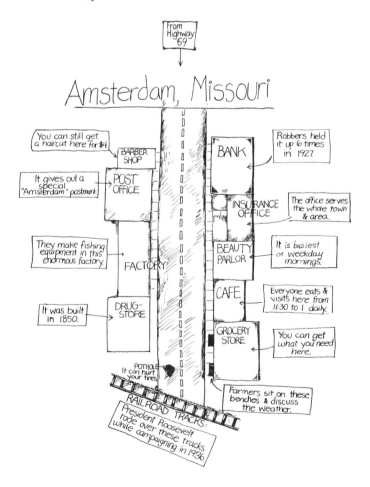

18.15 Reflecting: Read the next episode of the mystery story. Then find all the adjective clauses. Could the relative pronoun be taken out, added, or changed in any of these clauses? Could any of these clauses be reduced to phrases? Can you find any adjective phrases which could be replaced by adjective clauses?

> I needed the name of the woman who had called Deanne Miller. The phone call Mrs. Miller had received bothered me. Why did someone think she was hiding her husband? Why did Carl Miller need to be hidden?
>
> I made a list of all the names of the women in my files on the case. There were about 20. Next I looked up their phone numbers. I decided that I would call every one of them and tape record their voices. Then Deanne might be able to identify the woman who had called her.
>
> I couldn't find the numbers for three of the names written on my list. That still left me 17 women to call.
>
> The first name belonged to Sandy Brewer, a nurse working for Dr. Weber. I found her at the hospital.
>
> ''I'm looking for Carl Miller,'' I told her. ''He works for the insurance company that carries Dr. Weber's malpractice insurance.''
>
> ''He isn't here,'' she said.
>
> ''Yeah, I know. He has disappeared. Have you seen him?''
>
> ''No. The other person you should talk to is Abby Goldman. He talked to her about the case.''
>
> Abby Goldman was another nurse, and she was already on my list. I thanked Ms. Brewer and hung up and turned off my tape recorder.

18.16 Real-World Work

THINK/PRACTICE

Go to a place where there are many people—perhaps a student cafeteria. Make up sentences about what some of the people are doing or about what they are like. Use an adjective clause or phrase in each sentence. Examples:

The woman in the blue sweater is talking to the man with long hair.
The man who is talking to the woman in the blue sweater has long hair.

LOOK/LISTEN

In newspaper writing, adjective clauses are usually reduced to phrases whenever possible. Look at a newspaper, and try to find five nouns followed by adjective **phrases**. Try to change the phrases to **clauses**. Examples:

According to the proposal made by the Secretary of State . . .
According to the proposal which was made by the Secretary of State . . .

USE

Adjective clauses and phrases are powerful language tools. With them you can make it very clear what you are referring to. Has the work in this chapter been difficult for you? If so, this probably indicates that you make adjective clause errors or avoid using adjective clauses in your speech. Before you are out of practice, try to improve your use of adjective clauses. Often you must tell someone *which one* you prefer, want, mean, and so on. Sometimes you can give that information with an adjective or a determiner—for example, *Fred's car* or *the green book*. Often, however, you will need to use an adjective clause to provide enough information. Example:

. . . *the book that you recommended to me last week.*

19

More Adjective Clauses

REVIEW

The sentences in this paragraph contain the kinds of adjective clauses that you learned to use in the last chapter. *Write one word in each blank.*

When I arrived in New York City, the people _____ were supposed to meet me didn't show up. The plane _____ _____ I had just arrived was on time, so I couldn't figure out why my friends weren't there to meet me. I had their address in a little book _____ I always carry with me, so I called a cab. The cab driver was a strange fellow _____ could not seem to find the address. We finally reached the building _____ my friends lived. I paid an amount of money _____ seemed very unreasonable, and then I went up and knocked on the door. When my friend came to the door, he was so surprised to see me that he dropped the frying pan _____ _____ he was making lunch. "We thought you were coming tomorrow," he said sheepishly.

PREVIEW

In this chapter, we will look at some more grammar problems involving adjective clauses. You will learn about the kinds of clauses found in the pretest on the next page.

Choose the best answer to complete these sentences:

1. Anderson, _____ profession is carpentry, is a practical joker.

    a. who   c. who his

    b. who the   d. whose

2. He makes a dozen gadgets a year, _____ have some bizarre trick built into them.

    a. all   c. all of which

    b. of which   d. all of them

3. Last year he built a chair _____ cushion made a squealing noise every time you sat down.

    a. that the   c. whose

    b. which the   d. its

4. His customers, _____ know nothing about Mr. Anderson's unusual sense of humor, are often surprised when they start using his products.

    a. most of whom   c. most of them

    b. who most   d. that most

19.1 Adjective Clauses with *Whose*		
Complete these model sentences.	Check.	Complete these rules.
a. **The man _____ phone is ringing is getting some coffee.**	whose	The possessive relative pronoun is _____.
b. **The plant _____ leaves are shriveling seems to be dying.**	whose	***Whose*** is used more often for people than things, but it can refer to both people and things.
c. **The man _____ daughter you met last night works in this office.**	whose	The noun which refers to the person or thing possessed— for example, *daughter*—comes immediately _____ ***whose*** even if it is an object in the adjective clause. And ***whose*** comes immediately _____ the noun that it stands for—for example, *man*.

Oral Practice 1:   First, with your classmates, find the differences in the three men's work spaces. Look at desk drawers, wastebaskets, picture frames, plants, and chairs. Then take turns telling what one of the three men is doing. Identify the man you are referring to with a ***whose*** clause. Try to identify each man in all the ways possible using the picture. Example:

The man whose wastebasket is full is knocking on the boss's door.

Written Practice 1:   Rewrite, changing the sentences in parentheses into adjective clauses.

1.   That is the woman. (We saw her picture in the paper yesterday.)
2.   She has formed a political group. (Its philosophy is very conservative.)
3.   Even people (Their beliefs are different from hers.) praise her for her honesty.
4.   Everyone profited from the seminar, even students. (Their minds were elsewhere.)
5.   Everyone thinks Adam is a great lawyer, especially clients. (He has won their cases.)

19.2 Nonrestrictive Adjective Clauses		
Complete these model sentences.	Check.	Complete these rules.
a. Harry, _____ girlfriend just left him for another man, has no picture in his picture frame.	whose	In sentence **a**, we identify the person with the empty picture frame by giving his name. We are *not* identifying the person with the _____ clause. The name for adjective clauses which are not used to identify persons or things is **nonrestrictive adjective clauses.** They are set off from the rest of the sentence with _____. Nonrestrictive adjective clauses are used more often in writing than in speaking.
b. Dick, _____ was looking out the window, is now watering his plant. Harry, _____ the boss likes best, may get a promotion this year.	who whom	In sentences **b**, we again identify the people by giving _____ _____. In nonrestrictive adjective clauses, the subject relative pronoun for people is always _____. The object relative pronoun for people is _____. Do not use the relative pronoun *that* or leave out the relative pronoun in nonrestrictive adjective clauses.
c. Dick's plant, _____ he usually forgets to water, probably won't survive.	which	In sentence **c**, we identify the plant we are talking about by telling to whom it _____. In nonrestrictive adjective clauses, the relative pronoun for things is _____. Again, we normally do not use the relative pronoun _____ or leave out the relative pronoun.

Oral Practice 2A: Think of two facts about a classmate. Jot them down. Then underline the fact that you consider the most important or the most interesting. Example:

> *Ingrid is in my English class.*
> <u>*She is a member of the cross-country team.*</u>

Now express those ideas in a single sentence. The underlined sentence should be the main clause. The other idea should be in the adjective clause. Example:

> *Ingrid, who is in my English class, is a member of the cross-country team.*

Oral Practice 2B: Tell the class something about the last person you borrowed something from. Be sure to tell what you borrowed. Example:

> *Andy, whose car I borrowed, is a golf fanatic.*

Written Practice 2A: Combine these pairs of sentences, changing the sentences in parentheses into adjective clauses. Notice that they are **nonrestrictive** adjective clauses.

1.   Our dog barked furiously. (It was too excited to be calmed.)
2.   You should talk to Mr. Worth. (He advises foreign students.)
3.   It takes 88 days for Mercury to go around the sun. (Mercury is 36 million miles from the sun.)
4.   (Christopher Columbus made four voyages to the new world.) Christopher Columbus discovered Martinique on his final trip.
5.   This area of the house will be converted into a studio. (I have never liked this area.)
6.   Marjorie works at a local bank. (Her hobbies include skiing and fishing.)

Written Practice 2B: Add commas to these sentences wherever they are needed. *Some sentences may not need any commas.*

1.   My father who is an honest man works very hard.
2.   Anyone who wants to go on this trip should meet the bus here at 9 A.M.
3.   People hardly worry anymore about polio which killed and crippled many children and adults in the first half of this century.
4.   There are many diseases which have been practically eliminated.
5.   Jackson Burroughs who is a very famous sculptor made this statue.
6.   My English structure teacher who usually demands a lot of homework gave a very short assignment for this weekend.

19.3 *The . . . of Which/Whom*		
Complete these model sentences.	Check.	Complete these rules.
a. Tom, Dick, and Harry work for a large company, the president _____ _____ is their father. **The company, the name _____ _____ is Peterson and Sons, does accounting work for many small firms.**	of which of which	According to Rule Builder 19.1, we use the relative pronoun *whose* more often for _____ than for things. For things, a more common structure is: _____ + *noun* + *of* + _____ This structure usually occurs in **nonrestrictive adjective clauses**.
b. These firms, _____ largest _____ _____ has only 10 employees, cannot afford to hire their own full-time accountant. **Mr. Peterson has three sons, _____ oldest _____ _____ is Tom.**	the, of which the of whom	Another common adjective clause structure in formal English is: _____ + **superlative** + _____ + *which/whom*. If *whom* or *which* refers to only two persons or things, the **comparative** form should be used after *the*. Example: **He has two brothers, *the older* of whom is in college.**

Oral Practice 3A: Tell the class where you are from—country, state, province, and so on— and mention what the capital is in an adjective clause. Example:

> *I am from Canada, the capital of which is Ottawa.*

If everyone in class is from the same place, you can mention places you have visited or would like to visit.

Oral Practice 3B: Tell the class the name of your favorite novel or a novel that you have read recently. Mention the name of the author in an adjective clause. Example:

> *My favorite novel is One Flew over the Cuckoo's Nest, the author of which is Ken Kesey.*

Oral Practice 3C: Do you have more than one brother, sister, cousin, or roommate? Tell how many you have; then—in an adjective clause—give some additional information about the oldest and the youngest. Remember that if there are only two, use *older* and *younger*. Example:

> *I have two sisters, the younger of whom still lives with our parents.*

Written Practice 3A: Complete these sentences.

1. (Put the name of your country in the first blank.)

    I am from _____, _____ capital _____

    _____.

2. My favorite novel is _____, _____ author

    _____.

3. Dick, in the cartoon accompanying Rule Builders 19.1 and 19.2, has two brothers,

    _____ older _____

    _____.

4. I am taking _____ courses, _____ difficult _____

    _____.

5. In my English class there are _____ women, _____ youngest _____

    _____.

Written Practice 3B: Finish sentence B. It should have about the same meaning as sentence A.

1. A.   This part of the book has five chapters. The longest of these is on definite determin-

        ers.

    B.   This part of the book has five chapters, the _____

        _____.

2. A.   Halloween is now mainly an evening of fun for children. Its origin was religious.

    B.   Halloween, the _____, is now mainly

        an evening of fun for children.

3. A.   The earth has one natural satellite, the moon. Its radius is about 1,740 kilometers.

    B.   The earth's one natural satellite is the moon, _____ which

        is about 1,740 kilometers.

4. A.   Since 1900 Florida has been hit by several hurricanes. The most intense struck in

        1919.

    B.   Since 1900 Florida has been hit by several hurricanes, _____

        _____.

19.4 Adjective Clauses Which Begin with Quantity Expressions		
Complete these model sentences.	Check.	Complete these rules
a. In the office there are three **wastebaskets, one _____ _____ is full.**	of which	An adjective clause can begin with a quantity expression. Just as we can say, ''one of them,'' we can say, ''one of which.'' The quantity expression is followed by the preposition _____ and a relative pronoun. In this structure, the relative pronoun for things is always _____.
b. Three accountants, all _____ **_____ enjoy their jobs, work in this office.**	of whom	In this structure, the relative pronoun for people is always _____. Some of the quantity expressions which are used in this structure are numbers (_____, *two*, *three*, and so on.), *some*, *much*, *many*, *both*, _____, and so on.

Oral Practice 4A: Write down something that two or more classmates have in common. Then write down something that is true for one or some, but not all, of these people. Example:

> *There are three students from China.*
> *Two of them are graduate students.*

Combine these sentences into one sentence, making the second an adjective clause. Example:

> *In this class, there are three students from China, two of whom are graduate students.*

Oral Practice 4B: Think of two things that you have of the same kind. Mention the two things, adding a detail about one of them. Example:

> *I have two cats, one of which is very ferocious.*

Written Practice 4:   Combine these sentences, replacing the underlined words with relative pronouns.

1.   The Hendersons' cats are still very playful. All of <u>them</u> are over 10 years old.
2.   Mrs. Jones and Mrs. Dempsey are excellent players. Both of <u>them</u> belong to a tennis club.
3.   Walid has four classes. He finds two of <u>them</u> very interesting.
4.   Sam has three part-time jobs. He hates two of <u>them</u>.
5.   Carlson delivers mail to hundreds of houses. Only nine of <u>them</u> have vicious dogs.
6.   The university has many computers. Most of <u>them</u> are located in the math building.

19.5 Chapter Check: Finish sentence B with an adjective clause so that it has about the same meaning as sentence A. Be very careful about punctuation. *You will need commas in some of your sentences.* If you are unsure of an answer, check the indicated model sentences and rule.

1. A. Chicken pox is usually a mild disease. It strikes millions of people each year.

    Chicken pox _____

    _____ is usually a mild disease.   [19.2c]

2. A. But it is life-threatening to children with leukemia, because their immune systems

    are suppressed.

    B. But it is life-threatening to children _____ immune systems are sup-

    pressed because of leukemia.   [19.1a]

3. A. A new vaccine was recently tested in Philadelphia. Japanese researchers

    developed it.

    B. A new vaccine _____ was

    recently tested in Philadelphia.   [19.2c]

4. A. It was given to 467 healthy children. None of them contracted the disease during

    the nine-month follow-up period.

    B. It was given to 467 healthy children, none _____

    _____ during the nine-month follow-up period.   [19.4b]

5. A. The Japanese scientists were quite pleased with the results. They had been working

    on the vaccine for several years.

    B. The Japanese scientists _____

    _____ were quite pleased with the results.   [19.2b]

6. A. The results are good news for parents of leukemia victims.

    B. The results are good news for people _____ children are victims of

    leukemia.   [19.1a]

7. A. The Larsen Appliance Store has a wide variety of washing machines. The smallest

    of these is the new compact model.

    B. The Larsen Appliance Store has a wide variety of washing machines, the

    _____.   [19.3b]

8. A. Our new compact model is on sale through July 31st. It is only 24 inches wide.

    B. Our new compact model _____

    is on sale through July 31st.   [19.2c]

9. A. This is the perfect machine for people who have small apartments.

    B. This is the perfect machine for people whose _____

    _____.   [19.1a]

10.   A.   This washer has five temperature combinations. One of them is perfect for every

kind of fabric.

B.   This washer has five temperature combinations, one _____

_____.   [19.4a]

11.   A.   My father has offered me a job when I graduate. He owns a large business.

B.   My father _____ has

offered me a job when I graduate.   [19.2b]

12.   A.   Over 700 people were interviewed in the survey. Most of them lived inside the city

limits.

B.   Over 700 people _____

_____ were interviewed in the survey.   [19.4b]

13.   A.   Carol will soon have her hands full. Her doctor has just told her she is going to

have twins.

B.   Carol _____

_____ will soon have her hands full.   [19.1a, 19.2a]

19.6 Warm-up: Everyone in class should describe one of his or her possessions. Example:

My car is brown.

The teacher will make a list on the board of these possessions. Example:

brown car

After the list is complete, try to remember the owner of each thing. Check your memory by asking questions or making statements with ***whose*** clauses. Example:

Aren't you the person whose car is brown?
Walid is the person whose car is brown.

19.7 Communication: Think of a person in the class. On a piece of paper, write down three or four sentences that begin "His . . ." or "Her . . ." Example:

Her native language is Arabic.

When it's your turn, make a statement about the person that contains a ***whose*** clause. Example:

I'm thinking of a person whose native language is Arabic.

Call on a classmate to make a guess. If your classmate does not guess the right person, give another clue, again beginning, "I'm thinking of a person whose . . ." After your classmate has figured out who you were thinking of, he or she will tell the class something about another person, and the game will continue.

19.8 Communication: For this activity, you should bring some photographs to class. They can be pictures either of members of your family or of places you have been to.

Show your pictures to your classmates. If you have pictures of your family, identify each person by name, and then tell your classmates something else about him or her. Begin with ***this is.*** Example:

This is my Uncle Samuel, who teaches high school.

If you have pictures of different places you have visited, identify each place by name or description, and then tell your classmates what you did there. Begin each description with ***this is.*** Example:

This is Lindsborg, Kansas, where we visited some Swedish crafts shops.

19.9 Sentence Completion: Complete these sentences.

1.   This semester I am taking _____ courses, one of which _____

        _____.

2.   This semester I bought _____ textbooks, most _____.

3.   In this class there are _____ students, _____ are from _____.

4.   I own many _____, several _____.

5.   I have _____ cousins, _____ of _____ are in high school now.

6.   My native country has _____ important natural resources, one _____

        _____.

19.10 Sentence Writing: Tell some interesting facts about three of your classmates and friends. Give some additional information about each person in a nonrestrictive adjective clause. Try to use ***whose*** in at least one of your sentences. Example:

Mieko Tanaka, whose brother is a good friend of mine, recently won a scholarship to Stanford University.

19.11 Paragraph Writing: In this exercise you will write another paragraph about Amsterdam, Missouri (chapter 18, 18.14 Paragraph Writing). This paragraph will be about the year 1927 in that town. The title of the paragraph is "**A Memorable Year in Amsterdam, Missouri.**"

On the following page is the information that should be included in the paragraph. For each building mentioned, there is one piece of information that is directly related to the topic—the year 1927—and a piece of additional information. The information that supports the topic should be in the main clause, and the additional information should be in a **nonrestrictive clause**. The first step is to *circle* the information that will be in the main clause of each sentence.

Bank	All of the people in town kept their money in it.	It was held up six times in that year.
Post Office	It was rebuilt in 1927.	It burned down the previous year.
Drugstore	It had been built in 1850.	It established the first soda fountain in town that year.
Barber Shop	It raised its price for a haircut from 25 to 30 cents.	It is next to the post office.
Factory	It had begun making fishing equipment just five years before.	In 1927 it was expanded to double its original size.
Grocery Store	It installed its first refrigerated case in 1927.	The name of this store has changed many times over the years.

Now complete the following paragraph. Remember to put the circled information in the main clause in each sentence. Put the additional information in an adjective clause.

A Memorable Year in Amsterdam, Missouri

Nineteen twenty-seven was a very memorable year in the small town of Amsterdam, Missouri. The bank, in which all the people in town kept their money, was held up six times in that year. The post office, which had burned down . . .

19.12 Paragraph Writing: The following paragraph sounds rather awkward because almost all of the sentences are simple; there is not much variety in the kinds of sentences used. Rewrite the paragraph, trying to improve it by turning some of the sentences into adjective clauses and phrases.

Ed's Bait and Tackle Shop has stood on the same spot for 39 years. It is a dirty little building. Its windows have been cracked by rocks. Ed thinks the rocks were thrown by neighborhood kids. All of the kids around are afraid of Ed. Ed is a big fellow. He has enormous hands and a rough voice. His voice can be heard for blocks when he is angry. But Ed doesn't get angry very often. His nature is usually mild. Sometimes he gets a little annoyed with his customers. Some of them ask very silly questions about fishing. Recently, Ed received a letter. The letter was from the city commission. The city commission told him that they had heard some complaints. The complaints said that the bait in his shop made the neighborhood smell awful.

19.13 Reflecting: Read the next episode of the mystery story. Then check it for adjective clauses. Some of these clauses are set off with commas; others are not. Do you understand why? Examine the structure of the ***whose*** clauses.

At the end of two hours' telephoning, I had talked with 14 women, all of whose voices I taped. Later I wanted to play the tape for Mrs. Miller to see if she could recognize the woman whose voice she had heard. I dialed her number, which was busy. Maybe she was getting another threatening phone call.

Then I called Lieutenant Farmer, who was in his office.

"Somebody called Deanne Miller," I told him. "The caller, who was a woman, asked where Deanne was hiding her husband."

"That's interesting," Farmer said. "Why would Carl Miller want to hide?"

"That's the same question that occurred to me," I said. "Maybe he wants to hide because somebody who isn't very nice wants to find him."

"But who is mad at Miller?"

"Miller seemed to think Dr. Weber didn't do anything wrong," I said. "Miller's boss said he hadn't found any evidence against the doctor. That could have made the guy who wanted to sue Weber angry."

"Troy Daniels," Farmer said.

"Yes," I said. "Miller's report would mean that Weber's insurance company wouldn't give Troy Daniels any money. Usually in malpractice cases there's a lot of money involved—maybe a couple of million dollars. That could make anybody upset."

"Daniels is married."

"Then his wife could have been the woman who called Mrs. Miller," I said. "I think I will go see the Danielses."

19.14 Real-World Work

THINK/PRACTICE

As you are walking along today, make sentences like these about groups of things or people that you see. Practice making adjective clauses that begin with superlatives.

I see three young men, the tallest of whom is wearing a blue shirt.
I see many cars, the most expensive of which is a new Mercedes.

LOOK/LISTEN

1. **Nonrestrictive adjective clauses** are used much more in writing than they are in speaking. Look at several paragraphs in today's newspaper, a magazine article, a textbook you are using, or a short story or novel you are reading. Look for adjective clauses that are set off with commas. Do these give additional information about something in the main clause? Do you understand why the author chose to put these particular pieces of information in adjective clauses?

2. Here is a good exercise you can do with the nonrestrictive sentences that you found. Rewrite some of the sentences, turning the adjective clauses into separate sentences. (Is that the way you would probably give the information if you were speaking?) Then without looking at the original sentences, try to change your separate sentences back into single sentences with nonrestrictive adjective clauses. Finally, check what you have written.

USE

1. When you are showing someone pictures of your home and family, you have a chance to use **nonrestrictive adjective clauses.** Examples:

   That is my Uncle Josef, who works as a . . .
   This is a picture of my family's house, which sits on a little hill near . . .

2. Look at a composition that you have written. Can you find any nonrestrictive adjective clauses? If not, it could mean that you do not provide interesting additional information about the people or things you mention. Or it could mean that you put that additional information in separate sentences. Use what you have learned in this chapter to make your writing more interesting and effective.

20

Noun Phrase Review II

20.1 Part Four Check: Write *the* in the blanks wherever it is necessary. *Some of the blanks should remain empty.* If you are unsure of an answer, check the indicated model sentence and rule.

1. I think my country has one of _____ most pleasant climates in _____
   world. [17.5a, 17.3a]

2. _____ unit that we finished yesterday was very difficult. [17.3b]

3. _____ problem of _____ pollution must be solved; otherwise, _____ life will
   become very unpleasant. [17.3b, 17.3e]

4. I didn't understand _____ first problem of the assignment, but all _____ others were
   easy. [17.3b,17.4b]

20.2 Part Four Check: Complete these sentences.

1. The island of Greenland is 840,000 square miles in area; the area of Manhattan Island is
   22 square miles. Greenland is _____ larger _____
   Manhattan. [16.1a]

2. Lake Huron has an area of 23,010 square miles; Lake Michigan is 22,178 square miles in
   area. Lake Michigan is almost _____ Lake
   Huron. [16.3a]

3. The man to _____ the President was speaking is the Secretary of

    State.   [18.3a]

4. I think this is the dorm _____ Hugo lives in.   [18.4]

20.3 Part Four Check: Finish sentence B so that it has about the same meaning as
sentence A.

1. A. That restaurant is not nearly as good as this one.

    B. This restaurant is much _____

        that one.   [16.1d]

2. A. Is he the professor who taught our physics course last semester?

    B. Is he the professor _____ physics course we took last

        semester?   [19.1c]

3. A. I didn't care for the music he was listening to.

    B. I didn't care much for the music to _____

        _____.   [18.2b]

4. A. Thousands of people became ill. Most of them were small children.

    B. Thousands of people _____

        _____ became ill.   [19.4b]

5. A. Tennessee is only slightly larger than Virginia.

    B. _____ is almost as _____.   [16.3a]

6. A. Those are our children.

    B. Those children are _____.   [17.1d]

7. A. This is the town my wife and I were married in.

    B. This is the town _____ were married.   [18.4]

8. A. I would like to study with Professor Brown.

    B. Professor Brown is a teacher I would _____.   [18.3b]

9. A. Peter is extremely clever. As a result, he finished college in three years.

    B. Peter is _____ that he finished college in three

        years.   [16.7a]

10. A. Enrique's mother is coming to the U.S. this fall. She is a famous singer in Costa

        Rica.

    B. Enrique's mother _____

        is coming to the U.S. this fall.   [19.2b]

11. A. Arizona is hot, but it is not as humid as Kansas.

    B. Arizona is hot, but it is _____ than Kansas.   [16.1c]

12. A. The man Mr. Peterson spoke to yesterday is the assistant director.

B. The man to _____ is the assistant

director.   [18.3a]

20.4 Part Four Check: Complete these sentences about the three women pictured.

1. One of the _____ is much _____ than _____ other

two.   [16.1a, 17.4b]

2. The one _____ is sitting next to the window is sleeping.   [18.1a]

Now change the adjective clause into a phrase.

The one _____ is sleeping.   [18.1c]

3. The one _____ baby is crying seems _____ exhausted

_____ the woman by the window.   [19.1a,16.1e]

4. Her baby does not seem _____ content _____ other one.   [16.3b,17.4a]

5. The woman _____ is in the middle is wearing a hat.   [18.1a]

Now reduce the adjective clause to a phrase.

The woman _____ is wearing a hat.   [18.1c]

20.5 Sentence Writing: Each year the city holds a contest and gives an award to the most wonderful grandmother in the city. This year Mrs. Bates won. Following the examples given, describe her wonderful qualities and compare her to the other contestants. Write five sentences with each of these adjectives:

kind
patient
wise

Example for the adjective **generous:**

a. Mrs. Bates is very generous.
b. She is more generous than the other contestants.
c. They are not as generous as she is.
d. She is so generous she gives lots of money to charities.
e. Mrs. Bates is the most generous grandmother in town.

20.6 Sentence Writing: Think of a result or consequence of the facts given in these sentences. Then expand each sentence into a **so . . . that** sentence. Then restate the idea with **such . . . that**. Example:

> *The line in front of the movie theater was long.*
> *The line in front of the movie theater was so long that we had to wait an hour for a ticket.*
> *There was such a long line in front of the movie theater that we had to wait an hour for a ticket.*

1. The theater was crowded.
2. The people sitting behind us talked loudly.
3. The popcorn tasted salty.
4. The seats were comfortable.
5. The movie was good.

20.7 Sentence Writing: If your home country is not the United States, compare the prices of different kinds of food here and at home. Or compare the food prices of any two places that you are familiar with. Write at least five sentences. Examples:

> *A steak costs about half as much here as in my home town.*
> *A pound of coffee is much more expensive here.*

20.8 Paragraph Writing: Rewrite the following paragraph. Improve it by turning some of the simple sentences into adjective clauses.

> Yesterday on my way to work I saw a man. He was sitting at a bus stop. He was holding an umbrella. In his lap there was a sack. The sack was full of groceries. On the bench next to him were two packages. One of them was very large. After a few minutes, a bus came, but it didn't stop for him. The bus was very crowded. The man stood up and started walking. He had a disgusted look on his face.

20.9 Paragraph Writing: The following paragraph doesn't have many details.

> Stan is a member of a jazz quartet. The group is going to make a record soon. They hope the record will sell well. The performers want to become full-time professionals.

Rewrite the paragraph. To each of the four sentences, add a nonrestrictive adjective clause which answers one of these questions:

1. How do you know Stan?
2. Where does the group usually play?
3. When will the record be produced?
4. What instruments do they play?

You might begin this way:

> *Stan, whom I met in a bar one night, . . .*

20.10 Letter Writing: You have just received a letter from your cousin saying that she and her family are going to come to town to visit you toward the end of next month. You don't really want them to visit. Write a polite letter to your cousin explaining why they should consider not coming. Think of a better place for your cousin's family to visit, and try to convince them to go there instead by comparing this town with the other place you suggest.

20.11 Reflecting: Read the next episode of the mystery story. Then go back and mark all of the nouns. Look at the various things that go with each noun to make a noun phrase—articles, quantifiers, adjectives, adjective phrases, and adjective clauses. There are four adjective clauses which are set off from the main clause with commas. Do you understand why these clauses are nonrestrictive?

> When I finished talking to Lieutenant Farmer, I dialed the number of Troy Daniels, who wasn't home. His wife answered the phone. I added her voice to my collection of tape-recorded voices, which already filled up one side of a cassette.
>
> She told me I could come over when I said I was investigating her husband's case. I went out to my green Chevrolet, which was illegally parked by a fire hydrant. So far there was no parking ticket. This was my lucky day. Maybe I would find Carl Miller by the end of the day.
>
> I drove out to the Danielses' place. They owned a medium-large house with a yard that would take five hours to mow. Big houses are nice because there are plenty of places to park in front. I walked up to the front door. When I rang the bell, which played a little song, a big dog started barking.
>
> Mrs. Daniels came to the door. She was a pretty black woman in her mid-thirties. She invited me in. I looked around for the dog and then stepped inside.

21

More Present and Future Time

REVIEW

The following passage concerns the present and the future. Read it and then write the proper form of each verb in the blank.

Every day Stan (*dream*) _____ of becoming a famous saxophone

player in a great jazz band. He (*know*) _____ that to reach this goal he

(*must*) _____ (*spend*) _____ several hours practicing daily. However, his life

(*be*) _____ so hectic right now that he (*can + not*) _____ (*find*) _____

enough time to play the saxophone. His friends (*be*) _____ a little concerned about what

(*happen*) _____ if Stan (*achieve + not*) _____

_____ his goal.

Stan (*want*) _____ to get his life a little more organized. As soon as he (*finish*)

_____ school, he (*intend*) _____ to get a part-time job so that he (*can*)

_____ (*spend*) _____ the rest of his time practicing.

PREVIEW

If you were able to write the correct forms in the preceding passage, you have learned a great deal about verbs that refer to the present and the future. But there is more to learn. Try this pretest.

Fill in the blanks with the correct form of the verbs given.

1. Stan started practicing at 10:00 P.M.; it's 11:00 P.M. now, and he is still playing. He (*play*) _____ for one hour.

2. In an hour, it will be midnight. By that time Stan (*play*) _____ _____ for two hours.

3. Stan is a musician. If Stan (*be* + *not*) _____ a musician, he (*be* + *probably*) _____ a school teacher.

4. Sometimes Stan wishes that he (*have*) _____ more time to practice.

Notice the items that you had trouble with. You will study these structures in this chapter.

21.1 Present Perfect Progressive and Present Perfect with Action Verbs		
Complete these model sentences.	Check.	Complete these rules.
a. Right now I (*do*) _____ _____ **my English homework.**	am doing	**Review:** Verbs that can be used to tell what is happening are called **action verbs**. An example is _____. When you are talking about "right now," put an action verb into the present _____ tense.
b. I have _____ _____ **my English homework since** _____ **o'clock. In other words, I** _____ _____ _____ **my English homework for** _____ **minutes.**	been doing have been doing	When these verbs are used to answer the question "how long" about something that is happening, we use the **present perfect progressive**: *have/has* + _____ + **the** _____ **form** We can indicate how long something has been going on by telling when the starting point was. The word used before the starting point is _____. We can also simply tell the length of time that something has been happening. The preposition used before the length of time is _____.

21.1 Present Perfect Progressive and Present Perfect with Action Verbs (Continued)		
c. I (*work*) _____ _____ _____ **very hard on my English recently.**	have been working	We also use the present perfect progressive to tell what has been going on recently. A common way to begin a conversation is to ask. ''What have you been _____ lately?''
d. Tank has several bad habits; for example, he (*smoke*) _____ .	smokes	**Review:** When we use action verbs to refer to present *habitual* actions, we use the _____ _____ tense.
e. Tank _____ _____ **since he was 13 years old.**	has smoked or has been smoking	To tell how long someone has done something habitually, we usually use the simple present perfect: ***has/have*** + **the** _____ **participle** We can also use the present perfect progressive.

Oral Practice 1A: Find out what your classmates have been doing recently.

Oral Practice 1B: Think of three things that are happening in this classroom, this town, this region, or in the world now. Report the event and tell how long it has been going on. Example:

>   *It's raining right now.*
>   *It has been raining since yesterday afternoon.*

Oral Practice 1C: Tell your classmates something that you do as a hobby. Tell how long you have done this. Example:

>   *I collect stamps.*
>   *I have collected stamps for over 10 years.*

Oral Practice 1D: Mention a habit that you used to have but don't have anymore. Tell how long you have *not* done this. Example:

>   *I used to smoke, but I don't smoke anymore.*
>   *I haven't smoked for nine months.*

Written Practice 1A: Complete these sentences.

1.   Stan (*play*) _____ the saxophone since he was 10.
2.   The Joneses (*think*) _____ about looking for

   another place since their first week in their apartment.

3.   I (*study*) _____ English for _____.

4.   Irma's brother (*read*) _____ poetry _____ he was very young.

5.   Some people in the audience are about to fall asleep. The speaker (*talk*)

_____ for over two hours.

Written Practice 1B: Finish sentence B. It should have about the same meaning as sentence A.

1.   A.   Mr. Robbins is raking leaves in his yard. He started two hours ago.

     B.   Mr. Robbins _____

     _____ two hours.

2.   A.   The snow began to fall at six this morning, and it hasn't stopped.

     B.   The snow has _____ six this morning.

3.   A.   My friend Pat is staying with me. He arrived almost a week ago.

     B.   My friend Pat _____

     almost a week.

4.   A.   Ralph started working on his dissertation nearly four years ago, and he hasn't

     finished yet.

     B.   Ralph _____

     nearly four years.

5.   A.   People began streaming into the stadium at 11 A.M.; they're still coming.

     B.   People _____ 11 this morning.

21.2 Present Perfect with Stative Verbs to Tell How Long		
Complete this model sentence.	Check.	Complete these rules.
Stretch (*know*) _____ _____ **Tank since they were in high school.**	has known	Verbs that refer to situations rather than events—for example, _____—are called **stative verbs**. These verbs don't normally go into the progressive. To answer the question ''how long'' concerning a present state, we use the simple present perfect: _____ / _____ + **the** _____ **participle**

Oral Practice 2A: Mention to your classmates something special that you have. Then tell them how long you have had it.

Oral Practice 2B: Does anyone you know have an interesting job or profession? How long has he or she had that job? Example:

My brother-in-law has been a boxing referee for many years.

Oral Practice 2C: Mention something that you have liked, wanted, or needed for some time. Example:

I have wanted a computer for years.

Written Practice 2:   Complete these sentences.

1. Mr. and Ms. Jones (*know*) _____ each other _____ 20 years.

2. Stan (*be*) _____ in a bad mood _____ several days now.

3. _____ (*be*) _____ an independent country since _____.

4. I (*trust + not*) _____

     since _____.

5. I (*have*) _____ this book since _____.

6. _____ and _____ (*be*) _____ roommates for _____.

7. I (*like*) _____ since I _____.

8. I (*see + not*) _____ since _____.

21.3 The Future Perfect		
Complete these model sentences.	Check.	Complete these rules.
a. It's now 6:00 P.M. Ms. Jones is work-ing late tonight; she won't be home until 8:30. Mr. Jones has a meeting at 8:00, so by the time Ms. Jones gets **home, Mr. Jones _____** **_____ already left.**	will have	The present perfect is used to show that an action has been completed at some time before now. If we are thinking about some point in the future and want to show that something will be completed before this future time, we can use the **future perfect**. The structure is: *will* + _____ + **the** _____ **participle**
b. Ms. Jones is working on a long re-port. **She started working on it at 1:00 P.M.** **She won't be finished by 7:00 P.M.. By** **that time she _____** **_____ _____ working** **on it for six hours.**	will have been	If an action will be in progress at some future time, we can also talk about how long it will have been going on with the **future perfect progressive**. The structure is: _____ + _____ + _____ + **the -*ing* form**

Oral Practice 3A: Think of a time in the future. Think of something that will be true for you in the future. Tell how long this will have been true by then. Example:

In the year 2000, I will have been married for 10 years.
In the year 2010, I will have been working in my father's company for at least 15 years.

Oral Practice 3B: By the year 2000, what will have already happened in your life?

Written Practice 3:   Complete these sentences.

1. It's 10:00 P.M., and Stan has just started practicing his saxophone. By the time the Joneses finally fall asleep at 11:30, Stan _____ an hour and a half.

2. Oscar asked Sadie out for a date for the first time nine months ago, and they are still going out. In three months, they _____ a year.

3. In a week, we _____ already finished this chapter.

4. By the time I graduate in _____, I _____ studying at this school for _____.

5. I will have accomplished many things by the end of this century. For example, I will have _____ and _____. However, I will probably not _____.

Amsterdam, Mo. Post Office				
	Jan	Feb	Mar	Apr
LETTERS DELIVERED	107	98	104	93
PACKAGES DELIVERED	10	8	12	13
STAMPS PURCHASED	193	241	169	254
POSTCARDS PURCHASED	73	77	75	72

(See page 272, Rule Builder 21.4)

21.4 Passive Sentences		
Pretend that it is May 1 today. Refer to the preceding chart to complete these model sentences.	Check.	Complete these rules.
a. Usually about 100 letters _____ **delivered every** **month.**	are	Most of the time, the subject of a sentence performs the action of a verb; that is, the subject *does* something. Sentences like this are in the **active voice**. But as you saw in Rule Builder 8.7, sometimes the subjects of sentences *receive* the action of the verb; that is, they are in the **passive voice**. The structure for the **present tense** in the **passive voice** is: *am/is/are* + **the** _____ **participle**
b. In March _____ **stamps** _____ **purchased.**	169 were	Sentence **b** is also in the passive voice, but it is in the _____ _____ tense. The structure is: *was/* _____ + **the** _____ _____
c. Since January 1, _____ **packages** _____ _____ **delivered.**	43 have been	Sentence **c** is in the present _____ tense. The passive structure is: _____ */has* + _____ + **the** _____ **participle**
d. If May is a normal month, about 75 **postcards** _____ _____ **purchased.**	will be	*Will* is a _____ verb. When modals are used in the passive voice, the structure is: **modal** + _____ + **the** _____ _____

Oral Practice 4: The following chart provides information about the bank in Amsterdam, Mo. Using this chart and the post office chart, ask your classmates questions about the past, present, and future transactions at the Amsterdam post office and bank.

Amsterdam, Mo. Bank				
Transactions	Jan	Feb	Mar	Apr
ACCOUNTS OPENED	10	8	9	9
ACCOUNTS CLOSED	6	8	7	4
LOANS MADE	21	31	20	24
LOANS TURNED DOWN	13	12	16	13
CHECKS DEPOSITED	129	114	136	141
CHECKS CASHED	216	198	205	231
AMOUNT OF INTEREST GIVEN	$946	$912	$898	$994

Written Practice 4A: Referring to the chart which provides information about the bank in Amsterdam, Mo., complete these sentences.

1. In January _____ accounts _____.

2. In an average month, about 24 loans _____.

3. Since January 1, _____ accounts _____ closed.

4. If May is an average month, about _____ checks _____.

Written Practice 4B: Write six more passive sentences about Amsterdam bank transactions.

21.5 Unreal Conditional Sentences: Present and Future		
Complete these model sentences.	Check.	Complete these rules.
a. Tank makes poor grades, so the football coach always worries about him. If Tank _____ better grades, his coach would not worry so much.	made	In chapters 7 and 9 we used adverb clauses beginning with *if* to refer to conditions that are sometimes true or that might be true in the future. We can also use *if* clauses to describe conditions that are untrue or very doubtful. The verb in such *if* clauses is in a _____ tense—simple past or past progressive—even though it refers to the present or the future. The use of the past tense form shows that the situation is unreal or doubtful.
b. If Tank _____ smarter, he would not have so much trouble with his classes.	were	When the verb in the unreal *if* clause is *be*, we use the form _____ even when the subject is singular.
c. If Tank _____ to try harder next semester, he might not flunk out of school.	were	Both future and present unreal conditions are expressed with the past tense. To make it clear that a condition is future, use this structure: _____ + **infinitive**
d. If Tank were skinnier, he _____ not be such a good football player. Tank is in training, so he can't eat whatever he wants. If Tank _____ not in training, he _____ eat whatever he wanted.	would were could	The main clause in an *if* sentence is often called the **result** clause; it tells what the result would be if the unreal condition were actually true. In these clauses we use a past form of a _____ verb, such as ***would*** or _____. REMEMBER: A verb after a modal is always in the _____ form.

Oral Practice 5A: Tell how things would or might be different now if you were not a student.

Oral Practice 5B: This is surely impossible, but, just for fun, tell what would happen if you were to flunk out of school.

Written Practice 5:   Complete these sentences.

1. If Stretch _____ shorter, he _____ such a good basketball player.

2. If Stretch weighed more, _____ play football, too.

3. If Tank _____ smarter, he _____ fail his courses.

4. If Tank _____ a lot taller, _____.

5. If Tank _____, his father wouldn't get so angry at him.

6. If Stretch _____ to help Tank study for his next test, Tank _____ get a better grade.

7. If I had twice as much money as I do, _____.

8. I would feel better if _____.

9. Students would study harder if _____.

10. If I were to _____.

21.6 *Wish* versus Hope		
Complete these model sentences.	Check.	Complete these rules.
a. Mr. Jones is too busy. He wishes that _____ _____ **a little more free time.**	he had	We usually use the verb ***wish*** to talk about our fantasies—events or situations that are unreal or very unlikely but that we would like to be real. The verb in the noun clause is in a _____ tense form (simple past or past progressive), although the meaning may be present or future. Notice the similarity between these sentences and ***if*** clauses.
b. He wishes that his job _____ **get easier soon, but he knows it won't.**	would or could	We can use ***wish*** to express unrealistic desires for the future. In the noun clause we use the past forms of *will* or *can*, that is, _____ or _____.
c. He hopes that eventually _____ _____ _____ **a little more time.**	he will have or he has	If we think that an event or situation in the future has a real possibility of happening, we usually don't use the verb *wish*. Instead we use the verb _____. In the noun clause we don't use an ''unreal'' verb form. We can use a modal verb—_____ or ***can***—or the present tense.

Oral Practice 6:   Tell the class something you hope or wish for. Use an *if* sentence to explain the result of this hope or wish. For example, if you think you will be able to save money this semester:

> *I hope I can save some money this semester. If I save some money, I will be able to take a good trip in the summer.*

This is a real possibility.

If you think it's unlikely, however, say:

> *I wish I could save some money this semester. If I were to save some money, I would be able to take a good trip in the summer.*

This is an unlikely situation.

Written Practice 6A: Complete these sentences.

1.   Most people _____ that they had more money.

2.   All parents _____ that their children will live happy lives.

3.   I'm getting tired. I wish this movie _____ end soon.

4.   I enjoy being with Karl. I hope he _____ to the party tomorrow.

5.   I wish you _____ change your mind.

6.   Stan _____ that he will become a better saxophone player. He _____ that he were able to practice more.

7.   John wishes that he _____ a little more patience with his students. He hopes that he _____ learn to be more patient.

8.   I wish _____ come to your party, but I can't. When is the next party? I _____ I can make it to that one.

9.   I wish I _____ fly an airplane.

10.   The students hope they _____ on tomorrow's exam. They wish that they _____ a few more days to study.

Written Practice 6B: Finish sentence B. It should have about the same meaning as sentence A.

1.   A.   We are sorry you can't stay longer.

     B.   We wish _____.

2.   A.   They hope to get there before midnight.

     B.   They hope that _____.

3.   A.   Tank regrets that he doesn't have more friends.

     B.   Tank wishes _____.

4. A.   Nasser is sorry that he has to go to summer school in order to graduate.

    B.   Nasser wishes _____

    _____.

5. A.   Nasser hopes to find an air-conditioned apartment.

    B.   Nasser hopes that _____.

21.7 Chapter Check: Complete these sentences. If you are unsure of an answer, check the indicated model sentence and rule.

1. The team hopes that it _____ rain on the day of the game.   [21.6c]

2. Eduardo wishes that it _____ raining; he would like to be playing

    tennis.   [21.6b]

3. If it _____ to stop raining soon, Eduardo _____ still get in a tennis

    game before dark.   [21.5c&d]

4. Stretch _____ playing basketball since he was five years old.   [21.1b]

5. Oh, sure. I know Clarence. I _____ him for years.   [21.2]

6. If I _____ so tired, I would finish this homework tonight.   [21.5b]

7. No, Stretch doesn't hate tacos. If he hated tacos, he _____ eat-

    ing them right now.   [21.5d]

8. By the end of this year, Stan _____ spent more than $3,000 on

    music lessons.   [21.3a]

21.8 Chapter Check: Finish sentence B so that it has about the same meaning as sentence A.

1. A.   Someone stole the mayor's car last night.

    B.   The mayor's car _____.   [21.4b]

2. A.   The police have not found the car yet.

    B.   The car _____.   [21.4c]

3. A.   The mayor hopes that they will find it soon.

    B.   The mayor hopes that it _____.   [21.4d]

4. A.   It would be great to win the prize, but I don't think I will.

    B.   I wish I _____, but I probably won't.   [21.6b]

5. A.   I would jump for joy if I won the prize.

    B.   If I _____ to win the prize, I would jump for joy.   [21.5c]

6. A.   I would have to be taller to play basketball.

    B.   If I _____.   [21.5c&d]

7. A.   He hopes to graduate in May.

    B.   He hopes that he _____.   [21.6c]

8. A.   Some people have written angry letters to the newspaper about the incident.

    B.   Some angry letters _____ to the

         newspaper about the incident.   [21.4c]

9. A.   Unfortunately, it's late; otherwise, we could play another game.

    B.   If _____ so late, we could play another game.   [21.5b]

10. A.   I will learn a lot more English before the end of the semester.

    B.   By the end of the semester, I _____ learned a lot more English. [21.3a]

21.9 Warm-up: With your classmates, discuss what you would do if you suddenly received $50,000—perhaps from an unexpected inheritance or a winning lottery ticket.

21.10 Communication: Get together with a small group of your classmates. Work together on a "conditional chain" which you will then present orally to the rest of the class. The first step is to imagine a world without something that you consider important. Here are some possibilities:

A world without paper
A world without money
A world without war
A world without music
A world without electricity
A world without telephones
A world without computers
A world without automobiles

Your group can probably think of other possibilities. Tell your teacher what you have chosen before you continue.

Now make an *if* sentence beginning with *If there were no* or *If we had no*. The result of that condition then becomes the *if* clause in the next sentence, and so on. Example:

If we had no alarm clocks, we would sleep late every morning.
If we slept late every morning, we would miss early classes.
If we missed our early classes, we would fail those courses.
If we failed those courses . . .

Your group should try to make the best conditional chain in the class.

21.11 Paragraph Completion: In 18.13 Paragraph Writing, you worked on a paragraph about making wood into paper. The passive was used to describe the process. The passive is often used to describe research or industrial processes or procedures. Put the following steps in their appropriate place in the paragraph. The verbs should be in the passive voice. The first one has been done for you.

(1) *take logs to a mill*
(2) *take off the bark*
(3) *cut the wood into chips*

(4) *cook these chips with a chemical*
(5) *form the wet pulp into a sheet*
(6) *wind the finished paper onto a big roll*

There are many steps in making wood into paper. First, (1) _____ ***logs are taken to a mill*** where (2) _____ and (3) _____. Then (4) _____ until the wood fibers, or pulp, separate. On a bronze screen (5) _____ which goes between rollers that squeeze out some of the moisture. The sheet then passes over a series of heat rollers that dry it out. Finally (6) _____.

21.12 Paragraph Writing: Using 21.11 Paragraph Completion as a model, write a paragraph about a simple laboratory procedure or other research or industrial process that you are familiar with. If you cannot think of a process that you are familiar with, describe an everyday procedure that you know. Here are a few possibilities:

washing and drying clothes with coin-operated machines
making coffee with an automatic drip machine
bathing a baby
repairing a bicycle tire

Even if you are describing an everyday procedure, write the paragraph in the academic style, using the passive voice.

21.13 Sentence Writing: Mention three things that you know, understand, believe, remember, need, or own. Tell how long you have known this, understood this, and so on.

21.14 Paragraph Writing: Read the following paragraph.

Before you drive a car in Britain, you should learn some terms that are used differently in British English. Here are a few examples. A generator is called a *dynamo* in Britain, and a muffler is known as a *silencer*. The word *bonnet* is used by speakers of British English instead of the American English word *hood*. And, of course, the fuel that goes into British speakers' cars is referred to as *petrol* rather than *gas*.

1.   Reread the paragraph, underlining all of the passive verb constructions.
2.   Now write a paragraph for a *British* audience, explaining the difference between the following food terms. Use several passive verbs.

American English	British English
dessert	pudding
pudding	custard
custard	egg custard
jello	jelly
jelly	jam
cookie	(sweet) biscuit

Your paragraph may start something like this:

> Before you go to a restaurant in the U.S., you should know a few things about differences in food words used in the U.S. and Britain.

21.15 Paragraph Writing: Write a paragraph describing the activities that you might be involved in and the things which may be happening to you in five years.

21.16 Paragraph Writing: Write a paragraph entitled "My Fantasies." Mention three or four things that you wish were true for you. Then explain each of your wishes with a conditional sentence—an *if* sentence. Example:

> *I wish I lived in Paris. If I lived in Paris, I could spend hours in the Louvre every week.*

21.17 Reflecting: Read the next episode of the mystery story. Then examine the use of these structures: the present perfect progressive, the passive voice, unreal conditional sentences, and *wish* sentences.

> "If you wanted a cup of coffee, it wouldn't be any trouble," Mrs. Daniels offered.
>
> "That would be nice," I said. "I've been talking on the phone a lot today and I'm beat."
>
> The coffee was carried in on a blue enamel tray, and she set it on the coffee table between us. "Normally Troy is home by now," she explained. "But he's been working a lot of overtime. They've been talking about promoting someone, and I guess he wants to impress the boss. I wish he were home more."
>
> "I'm sure you can answer my questions," I said. I tasted the coffee. It wasn't as strong as I normally drink it, but you can't have everything. "Could you tell me about the lawsuit your husband is involved in?"
>
> "I wish he would forget about all of that," she said. "You can't raise the dead. But trying to change Troy's mind is like beating your head against a brick wall. He's sure that mistakes were made during the operation on his mother."
>
> "Why would he think that?" I asked.
>
> The big dog started barking in a bedroom or somewhere. Troy came in, and Mrs. Daniels introduced us.

21.18 Real-World Work

THINK/PRACTICE

1. If you enjoyed 21.10 Communication, make up some more conditional chains as you walk or ride along today.
2. Practice using the present perfect to tell how long something has been going on. Think of things that are true for you. Then tell yourself how long they have been true. Examples:

    I am studying English. I have been studying English for two years.
    I am in the U.S. I have been in the U.S. for three months.

LOOK/LISTEN

1. Find instructions in English for a board game that you know how to play. Read the instructions and look for sentences with a verb in the passive form. Ask yourself why these sentences are written in the passive rather than the active voice.
2. Look at an instruction manual for any piece of equipment you own. Check for passive verbs. Think about why the passive voice is used.
3. Newspapers are another good source of passives.

USE

1. A situation that often occurs in conversations with friends is that we want to talk about our fantasies—things that aren't true but that we wish were true. Remember that in English, when we discuss unreal or hypothetical things, we use the past tenses. Examples:

    I wish I <u>were lying</u> on the beach right now.
    Weekends <u>would</u> be a lot more fun if I <u>had</u> a car.

2. When someone asks you to explain a word in English, you can give a meaning for the word, and then you can tell a way or two in which it is used. This will give you a chance to use the passive form. Example:

    The word *hunk* has a couple of meanings. It's used to talk about a piece or chunk of something, such as a piece of metal. It's also used in slang to talk about a strong, muscular man.

22

More Past Time

REVIEW

In chapter 21 you practiced using a variety of structures to say things about the present and the future. Let's review a few of those structures.

Complete these sentences.

1. Stan _____ worrying about his classes _____ several weeks now.

2. He hopes that _____ fail any of his courses.

3. Sometimes he wishes that he _____ a bird.

4. If he _____ a bird, he _____ fly away from all his problems.

PREVIEW

In this chapter we will work with some new structures that are useful in speaking and writing in the past. Most of these are related to the chapter 21 structures. In the following sentences, try to fill in the blanks with the correct forms of the verbs given.

1. A few months ago Sadie and Oscar went to a movie together. They (*meet*)

    _____ just the week before.

2. They must (*have*) _____ a good time because they decided to go out

    again the following week.

3.   They wish that they (*meet*) _____ a long time before then.

4.   If they (*meet*) _____ earlier, they (*be + not*) _____

_____ so lonely for the past few years.

A crime has been committed in a student's apartment. Someone has stolen the student's valuable necklace. This picture shows the student's apartment as she found it when she returned from the library that night.

22.1 Past Perfect		
Complete these model sentences.	Check.	Complete these rules.
a. When the student got back to the apartment, she saw that someone _____ _____ **her valuable necklace.**	had stolen	When our attention is focused on a certain point of time in the past—in a story, for example—we may want to refer to something that happened **before** that moment. In this case we use the past perfect tense: _____ + **the past participle**
b. or . . . she saw that her valuable necklace _____ _____ **stolen.**	had been	The past perfect also has a passive form: _____ + _____ + **the** _____ **participle**

Oral Practice 1A: When the student got back home she saw that many things had happened in her apartment. Mention some of the things that had happened. Use both active-voice and passive-voice sentences.

Oral Practice 1B: Think back to the time when you had just arrived in this country, in this city, or at this school. Was anything different from what you had been told? Example:

I made a lot of friends quickly. This surprised me because a friend had told me that it was difficult to make friends here.

Written Practice 1:   Fill in the blanks in sentence A. Then finish sentence B. It should have about the same meaning as sentence A. The first one has been done for you.

When the girl got home, she saw that many things had happened . . .

1. A.   Someone ___*had stolen*___ her university T-shirt.

    B.   Her university T-shirt ___*had been stolen*___.

2. A.   Someone _____ the clock.

    B.   The clock _____.

3. A.   Someone _____ her baseball hat and _____ a French beret on

    her hat rack.

    B.   Her baseball hat _____ and a French beret

    _____.

4. A.   Someone _____ her jar of jelly.

    B.   Her jar of jelly _____.

5. A.   Someone _____ a glove on her table.

    B.   A glove _____ on her table.

Jelly on hands

missing button...

Mud on shoes

22.2 *Must, May, Might,* and *Could* + Perfect			
Complete these model sentences.	Check.	Complete these rules.
a. The man at the right is Pierre, a notorious international jewel thief. The police have just captured him. They have come to this conclusion:		When we have some good evidence that something happened, we can use this structure:
Pierre must _____ taken the necklace.	have	_____ + _____ + **the** _____ **participle**

b. The police aren't sure, but the dog _____ **have torn the button from Pierre's jacket.**	may/might/ could	When we aren't sure that something happened, but we think that it is possible that it happened, we can use this structure: _____ _____ } + _____ + **the past participle** _____
c. *or* . . . **the button may have** _____ _____ **off by the dog.**	been torn	In the passive voice, the structure is: **modal** + _____ + _____ + **the past participle**

Oral Practice 2A: Talk about what may/might/could/must have happened the night of the burglary.

Oral Practice 2B: Talk about some things that might have happened in the world since the last time you saw the news.

Oral Practice 2C: A friend has lost his or her glasses. Make some suggestions about what might have been done with them, or what your friend might have done with them.

Written Practice 2:   Complete these sentences. Use a modal verb in every sentence.

1.   The burglar alarm didn't go off. Pierre _____ through the window.

2.   The clock _____ unplugged when Pierre tripped over the cord.

3.   Pierre _____ dropped the jelly when he tripped over the clock cord.

4.   I didn't see her at the party, but she _____ been there.

5.   The sidewalk was all wet this morning; it (*rain*) _____ last night.

6.   In the middle of the movie, the screen went blank; the film (*break*) _____.

7.   My cat escaped; the door (*leave*) _____ open.

8.   I can think of three possible explanations for why the tree is no longer there: It (*blow down*) _____ by the wind; it (*use*) _____ for firewood; or it (*remove*) _____ because it was too close to that new driveway.

22.3 *Should* + **Perfect**		
Complete these model sentences.	Check.	Complete these rules.
a. Pierre wasn't careful enough. He _____ **have been much more careful.**	should/ could/might	To indicate that something that did **not** happen would have been a good idea, we can use this structure: *should* + _____ + **the** _____ **participle** This represents advice that is too late. You can soften the suggestions—that is, make them more polite—by using the modal _____ or _____ instead of *should*.
b. For one thing, he _____ _____ **have decided to have a snack in the apartment.**	should not	To indicate that something that **did happen** was not a good idea, we can use this structure: *should* + _____ + _____ + **the past participle**

Oral Practice 3A: What are some other things that Pierre should/could/might have done or should not have done?

Oral Practice 3B: Tell the class about a mistake you made or a problem you have had recently and what you should or should not have done to avoid it.

Oral Practice 3C: Tell the class some things you should have done to prepare yourself better for study at this university.

Written Practice 3:   Write five sentences about what Pierre and the student should and should not have done. Examples:

> *The student who lost the necklace should have locked her window.*
> *She should not have brought such a valuable piece of jewelry to the university.*

22.4 Past Unreal Conditional Sentences and *Wish* Sentences		
Complete these model sentences.	Check.	Complete these rules.
a. If Pierre _____ not made a sandwich, he would not have taken off his gloves. *or* **Pierre would not have taken off his gloves if he _____** **_____ _____ a sandwich.**	had had not made	If the conditions weren't right for something in the past, we can show that something different would have happened under different conditions. We describe the different, unreal condition in an adverb clause beginning with *if*. This is the structure: *if* + **subject** + _____ + **the** _____ **participle** REMEMBER: Adverb clauses such as *if* clauses can go either before or after the main clause. We separate the two clauses with a comma when the _____ clause comes before the _____ clause.
b. If he had not taken off his gloves, he **_____ not _____ left fingerprints all over the room.**	would, have	In the **main clause** of a past conditional sentence, we often use this verb structure: _____ + _____ + **the** _____ **participle**
c. If he had not left fingerprints, Pierre **_____ not have been caught.**	might	If we are not very sure that a certain thing would have happened under different conditions, we can use the modal _____ rather than *would*.
d. If Pierre had not taken that necklace, **he _____ _____ a free man today.**	would/could/ might be	Often an unreal condition in the past would have **present** results if it had really happened. As we saw in Rule Builder 21.5d, we use this verb structure for present or future results of unreal conditions: _____ *could* ⎱ + **the** _____ **form of the** *might* ⎰ **verb**

22.4 Past Unreal Conditional Sentences and *Wish* Sentences (Continued)		
e. Pierre wishes that he _____ _____ _____ **that necklace.**	had not stolen	In Rule Builder 21.6 we saw how the verb ***wish*** was used to talk about present and future fantasies. People have desires and dreams about the past, too. In such cases the verb in the noun clause is in the _____ _____ tense. Notice the similarity between ***wish*** sentences and ***if*** clauses.

Oral Practice 4A: What are some things Pierre wishes that he had or had not done during the burglary? How would things have been different if he had or had not done these things?

Oral Practice 4B: Think of something that you regret about the past—something that you wish had turned out differently. Tell the class how you might have changed this event, and what the effects on your life would have been. Example:

> *I wish I had studied English harder in high school.*
> *If I had done that, I wouldn't have had to take ESL courses in college.*

Written Practice 4:   Complete these sentences. *Some of them will make more sense if you make them negative.*

1.   If it (*rain*) _____ yesterday, we would have gone on a picnic.

2.   I wish it (*rain*) _____ yesterday; a picnic would have been fun.

3.   If I had bought that stock, I _____ made a lot of money.

4.   If I had bought that stock, I _____ a wealthy person right now.

5.   I wish _____ that stock.

6.   If Christopher Columbus (*discover*) _____ the New World, he (*become*) _____ such a famous man.

7.   If Christopher Columbus (*discover*) _____ the New World, who (*live*) _____ in the Americas today?

8.   Oscar and Sadie (*go out*) _____ many times by now if they (*meet*) _____ a long time ago.

9.   If they _____ a long time ago, they (*be*) _____ married now.

10.   Oscar and Sadie wish _____ a long time ago.

22.5 Chapter Check: Complete these sentences. If you are unsure of an answer, check the indicated model sentence and rule.

1.   The police _____ captured Pierre! He's at the police station now.   [8.2a]

2.   He (*confess*) _____ to his crime at 3 o'clock this morning.   [8.1a]

3. Pierre never used (*make*) _____ mistakes, but he makes a lot of

    mistakes now.   [8.4c]

4. The student (*study*) _____ at the library when Pierre (*break into*)

    _____ her room.   [8.5]

5. By the time the student got back to her room, Pierre (*leave + already*)

    _____.   [22.1a]

6. Judging from the evidence, Pierre must (*get*) _____ into

    the room by climbing in the window.   [22.2a]

7. We don't know, but Pierre (*have*) _____ an accomplice.   [22.2b]

8. If Pierre (*be*) _____ more careful, the police (*catch*) _____

    _____ him.   [22.4a&b]

9. Poor Pierre (*be*) _____ more careful that

    night.   [22.3a]

10. Sadie and Oscar had only coffee at Mike's because they (*eat + already*)

    _____.   [22.1a]

11. Mike didn't serve Sadie and Oscar himself because when Oscar and Sadie arrived, he

    (*leave + already*) _____.   [22.1a]

12. Oscar and Sadie had a date last night, and they are going out again tonight. They must

    _____ a good time last night.   [22.2a]

22.6 Chapter Check: Finish sentence B so that it has about the same meaning as
sentence A.

1. A. *Godzilla* was playing in town last night. Sadie and Oscar didn't go only because

        they didn't know about it.

    B. *Godzilla* was playing last night. Sadie and Oscar _____ to see it

        if they _____ about it.   [22.4a&b]

2. A. It would have been a good idea for them to look at the movie schedule in the paper.

    B. They _____ at the movie schedule in the

        paper.   [22.3a]

3. A. Wilt is sorry that he got home so late.

    B. Wilt wishes _____ earlier.   [22.4e]

4. A. While Peter was at the concert, his dog chewed holes in his shoes. Peter discovered

        this when he got home.

    B. When Peter got home from the concert, he discovered that his dog

        _____.   [22.1a]

5.   A.   Sam missed the review class. That was a bad idea.

       B.   Sam should _____ the review class.   [22.3b]

6.   A.   It is possible that someone else wrote this composition.

       B.   This composition might _____ by someone

            else.   [22.2c]

7.   A.   The only reason Charley was given that job was that his uncle was on the hiring

            committee.

       B.   If Charley's uncle had not been on the hiring committee, Charley

         _____ that job .   [22.4b&c]

8.   A.   Pete regrets buying his $2,000 computer.

       B.   Pete wishes _____ his $2,000 computer. [22.4e]

22.7 Warm-up: Think back to the time before you started going to school here. What are some things you could have done then besides coming to this school? What would you have probably done if you had not come to this school?

22.8 Communication: Form a small group with a few classmates. Think of an important event in your life. Tell how your life would have been different if that event hadn't happened. Example:

> My family moved from a small town to the capital of my country when I was in high school. If we hadn't moved, I would probably have started working in my uncle's store. I would not have continued my education, and I wouldn't be studying here now.

Take some notes on the following form. Then work with the other members of your group on a short report on what you have learned about each other. One person in the group can act as secretary, writing the information down. Everyone in the group should check the secretary's work; make sure that the verb forms are correct.

Name	*Important Event*	*How Life Would Have Been Different*
_____	_____	_____
	_____	_____
		_____
		_____
		_____
_____	_____	_____
	_____	_____
		_____
		_____

22.9 Sentence Writing: The police were able to prove that Pierre was the thief because Pierre did some foolish things. Mention three things that Pierre **should** or **should not have done**. For each one, indicate what **would** or **would not have happened** if Pierre **had** or **had not done** this thing.

22.10 Sentence Writing: Think of two bad things that you did or that happened to you because of a mistake that you made. For each of these things write four sentences.

a.   Tell what happened.
b.   Tell what you wish had happened.
c.   Explain what you should or shouldn't have done to prevent this from happening.
d.   Tell what would have happened if you had or had not taken the action explained in sentence **c**.

22.11 Paragraph Writing: In Rule Builder 21.4 you worked with the passive voice. In the following passage about the assassination of John F. Kennedy, some of the sentences would work better in the passive. Rewrite the paragraph, changing the underlined sentences from active to passive voice. In some sentences you will want to use a **by** phrase to tell who the action was performed by. In other sentences, the person or people who performed the action are much less important than the action itself, and you will leave out the **by** phrase.

> In November of 1963, President Kennedy set out on a speaking tour through Florida and Texas. On November 22, he and wife were driving in a procession through Dallas. Governor Connally of Texas accompanied them. At 12:30 P.M. people heard a rifle shot; the President and the governor slumped. Someone rushed them to the hospital. At 1:00 P.M. someone officially announced the President's death, and the nation went into mourning. That same day the police arrested Lee Harvey Oswald. Two days later, before he could testify about the crime, Jack Ruby murdered him in the Dallas Police building.

22.12 Paragraph Writing: Think of an important event in your home country's history. Briefly tell what happened. Then tell how things might have been different and might be different today if this event had not occurred.

22.13 Reflecting: Read the next episode of the mystery story. Then examine the way these structures have been used: the past perfect, modal + perfect, past unreal conditional sentences, and **wish** sentences.

I explained to Troy Daniels that I was working on his case and that I wanted to hear his side of the story. He joined his wife and me for a cup of coffee and stretched out in a lounge chair to talk.

He said that he had been at the hospital when Dr. Weber had operated on his mother. ''She had to have one of her kidneys removed,'' he said. ''It was a dangerous operation, sure, and I was hanging around in the waiting room. I was nervous. It must have been about four in the afternoon when one of the nurses came out and told me my mother had died. I couldn't believe it at first. But then she said I could talk to the doctor if I wanted.

''She took me into an office. I was really upset and wasn't able to think too straight. If I had been in shape, this thing probably would have been wrapped up without any trouble. But I didn't realize I was talking to the guy who had just operated on my mother; I thought it was a psychiatrist or something. He just asked if I was feeling okay a couple of times.''

''What was wrong with that?'' I asked.

''He stank of alcohol,'' Troy Daniels said sharply. ''He must have been drinking before he did that operation, Mr. Stern. I could have made them give him a test or something to see. I wish I had been thinking straight.''

22.14 Real-World Work

THINK/PRACTICE

Many of the structures you have been working on in this chapter require a lot of practice. As you are walking along, think of more unfortunate things that have happened to you (like those in 22.10 Sentence Writing). Tell yourself what happened, what you wish had happened, what you should or should not have done, and what would or would not have happened if you had or had not done this.

LOOK/LISTEN

In a newspaper, look for examples of past conditionals, afterthoughts (**should have**), and **wish** sentences about the past. You will probably not find very many examples; you may find some on the opinion page and in advice columns such as Ann Landers. It is probably true that these structures are used much more in conversation than in writing. Newspapers deal mostly with present and past facts and real possibilities in the future. In our conversations with friends and family, we can talk about what might have been, what we should have done, and what we wish had happened. In other words, we can talk about the world not only as it was and is, but also as it would have been if things had been different.

USE

1. Start an English conversation with another international student on the subject of what you both would/might/could have done and would/might/could be doing now if you had not come to this university to study.

2. Learners of a second language should always pay attention to the reactions of their listeners as they speak. If you notice that someone looks puzzled or confused after you have said something, remember what you have said. Ask the person you are talking to, or a friend later, what you could or should have said in the situation.

23

Modal Summary

REVIEW

You have worked with **modal verbs** in several previous chapters. For example, in chapter 4 you used modals in requests, offers, and suggestions.

1. _____ you give me a ride to school, Ted?

2. _____ I help you get things ready for the party?

3. _____ you mind closing that window?

4. _____ we take a break for lunch?

5. I _____ let Helen know that you are coming.

In chapter 9, you used modals to talk about the future.

6. We don't know how long the drive _____ take; we _____ be a little late.

7. Don't worry; we _____ start the meeting until you arrive.

8. We have a good team; we _____ probably win.

   or We have a good team; we _____ win.

In chapters 21 and 22, you used modals in drawing conclusions from evidence, stating the results of conditions, and giving advice.

9. They aren't here anymore; they _____ left.

10. If we had hurried, we _____ missed them.

11. You're right. Wc _____ hurried.

PREVIEW

In this chapter, you will review much of what you have already worked on. You will use modals to make **guesses** and **predictions,** and to express such notions as **expectation, ability, advisability, obligation,** and **necessity.**

A murder has been committed, and Sherlock Holmes has been called in. While Holmes is talking with a suspect named Clara Bentley, he is looking carefully for clues and drawing some conclusions.

23.1 Making Guesses and Drawing Conclusions		
Complete these model sentences.	Check.	Complete these rules.
a. He notices that Clara has a pencil stuck in her hair. She may _____ **in an office, or she might** _____ **a teacher.** She does not have a wedding ring. **She must** _____ _____ **married.**	work be not be	To say that it is possible or probable that a situation exists—for example, Clara is a teacher—or that an event occurs regularly—she works in an office—use this structure: *may/might* *could* } + the _____ form of *must* the verb To make a modal verb phrase negative, put ***not*** immediately _____ the modal.

b. She is not paying attention to Holmes's questions. She may (*think*) _____ _____ **about the murder.** **She is holding her purse very tightly.** **She must** (*hide*) _____ _____ **something in it.**	be thinking be hiding	To say that it is possible or probable that an event is occurring—she is *hiding* something—use this structure: *may/*_____ _____ + _____ + **the** _____ _____ **form**
c. She has a small ink stain on her fin- **ger. She must** (*write*) _____ _____ **a letter recently.**	have written	To say that is is possible or probable that a situation existed or that an event occurred—she *wrote* a letter recently—use this structure: *may/might* *could* + _____ + **the past** *must* **participle**
d. There is an open bottle of ink on the **table. She might** (*write*) _____ _____ _____ **a letter** **when Holmes arrived.**	have been writing	To say that it is possible or probable that an event was occurring—she *was writing* a letter—use this structure: *may/might* *could* + *have* + _____ + **the** *must* _____ **form**
e. Holmes looks at her purse again. **The letter may** (*put*) _____ _____ _____ **in the purse.**	have been put	To say that something in the past was possibly or probably done—the letter *was put* in the purse—use this passive structure: *may/might* *could* + *have* + _____ + **the** *must* _____ **participle**

Oral Practice 1A: What are some things your classmates may or must have done since yesterday morning?

Oral Practice 1B: Think of something you used to have but don't have anymore. What might have happened to it? Example:

> I used to have a stuffed bear. My little sister may still have it, but it might have been thrown in the trash.

Oral Practice 1C: Without looking, tell what might be going on outside the building right now.

Oral Practice 1D: At the moment when the police arrived at Pierre's hotel room to arrest him for the burglary (chapter 22), what might or must he have been doing?

Oral Practice 1E: Think of several things that may, might, and must have been done in this classroom in previous semesters.

Written Practice 1:   Complete these sentences. *Use a modal verb in each sentence.*

1. Where is Mr. Jenkins right now?

    I'm not sure, but he _____ at home.

2. What do you think he's doing there?

    He might _____.

3. He looked tired this morning. What did he do last night?

    I don't know that either, but he _____ to Sam's

    party.

4. How did the cat get out?

    Someone must _____ the window open.

    or The window _____ open.

5. I didn't hear the phone ring. I must (*take*) _____

    _____ a bath when you called.

23.2 Making Predictions and Expressing Expectations		
Complete these model sentences.	Check.	Complete these rules.
a. My father has not made a decision yet. **He _____ retire next year.** **But he _____ _____ retire until the year after that.**	may/might/ could may not/ might not	When making predictions about the future, we indicate possibility by using the modal _____, _____, or _____. To say that it is possible that something will not happen, use _____ _____ or _____ _____.
b. It _____ not snow tomorrow; I'm sure of it!	will	We indicate *certainty* about the future by using the modal _____.

c. **Have dinner ready by 6:30. The guests _____ be here by then (but they may be a little late).**	should	We indicate that we expect that something will happen or be true by using the modal _____. We don't normally use *should* if we expect something bad to happen. For example, if we expect good weather on our trip, we may say, "The weather _____ _____ nice there this time of year," or "We _____ _____ _____ any trouble with the weather." But if we expect bad weather, we don't use *should*; we may say, "The weather will probably be rather nasty."

Oral Practice 2:   Make some predictions about your near future. Use ***may/may not, should/should not***, and ***will/will not***. Remember to use ***should*** only for positive things.

Written Practice 2A: Write three sentences about things that may or may not happen in the next few years. *At least one of your sentences should be negative.*

Written Practice 2B: Write three sentences about things that you expect or don't expect to happen in the next few years. Use ***should*** with events that you anticipate with pleasure; use ***will probably*** for predictions that make you unhappy. *At least one of your sentences should be negative.*

Written Practice 2C: Write three sentences about things that you are certain will or will not happen in the next few years. *At least one of your sentences should be negative.*

23.3 Talking about Abilities		
Complete these model sentences.	Check.	Complete these rules.
a. Reggie has a job as a typist. He **hopes he can** (*find*) _____ **a more interesting job soon.**	find	We often use the modal _____ when talking about having the potential to do something specific.

b.   When Reggie graduated from college,
 	
he _____ **not find a job in his**
field. Finally, after weeks of job
 	
hunting, he was _____ ____ **find**
a job as a typist.
 	
or . . . He managed ____ _____
a job as a typist.
	could
	
	able to
	
	to find
		We use _____ *not* to mean "failed" or "was unable." *Could,* however, does *not* normally mean that someone succeeded. To express this, we use this structure:
		
		   was/were _____ + **the infinitive**
		If it was somewhat difficult to succeed, we often use this structure:
		
		  _____ + **the infinitive**

c. If he had been willing to move to **another city, he** _____ _____ **found a job in his field.**	could have	We might want to say that someone had the potential to do something, but did not do it. We use this structure: ***could*** + _____ + **the** _____ **participle**
d. When Reggie was in college, he _____ **type only 60 words per** **minute. Now he** _____ **type** **over 85 words per minute.**	could can	We also use the modal ***can*** when talking about having a skill or knowing how to do something. With this meaning we **do** use _____ to refer to past skills or abilities. Don't make the mistake of using *could* to refer to present skills or abilities; use _____.

Oral Practice 3A: Tell the class something that you could do when you were young but can't do now.

Oral Practice 3B: Think of something that you learned after a lot of difficulty. Tell the class about what you tried to do, couldn't do at first, but finally succeeded in doing. Use ***couldn't, was able to,*** and ***managed to*** correctly. Example:

     I played basketball for the first time in my life recently. At first, I couldn't even come close to making a shot, but eventually I was able to make a basket. *or . . .* I managed to make a basket.

Oral Practice 3C: Last Wednesday you had to go to school. Suppose that you hadn't had to go to school. What are some things you could have done?

Written Practice 3:   Fill in the blanks with *can/cannot, could/could not,* or *managed to.*

1. My roommate _____ speak four languages fluently: French, Italian, Spanish, and English.

2. When she was a child, she _____ speak German, but now she _____ say only a few words in that language.

3. Last night I was trying to read the owner's manual that came with my French bicycle. I _____ understand much of it.

4. When my roommate got home, I said, ''_____ you help me read this?''

5. With my roommate's help, I _____ find out what I needed to know in order to start enjoying my new bike.

6. Everyone has some special skills and abilities. There are some things that I _____ do well that are difficult for my roommate.

7. For example, as a child, I _____ do gymnastics very well.

8. I'm out of practice now, but I _____ still do a perfect cartwheel.

9. My roommate asked me to help her learn to do a cartwheel. She tried and tried, but for a long time, she _____ do it.

10. Finally, however, after hours of practice, she _____ do one good cartwheel.

11. Neither my roommate nor I _____ cook very well.

12. Last week we invited one of our professors to have dinner at our apartment, but we _____ figure out what to serve.

13. We finally decided to serve Italian food. It wasn't easy for us; we had to consult cook-books and call friends for help. In the end, somehow we _____ put a dinner on the table.

23.4 Talking about Obligations, Necessities, and Afterthoughts		
Complete these model sentences.	Check.	Complete these rules.
a. Anyone from another country _____ **get a visa before studying in the U.S.**	must/has to	The modal that expresses obligation or necessity is _____. Another expression that has about the same meaning is _____ _____.
b. For example, I _____ _____ **get a visa before coming here.**	had to	*Must* has no past form. To refer to an obligation or necessity in the past, use the expression _____ _____.
c. While in the U.S. a foreign student **must _____ work without permission.** or **A foreign student** _____ _____ **work . . .**	not may not/ cannot	Prohibitions can be expressed with the expression _____ + *not*. About the same idea can be expressed with *cannot* or _____ _____.
d. A student _____ have enough money before coming to the U.S. **A student _____** _____ **come to the U.S. without enough money.**	should/ ought to should not	To give advice, that is, to say that something is a good idea, use the modal _____ or _____ _____. To say that something is not a good idea, use the expression _____ _____.
e. I should _____ _____ **English before I came here, but I didn't.**	have studied	To give advice that is too late, we use this structure: _____ + *have* + the _____ participle

Oral Practice 4A: What are some things a student from your hometown must or should (ought to) do before leaving to study at this school?

Oral Practice 4B: What are some things a student who wants to be successful must not or should not do at this school?

Oral Practice 4C: Besides the things that any student must do before coming to this school, mention something special that you had to do.

Written Practice 4:   Fill in the blanks with *must, have to, has to, had to, ought to, should,* or *should have. Some of the sentences will have to be negative.*

1. Last summer, poor Mrs. McGill _____ spend a very boring week at the beach because of her husband.

2. I think she _____ refused to go.

3. Mr. McGill _____ try to be more considerate in the future.

4. In Mr. Jones's opinion, Stan _____ play his saxophone at midnight.

5. Last night Mr. Jones _____ put a pillow over his head in order to sleep.

6. Ms. Jones thinks they _____ look for another apartment.

7. Bernard _____ get off the elevator on the fourteenth floor because he cannot reach the higher buttons.

8. Elevator designers _____ think about children.

9. Pierre _____ stay in prison until the year 2000 because of his crimes.

10. Now Pierre probably says to himself, ''I _____ become a thief. I _____ listened to my mother and gone to law school.''

23.5 Chapter Check: Complete these sentences. If you are unsure, check the indicated model sentence and rule.

1. Our friend Sadie has written a book about manners. According to Sadie's book, one _____ talk with one's mouth full.   [23.4c or d]

2. She also says that a man _____ to take off his hat when entering someone's house.   [23.4a or d]

3. At first Pierre _____ not open the apartment window. But finally, after working for an hour, he _____ to get it open.   [23.3b]

4. Pierre received a harsh sentence from the judge, but since Pierre is not a trouble-maker, he _____ get time off for good behavior.   [23.2a]

5. Ten years ago, I _____ run 26 miles and feel great, but I _____ do that anymore. Last month I entered the local marathon race. After ten miles I _____ run anymore. However, I _____ to finish the race through a combination of walking and jogging.   [23.3]

23.6 Chapter Check: Finish sentence B so that it has about the same meaning as sentence A. Use the modal verb **must** in all of the sentences in this exercise.

1.   A.   I hear saxophone music coming from that apartment building. I suppose that Stan is practicing.

   B.   I hear saxophone music coming from that apartment building. Stan _____

   _____.   [23.1b]

2.   A.   Jerry's never late. I'll bet he forgot.

   B.   Jerry is never late. He _____.   [23.1c]

3.   A.   The police have come to the conclusion that the victim was strangled.

   B.   According to the police, the victim _____

   _____.   [23.1e]

4.   A.   The telephone is off the hook. The victim was probably talking on the phone when the crime was committed.

   B.   The telephone is off the hook. The victim _____

   on the phone when the crime was committed.   [23.1d]

5.   A.   Harry washes his car at least twice a week. I guess he loves that car.

   B.   Harry washes his car at least twice a week. He _____

   _____.   [23.1a]

23.7 Chapter Check: Finish sentence B. It should have about the same meaning as sentence A.

1.   A.   For months I tried to get an appointment with the governor; finally, last week I succeeded.

   B.   I finally _____ get an appointment with the governor after months of trying.   [23.3b]

2.   A.   Mr. McGill cannot read nearly as fast now as in his days as a student.

   B.   When Mr. McGill was a student, he _____ much faster than he can now.   [23.3d]

3.   A.   We couldn't leave last night only because you took the car key with you.

   B.   If you had not taken the car key, we _____ last night.   [23.3c]

23.8 Warm-up: Stan has had some bad luck recently. Here is a list of the bad things that have happened to him. Notice that each of the misfortunes was the result of the one before.

He overslept because he didn't set his alarm clock.
He had to hurry when he shaved.
He cut himself with his razor.

He got blood on his shirt.
He took time to change his shirt.
He missed his bus.
He walked to work.
He was late to work.
He lost his job.
He stopped paying rent on his apartment.
He gave up his apartment.
He moved in with his parents.
He feels silly living with his parents at the age of 29.

Go backwards through the list, following this structure:
Student A: Stan feels silly because he has moved in with his parents.
Student B: Well, he shouldn't have moved in with them.
Student C: He moved in with them because he gave up his apartment.
Student D: Well, he shouldn't have given it up.
Student E: He gave it up because . . .

23.9 Communication: Form small groups and read one of the following passages. Prepare a report in which you tell the class the following:

1. Tell what happened.
2. Tell what that person could have or should have done to avoid the problem.
3. Tell what he or she could have or should have done in the situation after it arose.

1. Philip and his friends live in a little house in the suburbs. They don't know any of their neighbors. Last week, Philip was the only one at home at 9:30 A.M. when he went outside to get the newspaper. He was barefoot and was wearing his bathrobe. As he picked up the paper, the wind blew the front door closed and it locked. He didn't have a key, so he tried to open a window. It was locked, so he broke it and cut his hand. He crawled in through the window, but in a few minutes a police car arrived because a neighbor had reported that someone was breaking into the house. Philip was taken to the police station. He had to stay there until 5 P.M. when his housemates arrived and identified him.

2. Sara drove her car downtown recently to see a movie. She parked in a place that had no time limit after 5:30 P.M., but which had a one-hour limit during the day. When she went back to the car after the movie, she found that she had a flat tire. She knew that her spare tire was flat, too, so she left the car and took the bus home. The next day she went to work, and after work she went back to the place where she had parked her car. It was gone; it had been towed away. It cost Sara $47 to get her car back.

3. Last month, Rolando started college in a town about 75 miles from Kansas City. He had to fly from Miami to Atlanta, and then from Atlanta to Kansas City. His flight to Atlanta was late, so he missed his flight to Kansas City and had to take a later flight. Some friends were supposed to meet him in Kansas City, but they left after waiting for two hours. When Rolando got to Kansas City, he didn't know what to do. He saw a taxi, so he got in and told the driver to take him to the town where the school was located. The taxi ride cost $83.

4. Frank had a test on four chapters in his Asian history class last Thursday. He hadn't been studying regularly. He decided that his only chance to do well on the test was to stay up all night and try to read the four chapters and memorize everything in his notes. During the night, he drank 9 or 10 cups of coffee and felt worse and worse. About 6 A.M., he finally decided to get a couple of hours of sleep. When his alarm went off at 8, he didn't hear it, so he overslept and missed the test.

5. Ying had a test in a math class last semester. During the test, she noticed that the boy sitting next to her was looking at her paper. She didn't tell the teacher about this or try to cover her paper. When the teacher saw that the two test papers were identical, he gave both students F's. Ying felt very sad, but she was also afraid and embarrassed, so she decided not to argue about the grade.

23.10 Sentence Writing: Each of the following sentences explains a difficult situation that you might find yourself in. For each situation write two sentences. In the first one, tell what you should or must do in the situation. In the second sentence, tell what you should have done to avoid being in that situation.

1. You have just eaten dinner in an expensive restaurant, and you realize now that you left your money at home.
2. You realize that your visa expired last month.
3. You have spilled a bottle of ink on the floor of your apartment.
4. You realize that you have left your backpack on the bus. Your wallet, which contains more than $100 in cash, is in the backpack.

23.11 Sentence Writing: Write about three things that you couldn't do 10 years ago but can do now. Use *could* and *can* in each sentence.

23.12 Paragraph Writing: An archeologist has found these parts of a game during her excavations. She has asked several people, including you, to make some guesses about how these things might have been used in the game. Write a short report to give her some ideas. Use *may, might, could,* and *must.* Use the passive voice.

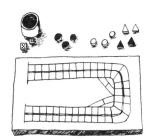

23.13 Paragraph Writing: Write a paragraph about what you had to do before coming here to study. Then mention two or three things that you should have done but didn't do.

23.14 Paragraph Writing: Pretend that this happened to you last week. You and your friend were taking a test in your late afternoon class. The test was long, and the teacher let you stay a few minutes late to finish. When you and your friend left the classroom, your friend realized that she had missed the last bus. It was getting dark, and she was not happy with the idea of walking the 10 blocks to her apartment. You had your moped, and you offered to give your friend a ride. She accepted, but on the way to her place, a policewoman stopped you and gave you a ticket for giving your friend a ride. According to the law, only one person may ride on a moped. The fine for breaking this rule is $20.

You have decided to appeal. You have gone to the traffic office and been given the following form to fill out. In your paragraph giving the reasons for the appeal, try to use several modals and expressions that you have reviewed in this chapter.

BOARD OF PARKING AND TRAFFIC APPEALS

I, _____, **want to appeal a parking/traffic ticket which I received.**

DATE OF TICKET: _____

CURRENT ADDRESS: _____

TELEPHONE NUMBER: _____

LICENSE PLATE INFORMATION: _____

PLEASE INDICATE:

FACULTY _____ **STAFF** _____ **STUDENT** _____ **STUDENT NUMBER** _____

IMPORTANT:

1. This appeal form may be used as evidence in your hearing.
2. If reasons for appeal are stated below, they should contain relevant facts including reasons for requesting review, and the nature of the evidence you are prepared to present.
3. False statements on this form or in court will result in disciplinary action.

REASON FOR APPEAL:

_____

_____

_____

_____

_____

_____

_____

_____

_____

_____

_____

_____

_____

23.15 Reflecting: Read the next episode of the mystery story. Then go back and look at all the modal structures. Do you understand exactly what they mean? Think of other ways of expressing the same ideas.

> Troy Daniels told me he had given Carl Miller this information about the doctor's drinking the day before Miller had disappeared. "You should have told somebody that Doctor Weber smelled like alcohol," I agreed with Troy. "The case probably would have been settled right away."
>
> I had thought that Daniels might have been involved in Miller's disappearance. But he didn't seem angry enough to have done something so drastic. I was beginning to think about the case differently. I asked myself what Miller would have done after he talked to Daniels. He would have needed to find out if Dr. Weber had really been drinking before the operation. But how could he have done that?
>
> I left the Daniels' apartment with a new angle on my case. If I tried to prove the same thing, then I should get some hint of what Miller had done.
>
> But I could only do so much work. I was tired. I could have kept at it that night; instead, I decided to give Linda a call. Maybe she would forgive me.

23.16 Real-World Work

THINK/PRACTICE

1. As you walk or ride around today, look at people and things and draw some conclusions. Example:

    That student is late to class. That student must have overslept.
    That building may have been built in the last century.

2. Think of some things that you regret doing or not doing recently. Tell yourself what you should have done or should not have done.

3. Think of some more things that you can do now but couldn't do 10 years ago, and vice versa.

4. Think back over your life. Remember some big decisions that you or your parents have made. What were the alternatives? Express these alternatives with **could have**. Example:

    I came to the U.S. to study.
    I could have gone to England, or I could have stayed home.

LOOK/LISTEN

1. Look at a book, magazine, or newspaper. Try to find five *different* modals. Read the paragraphs that these modals are in, and try to paraphrase the modal sentences. Example:

    This may have been the last good opportunity to avoid a crisis.
    Paraphrase: Perhaps this was the last good opportunity to avoid a crisis.

2. Listen to or read a news account of an accident that has happened recently. If the causes of the accident are unknown, investigators will try to reconstruct them. Observe carefully what is said or written. What modal verbs do you hear? What do these tell you about the certainty of the investigators' conclusions?

USE

1. Find out, by reading the school catalog and/or by asking questions, about the requirements and options that students have in a program of study that you are interested in. Find out about what job possibilities there are in this field. Be prepared to report what you have found to the class.

2. Talk to some other students. Ask if there are things they feel they should or could have done before coming to this school in order to have been better prepared.

24

Sentence
Connections

REVIEW

In this chapter we will focus on the various ways that we show relationships between ideas. You have already done a lot of work with sentence connections. For example, in chapters 7, 8, 9, and 21 you worked with **time** relationships. In the following sentences, write an appropriate conjunction in each blank and *add any needed commas*.

1. _____ Mr. Jones goes to bed Stan is still playing the saxophone. In other words, Mr. Jones goes to bed _____ Stan is still playing.

2. I carry an umbrella _____ it is rainy.

3. As _____ _____ Stan has enough money in his savings account he is going to go to New York to study music.

4. _____ Oscar was working in his father's grocery store he bought a flower shop.

In chapters 7, 9, 21, and 22, you used sentences involving the relationship of **condition**. Supply the correct form of the verb in these sentences, and add any needed commas.

5. If the cold front (*move*) _____ faster than expected it (*start*)

    _____ raining early tomorrow morning.

6. If Tank (*be*) _____ smarter he (*fail + not + always*)

    _____ his classes.

7. Pierre (*leave + not*) _____ fingerprints if he

    (*take off + not*) _____ his gloves.

In chapter 16, you practiced showing another relationship: **cause-effect**. Complete this sentence:

8. Stretch is _____ tall _____ he hits his head on the ceiling.

PREVIEW

In this chapter the following sentence relationships will be emphasized: ***time, reason-result*** (cause-effect), ***unexpected result,*** and ***condition***. You will work with four types of connectors. Here are some examples of the four types of connectors. All of the following sentences are examples of the relationship of ***unexpected result***.

It was raining hard, <u>but</u> attendance was good anyway (coordinating conjunction)
<u>Although</u> it was raining hard, attendance was good. (subordinating conjunction)
It was raining hard; <u>however</u>, attendance was good. (conjunctive adverb)
Attendance was good <u>despite</u> heavy rain. (preposition)

Tom Bogard's father had an interesting experience last night. You will read three different versions of the incident: (1) the words that Tom used to tell the story to his friends, (2) the paragraph that Tom wrote about it in his English class journal, and (3) the article about it that appeared in the local newspaper. Read all three, and notice the different ways that the sentence relationships are expressed.

1. ORAL VERSION

"I've got to tell you what happened when my dad went to the Quick Shop last night. There weren't any parking spaces, *so* he left his car in the middle of the driveway. *While* he was in the store, a robber ran out of the bank carrying a bag of money. The robber wanted to escape in his truck, *but* he couldn't *because* my dad's car was in the way. He tried to escape on foot, *but* the police caught him. *If* my father hadn't parked his car in the driveway, the man would have escaped. The police gave my dad a ticket *anyway*. Can you believe it?

2. JOURNAL VERSION

Last night my father had an experience at our neighborhood Quick Shop that he won't forget soon. *When* he arrived, there weren't any parking spaces. *Consequently*, he left the car in the middle of the driveway. He went into the store, which happens to be across the street from a bank. *Meanwhile*, a robber ran out of the bank and into the Quick Shop parking lot. Luckily, the robber couldn't escape in his truck *because of* my father's little "crime." He tried to escape on foot; *however*, the police caught him. It is a good thing that my father parked in the driveway; *otherwise*, the robber would have escaped. Unfortunately, *although* my father had stopped a crime, he received a parking ticket.

3. NEWSPAPER VERSION

Lincoln, Neb.—An armed bank robber was unable to escape from the scene of his crime yesterday *because* a grocery shopper had parked his car illegally.

The shopper, Jackson Bogard of Lincoln, was in the Oak Avenue Quick Shop yesterday at 2 P.M. *when* the robber, identified as Clarence Snide of Lincoln, ran out of the Oak Avenue Savings and Loan with a bag containing $6,000. Snide was unable to drive away in his truck *because* Bogard's car was blocking the only exit to the Quick Shop parking lot, where the truck was parked. Police captured the suspect *while* he was running down Oak Avenue.

Police admitted that the robber would have escaped *if* Bogard's car had been parked legally. *Nevertheless*, they issued a ticket to him.

Chapter 24   *Sentence Connections*

311

24.1 Coordinating Conjunctions		
Complete these model sentences.	Check.	Complete these rules.
There weren't any parking spaces, **_____ Tom's father parked in the driveway.** **The clerk gave the robber the money,** **_____ the robber ran across the street.** **Tom's father had stopped a crime,** **_____ he received a parking ticket anyway.**	so and but	*And, but,* and *so,* along with *or, nor, for,* and *yet,* are called **coordinating conjunctions.** When we connect two clauses with a coordinating conjunction, we usually put a _____ before the conjunction.

Oral Practice 1A: Tell the story of Tom's father's misadventure. Use **and, but,** and **so** to show the connections between the events.

Oral Practice 1B: Tell the class something that you wanted to do recently but couldn't do because of some problem. Example:

> *I wanted to play badminton yesterday, but I couldn't find anyone who had time to play.*

Oral Practice 1C: Tell the class about a feeling that you had recently and what you did as a result. Example:

> *I felt very homesick last Sunday, so I gave my parents a call.*

Written Practice 1:   Supply the appropriate coordinating conjunctions—**and, but,** or **so**—and *add any needed commas.*

1. I would like to see that movie tonight _____ I can't because of homework.

2. I have to do a long math assignment _____ then I must study for tomorrow's chemistry lab quiz.

3. The movie is going to be in town until next Tuesday _____ I will probably have a chance to see it.

4. Freddy is kind _____ I don't enjoy being around him very much.

5. Tuition is going up next semester _____ Bill is looking for a part-time job.

6. I worked very hard on that paper _____ I got only a C.

7. Last night was a typical evening at the apartment building: Stan practiced, Mr. Jones watched TV _____ Ms. Jones read a novel.

8. Very few students enrolled in that class _____ it was canceled.

9.   You should bring chips to the party _____ I'll provide the soft drinks.

10.   We wanted to go on a hike _____ it started to get cold in the afternoon _____
      we decided not to go.

24.2 Subordinating Conjunctions		
Complete these model sentences.	Check.	Complete these rules.
a. _____ there weren't any parking spaces, Tom's father parked in the driveway.	Because/ Since	Words such as *because, since, although, when, after* and *if* are called **subordinating conjunctions**. The most common subordinating conjunctions used to introduce a reason or cause are _____ and _____.
b. _____ Tom's father was in the store, the robber was holding up the bank. _____ the clerk gave him the money, the robber ran across the street.	When/While When/After/ As soon as	There are many subordinating conjunctions used to show **time** relationships. Among them are _____, _____, _____, _____ _____ _____, *before, since, until, whenever, as long as,* and *once.*
c. _____ Tom's father had stopped a crime, he received a parking ticket.	Although/ Even though	Certain subordinating conjunctions show that the result is not what you would normally expect from an action or situation. Use these words with the "cause" part of the sentence: _____ and _____ _____.
d. _____ Tom's father had not parked in the driveway, the robber would have escaped.	If	As you have already learned, the most common subordinating conjunction used to introduce a **condition** is _____.

e. You know that clauses introduced by subordinating conjunctions can go either before or after the main clause. Remember the punctuation rule:
 	
    Use a comma to separate the clauses only when the subordinate clause comes
 	
    _____ **the main clause.**		

Oral Practice 2A: Retell the story of Tom's father, this time using subordinating conjunctions to express the relationships between the events. Use *because, since, although, even though, while,* and *if.*

Oral Practice 2B: Explain why you have or don't have a car. Use *because* and *since.*

Oral Practice 2C: Think of someone you know who has done something surprising. This person might be rather young, old, small, intelligent, sophisticated, graceful, etc. to have done what he or she did. Use *although* or *even though.* Examples:

> *Although my roommate is very shy, he has made many friends in our residence hall this semester.*
> *My little cousin can read even though he's only five years old.*

Written Practice 2:   Supply the appropriate subordinating conjunctions and *add any needed commas.*

1. _____ I want to go to that movie tonight I've decided to stay home and study.

2. _____ I finish my long math assignment I have to study for a chemistry lab quiz.

3. I will probably have a chance to see the movie _____ it is going to be in town until next Tuesday.

4. _____ Freddy is kind I don't enjoy being around him very much.

5. Bill is looking for a part-time job _____ tuition is going up next semester.

6. I got only a C on that paper _____ I worked very hard on it.

7. _____ Stan practiced and Mr. Jones watched TV Ms. Jones read a novel.

8. That class was canceled _____ very few students enrolled in it.

9. _____ you bring chips to the party I'll provide the soft drinks.

10. _____ we really wanted to go on a hike we decided not to go _____ it started to get colder in the afternoon.

24.3 Prepositions that Show Relationships		
Complete these model sentences.	Check.	Complete these rules.
a. Because _____ **the lack of parking spaces, Tom's father parked in the driveway.** **or** _____ _____ **the lack of parking spaces, Tom's father parked in the driveway.**	of Due to/ As a result of	Notice in this model that the **reason** part of the sentence is not given in a clause—there is no verb. The reason is expressed in a noun phrase. Use *because* _____ with noun phrases. Other prepositional expressions that introduce reasons or causes are _____ ____ and _____ _____ _____ _____.
b. Tom's father was in the store _____ **the bank robbery.** _____ **the robbery, the robber ran across the street.**	 during After	Some prepositions that are used to show **time** relationships are *since, until, for, by, before,* _____, and _____.
c. _____ **the good results of his ''crime,'' Mr. Bogard received a parking ticket.**	Despite/ In spite of	When an event or situation has an **unexpected** result, use the preposition _____ or the prepositional expression _____ _____ _____.
d. The punctuation rule for these prepositional phrases is the same as that for adverbial clauses: **A comma is used only when the phrase comes** _____ **the main clause.**		

Oral Practice 3A: Retell the story of Tom's father, this time using these prepositions: *because of, due to, during, after,* and *despite.*

Oral Practice 3B: Think of something that you wanted to do recently but couldn't for some reason. Express the reason with *because of* and a noun phrase. Example:

  I wanted to play basketball last night, but I couldn't because of my hay fever.

Written Practice 3:   Complete these sentences with an appropriate preposition or prepositional expression and *supply any needed commas.* Try to use several different expressions,
rather than the same ones over and over again.

1.   _____ a strong desire to see that movie I stayed home last night and
     studied.

2.   I made an A on my chemistry lab quiz _____ my decision to stay
     home.

3.   _____ the quiz I thought, ''This quiz is easy! I'm glad I studied last
     night.''

4.   _____ my chemistry lab I went home and had a good nap.

5.   _____ Freddy's kindness I don't enjoy being around him.

6.   _____ the increase in tuition next semester Bill is looking for a
     part-time job.

7.   I got only a C on that paper _____ all my hard work.

8.   _____ Stan's practice session Mr. Jones tried to watch TV and Ms. Jones tried
     to read.

9.   That class was canceled _____ its small enrollment.

10. We wanted to go on a hike, but we decided not to do it _____ the cold
     weather.

24.4 Conjunctive Adverbs		
Complete these model sentences.	Check.	Complete these rules.
a. There weren't any parking **spaces; _____,** **Tom's father parked in the driveway.**	therefore/ thus/ consequently/ as a result	Words and expressions such as ***however, as a result, meanwhile,*** and ***otherwise*** can also connect sentences. One name for these words and expressions is **conjunctive adverbs.** Some conjunctive adverbs that are used to introduce a **result** are ***thus,***_____, _____, and _____ _____ _____.

24.4 Conjunctive Adverbs (Continued)		
b. Tom's father was in the store; _____ a robber was holding up the bank across the street. The clerk gave the robber the money; _____ the robber ran across the street.	meanwhile then	Two conjunctive adverbs that are used to show **time** relationships are _____ and _____. Other common time connectors are *since then, afterward, after that, before that, later, later on, next, subsequently, soon,* and *eventually.*
c. Mr. Bogard had stopped the crime; _____, he received a parking ticket.	however/ nevertheless	Two conjunctive adverbs that are used to introduce *unexpected results* are _____ and _____.
d. It is fortunate that Mr. Bogard had parked in the driveway; _____, the robber would have escaped.	otherwise	*Otherwise* is a conjunctive adverb that is used to introduce what will or would happen, or what would have happened, under different **conditions.** A paraphrase of model sentence **d** is: **The robber would have escaped if Mr. Bogard** _____ _____ _____ **in the driveway.**

e. When two sentences are connected with a conjunctive adverb, it is a mistake to use a comma between

them. You must use either a period or a _____. There is usually a comma

_____ the conjunctive verb. However, the adverb *then* does not require a comma after it. Nevertheless, it *is* a conjunctive adverb. Therefore, the following sentence has an error. Rewrite the sentence correctly.

First, I did my math homework, then I studied for the chemistry quiz.

_____

Oral Practice 4A: Tell the story of Tom's father's misadventure again. This time, practice speaking formally, and use conjunctive adverbs such as *therefore, nevertheless, meanwhile,* and *otherwise* to show relationships between events.

Oral Practice 4B: Think of a recent situation that had an unexpected result. Use *however* or *nevertheless.*

Written Practice 4:   Complete these sentences with an appropriate conjunctive adverb and *add any needed punctuation marks.*

1. I wanted to go to that movie last night _____ I decided to stay home and study.

2. My friends were enjoying a good movie _____ I was trying to figure out chemical formulas.

3. I stayed home and studied _____ I got an A on my quiz.

4. It's a good thing that I stayed home and studied _____ I probably would have done poorly on the quiz.

5. Freddy is quite kind _____ I don't enjoy being around him very much.

6. Tuition is scheduled to increase next semester _____ Bill is looking into the possibility of a part-time job.

7. I worked diligently on that paper _____ I received only a C for my work.

8. Mr. Jones watched a television show, and his wife read a novel _____ Stan practiced on his saxophone.

9. Very few students enrolled in that class _____ it was canceled.

10. The temperature fell suddenly _____ we decided not to go on the hike that we had been looking forward to.

24.5 Chapter Check: Study this cartoon story:

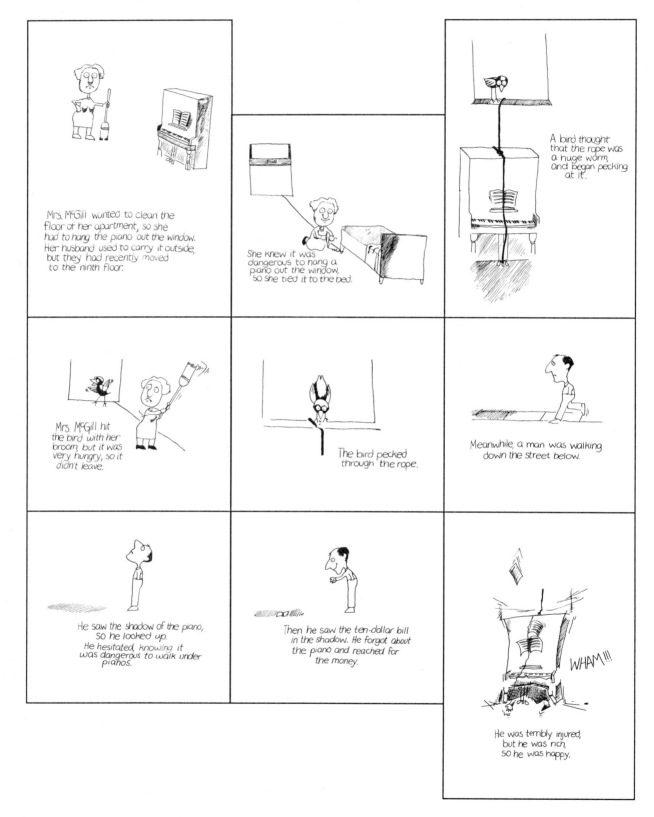

Complete these sentences. If you are unsure of an answer, check the indicated model sentence and rule.

1. Mrs. McGill had to hang the piano out the window _____ she wanted to clean her floor. [24.2a]

2. Mrs. McGill asked Mr. McGill to move the piano, _____ he refused. [24.1]

3. She knew it was dangerous to hang a piano out the window; _____, she tied it to the bed. [24.4c]

4. _____ Mrs. McGill hit the bird with her broom, it continued pecking at the rope _____ its extreme hunger. [24.2c, 24.3a]

5. _____ the piano was hanging from the rope, a man in the street below passed directly underneath it. [24.2b]

6. It is fortunate that the man had a very hard head. _____, he would have been killed by the piano. [24.4d]

24.6 Chapter Check: Finish sentence B so that it has about the same meaning as sentence A. Examine the punctuation of the B sentences carefully.

1. A. Since the McGills had recently moved to the ninth floor, Mrs. McGill could not put the piano out on the sidewalk.

   B. The McGills had recently moved to the ninth floor; _____, they could not put the piano out on the sidewalk. [24.4a]

2. A. Although it was dangerous, she hung the piano out the window.

   B. _____ the danger, she hung the piano out the window. [24.3c]

3. A. Because the rope looked like a worm, the bird began to peck at it.

   B. The rope looked like a worm, _____ the bird began to peck at it. [24.1]

4. A. It's too bad that the man forgot about the piano hanging above his head; otherwise, he would not have reached for the money.

   B. _____ the man _____ about the piano hanging above his head, he would not have reached for the money. [24.2d]

5. A. Even though the man was terribly injured, he was happy because he was $10 richer.

   B. The man was terribly injured; _____, he was happy because he was $10 richer. [24.4c]

6. A. While all these crazy things were happening, Mr. McGill was watching TV.

   B. Many crazy things were happening around the McGills' apartment; _____, Mr. McGill was watching TV. [24.4b]

7. A. After the man spent a few days in the hospital, he went to the best candy shop in town and spent his $10.

    B. The man spent a few days in the hospital; _____ he went to the best candy shop in town and spend his $10.   [24.4b]

24.7 Chapter Check: Finish sentences B and C. They should have about the same meaning as sentence A.

1. A. We had a substitute teacher one day last week because our teacher's wife had just had a baby.

    B. Our teacher's wife had just had a baby, _____

      _____.   [24.1]

    C. Our teacher's wife had just had a baby last week; _____

      _____. [24.4a]

2. A. Clara was quite ill; nevertheless, she went to the meeting to deliver the lecture.

    B. _____ ill, she went to the meeting to deliver the lecture.   [24.2c]

    C. Clara _____

      her illness.   [24.3]

3. A. The players were celebrating their victory; meanwhile, someone broke into their hotel rooms and stole cash, clothing, and jewelry.

    B. _____, someone broke into their hotel rooms and stole cash, clothing, and jewelry.   [24.2b]

    C. _____ the celebration after the victory, someone broke into the players' hotel rooms and stole cash, clothing, and jewelry.   [24.3b]

24.8 Warm-up: Form two groups. Each group will prepare a list of sentences about the events shown in the cartoons (24.5 Chapter Check). Group one should focus on the reasons and results. Find three sets of reasons and results, and think of many different ways to express these ideas. Group two should focus on events with unexpected results. Choose three events with unexpected results, and think of many different ways to express them. After a few minutes, the two groups can share their results.

24.9 Communication: Form two small groups. The goal of each group will be to produce a story which includes these words:

gorilla	consequently
elegant	even though
remember	due to
note	meanwhile
collapse	despite
loud	otherwise

Try to make your story as interesting as possible. Your teacher can help you decide how you will share your story with the people in the other groups. Perhaps you can read the stories aloud, or maybe they can be photocopied.

24.10   Punctuation Exercise: Add any needed punctuation to these sentences:

1. Before the bus arrived we had a nice long chat.
2. John had corrected his paper but then he lost it.
3. Edna fainted when she saw the man of her dreams.
4. The chef had been fired the day before consequently the meal was awful.
5. The committee had a short meeting before they started interviewing candidates.
6. We didn't receive the vaccine therefore we became ill.

24.11   Sentence Writing: Rewrite these sentences, changing the subordinating conjunction to a preposition or a prepositional expression—***because of, in spite of, despite***—and making other necessary changes.

1. They didn't come because it snowed.
2. Even though the climate is mild, it can occasionally get very hot.
3. Because the show got out late, we didn't get to bed until three.
4. He was accepted by the club although he had a bad reputation.

24.12   Sentence Writing: Rewrite the sentences, using the words ***therefore, however, as a result,*** or ***nevertheless.***

1. The night was so beautiful that no one wanted to go inside.
2. Although he felt embarrassed, everyone told him he had done a fine job.
3. The directions were clear, but John couldn't find the house.
4. She is a hard worker, so they give her frequent raises.

24.13   Sentence Writing: In this exercise, you are given a reason and a result. Connect them in four different ways, using (a) ***so***, (b) ***because***, (c) ***because of***, and (d) ***as a result***. For each reason and result you will write four sentences. Be careful with punctuation.

	Reason	**Result**
1.	It was raining.	The ball game was canceled.
2.	The phone was ringing constantly.	Stan couldn't sleep.
3.	The prime minister died.	The flags are at half-mast.

24.14   Reflecting: Read the next episode of the mystery story. Look for connectors—coordinating conjunctions, subordinating conjunctions, prepositions, and conjunctive adverbs. Think of other ways of expressing some of these ideas. Do some of these other ways of expressing the relationships seem better to you? Do you see any missed opportunities—any place where using a connecting word would make the relationship between two ideas clearer?

"I'm a nice person," Linda told me on the phone. "Otherwise, I wouldn't be talking to you now."

"I'm taking the night off," I said. "I thought we might see each other."

"I'll consider it, even though you are a rotten person," she said.

We made a date for eight o'clock. I had to run home to take a shower because I was wearing a day's sweat.

I have the habit of checking my answering machine right when I walk in the door. This time, however, I waited until after my shower because I was thinking about where I would take Linda to dinner. Since I had forgotten the last time, it would have to be someplace nice. Eventually, I decided on an Irish bar with good food.

When I got dressed, I listened to my calls.

"Stop looking for Deanne's husband," said a whispered voice on one of the messages.

24.15   Real-World Work

THINK/PRACTICE

1. Think of a recent situation in which many things happened—for example, a class, a party, or a morning at a job. Or remember a story—something you read, watched on TV, or saw in a movie. Tell yourself what happened. Use various time connectors: ***when, while, before, after, as soon as, during, then, meanwhile, afterwards***, and so on. Think of different ways you could express the time relationships.

2. Think of things that have happened recently. Why did these things happen? Practice expressing the reasons with various expressions—***because, since, because of, due to, therefore, as a result,*** and so on.

LOOK/LISTEN

1. Choose an article from a newspaper or magazine or a page from a textbook. Look for connectors discussed in this chapter. Mark them. Then try to think of different connectors that could be used to express the same ideas.

2. Some of your English textbooks may have given you difficulty because you haven't understood the logical connectors used. Choose a passage from a textbook with a lot of connectors, and practice changing the more unfamiliar structures into ones you are more familiar with: ***because, although,*** and so on.

USE

In your own writing, do you use too many short sentences that make your letters, reports, and essays seem rather simplistic? Perhaps you make longer sentences mainly by combining simple sentences with ***and, but,*** and ***so***. You can make your writing clearer, more interesting, and more persuasive if you are able to show relationships between ideas in a variety of ways. If you read a lot of good writing in English, you will develop a feeling for connectors and their usage, and you will improve your writing style.

25

About that raise, sir...
NO

Emphasis

REVIEW

There are many different ways that you can emphasize something you want to say in English. Look at this sentence:

He baked his mother a cake.

There are a lot of ways to say this sentence, and how you say it depends on the information that you want to stress or emphasize. Often we show emphasis with just the voice by putting stress on a word or a part of a sentence. How would you say the sentence if it were an answer to these questions?

a. *What did Larry do this morning?*
b. *Did Larry buy his mother a cake?*
c. *Did Larry bake his brother a cake?*
d. *Did Larry bake his mother a pie?*

There are other ways to show emphasis in English. In chapter 13, Rule 13.2d, you learned that you can emphasize a noun by putting a reflexive pronoun after it. For example, in answer to this question:

e. *Who baked that cake for Larry's mother?*

You could answer:

Larry _______________ *baked that cake.*

PREVIEW

Finish sentence A so that it has about the same meaning as sentence B. In the A sentences, emphasis is shown by underlining certain words. Read these sentence aloud, emphasizing the underlined words by giving them more stress. In the B sentences the same words are emphasized by using different structures.

1. A. I <u>turned off</u> the lights before I left the house.

    B. I _____ turn off the lights before I left the house.

2. A. I have <u>never</u> left the house without turning the lights off.

    B. Never _____ left the house without turning the lights off.

3. A. <u>Mike</u> forgot to turn them off.

    B. It was Mike _____ forgot to turn them off.

25.1 Emphasizing Positive and Negative Statements		
Complete these model sentences.	Check.	Complete these rules.
a. Oscar: I think I need a new car. **Sadie: I disagree. You do** **_____ need a new car, Oscar.**	not	We often use emphasis when we contradict what another person has said. When we negate someone's statement, we can do this more emphatically by *not* contracting the auxiliary verb + _____ and putting extra stress on ***not***.
b. Sadie: You haven't thought this over. **Oscar: I _____ thought it over!** **Sadie: But you don't really need another car, Oscar.** **Oscar: I _____ need one! The old one is in terrible shape!**	have do	To emphasize a positive statement, stress the auxiliary verb, for example _____. If the verb is in the **simple present**, use the auxiliary verb _____ or ***does*** + the **base form** of the main verb to emphasize the statement.
c. Sadie: But you never go anywhere! **Oscar: I _____ take a short trip last summer.**	did	To emphasize a **simple past verb**, use _____ + the _____ form of the verb.

Oral Practice 1:   Tell a classmate something he forgot to do earlier in the day. Make an "accusation," pretending to be serious. Your classmate should strongly disagree. Example:

> *You didn't wash the breakfast dishes!*
> *That's not true! I did wash them!*

Written Practice 1A: Contradict each of these sentences with an emphatic sentence. Add a form of *do* whenever possible. Example:

> *You don't have to go to the meeting.*
> *I do have to go!*

1. You always talk with your mouth full.
2. Carl said he could come tonight.
3. Bob doesn't try hard.
4. You don't want another piece of pie, do you?
5. Aaron will be glad to see us.
6. You didn't say thank you to Sharon.

Written Practice 1B: *Do* is often used for emphasis in sentences in which an affirmative statement is contrasted with a negative statement. Complete these sentences using *do* for emphasis. The first one has been done for you.

1. I don't like ___*American football*___ , but I ___*do like basketball*___ .

2. I don't speak the _____ language, but I _____

   _____ .

3. Oscar and Sadie don't enjoy TV, but _____ .

4. Our teacher doesn't let us _____ , but she _____

   _____ .

5. My native country, _____ , does not have _____

   _____ .

6. The house that I grew up in didn't have _____

   _____ .

7. _____ does not have much money, but _____

   _____ .

8. Athletes from _____ do not do very well in international athletic competition, _____ .

25.2 **Emphasizing Negative Adverbs**		
Tyrone, the used car dealer, is trying to encourage Oscar to buy a car from his lot.		
Complete these model sentences.	Check.	Complete these rules.
a. Oscar, I have a great deal for you! _____ **will you have a chance like this again!** _____ _____ **do I give customers deals like this. The last time was in 1969.**	Never Not often/ Hardly ever/ Very rarely/ Very seldom	Negative time adverbs—such as _____, _____ _____, _____ _____, *very rarely,* and _____ _____ can be emphasized by placing them at the beginning of sentences. If a sentence begins with one of these adverbs, *question* word order must be used. These are *not* questions, however.
b. _____ **for a friend could I make a deal like this!** _____ **once in a lifetime does an opportunity like this come along!**	Only Only	An adverbial phrase beginning with _____ has a negative meaning. When such a phrase is emphasized by putting it at the beginning of the sentence, question word order must be used, just as with the negative time adverbs in rule **a.**

Oral Practice 2:   The structure presented in Rule Builder 25.2 is definitely used more in writing than in speaking. However, sentences beginning with the expressions *hardly ever, very* or *only rarely,* and *seldom* are fairly common in conversational English. Often we use this structure to introduce a situation when we actually did this unusual thing. Think of something that you do rarely or hardly ever but that you did on a special occasion, and tell the class. Begin your sentence with the negative expression. Examples:

Very rarely do I cook, but last weekend I prepared a special dinner for some good friends of mine.
Hardly ever do I go to concerts, but I recently had the chance to see Itzhak Perlmann play, and I really enjoyed myself.

Written Practice 2:   Underline the negative expression in each sentence. Then rewrite it, putting the negative expression at the beginning.

1. You will never see skies like this in New York!
2. You can very seldom find the ocean this calm.
3. You hardly ever get any rest; you ought to take it easy!
4. She rarely gives her studies the attention they deserve.
5. You will see Halley's Comet only once in a lifetime.
6. Deer may be hunted only for a very short period of time in this state.

25.3 Emphasizing a Noun Phrase		
Sadie and Oscar are still arguing about Oscar's decision to buy a new car.		
Complete this model sentence.	Check.	Complete these rules.
a. Sadie: Oscar, you could have replaced your old furniture with that money. **Oscar: I wanted a new *car*, not new furniture.** **or It was a new _____ I wanted, not new furniture.**	car (that)	One way to emphasize a noun phrase is simply to put extra stress on the noun when you pronounce the sentence. Another way is to use this structure: _____ + *be* + **noun phrase** + **adjective clause**

Oral Practice 3A: The structure presented in Rule Builder 25.3 is often used to correct false statements. Turn back to the STUDENT INFORMATION SHEET in chapter 1. Make a false statement about a member of the class. Put a tag on it. Other students can correct your false statements. Example:

Hao plans to study electrical engineering, doesn't he?

No. It's Mourad who plans to study electrical engineering, not Hao.
or No, it's business that Hao plans to study, not electrical engineering.

Oral Practice 3B: Make a false statement about something you know about geography, and add a tag. Other students should correct you. Example:

Illinois lies just east of Kansas, doesn't it?
No, it's Missouri that lies just east of Kansas.

Written Practice 3: Review the chart on inventions and discoveries in chapter 8 (Oral Practice 7A). Then correct the misunderstandings expressed in the following negative statements. Use the *it + be + noun phrase + adjective clause* structure. Write three responses to each negative question following this example:

> *Didn't Morse invent the phonograph?*
> *No, it wasn't Morse who invented the phonograph.*
> *It was Edison who invented the phonograph.*
> *It was the telegraph that Morse invented.*

1. Didn't Priestly discover radium?
2. Didn't Kepler discover the law of falling bodies?
3. Didn't Marconi invent the phonograph?
4. Didn't Morse invent printing for the blind?

25.4 Chapter Check: Complete these sentences. If you are unsure of an answer, check the indicated model sentence and rule.

1. Seldom _____ visitors leave New York City without seeing the Statue of Liberty.

    [25.2a]

2. I don't like opera, but I _____ like symphonic music.

    [25.1b]

3. It's Stan _____ plays the saxophone, not Mr. Jones.

    [25.3]

4. I know you don't like pizza. If you _____ like pizza, I would have invited you to go with us last night.

    [25.1c]

25.5 Chapter Check: Finish sentence B. It should have about the same meaning as sentence A.

1. A. We have never had a more wonderful time than we had last night.

    B. Never _____ than we had last night.

    [25.2a]

2. A. We decided to leave only when the band stopped playing.

    B. Only when the band _____.

    [25.2b]

3. A. I was intoxicated because of the dancing, not because of the drinking.

    B. It _____ intoxicated me, not the drinking.

    [25.3]

25.6 Warm-up: In the following dialogue, the participants are arguing. People usually speak emphatically in an argument. With your classmates, try to make this dialogue more realistic by thinking about how the participants could speak more emphatically. Try to use the structures in this chapter to make all of the statements more emphatic.

MOTHER: I have never seen such a messy room.
KATHY: I didn't do it, so I don't have to clean it up.
MOTHER: You did it. You have to clean it up.

KATHY: Bill made this mess.
MOTHER: Did you do this, Bill? If so, you have to clean it up.
BILL: I cleaned it up. Kathy messed it up again.
KATHY: I didn't.

25.7 Communication: Team up with a classmate who comes from another country, area, or town. Without discussing this with your classmate, make a list of assumptions or beliefs you have about the place your classmate is from and the people who live there. You might consider geography, history, government, and customs. You and your classmate should read your lists to each other. Respond to each thing said by agreeing or disagreeing and explaining the response. The structures of emphasis in this chapter will be very useful. Examples:

> *Yes, many of the rural people <u>do want</u> to move to the large cities.*
> *Oh no, <u>it was Korea that had the 1988 Olympic games</u>, not Japan.*
> *No, that's not true. <u>Very rarely do people die in earthquakes</u>.*

25.8 Dialogue Writing: Rewrite the dialogue in 25.6 Warm-up. Make every statement more emphatic by using a structure from this chapter.

25.9 Essay Writing: Write a short essay on misconceptions about your country. Think of at least three things that people from other countries mistakenly believe about your country. Before writing the essay, review the structures of emphasis covered in this chapter. Try to use these structures in clearing up these misconceptions.

25.10 Sentence Completion: This exercise involves words that are used to express the idea of emphasis. Supply any needed prepositions. Some of the verbs are transitive; that is, they do not require prepositions. Refer to Appendix 2 if necessary.

1. We must emphasize _____ the importance of the issue.

2. We must put emphasis _____ the importance of the issue.

3. We must stress _____ the importance of the issue.

4. We must place stress _____ the importance of the issue.

5. We must underline _____ the importance of the issue.

6. At the meeting, we must focus _____ our attention _____ this issue.

7. At the meeting, we must keep this issue _____ focus.

8. We cannot overemphasize _____ the importance of this issue.

25.11 Reflecting: Read the next episode of the mystery story. Notice the structures that are used for emphasis.

> I called up Lieutenant Farmer to tell him about my strange phone call.
> "You got a threatening phone call?" he laughed. "Not very often have I heard anything that funny."
> "You have a great sense of humor," I growled at him. I told him I had the call on tape.
> "You can send it in, and I'll give it to the lab myself," he said. "I don't know what they'll do with it though."
> "You did know that Deanne Miller got a call, too, didn't you?"
> "You told me," he said.
> "I'm getting close to finding out what happened to Miller," I said.
> "If you ever do find him, let me know," Farmer said. "I would love to close that case. I have an awful lot of other things to do."

25.12   Real-World Work

THINK/PRACTICE

1. Think of things that never, almost never, or very rarely happen or that you very seldom do. Practice expressing these ideas emphatically by beginning the sentences with the negative expressions.

2. Think of a disagreement that you have had recently with someone. Try to remember what was said. Probably some of the statements were false. Think about how you could have contradicted those false statements with this structure: ***It + be + noun phrase + adjective clause.** Example:

No, it wasn't Carter who ran against Reagan in 1984; it was Mondale.

LOOK/LISTEN

1. In a newspaper, try to find a sentence that starts with a negative expression followed by question word order. Your teacher may want you to bring it to class to share with your classmates.

2. Listen carefully when you hear two friends have a disagreement about something. When two people disagree, or when someone corrects a statement that they think is false, you will almost certainly hear some of the things you have seen in this chapter. You may hear other ways of emphasizing things; pay close attention to these.

USE

In 25.7 Communication, you agreed with or contradicted things that a classmate said about your native country. This situation will probably occur many times when you meet Americans. You can say, for example:

I agree; the students in my country do take a more active role in politics than students here.

This is one situation in which you will need the emphatic structures used in this chapter.

26

Verb and Adverb Review II

26.1 Part Five Check: Complete sentence B. It should have about the same meaning as sentence A. If you are unsure of an answer, check the indicated model sentence and rule.

1. A. Stan started playing the saxophone at 10:00, and he's still playing.

    B. Stan _____ since

        10.   [21.1b]

2. A. Jimmy got that car three years ago, and he still has it.

    B. Jimmy _____ for three years.   [21.2]

3. A. Oscar is not at home, but his car is in the front of the house. I guess he's taking a

        walk.

    B. Oscar is not at home, but his car is in front of the house. He must _____

        _____.   [23.1b]

4. A. Tank is able to go to college only because he has a football scholarship.

    B. Tank _____ if

        _____ not have a football scholarship.   [21.5a&d]

5. A. The Joneses are sorry that they don't have a quiet apartment.

    B. The Joneses wish _____.

                                                                                 [21.6a]

6. A. Oscar retired four years ago. He met Sadie last year.

    B. Oscar _____ been retired for three years when he met Sadie.   [22.1]

7. A. The Joneses are an hour late. Maybe they forgot.

    B. The Joneses are an hour late. They might _____.   [22.2b]

8. A. These hamburgers are great! Mike himself must have made them.

    B. These hamburgers are great! They _____ by

    Mike himself.   [22.2c]

9. A. Hank didn't have enough money; otherwise, he would have gone to the concert

    with us.

    B. If Hank _____, he would have

    gone to the concert with us.   [22.4]

10. A. University rules require that all non-native speakers of English take a language profi-

    ciency test.

    B. According to university rules, all non-native speakers of English

    _____ a language proficiency test.   [23.4a]

11. A. My sister will probably graduate in May.

    B. My sister _____ graduate in May.   [23.2c]

12. A. I suggest that you not tell Margaret about this yet.

    B. You _____ Margaret about this yet.   [23.4d]

13. A. He had planned to go to the party, but he decided not to go.

    B. _____ he had planned to go to the party, he decided

    not to go.   [24.2c]

14. A. The thunderstorm prevented us from having a picnic.

    B. We couldn't have a picnic _____ the

    thunderstorm.   [24.3a]

15. A. Although the house is in poor condition, the Pearsons are interested in buying it.

    B. The Pearsons are interested in buying the house _____ its poor

    condition.   [24.3c]

16. A. If you don't hurry, you'll be late.

    B. You'd better hurry; _____, you'll be late.   [24.4d]

17. A. Mr. Benson left his house only on rare occasions.

    B. Only _____

    _____.   [25.2b]

26.2 Paragraph Completion: Fill in the blanks with an appropriate form of the verb given. *Many of the verbs will be passive.*

Three interesting objects (*find*) _____ recently _____ during an excavation in Heidelberg, Germany. A brass candlestick, a sword, and a pottery colander—a dish (*use*) _____ to drain water from foods—(*discover*) _____ in the ruins of a house a few hundred years old. At first archeologists (*puzzle*) _____ by the finds because normally this style of colander had (*own*) _____ by poor families. However, brass candlesticks had (*use*) _____ by wealthy families. The archeologists (*understand + not*) _____ why these objects (*unearth*) _____ in the same house. Finally, someone noticed that the sword was a kind that (*use*) _____ in fighting against the French during the Thirty Years' War. Thus, an answer to the mystery (*suggest*) _____. The house might (*belong*) _____ to a family that had been wealthy before the war, but whose wealth could (*lose*) _____ by a defeat during the war. So some of the discoveries indicated wealth, but others, poverty.

26.3 Sentence Writing: Here is another story about the McGills. First, read the story.

Mrs. McGill had spent the whole day cleaning. She was tired. She wanted to relax by playing cards with her friends.

Her husband <u>hates</u> card games. She had to make him leave the house. She knew he wouldn't leave for a card game.

She called her husband's best friend, John. She told John to invite her husband out for a drink. She called her friends and invited them over.

John and Mr. McGill went to a nearby bar.

Inside, there was a piano player who said he could play the piano blindfolded. Mr. McGill didn't believe him. They made a $20 bet.

Mr. McGill lost the bet. He was depressed. He wondered what he would tell his wife.

At home, Mrs. McGill was playing cards. Her friends wanted to play for money. She didn't want to, but they were her guests, so she didn't refuse.

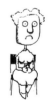

She won $20. She wondered what she would tell her husband.

Now fill in the chart.

Reason	Result
1. Mrs. McGill had spent the whole day cleaning.	_____
2. She was tired.	_____
3. Mr. McGill hates card games.	_____
4. She knew he wouldn't leave if she asked him.	_____
5. Mr. McGill didn't believe the piano player.	_____
6. Mr. McGill lost the bet.	_____
7. Mrs. McGill didn't want to argue with her friends.	**She agreed to** _____

Now write a sentence expressing each of the reason-result relationships in the preceding list. Use each of these expressions once: *so, because, therefore, as a result, since,* and *consequently*.

26.4 Sentence Writing: Each of these sentences explains a difficult situation that you might find yourself in. For each situation write two sentences. In the first one, tell what you should or must do in the situation. In the second sentence, tell what you should have done to avoid being in that situation.

1. As you are driving out of your driveway, you can't remember if you turned off your oven.
2. You realize that your best friend's birthday was last week and you forgot to say anything to him/her.
3. You are turning a corner in your car, and you hit another car parked along the street.

26.5 Paragraph Writing: The following sentences tell a story. But the story is difficult to read and boring because all of the sentences are short and simple, and there are no connecting expressions. Rewrite the story, using a variety of conjunctions, conjunctive adverbs, and relative clauses to connect the ideas.

> *Our janitor swept the hallway today.*
> *He usually does a very good job.*
> *He was in a hurry.*
> *He missed the corner.*
> *There was a banana peel in the corner.*
> *A dog saw the banana peel.*
> *Dogs don't eat banana peels.*
> *The dog picked it up in his mouth.*
> *He carried it to the top of the stairs.*
> *He saw our neighbor's cat.*
> *He dropped the banana peel at the top of the stairs.*
> *He chased the cat.*
> *I came out of my apartment.*
> *Normally, I'm very careful.*
> *I had a lot on my mind.*
> *I didn't see the banana peel.*
> *I stepped on it.*
> *I tried to grab the railing.*
> *I fell down the stairs.*

26.6 Sentence Writing: Review the story about the McGills (24.5 Chapter Check). Write five things that Mrs. McGill, Mr. McGill, or the man ***should*** or ***should not*** have done. After each of these sentences, write another sentence explaining what ***would*** or ***would not*** have happened if they ***had*** or ***had not*** done these things.

26.7 Paragraph Writing: Write a paragraph about what a student must and should do before coming to study in the U.S.

26.8 Paragraph Writing: Pretend that a guest recently visited the home of your parents or the home of a relative. Write a paragraph telling the things that the guest must have or might have seen/noticed/enjoyed/found out in this house.

27

Carelessy walking into the hole, WILSON was never seen again.

Participles

This chapter is about **participles**: **present participles**, which end in *-ing*, and **past participles**, most of which end in *-ed* or *-en*. Of course, these forms are not new to you. The *-ing* form is used as the main verb in **progressive** verb phrases; the **past participle** is used in **perfect** and **passive** verb phrases.

REVIEW

Supply the correct verb forms in this paragraph.

In the autumn of 1988, three California gray whales, which had (*be*) _____ (*try*) _____ to migrate south, were (*trap*) _____ by ice near Alaska's north shore. A small war was (*wage*) _____ to save them. Exotic equipment was (*bring in*) _____ from around the world, and hotels in the small town of Barrow were (*pack*) _____ with reporters and whale experts. Thousands of hours were (*devote*) _____ to breaking up the ice to free the whales.

Some experts argued that this whale species was not (*be*) _____ (*help*)

_____ by the massive rescue efforts. They said that the species was (*flour-

ish*) _____; in fact, gray whales were (*do*) _____ so

well that the environment could not support them all.

PREVIEW

In this chapter, you will use present and past participles as **modifiers**. Try to supply the correct forms of verbs in these sentences.

1.   The youngest and smallest of the (*trap*) _____ whales disap-

     peared a few days after the rescue attempt began.

2.   A special net (*build*) _____ to carry the whales was brought to the

     scene.

3.   (*concern*) _____ about the fate of these whales, hundreds of

     scientists, journalists, and other interested people converged on Barrow, Alaska.

4.   Before (*head*) _____ to Alaska to help in the rescue effort, several

     Soviet ships unloaded equipment for a research station at the North Pole.

5.   Scientists and volunteers spent thousands of hours (*attempt*) _____ to free

     the giant mammals.

	27.1 Participles Used as Adjectives	

Sadie and Oscar are driving home after watching a basketball game.

Complete these model sentences.	Check.	Complete these rules.

Sadie: Wasn't that a *(thrill)* _____ **game?**
Oscar: Yes! I was really *(excite)* _____ **during the last two minutes. How long have you been** *(interest)* _____ **in basketball, Sadie?**
Sadie: Oh, I've always thought basketball was a *(fascinate)* _____ **game.**
	thrilling
	
	excited
	
	interested
	
	fascinating
		When the **-ing form** of a verb is used as a modifier, it is often called a **present participle**. The **past participle** of many verbs can also be used as a modifier.
		    Like normal adjectives, the participle forms of many verbs can be used as adjectives before a noun or after a linking verb. Some examples are ***daring, broken, frozen, closed.*** Most verbs, however, cannot be used this way. You must learn these participle adjectives just as you learn other vocabulary.
		    Some of the most common verbal adjectives come from verbs of emotion—for example: ***thrill***, _____, _____, and _____. A list of some of these verbs follows. Be careful, because the two participle forms don't have the same meaning. The **present participle**, for example, _____, modifies the person or thing that causes the emotion. The **past participle**, for example, _____, modifies the person who experiences the emotion.

Here are some common verbs of emotion. The present and past participles of all of these verbs can be used as adjectives.

please	interest	surprise	frighten	bore	disappoint
satisfy	fascinate	amaze	alarm	tire	depress
amuse	stimulate	astonish	startle	annoy	disgust
inspire	thrill	shock	horrify	disturb	insult
	excite	embarrass	intimidate	irritate	
		confuse			
		puzzle			
		bewilder			

Oral Practice 1A: Pick a verb from the list below; then follow the directions.

bake	*steal*	*break*	*assign*
broil	*lose*	*tear*	*require*
steam	*hide*	*crush*	*finish*
freeze	*endanger*	*waste*	*forget*

1.   Make up an active-voice sentence. Example:

   The construction company has finished the bridge.

2.   Change the sentence to the passive voice.

   The bridge has been finished.

3.   Use the past participle as an adjective after **be**.

   We can use that bridge now; it's finished.

4.   Use the past participle as an adjective before the noun.

   Many people came to see the finished bridge.

Oral Practice 1B: The teacher or a student will pick one of the verbs of emotion in the list in Rule Builder 27.1 and ask the class to think of something that has that effect on them. Example:

   Think of something that bores you.

Everyone should be ready to make three sentences like these:

   Soap operas really bore me.
   Soap operas are really boring.
   I am really bored when I watch soap operas.

Written Practice 1A: Complete these sentences by adding present or past participles.

1.   If someone steals a computer, we can refer to the machine as a _____ computer.

2.   If a parent loses a child in a department store, the parent may go to the office to report a _____ child.

3.   Parents who understand and love their children are called _____ and _____ parents.

4.   If you put apples in the oven and bake them, you can then eat _____ apples.

5.   If the cold wind nearly freezes your fingers, you can describe the wind as _____ and your fingers as nearly _____.

6.   As snow falls, we can refer to it as _____ snow.

Written Practice 1B: Finish sentences B and C. They should have about the same meaning as sentence A.

1.   A.   His behavior annoys me.

    B.   I don't like his _____ behavior.

    C.   I _____ really _____ at his behavior.

2.   A.   The speaker's words inspired the young woman.

    B.   The young woman _____ by the speaker's words.

    C.   For the young woman, the speaker's words were _____.

3.   A.   The movie monster frightened the young children, so they put their hands over their eyes.

    B.   The _____ young children put their hands over their eyes so that they couldn't see the movie monster.

    C.   The children put their hands over their eyes because of the _____ movie monster.

4.   A.   The news startled me so much that I dropped my newspaper.

    B.   The news was _____ that I dropped my newspaper.

    C.   I _____ by the news that I dropped my newspaper.

5.   A.   The designs on this ancient pot fascinate me.

    B.   I _____ by the designs on this ancient pot.

    C.   The designs on this ancient pot are _____ to me.

27.2 Participle Phrases in Place of Adjective Clauses		
Complete these model sentences.	Check.	Complete these rules.
a. The man who is playing the saxophone is named Stan. *or* **The man _____ the saxophone is named Stan.** **A man who is named Stan is playing the saxophone.** *or* **A man _____ Stan is playing the saxophone.** **The people who are being bothered by his playing are named Jones.** *or* **The people _____** **_____ by his playing are named Jones.**	playing named being bothered	We saw a way to shorten adjective clauses in Rule Builder 18.1c. If the first word in the clause is a relative pronoun and is followed by a form of **be**, we can usually drop both the _____ _____ and the form of _____. Look at the phrase that remains. It can be a **participle phrase** that begins with either a **present participle**, such as _____, or a **past participle**, such as _____. And sometimes what remains is a **passive participle**: *being* + the _____ participle
b. Stan is interested in a new saxophone that costs over $500. *or* **Stan is interested in a new** **saxophone _____ over $500.**	costing	When an adjective clause with a stative verb modifies a noun that refers to a thing—for example, *a saxophone that costs $500*—it is usually possible to replace the adjective clause with a **present _____ phrase**.

Oral Practice 2A: Tell about a thing that you have or would like to have. Describe the thing with a participle made from one of these stative verbs:

cost	need	consist of	overlook
weigh	require	contain	resemble
		concern	

Example:

I would like a house overlooking the ocean.

Oral Practice 2B: Turn back to chapter 7 and look at the family scene (7.19 Paragraph Writing). Make up names for the people; then tell who each individual is, identifying him or her with a participle phrase. *Make some of the phrases passive.* Examples:

The girl <u>feeding the cat</u> *is named Sarah.*
The cat <u>being fed by the girl</u> *is named Ajax.*

Written Practice 2:   Finish sentence B. It should have about the same meaning as sentence A. *Write only one word in each blank.*

1. A. A man was trying to repair the window, and he broke the glass.

    B. A man _____ to repair the window broke the glass.

2. A. The students who are lined up in the hall are waiting for scholarship checks.

    B. The students _____ up in the hall are waiting for scholarship checks.

3. A. One of the people who are being nominated for the award lives next door to me.

    B. One of the people _____ _____ for the award lives

    next door to me.

4. A. The sculptor is working on a piece of stone that weighs over a ton.

    B. The sculptor is working on a piece of stone _____ over a ton.

5. A. The book which has that information is in the reference section.

    B. The book _____ that information is in the reference section.

6. A. The turkey which was baked slowly tasted better than the other one.

    B. The turkey _____ slowly tasted better than the other one.

7. A. Students who are living in apartments often do not eat as well as those who are liv-

    ing in residence halls.

    B. Students _____ in apartments often do not eat as well as those

    _____ in residence halls.

27.3	Participle Phrases in Place of Adverbial Clauses

Irving Thornapple, a noted art critic, is visiting a new exhibition in a museum. He is taking notes about the paintings. These are his notes.

Complete these model sentences. Write only one word in each blank.	Check.	Complete these rules.
a. Because I hope to rediscover the great artist Simarov, I have come to the Reynolds Gallery today. *or* _____ **to rediscover the great artist Simarov, I have come today to the Reynolds Gallery.** **As I stand in front of this painting, I am again reminded of Simarov's greatness.** *or* _____ **in front of this painting, I am again reminded of Simarov's greatness.**	Hoping Standing	In the first sentence, the subject of the adverb clause —*I*—is the same as the subject of the main clause. When this happens, the adverb clause can often be replaced by a **present participle phrase**. This happens with adverbials of *reason* or *time*. The most common position for these phrases is at the _____ of the sentence, but they can also be put at the end of the sentence. The participle phrase can go immediately after the subject if the subject of the main clause is a noun. **Irving Thornapple, *hoping to rediscover the great artist Simarov*, has come to the Reynolds Gallery today.**
b. Before (*leave*) _____ **the gallery today, I must record my thoughts in this notebook.**	leaving	The participle phrase can begin with time conjunctions—***when, while, after,*** and _____—to show clearly the relationship of the phrase to the main sentence.

27.3 Participle Phrases in Place of Adverbial Clauses (Continued)		
c. _____ **seen many other exhibition by this painter, I was excited about seeing his new show.**	Having	The **perfect participle** is used if the state or action of the phrase came earlier than the main clause. The structure is: _____ **+ the** _____ **participle** The conjunction **after** can be used with this structure. Example: **After having seen many other exhibitions . . .** The meaning is about the same.
d. (ignore) _____ **by critics for many years, Simarov almost quit painting.** *or* _____ _____ _____ **by critics for many years, Simarov almost quit painting.**	Ignored Having been ignored	Adverb clauses with passive verbs can also be reduced to participle phrases if the subjects are the same. The participle in these phrases is a _____ participle. To make it clearer that the first event occurred before the second, use this structure: *having* **+** _____ **+ the** _____ **participle**

Oral Practice 3A: Tell the class the name of your favorite song, piece of music, work of art, or TV show. Tell how it makes you feel when you listen to it, look at it, or watch it. Use a **present participle** to begin your sentence. Example:

> *Listening to Debussy's* Clair de lune*, I feel very romantic.*

Oral Practice 3B: Most people do certain things in the same order every day. Think of two things that you do one after the other. Express this relation in three ways, first with **before** and a participle, then with **after** and a participle, and finally with a perfect participle. Example:

> *Before doing my homework, I fix a cup of tea.*
> *After fixing a cup of tea, I do my homework.*
> *Having fixed a cup of tea, I do my homework.*

Oral Practice 3C: Think of something that was done to you recently. Perhaps you were told something, given something, injured, chosen or asked to do something, introduced to someone, invited to something—probably many things have happened to you. Tell what your immediate reaction was. First use a **when** clause; then replace that clause with a **perfect passive participle phrase**; finally, use a **past participle phrase**. Example:

> *When I was nominated to be president of the international club, I felt very honored.*
> *Having been nominated to be president of the international club, I felt very honored.*
> *Nominated to be president of the international club, I felt very honored.*

Which of these sentences seems more natural in speaking, and which seems to be "formal written English"?

Written Practice 3A: The following sentences begin with adverbial clauses. Some of these clauses can be replaced by participle phrases of the types in Rule Builder 27.3. Others, because the subjects are different, cannot. First, read each sentence and decide whether the clause can be replaced by a phrase. If it can, put a check in the blank before it. Then rewrite each of the checked sentences; each should begin with a participle phrase.

_____   1. As I wandered through this exhibition, I couldn't help but notice Simarov's brilliant choice of colors.
_____   2. When you visit this show, you will definitely be moved by the expressiveness of his work.
_____   3. After you have spent a few hours with Simarov's paintings, the world will fascinate you again, as it did when you were a child.
_____   4. Before you come to the Simarov exhibition, you should find time to read the article about him in last month's *Art World*.
_____   5. As I studied Simarov's works, his originality amazed me.
_____   6. Now that I have seen these latest works of Simarov, I am very eager to see what he does next.

Written Practice 3B: In Written Practice 3A, you should have rewritten four of the six sentences. The other two had different subjects in the adverbial clause and the main clause. Rewrite the main clauses of these two sentences without changing the meaning so that you *can* start the sentences with participle phrases in place of adverbial clauses.

27.4 Participles after Verbs of Position and Motion		
Complete this model sentence.	Check.	Complete these rules.
Yesterday Irving Thornapple was in the Reynolds Gallery looking at Simarov's new paintings. **He walked into the gallery** (expect) **_____ to enjoy the show.**	expecting	Verbs of position, such as **be, stand, sit,** and **lie,** and verbs of motion, such as **come, go,** **run,** and _____, are often used in this structure: **verb + adverbial of place + the** **_____ participle** The two situations or events are simultaneous; that is, they occur at the same time.

Oral Practice 4:   Did someone telephone you or knock on you door yesterday evening or sometime recently? Tell where you were and what you were doing when this happened. Use this structure: **verb of position + adverbial of place + present participle phrase** Example:

> *I was sitting at my drawing table working on my project when the telephone rang.*

Written Practice 4A: Finish sentence B. It should have about the same meaning as sentence A. *Write only one word in each blank.*

1. A. Mark lay in his bed and thought about the geography test that he was going to take the next morning.

    B. Mark lay in his bed _____ about the geography test that he was going to take the next morning.

2. A. My mother always jumped around and cleaned up all of the messes we children made.

    B. My mother always jumped around _____ up all of the messes we children made.

3. A. The last time I saw Henry, he was watching TV in the lounge.

    B. The last time I saw Henry, he was in the lounge _____ TV.

4. A. I sat for hours in front of my computer and tried to get my new program to run.

    B. I sat for hours in front of my computer _____ to get my new program to run.

5. A. The young Americans strolled through the streets of Hong Kong and took in all the delightful sights and sounds.

    B. The young Americans strolled through the streets of Hong Kong

    _____ in all the delightful sights and sounds.

Written Practice 4B: Rewrite each sentence using a present participle after the adverbial of place. Example:

> *Irving Thornapple is writing a review of the Simarov show in his study.*
> *Irving Thornapple is in his study writing a review of the Simarov show.*

1. Earlier today, he was in the Reynolds Gallery, where he took many notes on the paintings.
2. He stood motionless in front of one painting for several minutes and appreciated the sense of movement in the work.
3. When the gallery closed, Thornapple walked to his office. He hoped he could express his feelings about the show to his readers.

27.5 Present Participles versus Base Forms after Verbs of Perception		
Complete these model sentences.	Check.	Complete these rules.
a. I saw one of my teachers _____ **dinner at Mike's the other day.**	eating/having	Perception verbs, such as *watch, notice, observe, hear, listen to, feel,* and _____, are often followed by an object and the *-ing* form of the verb. A paraphrase of sentence **a** would be, "One of my teachers *was eating* dinner at Mike's the other day, and I saw her." In other words, you use this structure when you begin to perceive something that has already begun, that is, something in progress.
b. I heard her _____ **that she enjoys the atmosphere there.**	say	These same verbs can also be followed by an object and the _____ form of a verb. Use this structure when you observe an *entire* action from start to finish. A paraphrase of sentence **b** would be, "She _____ that she enjoyed the atmosphere there, and I heard her."

Oral Practice 5A: Go to the window and report to your classmates what you see happening outside. (If you can't see anything going on from your classroom, use your imagination.) Begin your sentence with "I see . . ."

Oral Practice 5B: Tell your classmates about something that you saw or heard your roommate do last night or this morning.

Written Practice 5:   Complete these sentences with a form of the verb in parentheses. In some of the sentences, the *-ing* form is appropriate. In other sentences, the base form gives the right meaning.

1.   It was so quiet that you could hear a pin (*drop*) _____.

2.   When I entered the bank, I noticed my old friend Beatrice (*stand*) _____ in line.

3.   Pete could hear a housefly (*fly*) _____ around his bedroom, but he never saw it (*land*) _____.

4.   When the children got out of school, they were delighted to see snow (*fall*) _____.

5.   Close the door quietly. My new roommate gets angry if he hears it (*slam*) _____.

6. I noticed your checkbook (*lie*) _____ on the kitchen floor.

7. When the lifeguard saw the boy (*drown*) _____, she acted very quickly to save his life.

8. When the lifeguard heard the boy's heart (*beat*) _____, she knew he was still alive.

NOTE: There are a few other verbs that occur in the structure **verb + object + present participle.**

Some of these can be called "verbs of interception" (because you observe something that has already begun):

> *find*
> *catch*
> *discover*

Others can be called "verbs of mental imagery":

> *imagine*
> *picture*
> *remember*
> *recall*

Examples:

> **The teacher caught Ralph cheating on the test.**
> **It's hard to imagine Ralph cheating on a test.**

Make up some more sentences with these verbs used with this structure.

27.6 Present Participles after Other Verbs and Expressions		
Complete these model sentences.	Check.	Complete these rules.
a. Let's go (*shop*) _____, **and then let's go** (*swim*) _____.	shopping swimming	Many leisure-time activities are expressed with **go** + the **-ing** form of a verb. Some examples are **go camping, go fishing,** _____ _____, and _____ _____.
b. We started (*shop*) _____ **at 7:30. We** **didn't finish** (*shop*) _____ **until after** **midnight.**	 shopping shopping	Verbs of beginning, such as **begin** and _____, verbs of continuing, such as **continue** and **keep**, and verbs of finishing, such as **stop** and _____, are often followed by the _____ form of the verb.

| c. **We always have fun** (*swim*)

 _____.

 or **We always have a** _____

 time (*swim*) _____.
 Sometimes we have difficulty (*find*)

 _____ **a good place to**
 swim.
 or **Sometimes we have a**

 _____ **time** (*find*)

 _____ **a good place to**
 swim. | swimming

 good

 swimming

 finding

 hard/difficult

 finding | Some expressions with *have*—for example,

 have _____ or *have*

 _____—are followed by the

 _____ form of the verb. |
| d. **In summer we spend most of our free**

 time (*swim*) _____. |

 swimming | *Spend* + an expression of **time** is followed by

 the _____ form of the verb. |

Oral Practice 6A: Tell the class a few things you have fun doing and a few things you have trouble doing.

Oral Practice 6B: Tell the class how you spend your evenings, your weekends, and your free time in general. Begin with "I spend . . ."

Oral Practice 6C: Think of an activity that you spent some time doing recently. Tell when you started/began doing it, how long you kept/continued doing it, and why you stopped doing it. Example:

> *My friends and I started playing basketball at 6:00 yesterday evening.*
> *We kept playing for two hours.*
> *We stopped playing at 8:00 because we all had homework to do.*

Written Practice 6:   Complete these sentences about your personal habits and pastimes. *Use an -ing form in each sentence.*

1.   When I need new clothes, I go _____.
2.   I always have a good time _____.
3.   I usually have fun _____.
4.   I rarely have trouble _____.
5.   Sometimes I have trouble _____.
6.   I spend a lot of my free time _____.

7. I spend a few hours each day _____ but only a few minutes

    _____.

8. I usually begin _____ at _____ every evening.

9. I usually stop _____ when I _____.

10. In the summer I like to go _____.

27.7 Chapter Check: Complete these sentences with the correct form of the verb given. If you are unsure of an answer, check the indicated model sentence and rule.

1. I just saw the teacher (*go*) _____ into the classroom.   [27.5]

2. We heard the roof (*collapse*) _____ during the storm.   [27.5b]

3. I've heard that teacher gives very (*challenge*) _____

    tests.   [27.1]

4. Let's go (*bowl*) _____ after class tomorrow.   [27.6a]

5. A concert pianist often spends eight hours (*practice*) _____ every

    day.   [27.6d]

27.8 Chapter Check: Finish sentence B. It should have about the same meaning as sentence A. *Write only one word in each blank.*

1. A. Harry was playing poker at one o'clock this morning; I saw him.

    B. I saw Harry _____ poker at one o'clock this

        morning.   [27.5a]

2. A. It amazes me that you have never tasted eggplant.

    B. I am _____ that you have never tasted eggplant.   [27.1]

3. A. That kind of behavior disgusts me.

    B. I think that is very _____ behavior.   [27.1]

4. A. My family has a very pretty little house that is surrounded by large trees.

    B. My family has a very pretty little house _____ by large

        trees.   [27.2a]

5. A. Because he had been seen by the police, Pierre had to wear a disguise.

    B. _____ been seen by the police, Pierre had to wear a dis-

        guise.   [27.3d]

6. A. Pierre was captured. Later, he sat in his jail cell and wished that he had chosen an-

        other career.

    B. _____ being captured, Pierre sat in his jail cell _____

        that he had chosen another career.   [27.3b,27.4]

7. A. We will not count any name on the petition that is not written in ink.

   B. Any name not _____ in ink on the petition will not be

      counted.   [27.2a]

8. A. I tripped and fell when I was running down the stairs.

   B. _____ down the stairs, I tripped and fell.   [27.3a]

9. A. After he took his date home, Ralph walked down the street and whistled a happy

      tune.

   B. After _____ his date home, Ralph walked down the street

      _____ a happy tune.   [27.3b,27.4]

27.9 Warm-Up: Tell the class about the last movie that interested you. Explain why you were interested and what was interesting about this film.

    Tell about the last piece of music or the last sports event that excited you. Describe what you found exciting in the music or game. When were you most excited?

    Tell about the last piece of news that disturbed you. Why were you disturbed? What was disturbing about the news?

27.10 Communication: Choose one of the verbs of emotion in Rule Builder 27.1. Interview other members of your class to find good examples of this emotional state. Take good notes so that you can write a paragraph about this emotion as part of your homework. Talk to as many of your classmates as you can in the time that your teacher gives you. Of course, they will want to interview you, too. Example:

    Mario, can you tell me about your most embarrassing experience?
    Well, I was really embarrassed one time when . . .

27.11 Communication: Interview two other students in the class to find out how young children between the ages of five and ten in your classmates' countries or regions or families spend their time. Think of some categories that you are interested in knowing about (for example, attending school, doing homework, watching TV, playing with friends, exercising). Write these activities in the column on the left. Then find out approximately how much time the average child spends doing these things every day. Take good notes so that you can write a report.

	_____	_____
Activity	*Country 1*	*Country 2*
_____	_____	_____
_____	_____	_____
_____	_____	_____
_____	_____	_____

27.12 Sentence Writing: Try to think of what was done to the following people and things to cause the unfortunate situations. You, your classmates, and your teacher may want to spend some time in class brainstorming before writing the sentences explained below.

1.   The librarian was unable to concentrate.
2.   The Nelsons couldn't find the house where the party was going on.
3.   Marcie's watch was stolen.
4.   Our tent was badly torn.
5.   All of the things on the clothesline are soaking wet.
6.   The painting took almost a year to repair.
7.   The huge oak tree split in half.
8.   Our neighbor had to be rushed to the hospital.

Now write a sentence with a participle phrase to explain the following situations. Try to use each of the structures in the following examples at least once.

> *Stan could not play very well.*
> *After being upset by the bad news, Stan could not play very well.*
> *Upset by the bad news, Stan could not play very well.*
> *Stan, upset by the bad news, could not play very well.*
> *Having been upset by the bad news, Stan could not play very well.*
> *Stan could not play very well, having been upset by the bad news.*

27.13 Sentence Writing: Add a **present participle phrase** to three of these sentences explaining what the subject was doing that caused the event or situation. Example:

> *John dropped the road map out of the window.*
> <u>*Leaning out to adjust the mirror,*</u> *John dropped the road map out of the window.*

1.   Samuel could not control the boat very well.
2.   The sparrow was caught by the hawk.
3.   We made poor time on the trip. (The expression *make poor time* means "travel more slowly than one had expected.")
4.   She missed the place where she should have turned.
5.   Our science teacher started a fire in the lab.
6.   Wilford Terrace did not answer his letters.

27.14 Paragraph Writing: Write a paragraph about the state of emotion that you talked to your classmates about in 27.10 Communication. You could begin like this:

> I asked six of my classmates to tell me about their most embarrassing moments. The first, Mario, was extremely embarrassed when he . . .

27.15 Paragraph Writing: Write a paragraph about the amount of time children from various countries, regions, or families spend on various activities. Use the information that you learned in 27.11 Communication.

27.16 Sentence Completion: When past participles are used as predicate adjectives, they are often followed by the preposition **by**. But some past participles are followed by other prepositions. Fill in the blanks with appropriate prepositions. When you have finished, check your answers with Appendix 2.

1.   The professor was very interested _____ her students' work.

2.   Few of the experts were satisfied _____ the quality of the wine.

3.   No one was very excited _____ the schedule change.

4.   I'm getting very tired _____ cafeteria food.

5.   My brother has become bored _____ his work.

6.   I was quite disappointed _____ the advice he gave me.

27.17 Reflecting: Read the next episode of the mystery story. Then look at the way participles are used. Can you find examples of present and past participles used to modify nouns? What about participle phrases at the beginning of sentences? How could the author have expressed the meaning of those participle phrases with adverbial *clauses*?

In the second paragraph, find the adverbial clause that begins with *after*. Change it to a participle phrase.

> Having showered and cleaned myself up, I jumped in the car and went to meet Linda for dinner. The case kept running through my mind. Sitting down to eat, I told Linda about everything that had happened. It was hard to concentrate because the restaurant was noisy.
>
> "So Carl Miller disappeared right after he talked to Troy Daniels," Linda said.
>
> "I think he found out something," I said. "Or he thought of something. And he went to investigate it. Then he disappeared."
>
> "You just have to find out what he did next, then," Linda said.
>
> "Right. But there's another problem. Somebody is making threatening phone calls." I told her about the call I had received, and also about the call Deanne Miller had gotten.
>
> "That means there are two groups involved. Somebody made Miller disappear, and somebody else wants to find him."
>
> "Right," I said. "It's confusing."
>
> Linda smiled at me. "Being such a smart guy," she said, "you'll figure it out."
>
> "But first I think I'll eat dinner," I smiled back.

27.18   Real-World Work

THINK/PRACTICE

The things which happen to us continually remind us of things in our past. Pay attention to the stimuli that awaken these memories. To report a memory, and how we are reminded of it, we often use a participle:

> *Hearing you say that, I thought about . . .*
> *Reading that book, I was reminded of . . .*
> *Seeing that picture again, I remembered . . .*

Today, pay attention to the things you remember and to what makes you think about them. Make sentences like the examples shown.

LOOK/LISTEN

Find a newspaper or magazine that you can mark up. Read through a long article or several short ones, looking for **-ing** and past participle forms. Many of these will be the main verb in the clause. Examples:

> *The results haven't <u>been</u> <u>tabulated</u> yet. (present perfect passive)*
> *They do not understand what the candidates are <u>talking</u> about. (present progressive)*

Look for **-ing** forms and past participles that are *not* main verbs. Think about whether they are being used as adjectives, in adjective phrases, in adverbial phrases, after verbs of perception, position, motion, or after certain other verbs or expressions, such as **finish, have difficulty**, and so on. Your teacher may want you to bring some interesting examples to class.

USE

1. Often when someone calls you on the phone, he or she will ask if the call has interrupted something you were doing. In this case it is common to give an answer such as:

   > *No, I was just sitting around doing nothing . . .*
   > or
   > *I was right beside the phone thinking about calling you . . .*

2. Sometimes in a conversation, the topic you are discussing will change several times. You may get an idea about one of the old topics (a party, for instance) too late—the subject has already changed. You need to say something to reintroduce the old topic. You might say,

   > *Going back to that idea for a party, I think we . . .*
   > *Thinking about the party, shouldn't we . .*

3. Before you write your next composition or paper, review Rule Builder 27.3. Participle phrases are very useful for showing relationships between events and situations without wasting words.

28

Gerunds

REVIEW

As you know, nouns and noun phrases can perform several roles: subject, object (including object of a preposition), predicate nominative, and noun modifier. For each of the following sentences, label the underlined words or expressions with **S** (Subject), **O** (Object), **OP** (Object of Preposition), **PN** (Predicate Nominative), or **M** (Modifier).

1. _____ <u>Many people</u> enjoy eating at Mike's.

2. _____ Mike's is <u>a small cafe</u> in the business district.

3. _____ A lot of people go to <u>the cafe</u> for lunch.

4. _____ I often have <u>a snack</u> there after a movie.

5. _____ I usually have a <u>cheese</u> sandwich.

PREVIEW

Words which are *not* nouns can also perform these functions in English. In chapters 28 and 29, we will practice using verbs—gerunds and infinitives—as subjects, objects, objects of prepositions, predicate nominatives, and noun modifiers. Identify each of the underlined words in the following sentences with **S, O, OP, PN,** or **M.**

1. _____ Peterson's favorite sport is <u>running</u>.

2. _____ He likes many sports, but he loves <u>running</u>.

3. _____ Peterson thinks about <u>running</u> all the time.

4. _____ He has to spend nearly $100 for a pair of <u>running</u> shoes.

5. _____ To put it simply, <u>running</u> is Peterson's life.

Complete these sentences with a form of the verb *eat*.

1. _____ is Brad's favorite activity.

2. Brad's favorite activity is _____.

3. He prefers _____ to almost everything else.

4. He thinks about _____ all of the time.

5. Mike's Cafe is Brad's favorite _____ establishment.

28.1 Gerunds as Subjects and Predicate Nominatives		
Complete these model sentences.	Check.	Complete these rules.

a. (look at) _____ ____
the customers at Mike's Cafe is always fun.
 	
(sit) _____ **at the counter**
 	
is more fun than _____ **at a table.**
	Looking at
	
	Sitting
	
	sitting
		All English verbs except modals have **-ing forms.** These **-ing forms** are used in **progressive** verb constructions (see Rule Builders 7.1 and 8.5):
		    Right now we are starting to study gerunds and infinitives.
		They are also used as modifiers (see Rule Builder 27.1):
		    That was a very frightening movie.
		Finally, **-ing forms** can be used to perform noun functions; these forms are called **gerunds.**
		A **gerund** can be used as a subject or an object in a sentence. In the model sentence **a**, the
		
		gerunds are being used as _____.

b. One amusing activity is *(watch)* _____ **the interaction between Mike and his customers.**	watching	Gerunds can also be used after the verb _____. In this position, the gerund is a predicate nominative. Don't confuse this structure with progressive structures. One of the following sentences has a predicate nominative gerund (G), and the other has a progressive form (P). Put *P* and *G* in the right blanks. _____ **His favorite pastime is jogging at the gym.** _____ **The athlete is jogging at the gym.**

c. Mike's *(run)* _____ **around and** *(joke)* _____ **with all the customers is always** **very amusing.**	running joking	If a gerund has a subject, telling who does it, then this noun or pronoun—at least in formal English—should be possessive. Put _____ on a noun, or use the possessive form of a pronoun.

Oral Practice 1A: Tell the class your favorite leisure-time activity. Example:

> *Bowling is my favorite activity.*
> *My favorite activity is bowling.*

Oral Practice 1B: Think of something that someone else does that amuses or annoys you, that makes you laugh or makes you angry. Express your idea with the possessive + gerund structure. Example:

> *My brother's complaining about everything really irritates me.*
> *One thing that really irritates me is my brother's complaining about everything.*

Written Practice 1A: Complete these sentences with *gerunds*.

1.   _____ is something my Aunt Gladys has done since she was very

young.

2.   _____ a plane was one of the first things she did after college.

3.   _____ a business is not one of Roger's plans.

4.   An activity many people enjoy at Christmas is _____ traditional

songs, called carols.

5.   _____ is not good for your health.

6.   Two things you can do on a train to avoid getting bored are _____ and

_____.

7.   One of Bill's favorite activities is _____ tennis.

8.   _____ in an apartment by oneself can cause loneliness.

9.   _____ for only five hours a night over a long period of time may lead

to fatigue and illness.

10.   _____ and _____ are essential skills for success

in high school and college.

Written Practice 1B: Complete each of these sentences with a *possessive and a gerund.*
Example:

My roommate's snoring keeps me awake.

1. _____ always makes me laugh.

2. _____ sometimes annoys me.

3. Something that really surprised me recently was _____

_____.

4. _____ after midnight really

irritates me.

5. _____ after he has been

drinking scares me.

6. One little thing about our teacher that annoys me is _____

_____.

28.2 Gerunds as Objects of Prepositions		
Complete these model sentences.	Check.	Complete these rules.
a. Last night at Mike's I was looking **forward** _____ (*eat*) _____ **a big, juicy hamburger.** **Suddenly, I heard a loud voice. A customer was complaining angrily** _____ (*find*) _____ **mayonnaise on** **his turkey sandwich. Instead ____** (*apologize*) _____ _____ (*put*) _____ **mayonnaise on the sandwich, Mike just repeated what was written on the menu, ''If you don't like it, you can scrape it off.''**	to eating about finding of apologizing for putting	If a verb is the object of a preposition, that verb should be a **gerund**—the _____ form. This is a very simple rule. The difficult thing is choosing the correct preposition. The choice of the preposition is often determined by the word or expression that comes before the preposition. For example, the expression *look forward* is usually followed by the preposition _____, and the verb *complain* takes the preposition _____. The most common preposition combinations are listed in Appendix 2.

b. **The customer accused Mike** _____ (*treat* + *not*) _____ _____ **his customers with respect and left the cafe.**	of not treating	To make a gerund negative, simply put _____ before it.

Oral Practice 2A: You and your classmates should discuss things you had to get accustomed to doing when you came to this school. Which of these things are you used to doing now, and which have you not gotten used to yet? Example:

   I had to get accustomed to studying after 10:00 at night.

Oral Practice 2B: Tell the class something that you are ***looking forward to doing***.

Oral Practice 2C: Tell the class something that you are ***worried*** or ***nervous about doing***.

Written Practice 2: Write the appropriate prepositions and the correct verb forms in these sentences. Check your answers with Appendix 2.

1. I was interested _____ (*eat*) _____ at Mike's.

2. In fact, I was excited _____ (*eat*) _____ there.

3. Last night, in addition _____ (*have*) _____ a good meal, I saw an amusing incident there.

4. The customer loudly claimed that Mike was not capable _____ (*make*) _____ a turkey sandwich properly.

5. He said Mike was responsible _____ (*ruin*) _____ his dinner.
   or He said that Mike was guilty _____ _____ his dinner.
   or He blamed Mike _____ _____ his dinner.

6. Mike is accustomed _____ (*hear*) _____ complaints.
   or Mike is used _____ (*hear*) _____ complaints.

7. It's impossible to keep customers _____ (*complain*) _____.

8. But Mike was tired _____ (*hear*) _____ complaints.

9. As the customer went out the door, Mike yelled, "Thank you _____ (*come*) _____ to Mike's!" Everyone laughed.

10. Mike succeeded _____ (*reduce*) _____ the tension.

28.3 Gerunds as Objects of Verbs		
Complete these model sentences.	Check.	Complete these rules.
a. I always enjoy (*eat*) _____ **at Mike's, but many people avoid** (*eat*) _____ **there.**	eating eating	Verbs can be direct objects of other verbs. Sometimes a verb that is used as a direct object is a **gerund**, that is, the _____ form of the verb. A **gerund** usually refers to something real or definite—something that definitely happens or definitely doesn't happen, is happening or isn't happening, happened or didn't happen. A gerund does not usually refer to something that just might happen.
b. I plan (*eat*) _____ _____ **at Mike's tonight.** **I want** (*get*) _____ _____ **there before six to avoid the crowds.**	to eat to get	In other cases, a verb that is used as an object may be an **infinitive**, that is, *to* + **the** _____ **form**. Often, it refers to an action or state that is possible or probable rather than real or definite. Often the **infinitive** is used instead of a gerund when it refers to an action that is later than the main verb in time. That is why we use the infinitive after such verbs as ***need***, _____, and _____. Test your understanding of the basic difference in meaning between infinitives and gerunds by doing the Self-Test which follows this rule builder.
c. I still remember (*come*) _____ **to Mike's for the first time several years ago. I must remember** (*write*) _____ _____ **an essay about that experience someday.**	coming to write	Rules **a** and **b** should help you to understand the difference between ***remember*** + **gerund** and ***remember*** + **infinitive**. If you remember something that you have already done, use the _____ after *remember*. If you remember something that you have to do later, use the _____.
d. Mike considered (*close*) _____ **his cafe last year. I'm glad he didn't.**	closing	Some verbs seem to go against the principle explained in rules **a** and **b**. One example is _____. Verbs like this cause the most trouble for students. Practice making sentences with these verbs until the structures seem natural to you. See the list of troublesome verbs which follows.

Troublesome Verbs

She *considered* eatING	She *imagined* eatING	She *managed* TO eat
She *discussed* eatING	She *dreaded* eatING	She *pretended* TO eat
She *suggested* eatING	She *anticipated* eatING	She *failed* TO eat
She *recommended* eatING		She *seemed* TO eat
		She *appeared* TO eat

Self-Test

Review Rule Builder 28.3. Then cover the answers and test yourself. Fill in each blank with either *to eat* or *eating*. Mark the ones you miss and practice using them in sentences until you know them.

		Answers
1.	She admitted _____	eating
2.	She wanted _____	to eat
3.	She detested _____	eating
4.	She appreciated _____	eating
5.	She decided _____	to eat
6.	She regretted _____	eating
7.	She expected _____	to eat
8.	She despised _____	eating
9.	She avoided _____	eating
10.	She seemed _____	to eat
11.	She hoped _____	to eat
12.	She prepared _____	to eat
13.	She recalled _____	eating
14.	She denied _____	eating
15.	She asked _____	to eat
16.	She risked _____	eating
17.	She needed _____	to eat
18.	She postponed _____	eating
19.	She appeared _____	to eat
20.	She would like _____	to eat
21.	She missed _____	eating
22.	She didn't mind _____	eating
23.	She resisted _____	eating
24.	She disliked _____	eating
25.	She agreed _____	to eat

Oral Practice 3A: Tell the class something that you and your friends have **discussed** or **considered** doing recently.

Oral Practice 3B: Imagine that you have a friend back in your native country who is having trouble learning English. Imagine that you are talking to this friend. What would you **suggest** or **recommend** doing or not doing?

Oral Practice 3C: What are some things that you **dislike, detest, hate,** or **avoid** doing? Looking on the brighter side, mention some things that you **hope, want, would like,** or **plan** to do.

Written Practice 3:   Complete each sentence with the gerund or the infinitive form of the verb given.

1. I remember (*go*) _____ to France when I was 10 years old.

2. Remember (*set*) _____ your alarm tonight.

3. I hope (*graduate*) _____ in four years.

4. Pierre denied (*steal*) _____ the necklace.

5. Stan promised (*stop*) _____ practicing at midnight.

6. The weatherman suggested (*take*) _____ an umbrella to the game.

7. I regret (*not + tell*) _____ Betty about our plan.

8. Old Mr. Ferguson is considering (*close*) _____ his store.

28.4 Passive Gerunds		
Complete this model sentence.	Check.	Complete these rules.
a. _____ **served by Mike himself is considered a great honor at Mike's Cafe.**	Being/Getting	Gerunds can be in the passive voice as well as the active voice. The passive structure is: _____ + **the** _____ **participle** In informal English, **getting** is often used instead of *being*.

Oral Practice 4A: Think of things that might happen to you that would be a great honor. Express these with passive gerunds. Examples:

Being put on the honor roll would be a great honor.

Oral Practice 4B: Think of things that other people could do to you that you enjoy or don't enjoy. Express these with passive gerunds. Example:

I don't enjoy being called up after midnight.

Written Practice 4:   Finish sentence B. It should have about the same meaning as sentence A. Use a gerund in each sentence.

1.   A. I don't like it when mosquitoes eat me alive.

    B. I don't like _____ alive by mosquitoes.

2.   A. They remembered the time when the bear chased them.

    B. They remembered _____ by the bear.

3.   A. Sally is resentful when someone tells her what to do.

    B. Sally resents _____.

4.   A. We were depressed when we were dropped from the team.

    B. _____ was depressing for us.

5.   A. It bothered him that so many people counted on him.

    B. _____ by so many people bothered him.

6.   A. Yolanda was awarded the top prize. She was very happy about that.

    B. Yolanda was very happy about _____.

7.   A. No one was surprised that Pierre was found guilty.

    B. Pierre's _____ surprised no one.

28.5 **Gerunds as Noun Modifiers**		
Complete this model sentence.	Check.	Complete these rules.
a. In the kitchen of Mike's Cafe, you will find many (*fry*) _____ **pans and** (*bake*) _____ **sheets.**	frying baking	Like most nouns, gerunds can be used to modify other nouns. Just as a beater for eggs is called an **egg beater**, a pan for frying is called a _____ **pan**. This gerund + noun structure is a true **compound noun**, like *paper clip* or *apple tree*. Therefore, pronounce a **gerund + noun** with greater stress on the first word, that is, the gerund.

Oral Practice 5:   You and your classmates should have a brainstorming session about gerund compounds. (Notice that the expression *brainstorming session* is a gerund compound.) Try to think of as many gerund compounds as you can under these headings:

Clothing	Schools/ Classes	Rooms	Equipment/ Machines
_____	_____	_____	_____

Examples: **running shoes**   **reading class**   **waiting room**   **adding machine**

Written Practice 5:   Complete each compound noun with an appropriate gerund. If you have trouble with any of the compounds, ask a native speaker for help.

Our Camping Trip

Last weekend some friends and I went camping. On the way we stopped at a nice motel that had a _____ pool. There was also a _____ pool, which is a very shallow pool for children.

I had prepared carefully for our trip. I had bought new, comfortable

_____ boots, a small tent, a _____ bag, and a

_____ pole.

We drove into the _____ area on a winding mountain road. We left the car in a very muddy _____ lot and walked the rest of the way to the campsite.

After the trip, we had a lot of dirty clothes, so before going home, we stopped at a laundromat. When we took our clothes out of the _____ machine, we noticed that it was getting very late, so we brought the wet clothes home. We put them on a

_____ rack in my _____ room. The next morning, everything was dry but very wrinkled, so I ironed all my shirts on a new

_____ board that my parents had given me for Christmas.

28.6 Chapter Check: Complete these sentences. If you are unsure of an answer, check the indicated model sentence and rule.

1. _____ to music is one of my favorite pastimes.   [28.1a]

2. I am still not used _____ in a residence hall.   [28.2a]

3. My doctor recommended _____ too much fatty

   food.   [28.2b, 28.3d]

4. The police accused Tom's father _____ his car in the store's

   driveway.   [28.2a]

5. Cecilia is considering _____ to another university next

   semester.   [28.3d]

6. Margaret is interested _____ a job as an English teacher in

   Japan.   [28.2a]

7. _____ playing his stereo at night makes it difficult for me to study

   or sleep.   [28.1c]

8. If a patient is having trouble falling asleep at night, a doctor occasionally prescribes

   _____ pills.   [28.5]

9. _____ by a ferocious dog would be terrifying.   [28.4]

10. The group failed _____ enough signatures on the petition to force a

new election.   [28.3d]

28.7 Chapter Check: Finish sentence B. It should have about the same meaning as sentence A.

1. A. At first it seemed very strange to be away from my country, but it doesn't seem

strange anymore.

B. Although it seemed very strange at first, now I am _____

_____ away from my country.   [28.2a]

2. A. Collecting insects used to be very interesting to me.

B. I used to be very _____.   [28.2a]

3. A. They decided not to leave until tomorrow.

B. They have postponed _____ until tomorrow.   [28.3a]

4. A. Helen thinks she might change her major.

B. Helen is considering _____.   [28.3d]

5. A. No one who has not lived abroad can understand the loneliness felt by a foreign

visitor.

B. No one who has not lived abroad is capable _____

_____ felt by a foreign visitor.   [28.2a]

6. A. I'm sorry that I was so abrupt.

B. I apologize _____.   [28.2a]

7. A. Mary will say what she believes no matter what you say.

B. Nothing you say can prevent Mary _____

_____.   [28.2a]

8. A. Somehow I succeeded in getting an A on the test.

B. Somehow I managed _____.   [28.3d]

9. A. Eating sweet food for breakfast still seems strange to me.

B. I am still not used _____ for breakfast.   [28.2a]

10. A. My grandfather owns an old-fashioned machine that adds.

B. My grandfather owns an _____ machine.   [28.5]

28.8 Warm-up: You and your classmates should mention some things that you enjoy
doing.

28.9 Communication: Form groups of four to six students. Each member of the group should tell whether they *love, enjoy, have no interest in, dislike,* or *detest* doing each thing in the following chart. Examples:

> *I enjoy playing sports.*
> *I have no interest in taking long walks.*

You may have come across an activity in the warm-up that you would like to add to the list. You will find two blank spaces in the chart where you can do so.

Put tally marks in the appropriate boxes to record each member's statements. When the groups have finished, report the results to the teacher or a classmate, who will record them on the board. Each member of the group can report on one activity. Example:

> *In our group, one person loves playing sports, two people enjoy it, one person has no interest in it, and one person detests it.*

Be sure to record the final count in the chart so that you can write an accurate paragraph about your classmates' attitudes toward various activities (28.13 Paragraph Writing).

Activities	Love	Enjoy	No Interest	Dislike	Detest
Play sports					
Take long walks					
Read novels					
Study for classes					
Watch TV					
Take naps					

28.10 Sentence Writing: Make a list of six things that you do. Then write a comment about that activity.

Activity	Comment
Example: I study electrical engineering.	It requires a lot of hard work.
Example: I play basketball.	It keeps me in shape.

Now write six sentences based on your lists. The subjects of these sentences should be gerunds. Examples:

> *Studying electrical engineering requires a lot of hard work.*
> *Playing basketball keeps me in shape.*

28.11 Sentence Writing: Osama is a very successful student of English as a second language. His friend Kiat is asking him for advice. Rewrite Osama's answers so that they include the structure *by* + **gerund**. Example:

> Kiat: How can I improve my ability to understand spoken English?
> Osama: You should talk to native speakers.

> *You can improve your ability to understand spoken English by talking to native speakers.*

1.   Kiat: But I don't know any Americans. How can I improve my listening by myself?
     Osama: You can listen to tapes in the lab.

2.   Kiat: How can I learn a list of new words?
     Osama: You should use them in sentences.

3.   Kiat: How can I learn to write more quickly and easily?
     Osama: You should keep a journal.

4.   Kiat: How can I find answers to my grammar questions?
     Osama: You can ask your teacher or use a grammar reference book.

5.   Kiat: How can I get good grades in English classes?
     Osama: You should go to class every day and study hard.

28.12 Sentence Writing: This exercise will help you review unreal conditionals and participles while you practice using passive gerunds. Finish sentence A. Then complete sentence B so that it has about the same meaning as sentence A.

1.   A. If I _____ chosen to be the student representative from this class, I

        would be (*surprise*) _____.

     B. _____ to be the student representative from this class

        would surprise me.

2.   A. We would be (*disappoint*) _____ if we were not met at the

        airport.

     B. _____ at the airport would be _____

        for us.

3.   A. If a teacher scolded me in class, I _____ very (*embarrass*)

        _____.

     B. _____ by a teacher in class would be very

        _____ for me.

   Now, using the sentences you have just completed as models, write three *if* sentences about things that would *frighten, amuse,* and *excite* you if they *were done to you*. Then paraphrase each of the three sentences with a sentence beginning with a passive gerund (*Being* . . .).

28.13 Paragraph Writing: Write a paragraph about the ways the people in your class enjoy spending their time (28.9 Communication). Mention at least four activities. Your paragraph might begin something like this:

> Today in our English class, we conducted a poll about how the 20 people in the class like spending their time. The most popular activity was playing sports. Fourteen students either love or enjoy playing sports, while only three dislike or detest doing it. Three people are not interested in playing sports.

28.14 Reflecting: Read the next episode of the mystery story. Then look for gerunds used as subjects and objects.

> Taking Linda home was the first thing I did after dinner. I wasn't ready to go to bed yet, so I went for a drive. Thinking is something that I do best while I'm driving. I listened to some late-night jazz on the radio as I drove around.
>
> Troy Daniels believed that Dr. Weber had been drunk when he operated on Daniels's mother. A good insurance investigator like Carl Miller would try to find some evidence that showed Weber had been drunk. I drove past the hospital where Weber worked. Down the street was a bar. I parked in the lot and got out. I could try asking around to see if Weber was known in any bars. I walked inside. I showed a picture of Dr. Weber to the bartender. "Do you know this man?" I asked.
>
> "Sure," the bartender said. "He comes in here all the time."
>
> I showed him Miller's picture. "What about this man?"
>
> "I remember talking to him," the man behind the bar said. "Hey, he was looking for Dr. Weber, too."
>
> The bartender held out his hand. I gave him a five-dollar bill. "Making money is my business," he said.

28.15   Real-World Work

THINK/PRACTICE

1.   Make a list of the verbs followed by gerunds that gave you trouble in Rule Builder 28.3. Perhaps **consider** and **suggest** are on the list, and there are probably more that you have a tendency to put infinitives after. As you are walking, riding, sitting, or standing around today, glance at your list and make up *meaningful* sentences with those verbs. Examples:

     I am considering going to California during spring break.
     My adviser suggested taking a pre-calculus course next semester.

2.   As you have seen, some expressions with the preposition ***to*** are followed by gerunds. The most common expressions used this way are probably *be used to* or *get used to, be accustomed to* or *get accustomed to,* and *look forward to.* Try to listen for other expressions that have *to* followed by a gerund. Practice thinking of things that you aren't used to, or things you are looking forward to. Be sure to use the gerund after these expressions!

     I am not yet used to eating dinner at 5:30.
     I am looking forward to seeing the new Woody Allen movie.

LOOK/LISTEN

Look in the yellow pages of an American phone book and see how many gerund compounds you can find among the categories. For example, under the letter *D*, you might find:

dancing instruction
dating services
dictating machines
dishwashing machines
driving instruction
duplicating machines

You and your classmates might want to try to put together a long list of these. You could divide the alphabet among you. One person could look under *A* and *B*, another under *C* and *D*, and so on.

USE

As you will see in chapters 31 and 32, clauses can be used as nouns. Look at this sentence, for example:

It shocked me <u>that he yelled so loudly</u>.

In this sentence you are saying that the *fact* that he yelled was shocking to you. ***That*** clauses refer to *facts*. Sometimes, however, you do not want merely to refer to the fact that something happened; you want to focus on the *action* itself—you want to focus on *its happening*. In cases like that, use a gerund, not a noun clause. Example:

<u>His yelling so loudly</u> shocked me. or <u>His loud yelling</u> shocked me.

In the second sentence, you are focusing not on the abstract fact that he lost his temper and yelled, but on the actual noise that came out of his mouth. Do you feel the difference between the two sentences?

When you are writing, you often have to make a choice between abstract noun clauses and more concrete gerund phrases. The choice, of course, depends on what you are trying to say and the effect you are hoping to achieve.

29

Infinitives

REVIEW

In chapter 16, you used the words **too** and **enough** with **infinitives** to express the ideas of excessiveness, sufficiency, and insufficiency. Fill in the blanks in the following exercise.

> Sadie has been writing a book of etiquette—a book that teaches the rules of politeness in a society. Sadie has ideas that many people would call old-fashioned.

1. According to Sadie, a 16-year-old girl is _____ young to go out on a date without a chaperon.

2. However, an 18-year-old girl is old _____ to go out alone with a boy.

PREVIEW

In chapter 28, you were given some guidelines for choosing between **gerunds** and **infinitives** after verbs. In this chapter, you will get more practice using infinitives as objects, and you will see that infinitives are used in many other structures. Try this preview exercise. In sentence A, fill in the blanks with the correct forms of the verb **go out**. Then finish sentence B. It should have the same meaning as sentence A.

1. A. A 16-year-old girl's _____ alone with a boy bothers Sadie.

   B. It bothers Sadie for a girl _____ alone with a boy.

2. A. When writing to girls, Sadie advises not _____ alone with boys

   until they are 18.

   B. Sadie advises girls under 18 _____ alone with boys.

3. A. If Sadie had a 16-year-old daughter, she would not allow her

   _____ alone with a boy.

   B. If Sadie had a 16-year-old daughter, she would not let her

   _____ alone with a boy.

In this chapter you will also work with infinitives after nouns, adjectives, and question words and learn about the **infinitive of purpose**.

Sadie's friend Oscar has been encouraging her to send her book of etiquette to a publisher.

29.1   Infinitives as Subjects

Complete these model sentences, which come from Sadie's book.	Check.	Complete these rules.
a. Putting one's elbows on the dinner table is impolite. *or* **To _____ one's elbows on the dinner table is impolite.** *or* **It is impolite _____** **_____ one's elbows on the dinner table.**	put to put	As we learned in Rule Builder 28.1, a gerund—the _____ form of a verb—can be part of a phrase that is the subject of a sentence. It is often possible to substitute an infinitive for the gerund. However, it is more common to put the infinitive phrase at the end of the sentence and put the word _____ in the subject position.
b. _____ a guest _____ **_____ the host that the soup is too cold would be rude.** *or* **_____ would be rude** **_____ a guest _____** **_____ the host that the soup is too cold.**	For, to tell It for, to tell	If we tell who or what does the action of the infinitive, write this subject of the infinitive as the object of the preposition _____.

29.1 Infinitives as Subjects (Continued)		
c. It is bad manners not _____ _____ **something nice about the host's food.**	to say	To make an infinitive negative, simply put _____ before it.
d. For many people, it is very embarrassing _____ _____ **asked their ages.**	to be	Infinitives can be in the passive voice. The structure is: _____ _____ **+ the** _____ **participle** In informal English, ***to get*** is often used instead of ***to be***.

Oral Practice 1A: Tell the other members of the class something that it is a very good idea to do the night before a major exam.

Oral Practice 1B: Now mention something that it is a good idea NOT to do the night before a major exam.

Oral Practice 1C: Think of something that someone did that surprised you. Express that idea with a gerund. Example:

Philippe's missing yesterday's class surprised me.

Then think of something that someone might do that would surprise you. Express that idea with an infinitive. Example:

For Philippe to miss another class would surprise me.

Written Practice 1:   Paraphrase each of these sentences with a sentence beginning with *it*. Example:

Arriving late for a dinner party is very discourteous.
It is very discourteous to arrive late for a dinner party.

1.   Talking with your mouth full demonstrates a lack of manners.
2.   A guest's asking a host how much a piece of furniture cost is rather rude.
3.   A guest's requesting the recipe for a delicious dish is considered a compliment to the cook.
4.   A dinner guest's not thanking the hosts is a very serious omission.
5.   Being invited to someone's house to eat should be considered a great honor.
6.   Not being complimented on the food served may hurt the hosts' feelings.

29.2 Three-Way Adjectives		
Complete these model sentences from Sadie's book on manners.	Check.	Complete these rules.
To have good manners is important. *or* _____ **is important** _____ _____ **good manners.** *or* **Good manners** _____ **important** _____ _____. **For a visitor to understand a different society's rules seems rather difficult.** *or* _____ **seems rather difficult** _____ _____ _____ ____ _____ **a different society's rules.** *or* **A different society's rules** _____ **rather** _____ **for a visitor** ____ _____.	It to have are to have it for a visitor to understand seem, difficult to understand	Many adjectives can be used in these two structures from Rule Builder 29.1: **infinitive + noun phrase + linking verb + adjective** ***It* + linking verb + adjective + infinitive + noun phrase** For some adjectives, which can be called **three-way adjectives**, the idea expressed by those two structures can also be expressed with this structure: **noun phrase + linking verb + adjective + infinitive** They are sometimes called three-way adjectives because they can be used in those three structures.
Some Three-Way Adjectives		

good	*important*	*easy*
nice	*essential*	*difficult*
pleasant	*necessary*	*hard*
delightful	*vital*	*possible*
wonderful		*impossible*

The **-ing** participles from the verbs listed in Rule Builder 27.1 (**exciting, interesting**, and so on) can also be used in these three ways.

Oral Practice 2: You and your classmates should make a list of things every college student should know. Use this structure:

noun phrase + linking verb + adjective (from the list above) + infinitive

Example:

Good study habits are difficult to achieve.

Paraphrase each statement with a sentence beginning with **it**. Example:

It is difficult to achieve good study habits.

Written Practice 2A: Paraphrase each of these sentences in two ways: first, with a sentence beginning with *it*, then with a sentence beginning with the noun phrase. Example:

> *For graduate students to maintain high grade-point averages is essential.*
> *It is essential for graduate students to maintain high grade-point averages.*
> *High grade-point averages are essential for graduate students to maintain.*

1. To study the principles of Newtonian physics is important.
2. For students to understand certain rules of English is difficult.
3. To climb that cliff looks very hard.
4. For me to pass Professor Benson's tests seems nearly impossible.

Written Practice 2B: Write three original sentences with three different three-way adjectives. Each sentence should have an infinitive. Then rewrite each sentence in the two other ways.

29.3 Infinitives as Objects		
Complete these model sentences from Sadie's book.	Check.	Complete these rules.
a. Remember _____ _____ **thank you to your host before leaving.**	to say	As we saw in Rule Builder 28.3, some verbs take infinitive objects and others take gerund objects. We commonly use an infinitive when we are referring to an action or state that occurs _____ the time of the main verb.
b. I advise you _____ _____ **a note of thanks to your host.**	to write	Many verbs are followed by a **noun** or an **object pronoun** + **an infinitive.** One example is the verb _____.
c. In your note say, ''I want _____ _____ **that I had a wonderful time,''** *or* **''I want you** _____ _____ **that I had a great time.''**	to say to know	Some verbs, such as _____, follow both rules; that is, they can be followed either by an **infinitive** or by a **noun/pronoun** + **infinitive.**
d. Oscar is eager _____ **Sadie** **(send)** _____ _____ **her book to a publisher.**	for to send	A few predicate adjectives—adjectives after linking verbs—also take infinitives. Among these are ***able, ready, anxious, willing,*** ***afraid, glad, happy,*** and _____.

Self-Test

Cover the answers in the right-hand box. On paper or orally, make sentences with the expressions given. Put the main verb in the past tense. If possible, put the infinitive immediately after the main verb. Then, if possible, put **me** before the infinitive. With some of the verbs in the list, both structures are possible. With others, only one of the structures is possible. Let the **meaning** of the sentence guide you. Look at these examples:

Verbs	Expressions	Answers	
ask	She . . . to go with them	She asked to go with them.	She asked me to go with them.
agree	She . . . to go with them	She agreed to go with them.	(impossible)
advise	She . . . to go with them	(impossible)	She advised me to go with them.

Now try these:

	Verbs	Expressions	Answers	
1.	**decide**	She . . . to go with them	She decided to go with them.	
2.	**convince**	She . . . to go with them		She convinced me to go with them.
3.	**encourage**	He . . . to come on time		He encouraged me to come on time.
4.	**refuse**	He . . . to come on time	He refused to come on time.	
5.	**forget**	He . . . to tell her	He forgot to tell her.	
6.	**remember**	He . . . to tell her	He remembered to tell her.	
7.	**remind**	He . . . to tell her		He reminded me to tell her.
8.	**offer**	She . . . to help	She offered to help.	
9.	**volunteer**	She . . . to help	She volunteered to help.	
10.	**agree**	She . . . to help	She agreed to help.	
11.	**urge**	She . . . to help		She urged me to help.
12.	**tell**	She . . . to help		She told me to help.
13.	**pretend**	She . . . to help	She pretended to help.	
14.	**learn**	They . . . to read fast	They learned to read fast.	
15.	**teach**	They . . . to read fast		They taught me to read fast.

	Verbs	Expressions	Answers	
16.	**want**	He . . . to see the show	He wanted to see the show.	He wanted me to see the show.
17.	**persuade**	He . . . to see the show		He persuaded me to see the show.
18.	**permit**	He . . . to see the show		He permitted me to see the show.
19.	**hesitate**	She . . . to open the door	She hesitated to open the door.	
20.	**order**	She . . . to open the door		She ordered me to open the door.
21.	**need**	She . . . to call him	She needed to call him.	She needed me to call him.
22.	**advise**	She . . . to call him		She advised me to call him.
23.	**force**	She . . . to call him		She forced me to call him.
24.	**ask**	He . . . to speak first	He asked to speak first.	He asked me to speak first.
25.	**allow**	He . . . to speak first		He allowed me to speak first.

Oral Practice 3A: Make a short list of things that you want or need to do and a short list of things you *want* or *need* a friend to do for you. Examples:

> *me*   go to a movie tonight   *my friend*   help me with my math assignment

Now share some of these thoughts with your classmates. Examples:

> *I want to go to a movie tonight.*
> *I need my friend to help me with my math assignment.*

Oral Practice 3B: Imagine that one of your friends is not happy with his progress in English, his living situation, and/or his ability to make American friends. What could you do for this person? (Use words such as *advise, convince, encourage, invite, offer, persuade, promise, remind, tell, urge,* and *volunteer*.)

Oral Practice 3C: Tell the class something that you are *able, ready, anxious,* or *eager* to do. Mention something that you would be *willing, glad,* or *happy* to do for someone else. Tell about something that you were *afraid* to try. Did you try? Were you *able* to do it?

Written Practice 3A: Assume that someone has said the following things to you. For each one, write a sentence describing what happened. In each sentence, use a verb from this list, and use each verb only once.

order	offer	volunteer	agree	urge
remind	permit	refuse	ask	encourage

Example:

> *Your teacher: "Remember to do the assignment on page 114."*
> *My teacher reminded me to do the assignment on page 114.*

1. Your roommate: "No, I won't wash the dishes."
2. Your friend: "Why don't I give you a ride to the airport?"
3. Your father: "You really should try out for the team."
4. A policeman: "Be at the police station at 10 tomorrow morning."
5. Your teacher: "Yes, you may leave class a few minutes early."
6. Two friends of yours: "We'll bring some chips and dip to the party."
7. The same two friends: "Could you bring some soda?"
8. Your mother: "You should come home this summer for a visit."
9. Your roommate: "Oh, all right. I'll wash the dishes."

Written Practice 3B: Write sentences beginning with the following phrases.

1. I am eager to
2. I used to be afraid to
3. I would be glad to
4. I am not willing to

29.4 Infinitives after Nouns		
Complete these model sentences from Sadie's book.	Check.	Complete these rules.
a. **A good conversationalist always gives the other person an opportunity** *(talk)* _____ _____. **A good conversationalist has the** **ability** *(listen)* _____ _____.	to talk to listen	Some nouns are commonly followed by infinitives; some examples are **right, chance,** and _____. Some adjectives and verbs that take infinitives have **noun** forms that also can be followed by infinitives. For example, the noun _____ is derived from the adjective **able**, and like *able*, it can be followed by an _____.

29.4 Infinitives after Nouns (Continued)					

The noun forms of the following verbs take infinitives. Give the noun forms. Use a dictionary if necessary.

able	*ability*	*agree*	_____	*offer*	_____
unable	_____	*attempt*	_____	*plan*	_____
eager	_____	*decide*	_____	*prefer*	_____
obligated	_____	*fail*	_____	*promise*	_____
willing	_____	*intend*	_____	*propose*	_____
unwilling	_____	*need*	_____	*refuse*	_____

b. A good conversationalist has a mental list of good questions (*ask*) _____ _____.	to ask	Infinitives can be put after many nouns to indicate what can be done or what should be done with the thing. For example, if you have a good book that you can read, you can say: **I have a good book** _____ _____.

Oral Practice 4A: Get together with another student. Each of you should tell the other about

> *something that you are able to do,*
> *something that you are unable to do,*
> *something that you are eager to do,*
> *something that you intend to do,*
> *something that you have decided to do,*
> *something that you have promised to do,*
> *something that you plan to do,*
> *something that you are unwilling to do.*

Example:

> *I am unwilling to lend my motor scooter to anyone.*

Then you and your partner should report to the class about what you were told. Your statements should begin with **He/she mentioned . . .** or **He/she told me about . . .** followed by a noun. Example:

> *She told me about her unwillingness to lend her motor scooter to anyone.*

Oral Practice 4B: Tell about something that you can or should do this weekend. *Use the structure shown in these examples:*

> *I have a good novel to read.*
> *I have a party to go to.*

Written Practice 4: Complete these sentences with appropriate infinitives.

1. A guest's failure _____ a note of thanks is very serious.

2. Mickey made his teacher a promise _____ in his assignment tomorrow.

3. The team's failure _____ the big game was a great disappointment.

4. I couldn't watch that show last night because I had a major paper _____ and a sink full of dirty dishes _____.

5. Jim's refusal _____ us any money for the party is understandable; he has some very large medical bills _____.

6. I believe that every person has the right _____ anywhere he or she wants.

29.5 Infinitives after Question Words		
Complete this model sentence.	Check.	Complete this rule.
Sadie's book explains how_____ **_____ a napkin properly and** **where_____ _____ it** **while you are eating.**	to use to put	Some verbs, such as *explain*, may be followed by a question word, such as *when, how,* or _____, + an _____.
Some Verbs That Can Be Followed by Question Words + Infinitives				
advise	teach	see	ask	remember
say	show	hear	wonder	forget
explain	learn	know	decide	
tell	discover	understand		
	find out			

Oral Practice 5A: What are some things that you know how to do, and what are some things you feel you need to find out how to do better?

Oral Practice 5B: What are some things a person needs to know before he can go through the enrollment process? Use *where, when, how, whom,* or *what* + **infinitive.** Example:

A person needs to know what time to go to the enrollment center.

Written Practice 5:   Tell what you might do to solve the following problems by completing the sentences. Use *infinitives* in your sentences.

1. What should you do if you're lost in your car in a big city?

    I should find out where _____ for information.

2. What should you do if you want to make a long-distance call but you don't know how?

    I should ask someone _____.

3. What should you do if someone asks, "Where is the business district?"

    I should explain how _____.

4. What should you do if someone asks you for your favorite recipe?

    I should tell him or her _____ this dish.

5. What should you do if you want to find out the time and temperature, but you don't know the telephone number?

    I should ask someone what number _____ for the time and temperature.

29.6 Verb Forms after *Let, Make, Have, Get,* and *Help*		
Complete these model sentences from Sadie's book.	Check.	Complete these rules.
a. Parents should not permit their children *(stay)* _____ _____ **up during a late party.** *or* **Parents should not let their children** _____ **up during a late party.**	to stay stay	The verb *let* has about the same meaning as *permit* or *allow*. Unlike those verbs, however, *let* requires this structure: *let* + object + the _____ form of the verb
b. They should require their children *(go)* _____ _____ **to bed at their regular time.** *or* **They should make their children** _____ **to bed at their regular time.**	to go go	The verb *make* has about the same meaning as *force* or _____ , but it requires the same structure as *let*. *Make* is sometimes called a **causative verb.**

c. Many parents always get their **children** (*go*) _____ _____ **to bed before the** **guests arrive.** *or* **Many parents always have their** **children** _____ **to bed before** **the guests arrive.**	to go go	The common verbs **have** and **get** can also be **causative verbs**. They are similar to **make** in meaning but are not as strong. Both can sometimes be paraphrased by *tell*, *select*, or *hire*; *get* often means ''persuade.'' The precise meaning of these causative verbs depends on the context. These are the patterns: **get + object + infinitive** **have + object + _____ form**
d. Most importantly, they should help **their children** (*understand*) _____ **the** **reasons for these rules.**	understand or to understand	With the verb **help** either of the structures can be used: **help + object + _____ _____** **help + object + _____**

Oral Practice 6A: Tell the class something a good parent should make his/her children do, something a parent ought to let his/her children do, and something a parent should help his/her children do. What is something that is difficult to get children to do?

Oral Practice 6B: Both **get** and **have** can appear in this structure:

> *causative verb + object + past participle*

Example:

> *I got my car fixed.* or *I had my car fixed.*

The meaning is about the same. The meaning is that you had somebody fix your car. Imagine that you suddenly had a lot of money. What are some things that you would have or get done? Examples:

> *I would have my shoes shined every day.*
> *I would get my car painted.*

Written Practice 6A: Fill in each blank with one of these verbs: **let, made, had, got.** Use *each verb only once.*

1. The policeman _____ the driver pull over to the side of the road.

2. The students _____ the teacher to postpone the test.

3. We usually _____ our dog come into the house on very cold nights.

4. I _____ the mechanic check my brakes.

Written Practice 6B: Complete these sentences.

1. I would never let my cat _____ on my sofa.

2. I ought to help my fellow students _____ their English.

3. The boss had the company doctor _____ all the employees.

4. He helped us _____ the house after the party.

5. He made his children _____ all of their vegetables.

6. I never let my mother _____ my laundry for me.

7. I always have my barber _____ my hair very short.

8. I'm going to get my neighbor _____ my mail while I'm gone.

9. I need to get my car _____ before winter.

10. We had our house _____ last year, but the paint is already peeling off.

29.7 **Infinitives of Purpose**		
Complete these model sentences.	Check.	Complete these rules.
Sadie is not writing her book so that she can make money. *or* **Sadie is not writing her book in** **order** _____ _____ **money.** *or* **She is not writing it** _____ _____ **money.**	to make to make	The **purpose** of an action can be expressed with this structure: *so that* + **subject** + $\begin{cases} \textit{can/could} \\ \textit{will/would} \end{cases}$ If the subject of the purpose clause is the same person as the subject of the main clause, this structure can be used instead: *in* _____ + **the infinitive** An even simpler way to express this meaning is just to use the infinitive. This is called the **infinitive of** _____.

Oral Practice 7:   What purposes do people have for traveling in foreign countries? Express your idea first with *so that . . . can/will*. Then paraphrase your statement with *in order to* or the simple infinitive of purpose.

   People travel in foreign countries so that they can . . .
   People travel in foreign countries (in order) to . . .

Written Practice 7A: Complete these sentences by explaining the purpose of the action.

1. John bought a new television set in order _____ better reception.
2. He wanted better reception in order _____ basketball games broadcast from a distant city.
3. John needs this recreation in order _____ after a hard day's work.
4. John works hard _____ lots of money.
5. He needs money _____ a new house.

Written Practice 7B: Complete each of these sentences. Then, if the subject of the purpose clause refers to the subject of the main clause, paraphrase the sentence using **in order to.** If the subject of the purpose clause is different, write, ''Different subject.'' Example:

Sadie is writing her book so that she can share her ideas with other people.
Sadie is writing a book in order to share her ideas with other people.

1. She wants to publish the book _____ the world _____ be a nicer place.
2. Children should practice the rules of politeness _____ they _____ learn self-control.
3. Adults should be polite _____ they _____ make other people comfortable in their presence.

29.8 Chapter Check: Complete these sentences. If you are unsure of an answer, check the indicated model sentence and rule.

1. Remember _____ a note of thanks after receiving a gift. [29.3a]
2. _____ is proper _____ the boy (*ask*) _____ the girl out. [29.1b]
3. The boy should invite the girl (*go*) _____ out at least one week beforehand. [29.3b]
4. Many times a boy does not know what (*say*) _____ to a girl. [29.5]
5. It's a good idea to let your date (*talk*) _____ about himself or herself. [29.6a]
6. I'm writing this book (*help*) _____ you (*feel*) _____ more comfortable in social situations. [29.7, 29.6d]
7. It is never too late (*become*) _____ a well-mannered person. [16.6a]
8. Should I have the package (*deliver*) _____ to your house or to your office? [Oral Practice 6B]

9.   It took several months _____ the sculptor (*finish*) _____ the

      statue.   [29.1b]

10.   I helped my friend (*find*) _____ a room _____

      live in.   [29.6d, 29.4b]

29.9 Chapter Check: Finish sentence B. It should have about the same meaning as sentence A.

1.   A. It appeared that the audience was moved by the music.

      B. The audience appeared _____

      _____.   [29.3a, 29.1d]

2.   A. It was very exciting to watch the championship games.

      B. The championship games _____ to watch.   [29.2]

3.   A. Our teacher usually allows us to stay after class to finish our tests.

      B. Our teacher usually lets _____ to finish our

      tests.   [29.6a]

4.   A. The corrupt politician forced his assistant to destroy the memo.

      B. The corrupt politician _____ his assistant destroy the memo.   [29.6b]

5.   A. It is not very difficult to understand these exercises.

      B. These exercises _____.   [29.2]

6.   A. He strongly suggested my dropping the course.

      B. He strongly urged me _____.   [29.3b]

7.   A. It is hard for an English speaker to pronounce some Russian words.

      B. Some Russian words _____

      _____.   [29.2]

8.   A. Riding motorcycles can be fun.

      B. It _____.   [29.1a]

9.   A. I was surprised that Jackson was willing to help.

      B. Jackson's _____ to help surprised me.   [29.4a]

10.   A. Carlos left school for a year so that he could earn enough money to study abroad.

      B. Carlos left school for a year in _____

      _____.   [29.7]

29.10 Warm-up: On the board there should be a list of the names of all the students in the class. Everyone in class should think of a desire that he or she has. Then each person should tell the class what that dream is, using one of these expressions:

I hope to
I would like to
I plan to
My dream is to

Example:

Someday, I would like to cross the Pacific in a sailboat.

In another column on the board, the teacher or a student should note each one of the students' dreams. Example:

cross Pacific/sailboat

The names and dreams should *not* be in corresponding order. After everyone has had a turn, you and your classmates should use your memories and try to match the student with the dream. Example:

Haryo hopes to cross the Pacific in a sailboat someday.

29.11 Communication: Think of some complex skill which you have or some complicated piece of machinery which you are able to operate. Try to think of something that not everyone can do and that might have bad results if it is not done well. Here are some examples:

skiing (snow or water)
mountain climbing
driving a car
using a chainsaw
jogging or doing aerobic exercises
butchering a sheep
word processing
administering CPR
diapering a baby

Find a student who has a skill that you don't have and who doesn't know how to do the activity that you can do well. Tell each other how to do these things without making any diagrams or drawing any pictures. Use only *words* to teach your skill. Explain what is **easy** to do and what is **difficult**. Tell what it is **important/necessary/essential** to do. Explain why it is important to do these things using **in order to**.

When the other student explains how to do something, take notes. You will use this information in a writing assignment.

29.12 Sentence Writing: What would you do in the following situations? Use **let, make, have, get,** or **help** in each sentence.

1.   Your bicycle is broken; your friend knows how to fix bicycles.
2.   Your roommate does not want to go out for pizza, but you really want to.
3.   You have a dog, and the dog is bothering your guest.

4. You see another student coming up the stairs in your building with a box that is too large for one person to carry comfortably.

5. Your windows are dirty. You don't have time to wash them yourself. A young boy who lives nearby likes to do that kind of work for pay.

6. A good friend of yours has to move out of his/her room on Friday and can't move into his/her new place until Sunday afternoon.

7. There are a lot of dirty dishes in your sink. Your roommate hasn't washed dishes recently.

8. The Office of Student Records at your school will send out transcripts upon request. You are thinking about transferring to another school, and the new school needs your transcript.

29.13 Sentence Writing:　Answer these questions with an **infinitive of purpose.**

1. Why are you taking this course?
2. Why did you come to this university?

3. Why are you planning to major in _____? (Fill in the name of your major.)
4. Why do you have to go to the bank sometimes?
5. Why do you hold up your hand in class sometimes?

29.14 Sentence Writing:　As you recall, Sadie has been writing a book about what is polite and impolite to do, according to her rather conservative American value system. Every society has different rules of conduct. Suppose that you know an American who is going to visit your native country. You want to tell that person what it is polite, impolite, necessary, illegal, and so on to do there. Write five sentences that you might say to that person. Begin each sentence with *It is* + **an adjective.** Here are some adjectives that you might want to use: *necessary, unnecessary, polite, impolite, acceptable, unacceptable, unusual, illegal.*

29.15 Paragraph Writing:　In 29.11 Communication, you and your partner told each other how to perform a certain task. Write two paragraphs, one about what you told your partner, and one about what you learned from your partner. Here are some expressions that you may want to use:

> *explained how to*
> *told me/her/him how to*
>
> *said that it was easy/difficult/hard to*
> *said that it was important/necessary/essential to*
>
> *told me/her/him (not) to*
> *warned me/her/him (not) to*
> *advised me/her/him (not) to*
> *reminded me/her/him (not) to*
> *encouraged me/her/him to*
>
> *said to be careful (not) to*

29.16 Reflecting: Read the next episode of the mystery story. Then look for infinitives. Some of the infinitives are objects of verbs. Others are used as adverbials to express purpose.

> To find a missing person you need patience, brains, and luck. I have lots of patience. When I talked to the bartender who had seen Carl Miller the day he disappeared, I got lucky.
>
> "Miller wanted to know about Dr. Weber, too," the bartender said. "He wanted to know if the doctor ever came in here to have a drink."
>
> "And you told him that Weber liked to drink here," I said.
>
> "Sure. The doctor comes in sometimes in the evening. He likes to talk. He tells me about how hard it is to be a doctor. Well, I listen to him, but I don't feel sorry for him. He gets paid to do that stuff."
>
> "Did Miller ask anything else?"
>
> "Yes, he asked me to tell him if Weber had ever come in during the day. I saw the doctor in here one time a couple of months ago. Right at noon. We watched the news together. It was the day after the election."
>
> I checked my calendar. That was the day Weber had operated on Troy Daniels' mother. So Carl Miller could have proved that Weber had been drinking before the operation. But then Miller disappeared.
>
> "Have you seen Weber recently?" I asked.
>
> "Sure. He came in the day Miller was here. I told him Miller had been asking about him."

29.17 Real-World Work

THINK/PRACTICE

By now you should know some of the expressions that cause you to make infinitive/gerund/base-form errors. For example, you may have trouble with the verbs that take the base form, that is, **let, make,** and **have**. Or perhaps you have trouble with **advise**, which takes an infinitive when there is an object noun or pronoun and a gerund when there is not an object. Example:

She advised me to be on time.
She advised being on time.

Maybe you forget to use the infinitive when you are referring to purposes. After you have identified the expressions that still cause you problems, you must practice them until the correct structure feels right and sounds natural.

LOOK/LISTEN

Infinitives are very common in both spoken and written English. Go over a composition that you have written fairly recently—not one that you have written for this chapter. Mark the infinitives that you find. You may find that most of the infinitives that you have used are objects of common verbs such as **want** and **need**. Now mark the infinitives you find on a page or two of a textbook. You will probably find infinitives used in a variety of ways: as subjects (perhaps moved to the end of the sentence and replaced with **it**), to show purpose (**in order to**), after adjectives, nouns, and question words. If you find that you are using infinitives in a very limited way, try to apply what you have learned in this chapter to your writing while it is fresh in your mind.

USE

If you are studying in the U.S. right now, you may want to use your journal to explore the differences between the rules of etiquette or politeness in this society and those of another society that you are familiar with. Which rules of politeness in your native culture would surprise someone born in the U.S.? Is there anything that people are expected to do in American society that seems silly to someone with another cultural perspective? This can be a very interesting area to think, talk, and write about.

30

Noun
Clauses

REVIEW

In chapters 28 and 29 you learned that infinitive and gerund phrases could act like nouns; that is, they could be subjects or objects in sentences, and gerund phrases are often objects of prepositions.

Underline the infinitive and gerund phrases in these sentences and tell if they are subjects (**S**), objects (**O**), or objects of prepositions (**OP**).

1. _____ I want to leave soon.

2. _____ Jogging is a free-time activity of millions of Americans.

3. _____ He is looking forward to hearing the concert.

4. _____ To listen to music is what he would rather do.

PREVIEW

In chapters 18 and 19 we saw that clauses—groups of words with subjects and verbs—can act like adjectives. In this chapter we will see that clauses can also act like nouns. The underlined expressions in the following sentences are **noun clauses**. Tell whether they are subjects, objects, or objects of prepositions.

1. _____ The fact that Mr. McGill is an old-fashioned man is obvious.

2. _____ His wife was thinking about why he believes the things he does.

3. _____ She doesn't know how she can change him.

In this chapter we will also work with some special kinds of noun clauses that come after verbs like ***recommend*** and expressions like ***it is important***:

It is important that Mr. McGill learn to think for himself.

30.1   Noun Clauses as Subjects

A 70-year-old woman (Sadie) has become a published author. That surprises nearly everyone—except Sadie and Oscar.

Complete these model sentences.	Check.	Complete these rules.
a. _____ **a 70-year-old woman has become a published author surprises nearly everyone.**	That	A statement, such as, ''A 70-year-old woman has become a published author,'' can be the **subject** of a sentence. The simplest way to do this is to put the word _____ in front of the clause and then put the entire clause before the main verb. This is not, however, the most common way.
b. The _____ **that a 70-year-old woman has become a published author surprises nearly everyone.**	fact	We often put the expression _____ _____ _____ in front of a **noun clause** that is used as the subject.
c. _____ **surprises nearly everyone** _____ **a 70-year-old woman has become a published author.**	It that	The most common way to make a sentence with a **subject noun clause**—especially in speaking—is to move the noun clause to the _____ of the sentence and put the word _____ in the subject position.

Oral Practice 1A: Tell the class a fact about Americans which surprises you.

Oral Practice 1B: Make a prediction beginning with one of these expressions:

It is certain
It is likely
It is probable
It is possible
It is unlikely

Example:

It is unlikely that I will get my degree in four years.

Written Practice 1:   Complete these sentences.

1. The fact that Mr. Arnold _____ annoys his neighbors.
2. _____ Mr. Johnson works in a factory is surprising.
3. _____ surprises most people that _____.
4. _____ Mr. Johnson _____ upsets his

   boss.
5. The fact _____ is not well known.
6. _____ Smith hates cats is not surprising.
7. It makes people sad that _____.
8. _____ hurts me that _____.
9. It makes me angry _____.
10. _____ will never be forgotten.

30.2 *It + Seems, Appears, Is Reported*, and so on		
Complete these model sentences.	Check.	Complete these rules.
a. The publisher seems to like Sadie's book. *or* **It seems** _____ _____ _____ **likes Sadie's book.**	that the publisher	The verb ***appear*** and _____ often appear in this structure: _____ + $\left.\begin{array}{c} \textbf{\textit{seems}} \\ \textbf{\textit{appears}} \end{array}\right\}$ + ***that*** + **clause** That structure can be paraphrased with this structure: **noun phrase** + $\left.\begin{array}{c} \textbf{\textit{seem}} \\ \textbf{\textit{appear}} \end{array}\right\}$ + **infinitive**

b. Sadie is rumored to be receiving a lot of money for her book.
 	
or _____ **is rumored**
 	
_____ **Sadie is receiving a lot of money for her book.**
 	
In fact, _____ **is believed that the contract assures Sadie of at least $100,000.**
or **In fact, the contract is believed**
 	
_____ _____ **Sadie of at least $100,000.**
	It
	
	that
	
	it
	
	to assure
		Several passive verbs can appear in this structure:
		
		_____ + **passive verb** + ***that*** + **clause**
		Here is a list of verbs that are commonly used in this structure. Notice that they are verbs of **believing** and **reporting**.
		
		   believe *report*
		   think *mention*
		   feel *say*
		   assume *rumor*
		   know
		Rumor is a very unusual verb; it is used *only* in the passive voice.
		   Like ***seem*** and ***appear***, these passive verbs can also be used in this structure:
		noun phrase + **passive verb** + **infinitive phrase**

Oral Practice 2A: You, your classmates, and your teacher should pick a topic (event, issue, problem, or crisis) of current interest in your school, your community, the country, or the world. Think of something you have heard about this topic or something that most people believe about it. Make a sentence beginning with one of these phrases:

It is believed	It is rumored
It is thought	It is reported
It is felt	It is said
It is assumed	It seems
	It appears

You may want to have someone write the sentences on the board or on an overhead projector transparency. Example:

It is reported that hundreds of people joined in the celebration.

Oral Practice 2B: Now paraphrase the sentences that were produced in Oral Practice 2A. Use the infinitive structure. If the verb in the ***that*** clause is in the present perfect or a past tense, you must use a **perfect infinitive**, i.e., ***to*** + ***have*** + **past participle.** Example:

*Hundreds of people are reported **to have joined** in the celebration.*

Written Practice 2:   Finish sentence B. It should have about the same meaning as sentence A.

1. A. The rebel troops are reported to have taken the third largest city in the country.

    B. It _____

        the third largest city in the country.

2. A. It appears that many soldiers on both sides have died in the heavy fighting.

    B. Many soldiers on both sides appear _____

        _____.

3. A. The rebels are believed to be within 10 miles of the capital.

    B. _____ that the rebels are within 10 miles of the capital.

4. A. It is rumored that the president has left the capital.

    B. The president is _____.

5. A. The leader of the rebels is said to be gaining in popularity among the peasants.

    B. It _____

        gaining in popularity among the peasants.

6. A. It is thought that many government soldiers have gone over to the rebel side.

    B. Many government soldiers _____ thought _____

        _____.

30.3 Noun Clause as Objects		
Complete these model sentences.	Check.	Complete these rules.
a. Bernard thinks _____ **the buttons in an elevator should be placed lower.** *or* **Bernard thinks the buttons in an elevator should be placed lower.**	that	Statements such as, ''Elevator buttons should be placed lower,'' can also become **object** noun clauses. The word _____ is often put before the clause, but it is not necessary. Some verbs take **infinitive** objects, some take **gerund** objects, and some take **noun clause** objects. With some verbs you have a choice: More than one pattern is possible. Try the self-test that starts on the next page.

b. He wonders _____ **the designers put the buttons so high. He doesn't know when**
 	
 _____ _____ **be able to reach the button for the twenty-second floor.**
	why
	
	 he will
		Information questions, such as ''Why
		
		 _____ the designers put the buttons so high?'', can also become noun clauses. When the noun clause is derived from an information question, we do *not* use the word *that* to introduce it. In a noun clause derived from an information question, the first word is usually the **question word**.
		   Answer this question: Are the words in these noun clauses in question word order?
		
		 _____, they are in
		
		 _____ word order.
		   Do *not* use a question mark after an embedded question unless the **main clause** is also a question. Compare:
		      I wonder why the buttons are so high.
		      Do you know why the buttons are so high?

c. He wonders _____ *(or* _____*)* **the elevators of the future will have buttons that kids can reach.**	if whether	**Yes/no** questions may also become noun clauses. The word _____ or the word _____ is used to introduce a noun clause derived from a **yes/no** question. Again the words in the clause are in _____ word order.

Self-Test

In the first part of the self-test you will give each verb an object. The object will always be the idea: ***I will be there***. After some of the verbs, this idea must be expressed in a **noun clause**; after some others, it must be expressed with an **infinitive phrase**. With some verbs, both structures are possible. Look at the examples. Then cover the answer box and make the sentence or sentences that are possible with each verb. After each verb check yourself by uncovering the answer. Mark the verbs that give you trouble, and practice making other sentences with these verbs until the correct structures feel natural to you.

Verb	Answer Box	
think	I think that I will be there.	(impossible)
plan	(impossible)	I plan to be there.
hope	I hope that I will be there	I hope to be there.

Now cover the answers and try these:

want		I want to be there.
prefer		I prefer to be there.
need		I need to be there.
hope	I hope that I will be there.	I hope to be there.
plan		I plan to be there.
have volunteered		I have volunteered to be there.
have offered		I have offered to be there.
hesitate		I hesitate to be there.
have refused		I have refused to be there.
have decided	I have decided that I will be there.	I have decided to be there.
have chosen		I have chosen to be there.
have said	I have said that I will be there.	
have promised	I have promised that I will be there.	I have promised to be there.
think	I think that I will be there.	
believe	I believe that I will be there.	
assume	I assume that I will be there.	
bet	I bet that I will be there.	
guess	I guess that I will be there.	
suppose	I suppose that I will be there.	
imagine	I imagine that I will be there.	

Verb	Answer Box	
expect	I expect that I will be there.	I expect to be there.
intend		I intend to be there.
know	I know that I will be there.	

The next part is just like the preceding one. This time the idea to be expressed in the object is ***She will be there***.

Examples:

think	I think that she will be there.	(impossible)
want	(impossible)	I want her to be there.
expect	I expect that she will be there.	I expect her to be there.

Now cover the answers and try these:

doubt	I doubt that she will be there.	
believe	I believe that she will be there.	
assume	I assume that she will be there.	
guess	I guess that she will be there.	
suppose	I suppose that she will be there.	
expect	I expect that she will be there.	I expect her to be there.
need		I need her to be there.
hope	I hope that she will be there.	
will permit		I will permit her to be there.
will allow		I will allow her to be there.
have persuaded		I have persuaded her to be there.
have encouraged		I have encouraged her to be there.
must remind		I must remind her to be there.

The last part of the self-test is like the preceding one. This time the idea to be expressed in the object is ***I was there***. Notice that you must choose between a **noun clause** and a **gerund**.

Examples:

Verb	Answer Box	
regretted	I regretted that I was there.	I regretted being there.
enjoyed	(impossible)	I enjoyed being there.
said	I said that I was there.	(impossible)

Now cover the answers and try these:

denied	I denied that I was there.	I denied being there.
admitted	I admitted that I was there.	I admitted being there.
enjoyed		I enjoyed being there.
disliked		I disliked being there.
remember	I remember that I was there.	I remember being there.
mentioned	I mentioned that I was there.	I mentioned being there.
declared	I declared that I was there.	
discussed		I discussed being there.

Oral Practice 3A: Tell the class some things you wonder about. Example:

I wonder why English has so many crazy rules.

Oral Practice 3B: Write an information question on a piece of paper. It should be a question that you would really like the answer to and that you think a classmate or the teacher could answer, e.g., when or what time something is, where something is, or how something is pronounced or spelled. Example:

When do we have our next test?

Now ask your question using the polite formula "Could you please tell me . . ." Example:

Could you please tell me when we have our next test?

Written Practice 3A: Finish sentence B. It should have about the same meaning as sentence A.

1.   A. Pierre admitted stealing the necklace.

     B. Pierre admitted that _____.

2. A. He genuinely regrets making a career of crime.

    B. He genuinely regrets _____ has made a career of crime.

3. A. He hopes to be out of prison in time for his mother's birthday.

    B. He hopes that _____ in time for his mother's birthday.

4. A. Stan has decided to go to a music school in New York City.

    B. Stan has decided that _____

    _____.

5. A. Stan's current teacher expects him to do well there.

    B. Stan's current teacher expects _____ will do well there.

Written Practice 3B: Answer the following questions with a *sentence that contains a noun clause*.

1. Where's the party?

    I don't know where _____.

2. Why is he always late?

    I don't know _____.

3. The bus fare should be lower, shouldn't it?

    Yes, I think _____.

4. Where can I get a map of the city?

    I'll tell you _____.

5. How much will the concert cost?

    I don't know _____.

6. How long can he stay?

    I haven't heard _____.

7. Do they have children?

    I don't know _____.

8. Is he coming?

    Who knows _____.

30.4 Noun Clauses after Nouns and Adjectives		
Complete these model sentences.	Check.	Complete these rules.
a. Stan's belief _____ he will succeed in the world of music makes him practice every night. The knowledge _____ it is very difficult to make a living as a jazz musician doesn't worry him.	that that	Certain nouns can be followed by noun clauses. Some examples are **idea, claim, theory, news, realization, suggestion,** **statement, proposal,** _____, and _____. Most of these nouns are derived from verbs that take noun clause objects. Using your dictionary if necessary, complete the following list.

Some Nouns That Take Noun Clauses

Verb	Noun	Verb	Noun
argue	**argument**	fear	_____
assume	_____	feel	_____
claim	_____	hope	_____
conclude	_____	realize	_____
discover	_____	recognize	_____
doubt	_____	suspect	_____
dream	_____	understand	_____

b. Stan is sure _____ he will succeed. His mother is afraid _____ he will be disappointed.	that that	Many adjectives of attitude or emotion, such as _____ and _____, allow this structure: **human subject + be + adjective + noun clause** See the following list of adjectives.

Some Predicate Adjectives That Take Noun Clauses

sure	happy	pleased	fearful	annoyed
certain	glad	amused	afraid	disturbed
doubtful	pleased	excited	frightened	irritated
aware	sad	thrilled		
	disappointed			

Oral Practice 4A: Tell the class something you are sure about and something you are not quite certain of. Example:

I am sure that I will get my B.S. degree.

Oral Practice 4B: One student should tell something he or she *believes, hopes, assumes, suspects, has realized,* or *has discovered*. Then another student should make a comment on the first student's *belief, hope, assumption,* etc. Follow this example:

> HENGKY: I believe that the world will become more peaceful.
> FAHAD: Hengky's belief that the world will become more peaceful is naive.

Written Practice 4:   Complete these sentences.

1.   This year the voters are confident that _____.

2.   The weatherman is certain _____ tomor-

row.

3.   The belief that _____ is common in my country.

4.   The idea _____ doesn't worry

me.

5.   I am afraid that _____.

6.   My parents are very proud that _____.

7.   The realization that _____

makes everyone in the world worry.

30.5 Noun Clauses with the Base Form of the Verb		
Complete these model sentences from Sadie's book.	Check.	Complete these rules.
a. I suggest that a boy _____ a girl out for a date at least a week before the night of a date.	ask	If the main verb describes suggesting, demanding, or anything in between—such verbs as *suggest, recommend, urge, ask, require,* and *demand*—the verb in the object noun clause is in the _____ form.
b. It is important that the children _____ in bed before the guests arrive.	be	The same thing is true after expressions such as *it is essential, it is necessary,* and _____ _____ _____.
c. I recommend that a guest _____ ask the cost of furniture and other items in the host's house. This is very impolite.	not	To make a base form negative, simply put _____ in front of it.

Oral Practice 5A: Tell the class things that a good parent should *insist, demand, require,* etc., that a child do or not do.

Oral Practice 5B: Mention things that it is *important, essential,* or *necessary* that a student do or not do if he or she wants to succeed.

Written Practice 5:   Complete these sentences.

1. It is essential that a guest _____ properly dressed for a formal dinner.

2. It is important that a guest _____ at a dinner party at the indicated time.

3. I strongly recommend that a guest _____ a thank-you note to the host.

4. It is necessary that you _____ alert in class.

5. I suggest that you not _____ during dinner.

6. Xavier's mother demanded that he _____ the garbage.

7. The hotel requested _____ all guests _____ of their rooms by noon.

8. Since there is no lifeguard, the pool rules require that children _____ accompanied by adults.

30.6 Clauses with *-ever* Words		
Complete these model sentences.	Check.	Complete these rules.
a. The person who got out that food should put it back. *or* _____ **got out that food should put it back.**	Whoever	You can refer to an unknown person, place, or thing with a clause that begins with a word made up of a question word and the ending *-ever*. The (unknown) person that = *whoever* The (unknown) thing that = _____ The (unknown) book that = *whichever* book The (unknown) place that = _____ The (unknown) time that = _____
b. If the host has not placed name cards on the table, the guests may sit anywhere they want. *or* . . . **the guests may sit** _____ **they want.**	wherever	These same words can give the idea of "any." For example, the sentence, "You can eat anything you find in the refrigerator," can be paraphrased this way: **You can eat** _____ _____ _____ **in the refrigerator.**

Oral Practice 6:   Tell the class some of the rules in the household you grew up in. Try to use **whoever, whatever, whenever, wherever,** and **however**. Example:

Whoever made a mess had to clean it up.

Written Practice 6:   Finish sentence B. It should have about the same meaning as sentence A. *Use an **-ever** word in each sentence.*

1. A. I don't know who did it, but that person should be ashamed.

    B. _____ did it should be ashamed.

2. A. You can go any place you want, but please be back here at noon.

    B. You can go _____, but please be back here at noon.

3. A. I don't know which route to take; I think I'll take the one Harry suggests.

    B. I think I'll take _____.

4. A. Anyone wanting to meet the author should be at the bookstore by nine o'clock.

    B. _____ to meet the author should be at the bookstore by

    nine o'clock.

5. A. I don't know when Kate will arrive, but she'll call us then.

    B. Kate will call us _____.

6. A. It seems that anything I say irritates Martha.

    B. It seems that _____.

30.7 Chapter Check: Complete these sentences. If you are unsure of an answer, check the indicated model sentence and rule.

1. I don't care where we go. We can go _____ you want to go.   [30.6b]

2. Mario's teacher recommended that he _____ the TOEFL soon.   [30.5a]

3. The claim _____ soldiers actually crossed the border has been de-

    nied.   [30.4a]

4. Chen was very _____ she won the scholarship.   [30.4b]

5. I'm looking for Mr. and Ms. Jones's apartment. Do you know _____ they

    live?   [30.3b]

6. Nothing looks familiar to me. I wonder _____ this is the right

    building.   [30.3c]

30.8 Chapter Check: Finish sentence B. It should have about the same meaning as sentence A.

1. A. Anyone who needs a ride should put his or her name on the list.

    B. Whoever _____ should put his or her name on the

    list.   [30.6b]

2.   A. The fact that many people enjoy eating at Mike's is rather surprising.

     B. It _____

         _____.   [30.1c]

3.   A. The fact that Sadie's book was published made her very happy.

     B. Sadie was very happy _____.   [30.4b]

4.   A. Stan's teacher advised him to go to New York.

     B. Stan's teacher recommended that _____.   [30.5a]

5.   A. My father has always said that I can do anything that I set out to do.

     B. My father has always said that I can do _____ I set out to

         do.   [30.6b]

6.   A. Charley Pierson may come home with us for Thanksgiving.

     B. _____ possible _____

         _____.   [30.1c]

7.   A. Our poor team will probably not win another game this season.

     B. _____ very likely _____

         _____.   [30.1c]

8.   A. Bob's forgetting an appointment was highly unusual.

     B. The fact _____

         _____.   [30.1b]

30.9 Warm-up: Everyone in class should think of a question about geography. Example:

   What is the body of water between Korea and China?

Someone can write these questions on the board. Now take turns making statements beginning with ***I would like to know***. Example:

   I would like to know what the body of water between Korea and China is.

Anyone who knows should answer the question, and the answers should be written on the
board.
     Finally, tell the class something that you have learned today. Example:

   I've learned that the Yellow Sea is between Korea and China.

30.10 Communication: Get together with a partner and think of three questions that some
people in class may know the answer to and others may not. They can be questions about
geography, history, current events, movies, music, a field of study, general facts—anything
that you and your partner decide on. Be sure to use correct noun clause structures in your
discussion. Example:

   Let's see if they know where the next World Cup games will be held.

List your questions in the chart.

Question	Predicted % Right	Right Answers	Wrong Answers	% Right
1.				
2.				
3.				

You and your partner should predict what percentage of your classmates will know the answer to each of the questions. Put that percentage in the second column in the chart. Example:

I think that about 90% of them will know where the World Cup will be held.

Now the class should be divided into two groups. You should be in one group and your partner should be in the other. Ask the three questions of as many people in your group as time allows: Begin the questions with **Do you know**. Example:

Do you know where the next World Cup games will be held?

For each right or wrong answer, put a tally mark (/) in the appropriate box. You might report any difference between your prediction and what you actually learned. Each pair can report on one interesting finding. Example:

> We thought that 90% of the class would know where the next World Cup games
> will be held. However, only 50% of the students in the class know that the next World

Cup games will be held in _____.

30.11 Sentence Writing: Imagine that you are planning to write a letter of advice to a friend who is going to study at this university. Write five sentences that might appear in such a letter. These sentences should begin, **I suggest/recommend/urge/etc. that you . . .** or **It is important/necessary/essential/etc. that you . . .** Use a different verb or expression in every sentence.

30.12 Sentence Writing: You probably know that Utah is one of the 50 states in the U.S. You may have some information about this state, but there are probably many things that you don't know about it. Write five sentences telling what you don't know about Utah. The sentences can begin with expressions such as **I don't know, I wonder, I would like to know, I have never heard**, and so on. Use a noun clause in each sentence. Use a different question word—**whether, where, what, when**, and so on—in each sentence.

30.13 Paragraph Writing: Write a paragraph about sometime in the past, such as your parents' or grandparents' generation. You can write about your own country or culture. Include information about peoples' beliefs or knowledge at that time.

30.14 Sentence Completion: Supply the correct prepositions. Notice that the prepositions in this exercise are followed by **noun clauses.** Refer to Appendix 2 if necessary.

1. Many poor families are very worried _____ how they will pay their fuel

    bills this winter.

2. Pay attention _____ what he says.

3. Our success will depend _____ whether we can convince the committee

    that we are right.

4. I am not familiar _____ how students are tested in that program.

30.15 Reflecting: Read the next episode of the mystery story. Then try to identify all of the noun clauses. Some of these clauses come from statements; others come from questions. Most are objects of verbs, but one of the noun clauses is the subject of a sentence, one follows an adjective, and one follows a noun. Can you find these three noun clauses?

> Even though it was late, I decided that I had to call Deanne Miller. What the bartender had told me gave me a good idea. I was sure that I knew why Carl Miller had disappeared.
> "I think I've figured everything out," I told Mrs. Miller.
> "Do you know where Carl is?" she asked.
> "Not exactly. That's what I need to talk to you about."
> "Do you think he's all right?" she asked.
> "I'm almost certain that he is," I said.
> I drove over to her house. She unlocked the door and let me in. She looked worried.
> "Tell me what you think," she said.
> "First let me explain what I've discovered," I said. I told her that I had spoken to a bartender who had seen her husband the day he disappeared. "He gave your husband proof that Dr. Weber was drinking before the operation. Then he told Dr. Weber about it."
> "Do you think the doctor did something to Carl? Did Weber kidnap him or something?"
> "No," I said. "I think Weber called your husband and threatened him. Your husband got scared, and he's hiding somewhere."
> I asked Deanne Miller if she knew where her husband might go to hide if he were afraid. She told me that they had a cabin at a nearby lake. "Usually we go there just in the summer," she said.
> "We're going to drive there now," I said. "I think that's where Carl is."
> "I don't understand why he wouldn't tell me where he was," Mrs. Miller said.
> "I think he wanted to protect you," I said. "If you knew where he was, Weber might threaten you. Instead, you went to the police and you hired me. So Weber would know that you were confused about the disappearance, too."
> It was midnight and the roads were empty. Except when she gave me directions, Deanne didn't speak. It took us an hour to get to the cabin at the lake. I stopped the car. We could see a small light was burning inside.
> Deanne knocked, and Carl Miller opened the door.

30.16   Real-World Work

THINK/PRACTICE

As you are walking along, think about things that you know or believe, that you have heard, and that you hope. Then think about things that you wonder about:

I wonder if my teacher will like the project I handed in yesterday.
I wonder when she will give us our grades on those projects.

Be careful to use **statement** word order in those noun clauses after "I wonder . . ."—**not** question word order.

LOOK/LISTEN

1. If you read news stories in American newspapers, you have probably noticed that this structure is used very often:

    It is reported/rumored/said/believed/thought/assumed/etc. + *that* + clause

2. Spend 15 minutes or so searching for noun clauses in a book, magazine, or newspaper. See how many of the following structures you can find:

    That + clause
    The fact that + clause
    It . . . *that* + clause
    verb + *that* + clause
    noun + *that* + clause
    adjective + *that* + clause
    verb + *wh-* clause
    -ever clause

    You and your classmates might want to have a contest. The winner is the student who finds examples of the most structures. Also try to find noun clauses with a verb in the base form (see Rule Builder 30.5).

USE

1. It often sounds more polite to use noun clause questions rather than simple questions. These polite sentences often begin with such phrases as **Could you tell me, Do you happen to know,** or **I was wondering.** Example:

    Excuse me. Could you please tell me where I could find a rest room.

2. Think about a dangerous situation in the world or a major event that is currently in the news. Start a conversation in English with someone concerning this news. You will find that you and the person you are talking with will use many noun clauses such as **I read that**, **I think that**, **I don't know if**, **I wonder when**, and so on.

3. Noun clauses beginning with **wh-** words, as well as ***that*** clauses, are very important in written English. Some ESL students make the common error of using question word order in noun clauses and using unnecessary question marks. Example:

    We didn't know when would they arrive?

    The corrected version:

    We didn't know when they would arrive.

    If that error appears in your own writing, make a special effort to apply what you have learned in this chapter to your next letter, essay, or report. Remember, however, that real questions can be used in writing. (See 2.10 Sentence Writing in chapter 2.) Be sure to use question word order and question marks with real questions. Example:

    Why do many people favor capital punishment? There are many reasons . . .

31

Reported
Speech

REVIEW

In chapter 30, we worked with noun clauses like those in the following paragraph. Complete these sentences.

When we finally arrived at the hotel around eight, the manager insisted that we

_____ dinner in the hotel restaurant. _____ that we were exhausted

didn't seem to make any difference to him. I wonder _____ he realized

_____ we felt. I didn't understand why _____ making us eat

there. Later I found out. The hotel requires that all guests _____ in the hotel res-

taurant because the manager is afraid that they will bring food into their rooms.

PREVIEW

We also use noun clauses when we tell the substance of what a person said without giving his or her exact words. We call this use of noun clauses **reported speech**. Use the underlined noun clauses in the following sentences to figure out what the speakers actually said.

1. The President said <u>that he felt much better.</u>

   "_____," the President said.

2. He wanted to know <u>when we were coming</u>.

   "_____?" he asked.

3. They wanted to know <u>if they were late</u>.

   "_____?" they asked.

31.1 **Pronouns in Reported Speech**		
Complete these model sentences.	Check.	Complete these rules.
a. **"I don't feel good," John said.** **John said that _____ didn't feel good.** **"You ought to get a haircut," my grandmother told me.** **My grandmother told me that** **_____ ought to get a haircut.** **Lily and her friends had been working all morning. "Let's go swimming," Lily said.** **Lily suggested that _____ go swimming.**	he I they	Pronouns in **quoted speech** refer to the world of the original speaker and listener. But _____ **speech** creates a new context—the world of the reporter and his or her listener or reader. Therefore, the pronouns used in quoted speech must sometimes be changed in reported speech. Exactly which pronoun is used depends on the new situation. Common sense should be your guide.

Oral Practice 1:   In certain situations, a person often says the same thing every time. Think about a person you know well: a teacher, classmate, roommate, friend, brother, sister, mother, father, etc. Tell what that person always says in a certain kind of situation. Example:

When he's hungry, my roommate always says that he could eat a horse.

Written Practice 1:   Complete sentence B. It should have about the same meaning as sentence A.

1. A. "You are working hard," my teacher said to me.

   B. My teacher observed that _____ was working hard.

2. A. "You don't seem happy," Jackson remarked to Amy.

   B. Jackson remarked to Amy that _____ didn't seem happy.

3. A. John said he didn't feel good.

   B. "_____ don't feel good," John said.

4. A. Amy asked me if I would come to the party.

   B. Amy said, "Will _____ come to the party?"

5. A. The teacher told the students that they had to stop writing in one minute.

   B. The teacher said, "_____ must stop writing in one minute."

6. A. Ted's friend Martha said, "You missed a great party, Ted."

   B. Martha told Ted that _____ had missed a great party.

7. A. "We will see you in September," Mr. and Mrs. Jablonski said to me.

   B. Mr. and Mrs. Jablonski told me that _____ would see _____ in September.

31.2 Reporting Verbs		
Complete these model sentences.	Check.	Complete these rules.
a. Tank was talking to Stretch and said, "I'm tired." Tank _____ that he was tired. *or* Tank _____ Stretch that he was tired.	said told	The most common verbs used to report **statements** are _____ and _____. When *tell* is used in reporting speech, it is always followed by a noun or a pronoun indicating the person spoken to.
b. Stretch said "Why are you tired?" Stretch asked _____ why he was tired. *or* Stretch _____ why Tank was tired.	Tank asked	The most common verb used to report **questions** is _____. It can be used with or without a noun or a pronoun indicating the person spoken to.
c. Tank said, "I studied until midnight." Tank explained _____ _____ had studied until midnight.	that he	There are many verbs that can be used instead of *say* and *tell* to report statements. An example is _____. These verbs have a more precise meaning and should be used only when the meaning is appropriate. A list of common reporting verbs follows.
Some Common Verbs of Reporting		
add *confess* *indicate* *point out* *reply* *swear* *admit* *declare* *inform (someone)* *promise* *report* *whisper* *announce* *emphasize* *maintain* *remark* *shout* *yell* *answer* *explain* *mention* *repeat* *state*		

Oral Practice 2:   The India Club on campus recently sponsored a Divali celebration. A newspaper reporter interviewed the president of the club. Use one of the verbs in Rule Builder 31.2 to report this woman's statements. You and your classmates can discuss which reporting verbs are appropriate.

As you will see in Rule Builder 31.3, the verbs in the noun clauses (the reported statements) can be kept in the tenses the speaker actually used or they can be changed. For example, the first one can be either "She explained that Divali *is* the New Year's holiday in India . . ." or "She explained that Divali *was* the New Year's holiday in India." Since you have not worked on this tense problem yet, use the original tenses in your sentences.

1. "Divali is the New Year's holiday in India and lasts for three days."
2. "The celebration of Divali involves food, dance, and an exchange of gifts."
3. "Traditionally, houses are cleaned and decorated with oil lamps and candles."
4. "Divali legends are interpreted differently throughout India. The club's event is a blend of different traditions."
5. "The celebration is three days long."
6. (When asked what kind of gifts are given) "New clothing is a traditional present."
7. (In a very low voice) "Gambling is often a major part of Divali parties."
8. "No illegal gambling occurred at this campus event."
9. "Two professional dancers were brought in for the celebration."
10. "We will have another Divali celebration next year."

Written Practice 2A: Report about seven of the statements above. *Use a different reporting verb in every sentence.*

Written Practice 2B: Sometimes statements can be reported with a verb + an infinitive. *Review Written Practice 3A in chapter 29 to find examples.* Then, using verbs from the list in that written practice, report what the following people said to you. Example:

> *Your adviser: "You should take Professor Hixon's geology course."*
> *My adviser urged me to take Professor Hixon's geology course.*

1. Your roommate: "I'll record that TV show for you."
2. Your teacher: "You may hand in your paper one day late."
3. The cashier: "No, I can't cash this check for you."
4. Your friend: "You should come to the Divali celebration with me."

31.3 Tense in Reported Speech		
Complete these model sentences.	Check.	Complete these rules.
a. "I'm not interested," Bernard stated. Bernard stated that he _____ _____ interested. "I'm not going," Angel told us. Angel told us that she _____ _____ _____. "I have been sick a lot," Freud wrote. Freud wrote that he _____ _____ sick a lot.	was not was not going had been	If a statement which was made in the past is put into reported speech, a present tense is usually changed to a _____ tense. That is to say, **simple present** → _____ _____, **present progressive** → _____ progressive, **present perfect** → _____ _____.

b. ''Rex left last week,'' said Larry. **Larry said that Rex _____ last week.**	left *or* had left	When the verb in the quoted speech is in the simple past tense, the past perfect tense is often used in reported speech. However, especially in spoken English, the verb commonly remains in the simple past tense in reported speech, especially if a time adverbial, such as _____ _____, makes the time clear.
c. ''The Ivory Coast is in Africa,'' William told me. **William told me that the Ivory Coast** **_____ in Africa.** *or* **William told me that the Ivory** **Coast _____ in Africa.**	was is	Of course, the statement made in the past may refer to things which are still true, or things which are still in the future. When this happens, we have the choice of using the original verb tense or changing the verb to a _____ form.

d. ''The world will end in the year 1000 A.D.,'' wrote a medieval prophet.
A medieval prophet wrote that the
 	
world _____ _____ in the year 1000 A.D.
''You can save yourselves only by becoming better people,'' he continued.
He also said that the people
 	
_____ _____ themselves only by becoming better.
''It may, however, be too late.''
The prophet cautioned that it
 	
_____ _____ too late.
	would end
	
	could save
	
	might be
		Modals must usually be changed when we are reporting what someone said in the past. If the events or situations that the person talked about are finished,
		
		   will becomes _____,
		
		   can becomes _____, and
		
		   may becomes _____.
		The modal **should** does not change.
		
		   Even if the events or situations referred to are still in the present or the future, the modals are often changed in past reported speech. For example, if last night Bill said to you, ''Hank can come with us tomorrow,'' you might say to Hank today,
		Bill said that you could come with us today.
		But it is not necessary to use *could*. You can also say,
		Bill said that you can come with us today.

e. ''You must believe me,'' he said. **The prophet told the people that** **they _____ _____ believe him.**	had to	The modal **must** has no past form. In past reported speech, change **must** to _____ _____ or **needed to.**

Oral Practice 3A: Tell the class about a short conversation you had yesterday or earlier today.

Oral Practice 3B: Think of some predictions that people made in the past but which have not come true. What did these people think would happen in the future?

Written Practice 3:   These are quotes from the fictitious presidential campaign of Senator Smith. Put his quotes into reported speech. Remember to use a variety of reporting verbs.

1. ''I have served in the U.S. Senate for over 10 years.''
2. ''I cannot comment on my recent conversation with the Soviet leader.''
3. ''I will address that problem early in my administration.''
4. ''I am convinced that the trade deficit will remain a serious problem.''
5. ''I do not favor lowering the dollar against foreign currency.''
6. ''Leaders from both parties must work together to solve these problems.''

31.4 Putting Imperatives into Reported Speech		
Complete these model sentences.	Check.	Complete these rules.
a. **''Board the plane quickly!'' the man at the airport said.** **The man at the airport told us** **_____ _____ the plane quickly.**	to board	When we report imperatives or requests, we can use a verb like ***order*** or _____ plus a noun or pronoun followed by an _____. A list of the verbs which permit this structure can be found in chapter 29—the right-hand column of the self-test on pages 375–376.
b. **''Close the door!'' Stan exclaimed.** **Stan demanded that I _____ the door.** **''I would like every student to be on time,'' the counselor said.** **The counselor urged that every** **student _____ on time.**	close be	Another way to report imperatives or requests is to use a more emphatic verb, such as _____ or _____. As you learned in Rule Builder 30.5, these verbs are followed by noun clauses which have verbs in the _____ form.

Oral Practice 4A: What are some things your mother or father always told you to do?

Oral Practice 4B: Tell someone across the classroom to do something. That person should pretend not to hear and should ask someone closer to you what you said. Example:

    MAY: *Please open the window a little bit, Amer.*
  AMER: *Luis, what did May say?*
   LUIS: *She asked you to open the window a little bit.*

Oral Practice 4C: What are some things you would tell someone to do if he or she were going to visit your country? Use both structures from Rule Builder 31.4. Examples:

> *I would urge the person to stay at a hotel on the beach.*
> *I would suggest that the person take scuba diving lessons.*

Written Practice 4:   Complete sentences B and C. They should have about the same meaning as sentence A.

1. A. "Take your seats!" he said.

    B. He told us _____.

    C. He insisted that _____.

2. A. "Turn the bolt the other way," Jimmy suggested to his father.

    B. Jimmy told his father _____.

    C. Jimmy suggested that _____.

3. A. "Look that word up in a good dictionary," the teacher said to Reynaldo.

    B. The teacher encouraged Reynaldo _____ in a good

        dictionary.

    C. The teacher recommended that _____

        in a good dictionary.

4. A. "Don't touch the works of art," the guide told the children.

    B. The guide ordered the children _____.

    C. The guide demanded that _____.

5. A. "Don't spend all of your time with other students from your country," the counselor

        urged Chin.

    B. The counselor urged Chin _____

        with other students from his country.

    C. The counselor suggested that _____

        with other students from his country.

31.5 Putting Questions into Reported Speech			
Complete these model sentences.	Check.	Complete these rules.
a. "Can you go to the basketball game?" Harold asked Sally. **Harold asked Sally** ____ _____ _____ _____ **to the basketball game.**	if she could go or whether she could go	Yes/no questions in reported speech begin with the word _____ or the word _____, and they use statement word order.
b. "Where is it going to be?" she asked with a frown. **She frowned and asked** _____ _____ _____ _____ _____ _____.	where it was going to be	Information questions in reported speech begin with the _____ word and use _____ word order.
c. "At the stadium. Will you drive?" Harold asked. **Harold told her it was going to be at the stadium and then requested that** _____ _____.	she drive	***Request*** is another verb which is followed by a noun clause with a verb in the _____ form. (See Rule Builder 30.5)

Oral Practice 5A: Pair off with a classmate. You and your classmate should quietly ask each other a question. Answer the questions; then report to the class what your partner asked you. You might also want to report your answer. Example:

She asked me if Indonesia was close to Japan.

Oral Practice 5B: We often use reported speech when we have to repeat what we have said. Think of something that you would really like to know about your teacher or a classmate (something that is appropriate to ask about in class). That person should pretend not to hear. When you repeat your question, begin with "I asked . . ." Example:

How long have you been teaching English?
Pardon me?
I asked how long you had been teaching English.
or I asked how long you have been teaching English.

Written Practice 5: A reporter was on the scene of a major fire last week. Complete these sentences about what the reporter asked the fire chief.

1. "Is the fire under control?"

   He asked _____.

2. "How did the fire start?"

   He then asked _____.

3. "When did the fire begin?"

   He wanted to know _____.

4. "How many firefighters are on the scene?"

   He asked _____.

5. "Could you please let me talk to one of the firefighters?"

   He requested that the chief _____ to one of the firefighters.

6. "Are there any people still in the building?"

   He tried to find out _____.

7. "Have you found any bodies in the building?"

   He asked _____.

8. "Please be honest with me, chief."

   He requested that the chief _____.

31.6 Chapter Check: Many states are considering establishing lotteries, games in which people buy tickets with the hope of winning a lot of money. In one state, debates are going on in the legislature concerning a proposed lottery. A debate was held on this issue last Thursday. These are some of the things legislators said. Finish sentence B so that it has about the same meaning as sentence A. If you are unsure of an answer, check the indicated model sentence and rule.

1. A. Senator Wilbur said, "Let the people decide whether to create a state-run lottery."

   B. Senator Wilbur encouraged his fellow senators _____

   _____ whether to create a state lottery.   [31.4a]

2. A. Senator Wong said, "I will vote for the lottery if advertising is prohibited."

   B. Senator Wong said that _____

   _____.   [31.1,31.3a&d]

3. A. Senator O'Brien asked his fellow senators, "Why do you want to legalize immoral behavior?"

   B. Senator O'Brien wondered _____

   _____.   [31.1, 31.5b, 31.3a]

4. A. Senator Schmidt said, "Let's stop arguing and schedule a vote."

B. Senator Schmidt suggested that _____

_____. [31.1, 31.4b]

31.7 Chapter Check: Finish sentence B so that it has about the same meaning as sentence A.

1. A. "Give me my car keys!" Angela said to me.

B. Angela demanded _____. [31.1, 31.4b]

2. A. She asked me if I needed any help finding the bank.

B. "_____ the bank?"

she asked. [31.1, 31.5a]

3. A. "When will you be back?" Sadie asked me a long time ago.

B. A long time ago, Sadie asked when _____

back. [31.1,31.5b,31.3d]

4. A. "I can do it!" I foolishly claimed.

B. I foolishly _____. [31.3d]

5. A. Father said that since it was raining, we could go on Friday.

B. " _____,"

Father said. [31.1,31.3a]

6. A. The janitor told us that he had been living in the basement for 17 years.

B. " _____,"

the janitor said. [31.1,31.3a]

7. A. "Will you please clean up this mess?" the boss asked her.

B. The boss asked her _____. [31.4a]

8. A. At the party last night, Martha turned off the music and said, "I must make an important announcement."

B. At the party last night, Martha turned off the music and said that

_____ an important announcement. [31.1,31.3e]

9. A. Before last night's concert, Mary asked, "What time does it begin?"

B. Before last night's concert, Mary asked what _____

_____. [31.5b,31.3a]

10. A. She then asked Jim, "Are we going to be on time?"

B. She then asked Jim whether _____. [31.1,31.5a,31.3a]

11. A. Jim replied, "I'm sure that we will."

B. Jim replied that _____. [31.1,31.3d]

31.8 Warm-up: Your teacher will tell you to say certain things to your classmates. Example:

> *Tell Gina that you like her new haircut.*
> *Ask Haryo if he could lend you a pencil.*
> *Ask Yanli to wait for you after class.*

Now tell one classmate to say something to another classmate.

31.9 Communication: Get together with another classmate. Choose a topic for a brief conversation. Suggestions:

> *Your families*
> *Your hobbies*
> *Things to do for fun in this town*
> *Your countries or cities*
> *A sports team or event that you are both interested in*
> *A field of study that you are both interested in*
> *A movie, TV show, or popular entertainer that you are both interested in*

Talk for a few minutes; then reduce the most interesting parts of your conversation to a short dialogue in which each person says three or four things. Practice the dialogue so that it is very smooth and easy to understand.

Your teacher will have some of the pairs perform their dialogues for the class. After each performance, try to write down the exact words of the dialogue. Use this format:

> ISMAIL: Have you ever played racquetball?
> CHANG: No, but I'd like to sometime.
> ISMAIL: Well, why don't we . . .

The next step, which could be done as homework, is to write reports on the dialogue. Example:

> *Ismail asked Chang if he had ever played racquetball. Chang replied that he hadn't, but that he would like to sometime. Ismail suggested that they . . .*

31.10 Sentence Writing: If you could interview a famous person, living or dead, whom would you choose?

> *If I could interview a famous person, I would choose* _____*.*

Think of five questions you would ask this person. Begin each of your five sentences with these words: *I would ask him/her* . . . Since you are using conditional sentences, use past tenses in your noun clauses. Example:

> *I would ask her where she was born.*

31.11 Sentence Writing: Watch at least a few minutes of a TV drama, comedy, or talk show. Write down six interesting quotes: two statements, two questions, and two orders or requests. Then put each of those into a reported speech sentence.

31.12 Paragraph Writing: A state legislature recently made it illegal for people under 21 to buy or drink alcohol. A local newspaper interviewed three people to find out how they felt about this new law. Read the following direct quotations, and then rewrite them to make them reported speech.

William Danley, 18 years old, an architecture student
''I think this is one of the dumbest things the legislature has ever done. Kids who are 18 are old enough to vote and to serve their country in a war. If they are old enough to take that kind of responsibility, then they should be allowed to drink.''

Jane More, 27 years old, a computer engineer
''The law is a good idea. When I was in high school, one of my best friends was killed by a young drunken driver. It was an awful tragedy. I think if more people had experiences like that, they would be grateful for this law.''

Carlyle Green, 45 years old, a senator who voted for the law
''The principle behind the law is a good idea. We have to do what we can to protect innocent drivers from others who are irresponsible. But children aren't the only problem here. I know a couple of *lawmakers* who have driven after they had a few drinks. While we were debating the bill, I tried to add a section which made it illegal for people over 40 to drink. I thought we should suffer right along with everyone else. That section didn't pass, of course.''

31.13 Paragraph Writing: Write a paragraph retelling a conversation you had with a parent or relative recently. Try to use some of the following verbs in your report:

advise	suggest
recommend	ask
insist	demand
request	say
tell	promise

Use mostly reported speech, but you might write a few sentences in quoted speech. Look at the example sentences in this chapter to see how to punctuate sentences in quoted speech.

31.14 Report Writing: Write a short paper summarizing either:

a. the main points of an interesting lecture you have heard recently, or

b. the main points of a book or article you have read recently. Be sure that it is always clear in your report whose ideas these are.

31.15 Reflecting: Read this final episode of the mystery story. Then reread it, noticing how the author uses both quoted speech and reported speech. Practice by putting the quoted speech into reported speech, and vice-versa.

> A few days later I was sitting in Lieutenant Farmer's office. He offered me a cup of coffee. ''How fresh it is?'' I asked him.
>
> ''I made this coffee two days ago. Just how you like it.''
>
> He sat down behind his desk. Then he asked me how I had solved the case. I told him that I solved it with my natural brilliance.
>
> ''Yeah,'' he said. ''But besides that?''
>
> ''I knew that Miller could prove Dr. Weber was guilty of malpractice. Weber was drunk when he operated on Troy Daniels's mother, and she died. Weber was going to have to pay a lot of money, and he would probably lose his job.''
>
> I explained that I had been confused by the threatening phone calls to Mrs. Miller and myself. ''The phone call to Deanne Miller was made by Dr. Weber's wife,'' I said. ''Deanne recognized her voice on a cassette I made.''
>
> ''But who called you?'' Farmer asked.
>
> ''Carl Miller called me,'' I said. ''He told me that he was afraid I would lead Dr. Weber to him. Dr. Weber had called Miller and threatened him and his wife.''
>
> Farmer asked me what I would do next, now that Weber had been arrested.
>
> I told him I was going to take a vacation with Linda. ''But first I'm going to drink another cup of coffee,'' I said. ''Very rarely do I get coffee this good.''

31.16 Real-World Work

THINK/PRACTICE

As you are walking, riding, or waiting today, remember a recent conversation you have had. Mentally, put it into reported speech.

LOOK/LISTEN

As you are reading, try to reconstruct what the writer actually said from reported speech, and practice turning quoted statements into reported statements. When you are reading a newspaper, pay close attention to the way that newspaper writers report speech. Many journalists try to alternate quoted speech with reported speech to make their stories more varied and interesting. There are also a number of difficult punctuation rules for sentences in quoted speech which you can learn in this way.

USE

1. The next time a classmate misses class, tell him or her what the professor said.

2. When talking with friends, you probably often tell them about conversations you have had recently, perhaps a long-distance telephone conversation with your family, a discussion with a teacher, or even an argument with another friend. If sometime soon you tell someone in English about a conversation, try to apply the rules you have learned in this chapter—rules for word order, pronoun use, and tense selection.

3. Often for a class you will have to attend a special lecture and take notes on what is said. You will also be asked to summarize a book or an article on many occasions. When you report what was said in a lecture or written in an article, you will have to use reported speech.

4. It is very important in English when you write or speak to give credit to the person from whom you get an idea, unless this idea is very common knowledge. If you borrow ideas without attributing them, you may be plagiarizing,which may be illegal and, at the least, can cause a paper to receive a bad grade. Make it a habit always to attribute correctly the ideas you mention even if you have not used exactly the same words as the author or speaker you got them from.